JURY TRIALS AND PLEA BARGAINING: A TRUE HISTORY

"At a moment when France is poised to adopt plea bargaining, McConville and Mirsky offer the best historical account of its emergence in mid-nineteenth century America, based upon exhaustive analysis of archival data. Their interpretation of the reasons for the dramatic shift from jury trials to negotiated justice offers no comfort for contemporary apologists of plea bargaining as more 'professional'. The combination of new data and critical reflection on accepted theories make this essential reading for anyone interested in criminal justice policy."

Rick Abel, Connell Professor of Law, UCLA Law School

"A fascinating account which traces the origins of plea-bargaining in the politicisation of criminal justice, linking developments in day-to-day practices of the criminal process with macro-changes in political economy, notably the structures of local governance. This is a classic socio-legal study and should be read by anyone interested in criminology, criminal justice, modern history or social theory."

Nicola Lacey, Professor of Criminal Law and Legal Theory, London School of Economics

Jury Trials and Plea Bargaining: A True History

MIKE McCONVILLE
and
CHESTER L MIRSKY

·HART·
PUBLISHING

OXFORD AND PORTLAND, OREGON
2005

Hart Publishing
Oxford and Portland, Oregon

Published in North America (US and Canada) by
Hart Publishing
c/o International Specialized Book Services
5804 NE Hassalo Street
Portland, Oregon
97213-3644
USA

Hart Publishing is a specialist legal publisher based in Oxford, England. To order further copies
of this book or to request a list of other publications please write to:

Hart Publishing, Salter's Boatyard, Folly Bridge,
Abingdon Road, Oxford OX1 4LB
Telephone: +44 (0)1865 245533 or Fax: +44 (0)1865 794882
e-mail: mail@hartpub.co.uk
WEBSITE: http://www.hartpub.co.uk

British Library Cataloguing in Publication Data
Data Available
ISBN 1 84113–516–X (hardback)

Typeset by Compuscript, Shannon
Printed and bound in Great Britain by
MPG Books, Bodmin, Cornwall

Preface

This book is a study of the origins and systematic adoption of plea bargaining replacing trial by jury as the principal method of disposition in criminal cases. The study is based upon detailed empirical analysis of original prosecution case files, court reports and statistical data in the leading criminal trial court in New York City between 1800 and 1865. As a backdrop to the research, we consider the explanations socio-legal commentators posit for the demise of the jury trial and the emergence and continued dominance of the guilty plea system. In attempting to determine whether the explanations advanced describe or obscure reality, we reflect on socio-legal history and the extent to which commentators and judges have misread it, perhaps in an effort to legitimate modern legal form.

Our other purpose here is to proceed to general social theory regarding the relationship between the state and the individual when considering the reasons for systemic social transformation. When examining this period in history we were forced to confront parallel changes within the wider society relating to how crime and social control came to be re-conceptualised with the emergence of machine politics and a new criminology. Thus, our analysis seeks to understand what the term 'legal rationality' means when applied to courtroom actors at a given point in time. Is this concept best understood through an evolving notion of the importance of evidence and proof, as synonymous with professional dominance and progress, ie, an improvement in earlier deficiencies of the fact-law conundrum with new-found competences and the capacity to provide solutions to what might appear to be contradictory demands? Or, on the other hand, can a clearer understanding be achieved through reference to the structural effect of socio-political forces within the wider society in defining criminal activity, the suspect population and the role of courtroom actors in relation to the method of case disposition?

As is apparent in the literature, no aspect of plea bargaining has gone unchallenged from its origins to its everyday practices. Critics in common law jurisdictions have contended that the demand for law and order legitimates an open alliance between police and courts which invites judges and lawyers to engage openly in guilty plea practices that are at variance from their expected role as neutral arbitrators or adversaries who guard both the interests of the individual and the concerns of the state. Guilty plea practice, it is argued, undermines the search for the truth, overturns traditional understandings of guilt based upon the burden of proof, marginalises the presumption of innocence and legitimates an administrative model of criminal justice through claimed savings in time and money. In the result, it is contended that the guilty plea system transforms criminal justice from one which seeks to determine whether the state has reliably sustained its burden of proof to another which seeks to determine whether the defendant, irrespective of guilt or innocence, is able to resist the pressure to plead guilty.

By contrast, defenders of plea bargaining maintain that the criminal justice system today depends for its very survival upon its continued practice where, for example, in America, more than ninety per cent of state and federal criminal cases result in pleas of guilty. Beyond contending that limited resources and burgeoning case loads necessitate such an approach to case disposition, defenders assert that the practice itself is better than a public trial and, in particular, the jury system it displaced. They contend that the courtroom actors are better able to address the interests of society and the individual informally through a settlement process without the need for the constraints of criminal procedure, evidence and proof. Indeed, some commentators contend that plea bargaining is 'a practice as old as justice itself'[1] and its introduction into the United Nations War Crimes Tribunal for the Balkans dealing with genocide has been described by the Tribunal's President as 'part of the court's coming of age.'[2]

This study seeks to address to what extent plea bargaining is defensible in its own terms and whether its adoption is indeed a sign of a system's maturity. Apart from theoretical considerations, the practical relevance of plea bargaining extends beyond America because the practice is already in place in both common law and civil law jurisdictions such Australia, England and Wales, Israel, Italy and South Africa and is being actively discussed in such diverse jurisdictions as Chile, China and Poland.

We are indebted to the United States National Science Foundation which provided the initial study grant,[3] as well as for additional support given by the Filomen D'Agostino Research Fund, New York University School of Law, the City University of Hong Kong, and the Research and Innovations Fund, University of Warwick.

In New York we owe a special debt of gratitude to Herman Eberhardt and wish to thank as well all the other students who provided research assistance in the course of this project: Deborah Applegate, Jim Fishman, Robert Franklin, Regina Lee, Mike Leggett, Jonathan Mirsky, Brian Murphy, Wendy Pollaert, Jim Rossman, Mark Smith, Paul Strauss, Claudia Trupp, Bruce Tulgan, Rebecca Willen, Terry Wildes, David Yamin, and Mark Zweifler. We were also fortunate to have help with data analysis organised by Jim Smith with the assistance of

---

[1] George Fisher, 'A practice as old as justice itself' *New York Times*, 28 September, 2003.
[2] 'Plea deals being used to clear Balkan War Tribunal's docket' *New York Times*, 18 November 2003, p A1, 14.
[3] Grant number: SES–9010178.

Craig Beezer, Cy Benson, John Crusadean, Wendy Dent, Mitchel Hurley, Hyung Paek, Barry Schindler and others too numerous to mention.

In Hong Kong we were given tremendous support by our able research assistants Alice Chan, Ka Yee, Paul Leung, and Po Sang whose technical skills and devotion to the research proved invaluable.

We also wish to record our thanks to those who have helped us in getting access to historical data, in particular: Mr Kenneth Cobb, the Librarian at New York City archives, Surrogates Court; the New York City Historical Society; the New York University School of Law Library; and the Empire State Library.

We are especially grateful to our friend and colleague Geoffrey Wilson, who undertook the labour of reading an initial and cluttered first draft and whose constructive comments and encouragement were of enormous benefit to us.

We would also like to thank the publisher's anonymous reader for the careful and perceptive report on the draft manuscript; our colleague Phil Thomas for his enthusiastic support for the project and, through him, the Journal of Law and Society for publishing some early findings; and the Criminal Law Area Group at New York University for their encouragement and constructive advice. We also take this opportunity to thank Richard Hart for his long-standing support and encouragement for our project and faith that we would eventually deliver a manuscript, and Mel Hamill, who served as our Editor and saw the book through to publication with patience and professionalism.

Throughout the project, Aileen Stockham at Warwick acted as Research Secretary and, together with Melina Jorge, Magalie Semexan and Dana Simonetti at New York University and Sandy Li at City University of Hong Kong, provided us with unfailing support and encouragement.

Our final thanks go to Sonia and Gloria for supporting us throughout the long period of the research: they were sorely tried but never exacted a bargain.

Summary of Contents

Contents

List of Tables

List of Figures

List of Illustrations

Chapter 1
Introduction

This book is a study of the transformation of the culture of criminal justice which, in the first half of the nineteenth century, celebrated trial by jury as the fairest and most reliable method of case disposition and then in the middle of the century dramatically gave birth to the guilty plea system or plea bargaining.[1] Focused upon the apprehension, investigation and adjudication of indicted cases in New York City's main trial tribunal in the nineteenth century—the Court of General Sessions—our study contributes to the growing body of knowledge that plea bargaining has a much longer history than generally understood and that it relates to structural factors which are at the very core of the culture of criminal justice.

The fact that at some point in the nineteenth century trials were replaced by guilty pleas in American state courts is well documented.[2] By the end of the century, cities such as New York, New Haven, Boston, Cleveland, Chicago, Dallas, and Philadelphia had substantial guilty plea rates. Thus, Albert Alschuler has reported that guilty pleas became the dominant mode of disposition in cities and counties after the Civil War (1865).[3] Likewise, Malcolm Feeley, from a review of court records in New York, New Haven, and London, has shown that guilty pleas accounted for approximately 50 per cent of all felony dispositions by 1860, and that by 1900 this figure had risen to 90 per cent.[4] Similarly, Theodore Ferdinand, Mary Vogel and George Fisher have reported that by the turn of the century, guilty pleas in Boston and Middlesex, Massachusetts amounted to 90 per cent of all felony dispositions.[5]

The waning of the jury and its replacement by the phenomenon of 'plea bargaining', however, has given rise to radically divergent explanations. The dominant theoretical approach, which we have collectively labelled as the professionalisation school, seeks to explain the transformation to plea bargaining

---

[1] The study was sponsored by the National Science Foundation, Study Grant Number: SES–9010178.

[2] AW Alschuler (1979); LM Friedman and RV Percival (1981); MM Feeley (1982); ME Vogel (1988) and (1999); A Steinberg (1989); T Ferdinand (1992); G Fisher (2000).

[3] Alschuler (1979).

[4] Feeley (1982).

[5] See below, present chapter.

within a legal framework hermetically sealed from the social context within which courts were operating. A less influential group of scholars, which we call contextualists, use various theoretical approaches which step outside the court-room and explain how changes in the wider society have explanatory force in understanding changes within the law. We briefly describe these divergent explan-ations to provide the reader with an understanding of the dominant themes in the plea bargaining literature which serve as important points of demarcation and departure in our own research and analysis.

PROFESSIONALISATION

Leading socio-legal commentators present a functionalist explanation rooted in a theory of professionalisation as having the greatest explanatory force in under-standing the abandonment of jury trials and the reliance on guilty pleas.[6] They contend that early reliance on jury trials was a function of the presence of amateur actors, while reliance on guilty pleas, which later came to displace trials, occurred because of the advent of professionalisation among police and lawyers. In this understanding, the new police were capable of producing reliable evidence of guilt and, with the emergence of lawyers who had the ability to assess evidence, courtroom actors were able to distinguish between cases where con-viction was certain and those where triable issues remained. In a context of cost-efficiency, everyday cases without triable issues gave rise to and became fodder for the guilty plea system.

'Amateur hour'

Lawrence Friedman has popularised the 'amateur-hour' thesis in a series of books and articles that seek to debunk the notion shared among intellectuals that between 1820 and 1860 there was a 'golden age' of American law in the United States.[7] According to Friedman, from an analysis of court docket entries in Alameda County (Oakland), California and Leon County (Tallahassee), Florida by the latter part of the nineteenth century:

> Most ... 'trials' were short, most of the defendants had no lawyer, and had
> to cobble together whatever they could say or do in their own defense, and
> there was not much quibbling about niceties of evidence.[8]

---

[6] L Friedman and R Percival (1981); L Friedman (1983); M Feeley (1982); M Feeley and C Lester (1994); G Fisher (2000); J Langbein (1979).

[7] The 'golden age' or 'formative era' of American law is depicted in writings of lawyers and oth-ers to cover the period 1820–1860 and best exemplified by Charles M Harr (1965).

[8] L Friedman (1993), pp 237–38.

Thus, lay jury trials were an unwitting and reflexive method of dispute resolution relied upon by people who lacked sophistication:

> In a system run by amateurs, or lawyers who spent little bits of their time and energy, with no technology of detection or proof, a trial was perhaps as good a way as any to strain the guilty from the innocent.[9]

In his overall analysis of the history of American criminal justice, Friedman contends forcibly:

> If we take a long-term view of the criminal justice system, from its beginnings in the colonial past to the end of the twentieth century, [professionalisation] is surely one of the master trends of the entire period. In the beginning ... there were no actors in the system who spent all their working lives in criminal justice. There were no police, professional prosecutors, public defenders, prison wardens, probation officers, detectives, social workers and the like. There were also few full-time criminals. Laymen, amateurs, and ordinary judges (some of them without any training in law) ran the system, together with a few lawyers, and a ragbag of constables, night watchmen, and haphazard jailers.[10]

Malcolm Feeley, basing his views upon transcripts in the Old Bailey in London and docket entries in New Haven, Connecticut, broadens the application of Friedman's thesis by depicting trials up to the middle of the nineteenth century as coincident to the English jury trial of the eighteenth century. According to Feeley:

> Defendants were not represented by counsel; they did not confront hostile witnesses in any meaningful way; they rarely challenged evidence or offered defenses of any kind. Typically when they or occasionally someone in their behalf did take the witness stand they requested mercy or offered only perfunctory excuses or defenses. Similar practices appear to have characterized trials in Connecticut during this same period as well.

> Perhaps what is most revealing about their substance is the speed at which these early trials were conducted. The record of proceedings in London reveals that the same judge and jury would hear several cases per day with hardly a pause between them. Similarly, the New Haven court register indicates that the same judge and jury might handle several cases in a one or two-day period; trial, deliberation and sentencing could all occur within the span of an hour or two. It should be emphasised that these cases usually involved felonies and that substantial sentences were often involved.[11]

---

[9] Friedman and Percival (1981), p 194.
[10] L Friedman (1993) p 67.
[11] Feeley (1982) p 345.

Central to this view is the understanding that, in the first half of the nineteenth century, there was an absence of lawyers in court and that whatever 'legal representatives' were present were untrained. This is captured in Feeley's description of English and American criminal courts:

> ... Frequently courts were staffed with part-time officers; often prosecutors and judges were not trained in the law ... Police officers often acting as prosecutors in court were unfamiliar with the rudiments of the law and cared even less ... Admissibility of evidence was capricious, points of law were treated with casualness.
>
> Historically, the modern trial by jury emerged when the criminal justice system was staffed by untrained amateurs who were charged with the task of trying to cope with the problem of accusing, trying and convicting or acquitting someone.[12]

In short, by the nineteenth century amateur actors did little more than 'muck about' with the available evidence,[13] before arriving at some precipitous outcome in jury trials.[14] Thus, Feeley concluded:

> There was no golden era of the jury trial, or if there was, it was a tarnished one. Thus if we are witnessing [today] the 'twilight of the adversary system', it is not at all clear when if ever there was a 'high noon'. To speak of 'twilight' is to foster a myth of a non-existent past. When trials were once extensively relied upon, they were, at least in the vast majority of ordinary offenses involving ordinary people ... brief perfunctory affairs that bear but scant resemblance to the contemporary jury trial.[15]

Synthesis of policing evidence

According to professionalisation commentators, the immediate precursor of the presence of lawyers and the transformation in the method of case adjudication was the reorganisation of police and its importance to the evidence-gathering function. They contend that when the task of evidence acquisition was lodged in the hands of a complainant or victim or voluntary community constables, the reliability, sufficiency and persuasiveness of evidence became problematic. Thus, commentators argue that at some point in the late nineteenth century, policing evolved into a skill and an occupation requiring 'different and more specialised skills as science became part of crime detection'.[16] The contention is that

---

[12] Feeley (1982) p 349.
[13] Feeley (1982) p 346.
[14] Feeley (1982) p 346.
[15] Feeley (1997) p 190.
[16] Hindus (1982) p 927.

scientism transformed the quality of evidence available at the trial while its reliability and persuasiveness assured its redundancy.

Under the professionalisation hypothesis, the significance of the police investigation and its relationship to the elements of proof had a synergistic effect upon the method of case disposition once lawyers skilled in assessing the weight and reliability of evidence became an essential part of the process and recognised the 'dead bang' from the 'triable' case, through what commentators describe as 'extensive pre-trial screening'.[17] This separation of wheat from chaff meant that 'dead bang' police-investigated cases became the fodder for plea bargaining without the concern for the legal form associated with witness examination, procedural and evidentiary rulings and argumentation. As Friedman and Robert Percival put it:

> Why go through a long and expensive process. Trials for the obviously guilty were a waste of good money and time.[18]

Case complexity

These commentators additionally contend that over time with the presence of trained lawyers came a change in the complexity of trials and ultimately in the need to streamline litigation into guilty pleas. Events which were once spontaneous occurrences became carefully choreographed set pieces, applying lawyers' practices to the application of common law rules of procedure and evidence. Such practices, including highly formalistic and nuanced pleadings, circumscribed the ability of the courtroom actors to establish the substantive elements of offences, the proof of which thus became increasingly technical and obscure. Hence, lawyered trials which at once were celebrated by commentators as a triumph of legal rationality were also dramatically more complex and time-consuming than their amateur predecessors. Furthermore, complexity itself motivated lawyers to avoid trials and to move instead to a simplified proceeding which, while unencumbered by rules of procedure and evidence, regarded those rules as the basis upon which negotiated justice could be achieved efficiently. This lawyer's dichotomy, which on the one hand, commentators contend, resulted in the strengthening of trials and improving upon the reliablity of outcomes, became, on the other hand, a reason to avoid trials altogether. As Feeley described it:

> ...[P]re-trial procedures and the rules of evidence expanded in number and complexity. These various rules were designed in large part to structure and restrict the power to lay decision makers, but they had the effect of giving greater authority to lawyers who could then exercise their expertise prior to trial. And as resources ear-marked for criminal justice expanded, these

---

[17] L Mather (1979).
[18] L Friedman and R Percival (1981), p 194.

professional decision makers had increased opportunity and incentive to use the pretrial process.[19]

Feeley contends that complexity led lawyers to the transformation in the method of case disposition whereby trials and guilty pleas became bargained-for dispositions as lawyers recognised that the new rules and procedures made the trial obsolete and cost-inefficient in routine cases:

> As the trial became more complex, the lawyers who were coming to dominate it developed an alternative. Ironically, just as the components of the modern jury trial were put into place, and the capacity to use them was developed, these very developments themselves undermined the process they were designed to enhance. As the trial came to be vigorous and complicated its centrality and the prominent roles of the judge and jury began to wane, displaced by a lawyer-dominated guilty plea process.[20]

A similar argument is advanced by John Langbein based primarily on his research in the Old Bailey, London in the eighteenth century:[21]

> Just as the want of plea bargaining helps explain the rapidity of the trial times, the rapidity of trial helps explain why there was so little use of guilty pleas. Modern plea bargaining entails the surrender of the defendant's right to trial in exchange for a lesser sanction. A plea-bargaining defendant effectively trades back to the state his right to put the criminal justice system to a time-and-resource-consuming trial. But when trials were short and rapid, the crown had no particular incentive to engage in the exchange, and thus the defendant had no bargaining chips.

For Langbein, the primacy of lawyers and increased complexity through rules of evidence 'ultimately destroyed the system in the sense that they rendered trials unworkable as an ordinary or routine dispositive procedure for cases of serious crime'[22] thereby necessitating the development and reliance upon a guilty plea system.[23]

Workload

Under the professionalisation hypothesis, therefore, time and efficiency become prominent values that extended beyond any commitment to the jury trial as a reliable and fair method of case disposition and serve as an important explanatory

---

[19] Feeley (1982) p 350.
[20] Feeley (1997) p 192.
[21] Langbein (2003) pp 18–9.
[22] Langbein (1979) p 265.
[23] Langbein (1978) pp 9–10.

force behind the method of disposition lawyers chose to adopt. In the parlance of professional dominance, a cost-efficient work day was the basis upon which lawyers could achieve and maintain monopoly status over case disposition. Whilst the amateur—the victim or the individual defendant—was concerned solely with the facts which gave rise to the criminal dispute, the professional had to become concerned with multiple or aggregate fact patterns representing a wide range of cases which out of necessity extended beyond and took precedence over the needs of any one individual. Such concerns meant that in a given work day a lawyer would have to consider the total number of hours available by which to adjudicate and dispose of cases while maximising the opportunity for remuneration commensurate with these efforts. This commodification process is according to these commentators best observed in the response lawyers made to 'caseload pressure.'

George Fisher is a leading proponent of the effects of caseload pressure on professional decision-making and the adjudicatory process in the nineteenth century. Whilst Fisher does not accept the arguments advanced regarding the linkage of plea bargaining to the replacement of amateurs by lawyers or increased complexity through the lawyerisation of trials, he contends that lawyers sought to plea bargain to enable them to continue to function in a cost-effective manner when confronted by rising caseload:[24]

> Prosecutors of the nineteenth century, like prosecutors today, plea bargained to ease their crushing workloads, made heavier in the nineteenth century both by their part-time status and utter lack of staff and by a caseload explosion perhaps set off by newly founded police forces and massive immigration.

So paramount is what Fisher describes as the 'general' case pressure concern, that lawyers will find cost-efficient expedient methods of case disposition whenever rules of criminal procedure can be exploited to eliminate the necessity for reliance on time-consuming jury trials. Thus, seriousness of the offence and wider societal concerns regarding social conduct become subsumed by a professional culture that is governed by the values underlying efficient and cost-effective methodologies. In this scenario, murder cases can be just as easily plea bargained as liquor law violations. What is dispositive is that the overall caseload of lawyers must be managed in the context of the available workday which would include the remunerative nature and hence importance of contemporaneous civil law practice which was part and parcel of professional practice of both part-time prosecutors and defence lawyers in the nineteenth century. To maximise these concerns, the lawyers would fasten upon a weak link in the criminal process which would enable inducements to be offered to defendants to avoid jury trials and the time consuming nature of evidence and proof thereby implied:[25]

---

[24] G Fisher (2000) p 865. See also, Fisher (2003).
[25] G Fisher (200) p 903.

Caseload pressure generally increased prosecutors' incentives to plea bargain. Once prosecutors felt a general incentive to lighten their workload, they struck plea bargains whenever they had the power to do so—that is, whenever rigid penalty schemes permitted them to manipulate sentences by manipulating charges.

Fisher, like the other proponents of the professionalisation hypothesis, constrains the explanation for plea bargaining to the functionalist concerns of courtroom actors, although workload may be a function of population growth and an increase in the incidence of criminality. Thus, under this theory, plea bargaining can be explained as occurring in a wide variety of jurisdictions without regard to the structure and ordering of society and their effects on the role of courtroom actors. Indeed, under the workload adaptation hypothesis, a historical sociology of the culture of plea bargaining which extends to the wider political economy is specifically rejected. As Fisher emphatically states:

> Often—perhaps usually—taking a broader focus improves the telling of history. I do not believe this is one of those times. The evidence overwhelmingly suggests that plea bargaining was the work of those who labored in the criminal courts and was the product of their personal interests and struggle for power.[26]

CONTEXTUAL ACCOUNTS

A less influential group of commentators has sought a wider context to account for the rise in reliance on guilty pleas by situating it within the political economy of the local state. These accounts range from a class-based analysis in which discretion and leniency is utilised in order to secure obeisance to and the authority of a ruling propertied elite to another which points to structural changes in the role and purpose of the courtroom actors and the local state.[27]

A prominent and detailed class-based account of the transformation of criminal dispositions in nineteenth century America is Mary Vogel's study of Boston's lower criminal courts between 1830–1860.[28] Vogel, borrowing from the earlier work of Douglas Hay in eighteenth century England,[29] argues that plea bargaining in Boston emerged between the third and fourth decades of the nineteenth century as an integral part of 'episodic leniency', a process of political stabilisation whereby elites sought to legitimate institutions of local government through ameliorative acts directed to the emerging underclass

---

[26] G Fisher (2000) p 904.
[27] D Hay (1975); M Vogel (1988) and (1999).
[28] M Vogel (1988) and (1999).
[29] Hay (1975).

during a period of social conflict wrought by industrialisation, immigration and urbanisation.[30]

Theodore Ferdinand in an earlier study of Boston's Municipal (superior) Court, which had been established in 1800 as a lawyers' court with an adversarial style and formal decorum, locates a principal reason for the emergence of the guilty plea system in the assumption of control by the public prosecutor of the judicial process. This included the power to settle cases through guilty pleas, building upon what had already occurred in lower police courts where there were no lawyers.[31] Ferdinand's study shows how structural changes in the role of the public prosecutor in Boston led to the infusion of expanded concern in the handling of everyday cases that extended beyond the narrow fact/legal issue of guilt or innocence and ultimately affected the method of case disposition.[32]

Allen Steinberg, in an important analysis of Philadelphia from the eighteenth to the early nineteenth century, explains how the American criminal justice system was not always guarded by public prosecutors and that both case law and social history suggest a complex transformation to a system of public prosecution and plea bargaining.[33] Steinberg argues that the emergence of a new American state concerned with macro issues of social control and policing replaced an earlier system dominated by private litigants and initiated by private prosecutors. The transformation to 'statism' incorporated the principal attribute of private prosecution—the exercise of discretion—and moulded discretion to accomplish wider political concerns regarding social order.[34]

The combined effect of this body of contextual research would suggest that at least in the northeastern United States, where the predominant American population existed in the first half of the nineteenth century, the professionalisation hypothesis may be of limited explanatory force in understanding the abrupt transformation from trials to plea bargaining. Certainly, without taking on board the societal context of criminal courts and their relationship to the emergent local state in the rapidly changing political economy of the nineteenth century one may be left with a very narrow understanding of the role of guilty plea practice in the ordering of social justice.

PURPOSE AND THEORY OF THE PRESENT RESEARCH

In this book, we argue that the culture of plea bargaining cannot be understood by confining analysis to the courtroom but instead can only be explained by

---

[30] M Vogel (1999). Her attempt, however, to distance guilty plea rates from caseload pressure has been powerfully challenged by George Fisher. See G Fisher (2000) pp 900–3.
[31] T Ferdinand (1992).
[32] T Ferdinand (1992) pp 97–8.
[33] A Steinberg (1984) and (1989).
[34] A Steinberg (1989) pp 230–31.

looking at the effects of changes in the wider political economy on the nature and purpose of criminal prosecutions, the role of courtroom actors and the method of disposition.

We found that the nature of criminal prosecutions in everyday indicted cases transformed from disputes between private parties resolved through a public determination of the facts and law to a private determination of the issues between the state and the individual, marked by greater police involvement in the processing of defendants and public prosecutorial discretion. As this occurred, the structural purpose of criminal courts changed—from individual to aggregate justice—as did the method and manner of their dispositions—from trials to guilty pleas.

Contemporaneously, a new criminology emerged, with its origins in European jurisprudence, which was to transform the way in which crime was viewed as a social and political problem. Our study, therefore, sheds light on the relationship of the method of case disposition to the means the local state utilised in securing social control of an underclass, in the context of the legitimation of a new social order which sought to define groups of people as well as actual offending in criminogenic terms.

We contend that it is essential to understand and appreciate the detail and context of facts both past and present, both inside and outside the courtroom, before drawing any conclusions regarding systemic change that have persuasive force at a theoretical level. We seek to demonstrate that a theory of system transformation for any jurisdiction must emerge from a close empirical analysis of the available records of that jurisdiction approximate to the period of transformation. Thus, our methodology, rather than proceeding from some abstract notion, part ideological and part factual, begins from the ground up to enable the reader to more critically confront transformative events as well as the horatory explanations that socio-legal commentators have advanced for the gap between law in the books and law in action.

As will become clear, our research raises basic questions about historical method and accounts of nineteenth century law practice in criminal cases. We were struck throughout by the fact that a whole generation of courtroom actors— lawyers and judges—prominent in the first half of the nineteenth century when jury trials predominated, seems to have gone unrecognised by many leading socio-legal historians despite the fact that evidence of their existence abounds. Moreover, the idea that the transformation to guilty pleas is an aspect of 'history as progress' brought forth by the rise of professionalism is troubling because the evidence abounds that the shift to a guilty plea system occurred rather abruptly and was not part of an evolutionary process which culminated in the birth of lawyers capable of distilling the wheat from the chaff.

Published accounts which suggest to the contrary are all the more distressing because they are promulgated by commentators who are celebrated as legal historians and historical sociologists, and thus their words are influential among students and colleagues who are often unprepared to consider critically assertions made about the relationship of law to the political economy.

The empirical basis

The basis for our research is a longitudinal analysis of data which systematically describes the structure of criminal cases and the practice of criminal law in prosecutions resulting in indictment and adjudication in General Sessions. The principal sources of data include: prosecution case files maintained by the District Attorney over the course of the nineteenth century; reports of cases in General Sessions prepared by nominative reporters; courtroom and case data included within the Court Minute Book; and criminal statistics reports issued by the Secretary of State of New York from 1838. We deal with the strengths and weaknesses of these data sources at appropriate points throughout the book.

The District Attorney's case files[35] provide a detailed account of the case for the prosecution. The files regularly include such matters as the record of the complaint, warrants issued to arrest and search, processes issued to compel evidence, the statements of witnesses, the response of the defendant, the indictment, lists of witnesses upon whom the prosecution proposed to rely, briefing notes by counsel, and sometimes tangible evidence likely to be introduced at trial. In 1865 the files contained transcripts of witness testimony at trial in cases ending in conviction. We analysed the District Attorney's case files at five yearly intervals from when the files were first preserved in 1804 over our study period through 1865.[36] We constructed our sample on the basis of all cases over a thirty-day period in the case files that were listed in the Court Minute Book as appearing on the daily docket.[37] In total, the basis of our sample consisted of 1,117 case files for the period 1805–1845 and 557 case files covering the period 1850–1865.

The Minute Books of the Court of General Sessions were another source of information.[38] They included daily docket entries, which we coded for thirty days of the year at ten year intervals, memorialising the type and number of indicted cases, the manner of motion practice, the method of case disposition, as well as the number of defendants and witnesses, and the frequency and type of jury verdicts, guilty pleas, and the time lapse between indictment and entry of a final

[35] The District Attorney's Files are part of New York City archives and deposited at Surrogates Court.

[36] As will subsequently emerge, where the records were incomplete for the relevant sample year we analysed cases drawn from the closest adjacent period.

[37] For comparative purposes we also drew samples of cases from the District Attorney's files that were not listed in the Minute Books.

[38] Our samples were drawn from the Minute Books relating to one Part (or Division) of the Court of General Sessions. There was only one Part of the Court at the outset of the century and it was not until 1839 that a second Part was added to help handle increased court business. General Sessions Minute Books are held at New York City's archives in Surrogates Court.

judgment. We also coded the Minute Book for the entire year, at five yearly intervals, to determine the frequency of lawyers and the outcome of trials in which lawyers were present. Arising out of this coding exercise, we sought to identify lawyers who appeared in the indicted cases and, to assess their background and status, we referred to biographical accounts of members of the Bar and directories of prominent citizens of New York.

A third important source of information analysed in the course of our research are accounts of trials in everyday cases in General Sessions that were prepared by named court reporters (the 'Nominative Reports').[39] These quasi-official reports over the period 1815–1825 are rich with data describing the role, activities and discourse of the courtroom actors. These reports were cited by General Sessions' actors as authoritative and were prepared by individuals present in the courtroom who were themselves lawyers, in some instances of considerable standing within the profession.[40] In addition to reporting cases, the nominative reporters included from time to time their own commentaries on issues presented by individual cases.[41]

Additionally, we re-analyse statistical information presented in Annual Reports prepared by the Secretary of State of New York over the period beginning 1838 to the end of our study.[42] The reports are an important source of caseload data and include the frequency of convictions and the incidence of guilty pleas and trials. In addition, these annual reports contain commentary regarding the state's contentions regarding the origins and nature of crime and criminality.

---

[39] The Nominative Reports in question are: D Bacon, *The New York Judicial Repository* (1819); D Rogers, *The New York City Hall Recorder, 1816* (1817), *The New York City Hall Recorder, 1817* (1818), *The New York City Hall Recorder, 1818* (1819), *The New York City Hall Recorder, 1819* (1820), *The New York City Hall Recorder, 1820* (1821), *The New York City Hall Recorder, 1821* (1822); JD Wheeler, *Reports of Criminal Law Cases Decided at the City Hall of the City of New York* (1823), *Reports of Criminal Law Cases*, vol 2, (1824), *Reports of Criminal Law Cases*, vol 3 (1825).

[40] These reporters provided a written record of the decisions and proceedings in General Sessions including detailed accounts, at trial, of the role of the District Attorney, private lawyers representing either the prosecution or the defence, and the judge and jury.

We cross-referenced the cases reported by the nominative reporters with the Minute Book. This enabled us to see the extent to which the docket entries of reported cases were the same or different from other cases on the same day which were not reported by the nominative reports. The measures we adopted included the number of witnesses per case, the identity of the lawyers present, whether the jury returned a verdict with or without retiring, and the number of cases tried in General Sessions on the same day. All these measures showed that the cases contained in the nominative reports were indistinguishable from other cases reported in the Minute Book during a typical court day.

[41] The Reports were not, of course, official court records and have their own limitations. As Michael Millender notes, written for the market place and sometimes edited by the lawyers whose words they reproduced, their accuracy is limited 'by the vanity or ambition of the practitioners who appeared in the trials': Millender (1996) p 17.

[42] The Reports were compiled by the Secretary of State on the basis of returns filed by county clerks regarding cases in which convictions were obtained in criminal cases: Secretary of State, *Annual Report of the Secretary of State on Statistics on Crime*, 1838–1865.

Longitudinal comparison

We organise our data around two longitudinal periods, 1800–1845, the mercantile laissez-faire era of individualised justice and jury trials and 1850–1865, the pre-industrial era, marked by aggregate outcome and the institutionalised guilty plea system.

In the first part of the book (chapters 2–8), dealing with the mercantile era, we provide an overview of the political economy of New York's criminal justice system, its structure, institutions, and key actors; the nature of crime prosecuted in General Sessions and the detection and investigation system relating thereto; how cases were screened prior to trial; the method of adjudication at trial; the method of disposition in guilty plea cases; and the sentencing principles and practices employed. In the second part of the book (chapters 9–13), dealing with the pre-industrial era, we examine criminal justice organisation and practice in General Sessions' prosecutions from mid-century until 1865 when guilty pleas became the dominant method of case disposition. We include in this account, an analysis of the political economy of criminal justice over this period; the nature of crime prosecuted in General Sessions; and the extent to which the rise of bargaining was explicable in terms of increased caseload. We consider the detection and investigation system then in place and the nature of criminal trial practice and explore the extent to which police evidence became more reliable and jury trials, during the ascendancy of plea bargaining, evidenced greater complexity and adversariness. We separately analyse the practice of plea bargaining to determine to what extent it was in conformity with principles of legal rationality. We then address the politicisation of criminal justice and its impact upon the suspect population, prosecutorial discretion and the rise of a new criminology. We conclude in the final chapter by reflecting upon our data over both periods and the theoretical implications these have for our understanding of plea bargaining and system transformation.

Chapter 2

The Political Economy of Criminal Justice in the Mercantile Era

INTRODUCTION

In this chapter, we provide an overview of the political economy of New York City's justice system in the early decades of the nineteenth century. We consider not only the structure of the City itself and its inhabitants but its method of governance and the role of its leading officials, the Mayor, Recorder and Aldermen, in the administration of local government. Our principal focus is on the nature of the legal system which underpinned the apprehension, prosecution and disposition of indicted individuals in the City's main criminal tribunal, the Court of General Sessions at this period of history. In this undertaking, we provide an overview of the institutions charged with this responsibility, the role and authority of the principal actors, and the nature of offences and offending prosecuted in General Sessions.

THE STRUCTURE OF SOCIETY

Over the first half of the nineteenth century, New York City grew from a sea trading port, with a population of about 60,000, clustered in a small area of lower Manhattan to become, by 1845, the largest city in the United States with a population of over 371,000, congested within the area south of 14th Street.[1] As the major point of entry into the United States, waves of immigration transformed New York City's population from one where, at the outset of the century, most of the inhabitants were born in North America to another where, by 1845, over 36 per cent of the population was foreign-born.[2]

---

[1] I Rosenwaike (1972) p 16. Despite this growth, it remained small in comparison to London whose population had already reached one million at the outset of the nineteenth century: Roy Porter (1982).

[2] I Rosenwaike (1972) pp 39, 42.

Even at the outset of the nineteenth century, New York was a far from homogenous society. New Yorkers were of Dutch and English ancestry as well as North Americans drawn to the busy trading port from New England, Long Island and other parts of New York State and New Jersey.[3] Enriching the mix were more recent immigrants from Scotland, England, Ireland and France. In addition, free blacks were attracted to the City by its manumission laws; between 1800 and 1820, the proportion of African Americans grew as rapidly as whites and comprised about ten per cent of the population.[4]

While New York began as a trading port, it quickly came to dominate the North American economy by becoming the major distribution centre for commercial activity in North and South America. The City itself spawned industries involved with manufacturing, refining and processing goods and products that were the basis of the commercial economy.[5] Supporting the mercantile economy were artisans, craftsmen, journeymen and labourers who supplied the infrastructure that sustained shipbuilding and trading and enabled commerce to grow.[6] Underpinning this was a thriving local economy based around retail shopping outlets, banks, transportation systems, inns, entertainment halls, gambling dens and the like.[7]

Not only were people from disparate backgrounds attracted to New York City, but also the very basis of the mercantile economy produced extreme social stratification. The bulk of the population comprised labouring and artisan classes on top of which was an elite composed of merchants, financiers, and landed gentry. In 1828, four per cent of the population controlled at least ninety per cent of the City's wealth.[8] At the bottom of society were slaves and free black people,[9] the latter of whom lived in segregated neighbourhoods and found it increasingly difficult to find regular employment, given the competition from whites and the attitude of the mercantile elite that free blacks were often lazy, feckless and prone to criminality.[10]

Over time and as the city rapidly expanded in size, economic and social conditions conducive to crime became more pronounced. A huge growth in small-scale manufacturing was fuelled by an army of unskilled and semi-skilled

---

[3] I Rosenwaike (1972) p 22.

[4] I Rosenwaike (1972) p 24. See L H Hirsch (1931); R Ottley and W Weatherby (1967). African Americans were heavily concentrated in the Collect neighbourhood known as Five Points: T Anbinder (2002) pp 16–17.

[5] I Rosenwaike (1972).

[6] A Pred (1966).

[7] Albion (1939).

[8] E Pessen (1973) p 34.

[9] Whilst slavery was not abolished in New York until 1827, it had long been in decline and most black people were free though still discriminated against and working in menial capacities. See L Hirsh, Jr (1931).

[10] R Ernst (1979) pp 40–41; P Gilge (1987) p 146; T Anbinder (2002) p 19.

labourers, the victims of low wages and fluctuations in employment, in place of the system of artisans and apprentices that had been the hallmark of the earlier era. With the casualisation of labour, low wages and cycles of unemployment and the swelling of the population through mass immigration, the poor began to cluster in increasingly sub-divided multi-occupation buildings that paved the way by mid-century for the construction of purpose-built tenements.[11] Growth of this magnitude brought with it social dislocation and conditions conducive to crime: unemployment, poverty, inequalities of wealth and a social welfare system that could not cope with the strains imposed.

Nevertheless, even at the outset of the century, crime was already part of the fabric of a city in which inter- and intra-class disputes were quite common.[12] Writing anonymously in 1812, as 'a citizen', Charles Christian,[13] one of the City's Special Justices, identified the sites of crime as including gaming houses, brothels, taverns and public baths, and those engaging in crime as including 'sharpers', pickpockets, men domesticated in brothels, the husbands of bawds, professional gamblers, dealers in junk, pawn brokers[14] and dealers in old clothes.

Thus, from the early decades of the nineteenth century, New York was, in effect, two cities:[15] one comprised of a proportionately small number of wealthy merchants[16] and landed individuals who lived in small enclaves, and the other an artisan and labouring class who, for the most part, were property-less and often lived in substandard housing.[17] Whilst Broadway was from early on, with its substantial brick built mansions housing wealthy ship owners and financiers, the paradigmatic street of fashion, the labouring classes became increasingly confined to overcrowded areas such as Five Points, Corlear's Hook, Bancker Street and Dutch Hill that were to become emblematic of urban poverty.[18]

---

[11] T Anbinder (2002) pp 16–18; 21, 23–5.

[12] See Bruce Smith (1996) pp 60 *et seq.*

[13] Charles Christian, *A Brief Treatise on the Police of the City of New-York*, 1812 (Reprinted 1870, Arno Press).

[14] *Cf.* Luc Sante (1991) p 65 who had identified pawnbroker shops as almost exclusively a feature of the Bowery with the first noted on Park Row around 1822. See also T Anbinder (2002) pp 219, 207–34.

[15] Whilst at the outset of the century New York, with its higgledy-piggledy street system and its blending of rich and poor residences, was said to resemble a market town of *ancien régime* Europe, by 1820, following the inauguration of the grid street plans in 1811, distinct boundaries between 'rich' and 'poor' neighbourhoods had emerged: Sean Wilentz (1979).

[16] It has been estimated that by 1800, the richest 20 per cent owned almost 80 per cent of the City's wealth, with the poorest half of the population owning less than 5 per cent: Burrows and Wallace (1999) p 351.

[17] E Pessen (1973) pp 33–8.

[18] R Ernst (1949); C Stansell (1987). Stansell remarks that in 1819 at one address in Corlear's Hook, 103 people lived in one building: p 9. See also Anbinder (2002) pp 15–37.

METHOD OF JUDICIAL GOVERNANCE

The inequalities of wealth were reflected in the governance of the City, where there was little by way of participatory democracy. Property qualifications, which were not abolished until 1843, severely limited those eligible to vote in municipal elections.[19] Furthermore, there were only a few elected offices; the City's top officials, the mayor, recorder (the City's permanent law officer), judges, chief constable, district attorney, and marshals, were appointed by the governor and/or his Council, while eligible voters elected only the aldermen and constables.[20] At the outset of the century, the mercantile elite not only dominated local government but also regulated the City's markets and controlled its charitable and cultural organisations under a paternalistic, communitarian ideology of consensus (the identification of a common good).[21] The elite took a leadership role in philanthropy by providing relief to the poor through ad hoc committees that engaged in door-to-door solicitations and donations.[22]

Government was centred in the Mayor's Court which had legislative (Common Council), civil (Common Pleas) and criminal (General Sessions) jurisdiction.[23] At the outset of the century, each branch of the Court was presided over by the mayor who sat with the recorder and aldermen, all of whom also were justices of the peace.[24] The mayor and recorder were some of the City's most prominent individuals. They came from the upper stratum of society with a background in classical education and the study and practice of law, often having served as either a state or federal legislator, Justice of the State Supreme Court and District Attorney.[25] Aldermen were also men of wealth and social standing, many of whom were either businessmen or lawyers.[26]

As members of the Common Council, the mayor and aldermen resolved market disputes, whilst as judges they presided over criminal and civil disputes. At the outset of the century, members of the Mayor's Court along with a State Supreme Court judge also presided over the Court of Oyer and Terminer which

[19]   C Williamson (1960) p 197; J G Wilson (1892) pp 378–79. In 1800, only five per cent of the population was eligible to vote for New York City officials. For a detailed account, see L P Curry (1997).

[20]   C Williamson (1960) p 162; Pomerantz (1938) pp 26–7, 64–70.

[21]   A Bridges (1984) pp 17, 70–73; M Heale (1968) and (1976) 63:23; C Griffin (1960); Anbinder (2002).

[22]   Bridges (1984) p 70; Pomerantz (1938) pp 37–52; P Weinbaum (1979) p 112. As the unremitting demands of charity grew, by the end of the second decade of the century there was a measurable shift in philanthropy from alleviation of poverty to active reform and in this way the focus of interest became the habits of the poor: R Mohl (1971).

[23]   C P Daly (1855); J W Brooks (1896) pp 198–99.

[24]   Scott (1909) p 97.

[25]   This point was emphasised by Daly (1855) p 64. For a biographical account of mayors and recorders who were prominent lawyers see: L B Proctor (1870); D McAdam, H. Bischoff *et al* (eds) (1897).

[26]   J W Brooks (1896) pp 198–99; Weinbaum (1979).

was convened to try criminal cases of the greatest gravity.[27] In addition, particularly when misdemeanour defendants could not afford bail, the Common Council authorised the members of the Mayor's Court to conduct non-jury trials in a Court of Special Sessions.[28]

By an Act of 1821, the Mayor's Court was divided into the Court of Common Pleas and General Sessions, after which the mayor ceased to preside over either court.[29] Trials in General Sessions were thereafter conducted by the recorder, as chief judge, along with the aldermen as associate judges. The recorder, by the constitution as amended in that year, was appointed by the Governor with the consent of the Senate and held office for a term of five years, while a separate judge also appointed by the Governor presided over Common Pleas.[30] After 1829 Special Sessions was presided over by the recorder and separate judges of Common Pleas and, by 1846, the police magistrates.[31]

General Sessions was the principal venue for jury trials in indicted cases. It was a court of record serviced by a Clerk who was responsible for taking notes of the proceedings and, if necessary, preparing an official record.[32] By 1800, the court sat six times a year and by 1821, it commenced on a monthly basis.[33] Originally housed in City Hall, in 1838 General Sessions moved to the Halls of

---

[27] By 1821, Oyer and Terminer met four times a year with a judge of Common Pleas as well as a justice of the Supreme Court and either the mayor, recorder or alderman who, by 1847, could be replaced entirely by the separate judges of Common Pleas: Colby (1868) p 56; Barbour (1852) p 296; Scott (1909) pp 389–90.

[28] 1801 *Compilation of the Laws of the State of New York*, Acts of the 24th Session, Chapter LXX, Section ix, p 305. Originally Special Sessions met at such time as the Common Council thought necessary, dependent upon the backlog of misdemeanour offences pending in General Sessions. Because of doubt about the constitutionality of a misdemeanor conviction without a jury, Special Sessions was infrequently convened before 1829: Bruce Smith (1996) pp 163–64.

In 1829, the Statute was amended to overcome these objections: *1829 Revised Statutes of the State of New York*, Part IV, Chapter II, Title III, Section 22, p 714. Thus, persons charged with a misdemeanour offence could not be detained longer than twenty-four hours without a non-jury, bench trial in Special Sessions. However, because of the importance attributed to a jury trial, a defendant convicted after a trial in Special Sessions could demand a *de novo* trial in General Sessions, by the same bench, but before a jury: *1829 Revised Statutes of the State of New York*, Part IV, Chapter II, Title III, Section 26–9, p 750. Otherwise, if the defendant was able to post bail or provide recognisance, the defendant could choose not to proceed in Special Sessions and, instead, demand a jury trial in General Sessions. See J Colby (1868) p 185.

[29] 1821 *Laws of the State of New York*, Chapter 72, Sections 1, 6, pp 64–6.

[30] See Daly (1855) pp 64–5; see also Barbour (1852) p 301; Gilje (1987) p 274.

[31] Barbour (1852) p 641; Colby (1868) p 35.

[32] 1813 *Laws of the State of New York*, Acts of the 35th and 36th Sessions, Chapter LXVI, Section xiii, p 338 authorised payment of the clerk for fees out of the forfeiture of recognisances when individuals failed to appear. See also eg *People v William Jarvis* (1816) Rogers, vol 1, 191 where, on a charge of perjury, counsel for the prosecution 'offered Robert Macomb, the clerk of this court as witness, with his book of minutes, to prove the existence of the former cause, during the trial of which the perjury was alleged to have taken place'; and *Robert Goodwin* (1820) William Sampson, p 191 in which a copy of the minutes of the trial were laid before the Supreme Court.

[33] Daly (1855) p 65; Brooks (1896) p 217.

Justice (The Tombs) which also housed the Police Office and a facility for pre-
trial detention.[34]

Whilst at the outset of the century, General Sessions could 'enquire by the oath
of good and lawful men the truth of any treason, murder or felony and all other
crimes or misdemeanors done in the locale of the court', those indictments punishable with death or life imprisonment or where the defendant was in jail were
to be delivered to the Court of Oyer and Terminer, with jail cases untried to be
remitted to General Sessions.[35] By 1813, the court acquired jurisdiction of all
offences including those punishable by life in prison and excluding only the few
offences punishable by death.

Activist role of mayor and aldermen

In addition to their role as judges and members of the Common Council, the
mayor and aldermen were regularly present fighting fires and quelling public disturbances,[36] thus further blurring the lines between socio-political and judicial
leadership.[37] An account of an assault case in our sample of nominative reports of
indictments prosecuted in General Sessions in 1816 illustrates the personal character of the role of the mayor and aldermen in the resolution of disputes involving wider issues of public order in the early decades of the nineteenth century.[38]
The defendants, Andrew Mickle, a merchant tailor, and his wife Elizabeth, held a
lease from William Edwards and his wife, 'coloured people, who keep an oyster-
cellar in the Park, near the Theatre' for a part of the building. The lease expired
on 1 May 1816. During the preceding February, Mickle had, according to custom,
put up a notice to let at the request of the landlord, it being understood by all the
parties that the part of the building occupied by Mickle was to be rented
to another person.

Prior to the expiration of the lease, a Frenchman, Lewis Thiery, leased the
premises from Edwards and, on 1st May, came to take possession, accompanied
by Mrs Edwards. Andrew Mickle refused to give up the key. The report continues:

> An application was then made on behalf of the landlord and his new tenant
> to Alderman Lawrence and the police-magistrates for advice and assistance.
> In the testimony of Thiery he called the Alderman, 'Comissaire de police',
> and 'un gros bel homme'. A police magistrate—a big handsome man.

---

[34] Smith (1996) pp 330 *et seq.*

[35] 1801 *Compilation of the Laws of the State of New York*, Acts of the 24th Session, Chapter LXX,
Section I, p 302; Chapter viii, Section x, p 175; Chapter viii, Section xvi, p 177.

[36] Whilst the direct involvement of the mayor and aldermen in fire fighting and similar activities
waned over the first few decades of the century, as late as 1834, the mayor, accompanied by a body of
watchmen, intervened to quell a riot over the beating by sailors of an Irishman: Anbinder (2002) p 28.

[37] Bridges (1984) p 70; Pomerantz (1938) pp 37–52.

[38] The account is taken from the court reporter, Daniel Rogers, *The New York City Hall Recorder*,
vol 1 (1816) p 96.

By reason of the great influx of foreigners, and divers other causes, on that day, much difficulty existed in every part of the city on account of tenancies. There were more tenants than tenements to contain them; and very many respectable families applied to, and were provided by, the corporation with rooms in the Alms-house until they could provide for themselves elsewhere. Applications [for leases] ... poured in from all quarters—all the constables and marshals were at the polls of the election—New York seemed to pour forth at once into her streets, her thousands of men, and women, and children, of all ages, colors and conditions—and carts loading and unloading—furniture piled here and there—houses turned upside down, and carriages and carts rattling, and chimney-sweeps crying, and tea-rusk horns blowing (by far the most villanous sound that every assailed mortal ear) made the tout ensemble, 'confusion worse confounded'. This was not, therefore, a fit season to procure much assistance or correct legal advice from the police or any other magistrates.

It appears, as a result of some 'hint or suggestion' from the Recorder, the official who had ultimately been consulted, that Thiery, Mrs Edwards and 'several colored men' including one called Johnson, came at four o'clock the same day to the door of the tenement occupied by Mickle, his wife and several of his journeymen who were packing up their furniture and the stock of the tailor's shop in preparation for the move.

The door was locked and access from without denied. The beseiged had several shelalahs and an old blunderbuss for defence. The defendant [Mickle] stood against the door on the inside, and Mrs Edwards and Johnson pressed for entrance on the outside. The Frenchman was behind the colored men, with a bundle, ready to take possession as soon as entrance could be obtained. The door was forced open, and in entering, a blow was aimed at the head of Johnson with the aforesaid blunderbuss which he fortunately avoided, and the intended death-doing blow fell on his shoulder. Mrs Edwards and her party then entered, and delivered (as was thought) peaceable possession to the Frenchman, who brought in some of his things, and with Johnson and the other black men, began to throw the furniture and the made and unmade cloth of the shop into the street, while the defendant was absent at the police to get assistance. Almost as soon as Thiery had entered, the defendant's wife ... saluted him in the face—with her fist. He was too much of a Frenchman to return the compliment with the same politeness. At first he stood amazed with his hands on his breast ... then ... he became more active in bundling the things into the street. In throwing out a bundle, either by accident or design, he repaid the blow of the fair assailant with interest, by sending it against her head, and knocking her down, with the side of her face against a wood-pile.

The defendant returned without legal assistance, and found a great part of his furniture and the materials of his shop in a woful pickle, and, as Edmund

Burke would say, 'trodden under the hoofs of the swinish multitude.' As he approached the scene of action, he cried out 'Huzza! Now I've the strongest party'. The people, seeing the things thrown in the street, and hearing the hubbub, collected to the number of two or three hundred. A re-entry was made by the defendant, who found his wife in possession, and a part of the goods remaining. An attack was then commenced by the defendant, and others, on the Frenchman, and he was beaten unmercifully, and two of his fore-teeth knocked out. He was immediately dragged or carried feet foremost into the street, by the people; and the cry of 'Kill the Frenchman and negroes', was vociferated right merrily. The Frenchman retreated and took refuge in the apartment of Mrs Edwards.

The Mayor, with several other officers, arrived near the scene of action about the time the Frenchman was dragged into the street, and ascertaining who had originally the peaceable possession, reinstated the defendant and restored order.

However, as their control over political life waned with the growth in population, leaders of the Mayor's Court and the mercantile elite came to reject an activist role in government along with the notion that society had a moral obligation to the poor.[39] Charity, formerly an expression of the social responsibility of the merchants and professionals of the new republic, came to be seen by the 1820s as an unwelcome imposition on the good will of the wealthy.[40] Instead, the elite came to advocate laissez-faire individualism, regulated by the market and protected by government.[41] For their part, artisans and labourers came to criticise the regulatory state for granting privileges to the mercantile class and thereby threatening the rights of all citizens.

Offences and offending

At the outset of the century there were few statutorily derived criminal offences that were the subject of prosecution in General Sessions. Essentially, as set out in the Laws of 1796, in addition to murder, treason and stealing from a church, offences punishable by death, there was the general category of 'felonies' (derived from the common law) in addition to petit larceny, obtaining property by false pretences and knowingly receiving stolen property.[42] As common law offences, these crimes were not differentiated according to degree (other than grand and petit larceny) and thus indictments charged people, for example, with forcible theft, burglary, rape or assault without reference to degrees of culpability other than the division between principal and accessory. By 1801 there was

---

[39] Anbinder (2002) pp 144 ff documenting the changes in Five Points.
[40] Stansell (1987) Chapter 2.
[41] Bridges (1984) pp 6–10; *cf.* L Harts (1968).
[42] 1796 *New York Session Laws*, Session 19, Chapter 30.

greater statutory definition of felony offences in which the elements of such crimes as arson, assault, robbery, burglary, forgery and perjury began to be enumerated.[43] With the reform of 1829, however, offences came to be defined according to degree with greater and lesser degrees carrying discrete sentences.[44]

The vast majority of indictable offences prosecuted in General Sessions involved localised disputes committed by males who constituted around 85 per cent of all defendants in our sample. No fewer than 65.0 per cent of our case files were property offences, while approximately 30 per cent were crimes against the person with the category of 'other offences' including miscellaneous public order prosecutions and quality of life offences. As in England at the same period, property crimes were prosaic both in nature and the manner of execution.[45] The vast majority of property offences in our sample consisted of a larcenous taking, the most common form of which was from a store or ship in port, although theft within houses by lodgers or servants was widespread. Most defendants were charged with either grand or petit larceny, charges appropriate to cover offences such as theft from the person, shoplifting, walk-in and other forms of burglary.[46] After 1820, some defendants faced charges of grand or petit larceny combined with charges of burglary or receiving.[47] Our analysis of the value of property taken, often an important distinction between grand and petit larceny, showed that in General Sessions between 1800–1830 petit larceny predominated while after 1830 grand larceny predominated, indicative of the greater reliance upon Special Sessions in misdemeanour prosecutions.[48]

There were comparatively few prosecutions involving thefts from the person, only thirty three such prosecutions falling within the samples over the period 1800–1845. By 1835, the predominant thefts from the person were classic pick pocket situations, typically where the prosecutor was part of a crowd in the park or in the fly market. In addition, many thefts from the person in the later samples (1835, 1839 and 1845) involved allegations against women who were in the business of selling sex. A small group of property prosecutions also involved

---

[43] 1801 *Compilation of the Laws of the State of New York*, Session 24, Chapter LVIII.

[44] 1829 *New York Revised Statutes*, Part IV, Chapter 1.

[45] See Langbein (2003) and Carolyn A Conley (1991).

[46] The first charge of burglary in our sample was faced by *Joseph Willets*, District Attorney's Files, 8 August, 1815 who broke into the dwelling-house of William Kerr, a grocer, and stole a firkin of butter. Burglary became more commonly charged, with 23.0 per cent of the 1835 sample comprising burglary cases, 16.0 per cent in 1839, and 35.8 per cent in 1845.

[47] In our sample, there were 20 such cases.

[48] Early statutory authority provided that individuals would be charged with petit larceny (a misdemeanour) where the value of the goods stolen was less than $12.50 (1801 *Compilation of the Laws of the State of New York*, Acts of the 24th Session, Chapter LVIII, Section v, p 254 and with grand larceny (a felony) for higher value thefts, though there were occasional exceptions; whereas by 1829, the Statute was revised to provide that petit larceny occurred when goods stolen were less than $25.00 (1829 *Revised Statutes of the State of New York*, Part IV, Chapter I, Title VI, Section 1, p 690.).

obtaining goods or money by some act of deception or fraud. Other acts of deception involved passing counterfeit notes.

In broad terms, our analysis of property offenders in our sample showed that between 1800 and 1845, 92 per cent of indicted defendants whose occupation was known were classified as labourers (13 per cent of whom were said to be skilled in some craft), while 4 per cent were merchants or businessmen and another 4 per cent were either unemployed or slaves. Indeed, it appears that people of colour, who comprised about ten per cent of the population, were disproportionately represented in property offence prosecutions in the early period of the nineteenth century.[49] Crimes were sometimes explained by the accused in terms of the social economy the individual confronted, ie, that he had stolen a bundle of twelve combs 'to get him some victuals having eaten nothing in two days' or that 'he has no house nor home—sleeps under the boards and trees at night'.

Although a 'propertied class' dominated as prosecutors, as one would expect, because they had the property to be stolen or protected, this does not tell the whole story: many of the prosecutors who were victims of property theft were without any considerable standing, power or wealth. Thus, whilst the standard prosecutor in property prosecutions was a person of some means, however, as our sample of case files make clear, the law could be invoked by working class victims. As in England in the seventeenth and eighteenth centuries, prosecution was far from being a preserve of the ruling class.[50] Thus, prosecutors were not infrequently 'free black men' or 'persons of colour', servants, gardeners, cartmen, cordwainers, and shipwrights. Equally, the law could be and was occasionally invoked against people of means and standing in society including Wall Street brokers and clerks.

The typical relationship of the parties in property offences prosecuted in our sample was between a defendant drawn from the labouring classes and a prosecutor drawn from the diverse mercantile classes, ie, merchant, small store owner, craftsman, master, ship owner, and the like.[51] There also appears to have been a marked difference between the age, experience, and educational standards of defendants and those of prosecutors, as is evidenced by their ability to sign legal documents.[52] Although most defendants were aged between twenty and forty, a

[49] For accounts of the lives of black people in the City over this period, see S White (1989); S White (1991).
[50] See for a discussion of the position in England: Langbein (1993) p 101–02; P J R King (1984); Conley (1991) pp 173–201.
[51] This was also not dissimilar from England: see J Brewer and J Styles (eds) (1980); P J R King (1984) and (2000).
[52] Some care should be exercised here because a small number of experienced defendants may have strategically elected to make a mark as a further way of making it difficult for the authorities to establish their identity. Thus, in the case of *Abel Smith (with Henry Holmes)*, District Attorney's Files, 15 December, 1809, Holmes stated at his examination that he could sign his name 'after a very bad fashion' adding 'but I generally make a mark when I am called to witness a paper'.

substantial portion was under the age of twenty.[53] By contrast, over three-quarters of victims/private prosecutors were petty merchants or small businessmen, with another 9 per cent skilled craftsmen, and 11 per cent professionals. Similarly, defendants signed their statements at their examination before the magistrate in only 40.0 per cent of cases in our sample, making a mark in 58.2 per cent and refusing to sign or make a mark in 1.8 per cent. By contrast, private prosecutors signed statements of complaint in 87.9 per cent of cases, making a mark in only 12.1 per cent of instances.

Whilst most property offenders prosecuted in General Sessions appear to have been opportunistic amateurs, nevertheless there was also a group of repeat offenders, often previously the beneficiaries of a pardon, whose activities posed greater problems for the policing system, some of whom demonstrated evidence of organisation and professionalism,[54] as in prosecutions for false or fraudulent documents the initial production of which required some planning and resources.[55] Occasionally, minor fraudsters used false documentation to support the deception, as in the petit larceny prosecution of John Brown[56] who tried to pass himself off as deaf and dumb with the support of false documentation:

[53] See also R Ernst (1979) p 57. Burrows and Wallace (1999, p 501) describe the problem of juvenile delinquency: 'With only half of the city's children in school and the old apprenticeship system in disarray, it was almost inevitable that thousands of ragamuffins would become a feature of the city scene—lolling about wharves, begging on the streets, thronging the shipyards, hanging about Brooklyn ropewalks on the Sabbath, playing cards and spouting profanity. Some edged into criminality.'

[54] No consistent information is available on the ages of those prosecuted in General Sessions. Early on, where reference is made to age, the defendants tend to be children of 12 or 13 years of age (*John Heyer and Lewis Eastwood*, District Attorney's Files, 6 April, 1805; *Frederick Romer, Amos Lafrege and John Barnes*, District Attorney's Files, 5 November, 1805) or young persons (*Samuel Burt*, District Attorney's Files, 5 February 1805, aged 19). Where more consistent information is provided, as in 1830, the ages of those charged with property crime for the most part fall within the band 15–30 years of age (79.6 per cent), with the heaviest concentration (59.2 per cent) in the band 17–24 years of age. In 1830, of those whose ages were known, the youngest defendants (aged 11 and 13) were given *nolles prosequi* almost certainly on the basis of their youth. Similarly, in 1835, of those defendants whose ages are revealed, 81.4 per cent were 15–30 years of age, with most (60.4 per cent) below the age of 25 years.

[55] See David Johnson (1979) p 43 who points out that counterfeiting was a complex and widespread crime at a time when the absence of a national monetary system and a profusion of local banks practically guaranteed success. Attempts to pass counterfeit notes, however, as in almost all the cases prosecuted in our sample, is not of itself evidence that the individual directly involved in the passing was a professional counterfeiter; and the very lack of a national monetary system meant that genuine mistakes could be made as to whether the notes were genuine or bogus. For examples of counterfeiting activities of an organised character see *Dennis Weaver* (1817) Rogers vol 2, 57; *Simeon van Houton* (1817) Rogers vol 2, 72.

[56] District Attorney's Files, 8 February, 1805. On his examination, Brown said that he had acquired the printed paper in Philadelphia from where he had arrived in the City about three months ago and had 'out of a joke represented himself to be deaf & dumb...'.

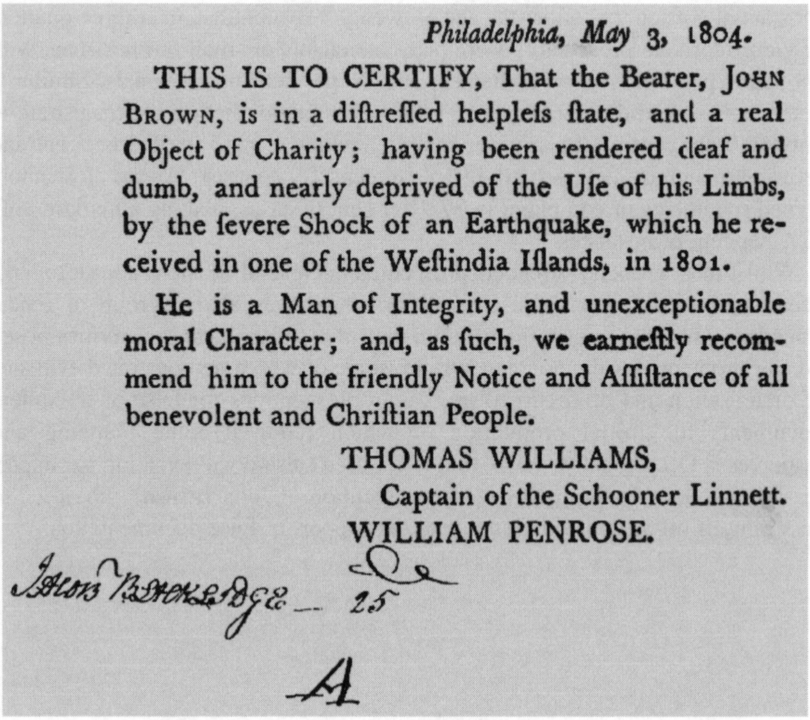

Philadelphia, May 3, 1804.

THIS IS TO CERTIFY, That the Bearer, JOHN BROWN, is in a diſtreſſed helpleſs ſtate, and a real Object of Charity; having been rendered deaf and dumb, and nearly deprived of the Uſe of his Limbs, by the ſevere Shock of an Earthquake, which he received in one of the Weſtindia Iſlands, in 1801.

He is a Man of Integrity, and unexceptionable moral Charaĉter; and, as ſuch, we earneſtly recommend him to the friendly Notice and Aſſiſtance of all benevolent and Chriſtian People.

THOMAS WILLIAMS,
        Captain of the Schooner Linnett.
WILLIAM PENROSE.

ILLUSTRATION 2.1: John Brown, District Attorney's Files, 8 February, 1805.

In the vast majority of offences against the person found in our sample the defendant was charged with assault and battery, the residual cases consisting of allegations of riot, assault with various intents and manslaughter. Assault and battery was an omnibus charge apt to cover acts that amounted to a technical invasion of the prosecutor's right to personal security such as 'threwing water' and 'mud and dirt' on the prosecutrix, or calling a next door neighbor, 'a little whore and a little hussey and such like names ...'; and for having 'pushed [the prosecutrix] out of doors, and otherwise grossly abused her'.

In the vast majority of cases in our sample, the complaint relied upon the common usage in the form of action for assault and battery, as in Samuel Clews[57] where the prosecutor swore the following complaint on 30 January 1805:

> John Duberay of Henry Street Innkeeper being duly sworn deposeth and saith that on the Twenty Ninth Instant at the Seventh ward of said City he was violently assaulted and Beaten by Samuel Clews of the said City Innkeeper without any Justification on the part of the said Samuel and therefore prays surety of the peace of the said Samuel.

[57] District Attorney's Files, 11 February, 1805.

When the complaint departed in some way from the formulaic construction, rich-er information was provided about the facts without, however, otherwise compli-cating the case, as where the prosecutrix alleged that 'some time in or about the month of July last' she was assaulted by the accused 'a black woman' who 'bruised [her] in such manner that she feels the effects of it yet ...'. In another case, the prosecutrix alleged that she had been 'cut in her arm with an axe so that she was nigh bleeding to death ...'.

In contrast to property prosecutions, the typical relationship of the parties in assault and battery cases was between people of the same occupational group such as labourers, carpenters, or innkeepers, or between those drawn from differ-ent occupations within the same class (eg cordwainer and cartman; physician and gentleman; attorney at law and gentleman; merchant and Counsellor at Law). Cross-allegations were not uncommon with all disputants separately prosecuted. Prosecutions could, however, transcend class or status divisions, being laid for example, against masters for correcting apprentices, police officers for acts of assault on civilians, and masters for beating slaves.

The vast majority of prosecutions for offences of personal violence (74 per cent) in our sample involved allegations of assault between males, 25 per cent of males assaulting females, with a further three cases where the male defendants were said to have assaulted unspecified victims.[58] In eleven per cent of cases, women were charged with assault on other women, while in a residue of four per cent with assault on men.[59]

Riots were a common feature of city life over the whole of the period 1800–1845.[60] Whilst much rioting, a common law offence, had its source in class, ethnic, racial and religious conflicts, in post-revolutionary times rioting was also viewed as a legitimate method of expressing public dissatisfaction over political, social and economic issues.[61] Increasingly over the early decades of the nineteenth century, however, rioting of all forms gave rise to prosecutions that were initiated upon the complaint of the watch, constables and marshals.

Several prosecutions for riot in our sample show the wide range of conduct covered by the charge including in one case where the defendant was charged with 'strolling up & down cursing & swearing & using very indecent language & shoved people about on the walk and behaving very disorderly' and in another case for drawing a sword, cutting and slashing, wounding the woman of the

[58] Of the whole sample, 23 cases (7.1 per cent) involved an allegation of assault on a police officer (watch or constable).

[59] The files do not ordinarily provide details of the age or race of the defendant and complainant in assault cases, although occasionally there is some reference to such matters, as in *Sophia Clarkson*, District Attorney's Files, 5 April, 1830 in which the defendant is said to be 'black' and the com-plainant 'mulatto'.

[60] See Paul Gilje (1987). For a contemporary view of riots see Philip Hone, *The Diary of Philip Hone, 1828–51* (ed A Nevins) vols I and II (1927).

[61] Several prominent lawyers, including Hugh Maxwell, were convicted after protesting at the refusal of Columbia College to grant a diploma to a graduating student: Gilje (1987) pp 115–16.

house in the face and putting in dread and fear for their lives all the females of the house.

A residual group of prosecutions memorialised in the our sample of case files consisted of a diverse range of offences mostly on the allegations of police officers or other officials, although citizen prosecutors did initiate many of these cases. These cases include: keeping a disorderly house, horse-killing, bigamy, libel, perjury, cruelty to animals, aiding escape from prison, extortion, illegal voting, liquor violations, and nuisance associated with animals.

Private prosecutors

Like the political economy, at the outset of the nineteenth century, the prosecutorial system leading to trials in General Sessions was at once private-entrepreneurial and publicly administered. The importance of the citizen in crime control functions in New York is traceable to the moral reformation project of mid-eighteenth century England in which reformers contended that the solution to the 'crime panic' was that citizens should take responsibility for apprehending offenders and co-operating with magistrates in the suppression of vice and in the execution of the laws against public offending.[62] In New York City, a private citizen who was aware that a felony had been committed had the responsibility to file a complaint at the Police Office.[63] Thus, the mainspring of the criminal justice system in the first half of nineteenth century New York was the private prosecutor. It was the private prosecutor—the victim or someone acting on his or her behalf—who initiated the overwhelming majority of complaints and in whose name complaints were launched.

Private prosecutors came from all walks of life many of whom were members of the underclass of labourers, servants and free blacks.[64] Without the moving force of the private prosecutor, many prosecutions would never have been brought or, if brought, would have failed through lack of evidence. As in England, there was statutory recognition of this in providing compensation for time and expenses to the citizen prosecutor and witnesses.[65] In addition, the administrative structure which supported the private prosecutor was itself based upon market principles: the marshals, constables, magistrates and part-time District Attorneys were compensated according to a schedule of fees for acts undertaken on behalf of the citizen.[66]

---

[62] See Rawlings (1999) p 29.

[63] O B Barbour (1852) p 515.

[64] See also Conley (1991). Writing about the English county of Kent in Victorian times, Conley writes: 'The citizens of Kent respected the rule of law, Even the working classes brought their complaints to court': Conley (1991) p 202.

[65] 1796 *New York Sessions Law*, Session 19, Chapter 30, p 670; 1801 *Compilation of the Laws of the State of New York*, Acts of the 24th Session, Chapter LX, Section xv, p 263. For a discussion of the English practice see Philip Rawlings (1999) p 29, citing the Disorderly Houses Act 1752 (25 Geo II C36).

[66] Barbour (1852) pp 481–82.

Upon a police magistrate's examination of the private prosecutor and the material witnesses, and upon a finding of probable cause, an arrest warrant would be issued.[67] An arrest warrant recited the accusation and commanded a constable or marshal to take the person accused into custody and to bring him before a magistrate without unnecessary delay.[68] However, a warrant was not essential and arrests by private citizens were statutorily authorised without a warrant when apprehending a perpetrator in the act of committing a crime or in hot pursuit and when a felony was committed outside the presence of the private person who had reasonable suspicion of the identity of the perpetrator. In any event, private citizens were statutorily directed to deliver arrested suspects to the watch house or directly to the magistrate at the Police Office.[69]

The private prosecutor (either before or after indictment) on a charge of assault or other misdemeanour had the statutory authority to settle or 'compound' the criminal case by acknowledging having received satisfaction and by appearing before a police magistrate or before the Court of General Sessions. Such practice when it occurred in General Sessions resulted in a nolle prosequi and discharge of the accused.[70] Moreover, in General Sessions no misdemeanour could be compounded without the District Attorney's approval.

At the same time the requirement that the accused was to be brought before a police magistrate (along with the private prosecutor and the witnesses) effectively challenged the notion that law enforcement was entirely a discretionary decision to be left to the individual.[71] Whilst private prosecutors would frequently be represented by private counsel at trial in General Sessions,[72] the bedrock of the criminal justice system lay in an elaborate public administrative structure that was applied to every prosecuted case and through which evidence was gathered and assembled according to uniform procedures. The policing system, magistrates' examination of witnesses, grand jury review and the District Attorney's overall responsibility for the case file and the prosecution of indicted cases formed the base of a vertically-integrated justice system through which all

---

[67] 1829 *Revised Statutes of the State of New York*, Part IV, Chapter II, Title ii, Section 2, p 706; Title ii, Section 20, p 709. See Colby (1868) pp 175–77.

[68] *Ibid*, Section 3, p 706; see Barbour (1852) p 536 indicating that under case law interpreting the Revised Statutes a constable could detain a person for up to twelve hours in order to locate a magistrate to hear the cause.

[69] 1829 *Revised Statutes of the State of New York*, Part IV, Chapter II, Title ii, Section 8, p 707.

[70] 1801 *Compilation of the Laws of the State of New York*, Acts of the 24th Session, Chapter LX, Section xviii, xix, 264; 1829 *Revised Statutes of the State of New York*, Part IV, Title IV, Chapter II, Sections 68, 72; see Colby (1868) pp 206, 258.

[71] For a discussion of similar policing strategies and the reciprocal relationship of the private prosecutor and the magistrate see Philip Rawlings (1999) p 30 discussing the work of the Fielding brothers in England.

[72] 1801 *Compilation of the Laws of the State of New York*, Acts of the 24th Session, Chapter XLVIII, Section 1, p 416 provided that 'every person of full age and sound memory ... may appear by attorney in every action or plea by or against him.'

indicted cases proceeded and which eventually articulated with the demands of the judges and lawyers of General Sessions.

Police organisation

The public element of law enforcement comprised the mayor, common council, high constable, police magistrates, constables, marshals, and night watch all of whom bore some responsibility for crime control although, as in other cities in the North East, individuals with means could hire private watchmen to secure their premises.[73] The mayor was the chief police officer, while the high constable was directly subordinate to the mayor and was the chief assistant in the maintenance of public order. The latter was directed by the Common Council to enforce all state laws affecting the peace and all City ordinances.[74] At the outset of the nineteenth century, there were sixteen constables, two elected annually in each of the first six wards and four in the seventh ward, while, by 1811, there were sixty marshals appointed by the mayor who held office at his pleasure. Constables and marshals, who often came from the ranks of artisans and tradesmen, were compensated according to a schedule of fees. They were generally responsible for maintaining the peace, detecting and apprehending criminals and idle and disorderly persons, although much of the marshals' time was taken up by attendance at the Mayor's Court and in service of process.[75] It was also the responsibility of constables and marshals to provide the police magistrate information regarding disorderly houses, gambling establishments, and taverns operating without license.[76]

The eighteenth century Montgomerie Charter (1731) provided a permanent citizens' watch in which all citizens had to serve or pay for a substitute.[77] Watchmen were drawn from the labouring classes and were paid a minimal wage, per evening of service. They served on alternate nights, while pursuing other occupations during the day. The watch was divided into two shifts each night and watchmen were required to wear leather helmets from which they derived the name 'leather heads'. A watchman who fell asleep while on duty could have his helmet taken from him, and this could serve as a ground for dismissal.[78] For both nightwatchmen and constables, income came to be supplemented through rewards obtained principally from recovering stolen property, a practice reformers contended led in America, as in England, to active collusion between thieves and law enforcement officers.

The night watch grew following the mid-1820s, which saw an increase in crime concomitant with a rise in immigration and the incidence of poverty.

---

[73] Richardson (1970) p 16. Our account in this section is indebted to Richardson.
[74] Minutes of the Common Council for 1801, vol ii, p 743; see Richardson (1970) p 16.
[75] Richardson (1970) pp 17–19.
[76] Pomerantz (1938) pp 302–03.
[77] Richardson (1970) p 9; see Christian (1812; reprinted 1970); Costello (1884).
[78] Richardson (1970) p 20.

Although the mayor originally had the power of appointment and removal of watchmen, this later became the responsibility of a standing committee of the Common Council.[79] The alderman of each ward kept a list of those persons liable for service, and the chief constable was responsible for accompanying the appropriate group of citizens each night for watch duty.[80] As private citizens, night watchmen could arrest with impunity only if a crime was committed in their presence or they were acting under the direction of a magistrate, marshal, constable, or justice of the peace.[81]

Special Justices

In contrast with the rest of the state, the City of New York did not have justices of the peace (an English institution dating from 1361 that had survived in North America in pre- and post-colonial days) until towards the end of the eighteenth century.[82] However, the mayor, recorder and aldermen, all magistrates and members of the Mayor's Court, possessed powers equivalent to or greater than those possessed by justices of the peace outside the City.[83]

By 1800, paid Special Justices were appointed by the Governor with the same powers as justices of the peace.[84] Like their predecessors and English counterparts, Special Justices had the authority to engage in summary proceedings for minor, 'quality of life' offences such as vagrancy and public intoxication and could require individuals to post recognisances to secure against a future breach of the peace.[85] Special Justices thus interfaced with those individuals whose behaviour, whilst not necessarily criminal or threatening, was unsettling to the ways of an orderly society predicated on compliance with prevailing norms related to work, industriousness and sobriety.

Under an Act of 1798, the Common Council acted to establish a Police Office to facilitate discovery and apprehension of offenders, comprising two Special Justices and a clerk.[86] Until 1812, the Police Office was in the basement of the

---

[79] The Common Council then comprised the mayor, recorder and one alderman and assistant elected from each of the City's wards: Richardson (1970) p 20.

[80] J Richardson (1970) p 9.

[81] J Richardson (1970) p 19; see Jerome Hall (1936) p 5.

[82] Note, 'Magistrates Courts of the City of New York: History and Organisation' 8 *Brooklyn Law Review* (December, 1937) 133, 139. See also Bruce Smith (1996) pp 19–49, 171–214.

[83] See 1801 *Compilation of the Laws of the State of New York*, Acts of the 24th Session, Chapter LXX, Section VIII, p 305.

[84] Pomerantz (1965) p 310. See also 1829 *Revised Statutes of the State of New York*, Part IV, Chapter 2, Title I, Section 1, p 704. Paid magistrates had been established a few years earlier in England: Middlesex Justices Act 1792 32 Geo 3, C53.

[85] For a detailed consideration of the summary jurisdiction of New York magistrates, see Smith (1996).

[86] The first Police Office was created by the Common Council in 1798 as means 'more effectually to discover and apprehend offenders' in the City of New York: Act of March 2, 1798 Chapter 25, 4 *New York State Laws* 164. See Smith (1996) p 68.

City Hall on Wall Street.[87] As in London, when the Police Office was in session, the Special Justice was seated at a desk next to or in close proximity to the clerk and separated from the public by a wooden bar. Constables, accused, lawyers, witnesses and the general public milled about the room and adjoining hallways.[88] At least one of the two Special Justices together with a clerk was required to 'daily and throughout the day (Sundays and convenient intervals for refreshment excepted) attend in the said police office for the execution of their respective trusts'.[89] Initially drawn from the ranks of aldermen, the first two Special Justices, Theophilus Beekman and Jacob De La Montagnie, were both men of substance with prior experience in local government.[90]

Where individuals were accused of offences prosecuted in General Sessions, Special Justices conducted committal proceedings by examining witnesses and the accused and binding the accused over to the Grand Jury and/or discharging the accused dependent upon the sufficiency of the evidence and charge severity.[91] The role of the Special Justice in examining witnesses, including the accused, originated in justice of the peace manuals of English origin which were widely distributed in the North Eastern United States by the mid-eighteenth century. These manuals provided Special Justices with a digest of rules and policies related to their common law and statutory responsibilities and contained basic articles on the manner and subject of criminal investigation and adjudication.[92] The Special Justice and his Clerk had the responsibility of maintaining all case records—witness examinations and tangible evidence in the Police Office itself which were later transmitted to the Grand Jury and District Attorney for use as the basis of an indictment and trial evidence in General Sessions. The role of the Special Justice thereby secured and resulted in the construction of the prosecution's case.

The 1801 statute requiring the Special Justice's examination of the accused was amended in 1829 to provide that before examining the defendant, the magistrate was to inform the accused of the charges against him, of his right to

---

[87] After 1812 the Police Office was moved to the new City Hall with a second Police Office being opened at Bowery and Third Streets in 1832.

[88] Frederick Trevor Hill (1912), cited in Smith (1996) p 301.

[89] The Act established a salary of $750 for each Special Justice together with such fees as were allowed to a justice of the peace, and an equivalent salary to the clerk, the costs of the salaries and the expenses of the police office to be part of the budget of the city and county.

[90] See Smith (1996) pp 69–70.

[91] 1801 *Compilation of the Laws of the State of New York*, Acts of the 24th Session Chapter LXX, Section vi, p 304; *James Robertson* (1824) Wheeler, vol 3, 180; see Barbour (1852) pp 552–57; Colby (1868) p 175; Eben Moglen (1997) pp 114–17.

[92] The manuals included: Giles Jacob, *The Modern Justice: The Business of a Justice of the Peace* (London, Sayer, 1716); William Nelson, *The Office and Authority of a Justice of Peace* (London, Sayer, 1710); Richard Burn, *Justice of the Peace and Parish Officer* (London, Linton, 1755). American justice of the peace manuals either reprinted large portions of the English manuals or contained in edition local statutes peculiar to justices of the peace in various jurisdictions. See E Moglen (1994) p 1097.

counsel and the right to remain silent.[93] Otherwise, the amended statute conformed with pre-existing practice: the magistrate could not examine the accused 'on oath'[94] so as to avoid concerns that the statement of the accused would be deemed involuntary and inadmissible at trial; all examinations were under oath and reduced to writing by the magistrate's clerk, who would read the examination to the prosecutor, the witnesses, and the defendant for possible corrections;[95] the examination could be delayed to permit the defendant a reasonable time to obtain and consult with counsel and to have counsel present and that counsel could assist in the examination of defence witnesses, for whom the defendant had the right to ask the magistrate to issue a subpoena.[96]

Special Justices were entrusted with the overall supervision of the watch as well as directing the activities of the marshals and constables. Every morning the Special Justices supervised the dismissal of the watch. They also maintained records of liquor law violations and a list of all licenses issued by the City.[97] The innovation in the role of police magistrates in New York City, as in mid-eighteenth century London under the initiatives of magistrates Henry and John Fielding, was to extend their function and authority to co-ordinating and supervising investigations into alleged criminal activity of a more serious nature including attending searches and seizures of property.[98] These Special Justices were often the critical players in providing an over-arching intelligence to disparate allegations and bits of evidence that filtered into the Police Office through private prosecutors, informants, constables and watchpersons. Indeed, their responsibilities led Special Justices to recommend policing initiatives that would address local problems that had surfaced through the course of their investigations.

Grand Jury

Before someone could be prosecuted in General Sessions, a case had to be presented before a Grand Jury that was empanelled at the commencement of each term.[99] The Grand Jury was an English institution designed to protect against the

---

[93] 1829 *Revised Statutes of the State of New York*, Part IV, Chapter 2, Title 2, Section 14–15, p 708.

[94] *Ibid.*

[95] *Ibid*, Section 16, p 708.

[96] *Ibid*, Sections 14, 15 and 17, p 708, although the magistrate had the power to commit the defendant until such time as the witnesses could be examined.

[97] *Laws of New York*, 21st Session, Chapter 24, March 2, 1798; see Pomerantz (1965) p 304.

[98] Smith (1996) pp 304–05. For a discussion of the Fieldings' efforts 'to bring system to the collection of information about crime and criminals' to Bow Street, see Rawlings (1999) pp 30–32; and Beattie (2001) at pp 81–2, 418.

[99] Goebel and Naughton (1944) showed that after 1684 accusation by grand jury became the predominant method of initiating prosecutions of persons suspected of felonies and serious misdemeanors: p 337.

arbitrary exercise of authority in arrest and prosecution.[100] Grand Jury screening occurred when the District Attorney, after reviewing the Special Justice's file, presented the private prosecutor and witnesses and instructed the Grand Jury as to the relevant law which would guide them in deciding whether there was sufficient evidence by which to indict. The District Attorney was present when the testimony of witnesses was given and could thus assess its probity and persuasiveness. Indictments returned by the Grand Jury were drafted by the District Attorney.[101]

Grand Jurors were chosen from a list of 600 persons proposed by the mayor, recorder and aldermen who the statute required 'must be of integrity, fair character, sound judgment and must be well informed …'[102] A Grand Jury comprised not more than 23 nor fewer than 16 persons with a Foreman to be appointed in every case.[103] Prominent members of society sometimes appeared as grand jurors as did merchants, lawyers and crafts people.

However, at least by 1841,[104] Grand Jury records of General Sessions show considerable diversification with a wide range of occupational groupings represented typical of the mercantile economy rather than being dominated by the propertied or landed elite. In the Grand Jury return for January 1841, for example, 24 potential jurors were called for service. Of these, 5 were excused (one of whom was ineligible by reason of being too old), 2 defaulted and one was not found. Those called for service and for whom details were available spanned a wide range of occupational groupings: merchant (n=11); grocer (n=2); ship carpenter (n=2); butcher; clothier; morocco draper; plumber.

The District Attorney

Although the prosecutorial function relied heavily on the initiative of the private citizen, first, in New York City General Sessions and Oyer and Terminer, a public prosecutor, the State Attorney General[105] (in other districts, Assistant Attorney Generals appointed by the Governor) and then by 1801 a similarly-appointed District Attorney, for the district including New York City and the counties of Queens, Kings, Suffolk, and Westchester, was available to represent the private

---

[100] For a discussion of grand juries in England, see John Beattie (1977); for America, see Richard D Younger (1963).

[101] The District Attorney's statutory authority to examine witnesses, give legal advice and to issue subpoenas first appeared in the 1829 *Revised Statutes of the State of New York*, Part IV, Title IV, Section 32, p 725.

[102] *Ibid*, Section 11, p 720.

[103] *Ibid*, Section 26, p 724.

[104] This was the first year for which we were able to obtain complete lists of Grand Jury members.

[105] Whilst the Attorney General was specifically limited from acting as attorney-solicitor or proctor in any private suit without state interest, such limitations in the practice of civil law did not apply to Assistant Attorney Generals or District Attorneys who were of the degree of counsel in the state Supreme Court and resident of the district: 1796 *New York Sessions Laws*, Session XIX, Chapter VIII, pp 643–45.

prosecutor in indicted cases prosecuted in General Sessions.[106] As part-time public prosecutors, Assistant Attorney Generals and District Attorneys were compensated through the state treasury after an audit by the Court of Exchequer based
upon a schedule of fees authorised by statute for issuance of subpoenas, for draft-
ing an indictment, and for a trial or demurrer or opposition to a motion.[107]

By 1813 it was the statutory duty of the District Attorney to manage and conduct all prosecutions in General Sessions and Oyer and Terminer. However, when
the District Attorney did not attend the prosecution, the court had the authority to
appoint one of the private lawyers in the court who would then prosecute and
could be compensated for services in the same manner as the District Attorney.[108]
In practice, our data showed that in General Sessions, private lawyers for the
prosecution quite commonly appeared either in lieu of the District Attorney or as
co-counsel. The District Attorney's responsibility began once the Special Justice
had bound the case over to the grand jury, although it did not extend to the Police
Office where cases were assembled by the Special Justice and Clerk or misdemeanour cases prosecuted in Special Sessions.[109]

Over this whole period, the District Attorney was an officer of the court and a
prominent lawyer in private practice. Until 1847, he was appointed by the
Governor's Council of Appointment and approved by the judges of the Court of
General Sessions.[110] During this period, the District Attorney's principal function
was to receive the case file assembled by the Special Justice, appear before the
Grand Jury and guide the case to conclusion in General Sessions actively representing the state at trial, when the prosecutor was not represented by a private
lawyer.[111] The District Attorney's right to terminate the prosecution of an indictment by entering a *nolle prosequi* because of the co-operation of the accused or
upon other extenuating circumstances became limited by the statute of 1829 to
those instances where the court considered such action appropriate.[112]
Prosecutorial conduct infrequently attracted criticism and adverse comment was
muted usually centring on the refusal of the District Attorney at trial to introduce
exculpatory statements made by defendants in the examination before the Special
Justice.

---

[106] *Ibid*; 1801 *Compilation of the Laws of the State of New York*, Acts of the 24th Session, Chapter
CXLVI, Section I, p 461.

[107] 1796 *New York Sessions Law*, Section XIX, Chapter VII, p 644.

[108] 1813 *Laws of the State of New York*, Acts of the 35th and 36th Session, 1812, 1813, Chapter
LXVI, Section VII, p 337, Chapter LXXXIX, Section IV, p 415.

[109] This was confirmed by our own analysis of the District Attorney's files. See also Smith (1996)
p 301.

[110] 1801 *Compilation of the Laws of the State of New York*, Acts of the 24th Session, Chapter CXLVI,
Section I, p 461. A Chester (1925) vol 2, 886–87.

[111] For discussion of the history of public prosecution see W Scott Van Alstyne (1952); Rita W
Cooley (1958); J Langbein (1973); A Sidman (1976); Jack Kress (1976); J Jacoby (1980); and
Carolyn B Ramsey (2002).

[112] 1829 *Revised Statutes of the State of New York*, Title IV, Section 68, p 730; Section 54, p 726.

Legal representation and the legal profession

Lawyers who appeared in General Sessions had to be licensed to practice in the court by the chief judge, based on good character and learning.[113] General standards of admission for attorneys, those lawyers whose actions were limited to preparing a case for trial, writing a brief or making preliminary motions,[114] were set forth by the state Supreme Court.[115] They included seven years of preparation at least three years of which was to be as a clerk or apprentice with a practising attorney provided the applicant had four years of a classical education obtained after age fourteen.[116] An additional three to four years of practice as an attorney was required before a lawyer could be admitted as a counsellor, someone fully qualified to represent a party in the trial of a case in General Sessions.[117]

As was underscored in 1815 by Richard Riker, the Recorder in General Sessions, with reference to Article 34 of the New York State Constitution:

> [I]n all criminal prosecutions the accused ought to be informed of the cause and nature of his accusation. To be confronted with his accusers and the witnesses against him. To have the means of producing his witnesses, *and the assistance of counsel for his defence*[118] (original emphasis).

Upon the defendant requesting counsel, the court would assign one of the lawyers admitted to practice in General Session.[119] The court sought to satisfy the right to counsel in indicted cases in this manner.[120] Counsel was provided access to the accused during pre-trial detention at the local Bridewell, as described in the trial of James Lent and James Williamson (1818):[121]

---

[113] New York State Constitution 1777, Article 27; 1823 *Compilation of the Laws of the State of New York*, Chapter 20, Section 19, p 215.

[114] G Martin (1970) Appendix B, p 385.

[115] See Henry Scott (1909) p 215.

[116] Rules of the Supreme Court, October Term 1797 (reprinted in *Attorney's Companion: Containing the Rules of the Supreme Court, Court of Chancery and Court of Errors of the State of New York* (Poughkeepsie, Potter, 1818) pp 7–8); A Z Reed (1921) pp 82–5; Wilson (1892), vol 2, note 28, p 618.

[117] *Attorney's Companion, ibid*, pp 7–8; Rules and Orders of the Court of Common Pleas for the City and County of New York (New York, Gould and Banks 1830) pp 25–26; 9 Wend. 427 October 1832. See also Alden Chester (ed) (1911) vol 1, p 306.

[118] New York State Constitution, adopted July 26, 1788 and quoted in *The matter of the Sheriff and Jailer of the City and County of New York on the complaint of Wm W McClelan, Gentlemen, one, etc*; Wheelers 1 (1823) pp 303, 311. While the New York State Constitution recognised the right to counsel in criminal cases beginning in 1777 (N Y Constitution of 1777 Article XXXIV) the implementing statute in effect at the outset of the century provided that 'every person of full age and sound memory other than defendants subject to punishment by corporal punishment, may appear by attorney in every action or plea by or against him': 1801 *Compilation of the Laws of the State of New York*, Acts of the 24th Session, Chapter XLVIII, Section 1, p 416.

[119] See eg *Terence Hughes* (1819) Rogers, vol 4, p 123 where the defendant charged with stealing requested counsel; 'the court accordingly assigned M C Paterson for that purpose.'

[120] It was not until 1881 that the Criminal Procedure Law was amended to provide that a defendant who appeared without counsel in response to an indictment was to be asked whether he wanted an attorney (Act of June 1, 1881, Chapter 442, 1881 New York Law 601, Section 8). If the defendant wished counsel, the court would appoint a lawyer on a *pro bono* basis (New York Criminal Procedure Law, Section 308). An 1893 amendment provided compensation for representation in homicide cases only (*ibid*).

[121] (1819) Rogers, vol 4, pp 56, 57; see also Wheelers 1 (1823) pp 303–14.

After the arguments of the counsel, the mayor charged the jury, that, as respected the public administration of justice, this case was important. Formerly a prisoner was not allowed the benefit of counsel; but now, according to the principles of our constitution, a different rule prevailed. The party accused is entitled to the assistance of counsel, who, in the case of the inability of the party, shall be assigned by the court. But this privilege would be nugatory—it would be a mere mockery, if counsel should be denied access, when employed by the prisoner or assigned by the court.

Minute Book entries reveal that, at least from 1810 onwards, almost every defendant in General Sessions exercised the right to be represented by a lawyer at trial irrespective of his standing in society or ability to pay a fee. It was not unusual for the judge to assign counsel even where the defendant was already represented, and it was common for more than one lawyer to be assigned to a single defendant. As Figure 2.1 shows, by 1810 there were over 400 recorded defence-lawyer cases, by 1821 the number had reached almost 1000[122] and thereafter it mostly levelled off at between 400–600 cases per year, until 1865:

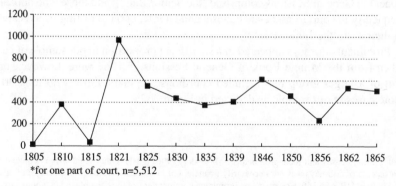

*for one part of court, n=5,512

FIGURE 2.1 General Sessions Minute Book—Number of Recorded Defence Lawyer Cases Over the Year*, 1805–1865

Private lawyers volunteered for court assignments and, when a fee was not forthcoming from the defendant or his family,[123] acted pro bono.[124] The same lawyers who were retained in fee-paying cases accepted court assignments when indigent defendants were without counsel.

---

[122] A similar analysis for the period January–August 1811 undertaken by Smith revealed that defence counsel was mentioned in 46 of 88 cases recorded in the Minute Book of General Sessions: Smith (1996) p 313.

[123] See *Report of the Trial of Henry Bedlow for Committing a Rape on Lanah Sawyer* (New York, 1793) for an account of a case in which a team of lawyers represented a gentleman in a notorious rape case.

[124] Aspects of the criminal bar at work in Manhattan are discussed by Michael Millender (1996), Chapter 3. Millender contends that the willingness to accept court assignments was part of an overall effort by the cadre of lawyers appearing in General Sessions to gain notoriety so that people of some means would be willing to retain them in the future. Millender points to the numerous pamphlets and nominative reports which the lawyers themselves authored and which demonstrated their familiarity

In the eighteenth century, the Mayor's Court attracted lawyers of ability and distinction. Originally a small group of these lawyers provided the entirety of legal representation but this was subsequently expanded to include all lawyers admitted to practice in the state Supreme Court. By the end of the eighteenth century, prominent lawyers continued to dominate and included such notables as Alexander Hamilton, Aaron Burr, Edward Livingston and the 'American Erskine', Josiah Ogden Hoffman.[125]

At the outset of the nineteenth century, the bar at the Mayor's Court was a broadly homogenous group that came together in social gatherings and clubs to exchange ideas and discuss the issues litigated in the courts.[126] Prominent among these was the Chancellor Kent's Club, which by 1828 became part of the New York Law Institute, formerly the Law Library and An Association of Lawyers, a small group of eminent attorneys.[127] Criminal practitioners of the day formed a barristerial class who would appear on either side of the case. They would frequently represent the private prosecutor in one case and the defendant in another whilst being bound by the attorney-client privilege. By 1821 prominent practitioners in General Sessions comprised 'the Senior Bar'[128] and those who appeared frequently in court as associate counsel and later went on to distinguished careers of their own 'the Junior Bar'.[129]

Prominent attorneys appeared in a significant proportion in our sample of cases taken from the Minute Book of General Sessions.[130] They were, however, only part of a larger group that included courthouse regulars, those who took 30 or more cases in our sample as depicted in Figure 2.2:

with criminal cases and their prominence: Millender (1996) p 108. Other legal writers contend that the success of attorneys was not necessarily financial but in moral virtue and in the service of others: Bloomfield (1976) p 146. However, one prominent commentator of the day contended, young lawyers with considerably less skill than the District Attorney may have earned their stripes as court assigned counsel: see Edward Livingston, 'Introductory Report to the Code of Criminal Procedure', in *The Complete Works of Edward Livingston on Criminal Jurisprudence* (1873) p 387. In our study, Minute Book entries and Nominative Reports show the frequent presence of more senior or associate co-counsel, and thus whoever the lawyer was did not appear to impact the method of case disposition or the manner in which trials were conducted.

[125] Proctor (1870) p 1; Scott (1909) pp 217–18; C H Hunt (1864) pp 48–54.

[126] As Michael Millender (1996) notes, the social identity of the bar became much more diffuse from the 1820s, as lawyers from outside the city as well as English and Irish radicals were attracted to New York.

[127] See E Patterson, *Catalogue of the Books in the Library of the New York Law Institute* (New York, Martin's Steam Printing House 1874) pp xxiv–xix. M Bloomfield (1976) p 140. By 1830, law students and junior lawyers founded the New York Law Association to provide regular lectures and meetings about law practice.

[128] See Daly (1855) p 65.

[129] See Daly (1855) p 65.

[130] The designation of the term 'prominent attorneys' derives from our analysis of Proctor (1870); C Warren (1911); D McAdam, H Bischoff *et al* (1897) New York Sun, *Wealth and Biography of the Wealthy Citizens of New York City* (1845).

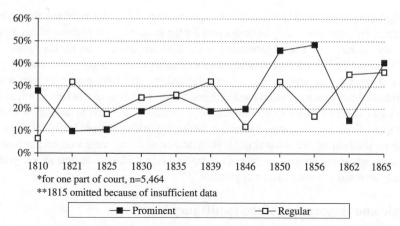

FIGURE 2.2 General Sessions Minute Book—Percentage of Regular and Prominent Identified Defence Lawyer Cases of All Defence Lawyer Cases Over the Year*, 1810–1865**

In the nominative reports of cases between 1818 and 1823, prominent and non-prominent lawyers appeared alongside one another, regulars and others who practiced occasionally in General Sessions on behalf of the defence and prosecution.[131]

Our sample of prominent lawyers included the regular presence of John Anthon, who drafted the Act of 1821[132] which established General Sessions as a separate court, 'one of the foremost lawyers of his day' and one of the most prominent lawyers practising at the Bar.[133] A founder of the New York Law Institute, he wrote widely on legal matters.[134] Another member of our sample, also a 'generous supporter' of the library of the New York Law Institute,[135] was James T Brady, who was recognised as 'one of the foremost criminal lawyers of the times, and was constantly engaged as counsel in the most important cases'. Brady, also described as 'one of the eminent leaders of the Bar in Civil suits,'[136] was appointed District Attorney in 1843 and afterwards was Corporation Counsel to the City.

David Graham, the father of a series of Grahams, all of whom appeared in our sample, was a prominent member of the Bar who emigrated from Ireland where he had been educated as a Presbyterian Clergyman.[137] 'Recognised as a brilliant

---

[131] In an analysis of appearances of lawyers noted by Daniel Rogers between 1816 and 1819, Millender found that 283 of the 354 lawyer appearances were by only fourteen of the more than fifty practitioners who occasionally appeared in General Sessions: Millender (1996) p 134.

[132] 1821 Laws of the State of New York, Chapter 72, Sections 1, 6 pp 64–6.

[133] D McAdam, H Bischoff *et al* (1897) vol 1, p 248.

[134] His publications included *Anthon's Law Student* (1810), *American Precedents* (1810), *Digested Index to the Reports of the United States Courts* (1813), *Reports of Cases at Nisi Prius in the New York Supreme Court* (1820), and *An Analytical Abridgement of Blackstone's Commentaries* (1832).

[135] D McAdam, H Bischoff *et al* (1897) vol 1, pp 266–67.

[136] D McAdam, H Bischoff *et al* (1897) vol 1, pp 266–67.

[137] Accounts of Irish emigres are provided by M Durey (1987); R Twomey (1989).

pulpit orator' he quickly became 'very prominent at the Metropolitan Bar being especially distinguished as an orator and for the masterly construction of his arguments'.[138] His son, David Graham Junior, who studied law under his father, in 1832 at the age of 24 was appointed to a committee of lawyers who drafted the new City Charter and in 1846 was selected by the Legislature to join with Arphaxed Loomis and David Dudley Field to compile a comprehensive and rationalised Code of Criminal Procedure. The proposed Code came to be known as the Graham Code because it was Graham Junior's work which primarily resulted in the production of the document.[139] Both father and son were said to have possessed 'great magnetism of manner, adroitness and other qualities which peculiarly adapted them for criminal practice'.[140]

Role and importance of the (petit) jury

The relationship between judges, lawyers and jurors is central to an understanding of the purpose and method of operation of General Sessions and, in particular, its reliance upon jury trials for the vast majority of dispositions in 'everyday' indicted criminal cases. Dating back to the colonial era, as incorporated in the New York State Constitution of 1777, a jury trial was held to be an inviolate right 'in all cases in which it had heretofore been used' including all indicted cases.[141] The trial or petit jury was to be composed of twelve white male freeholders drawn from twenty four 'good and lawful men produced by the sheriff'.[142] By case law, this supposedly 'blue-ribbon' panel[143] had the authority to decide both issues of law and fact.[144] It served, at least symbolically, as the ultimate protection against unrestrained state interest.

The jury trial tradition that was emulated in the first part of the nineteenth century authorised jurors to determine the law in a particular case where either there was the absence of a statute or English common law precedent or when there was a dispute as to the proper interpretation of a statute. In such cases, given the composition of the Court, law determination was not something unfamiliar to the

---

[138] D McAdam, H Bischoff *et al* (1897) vol 1, p 355.

[139] See 4 Report of the Commission on Practice and Pleading, Code of Criminal Procedure, 1849. See *People v Willis* 52 NYS 808, 809 (Supreme Court 1898). The Code was revised once and presented by the Committee on the Criminal Code to the legislature in 1855: see 1855 Assembly Doc 150. It was not adopted, however, until 1881.

[140] D McAdam, H Bischoff *et al* (1897) vol 1, pp 335–36. Graham Jnr also published *Practice of the Supreme Court of the State of New York* (1832), *New Trials* (1834), *Courts of Law and Equity in the State of New York* (1839) and he annotated *Smith's Chancery Practice* (1842).

[141] New York State Constitution 1777, Article XLI.

[142] 1801 *Compilation of the Laws of the State of New York*, Acts of the 24th Session, Chapter lxx, Section ii, p 303. See Goebel and Naughton (1944) pp 465–66; Colby (1868) p 332. Similarly, until 1843, property disqualifications limited the eligible voters to this group of individuals: J G Wilson (1892) vol 11, pp 378–9.

[143] Goebel and Naughton (1944) p 467.

[144] For a discussion of the similar authority of jurors in another common law state, see W Nelson (1975) pp 28–29, 170–71; see also Jeffrey Abrahamson (1994) pp 69–95.

judicial actors who, after all, as members of the Common Council had gathered to enact statutes and regulations governing the City. Each then, mayor, recorder and alderman, were well placed to consider the application of criminal law in any given case and to attempt to settle the law through their charge to the jury where, as in commercial crimes, a need existed for interpretive clarity.[145]

The decision-making process was not, however, captive to those members of the mercantile elite who controlled most of the City's wealth and may have had a clearly defined canon of conduct but instead involved craftsmen and others of modest means who were also part of the wider economy. The Sheriff's inventory of prospective jurors and an analysis of those who actually served showed that those who were called to serve on the petit jury in the Court of General Sessions were not exclusively or even mostly members of an elite class, despite the statutory constraints on jury service.

Thus, for example, whilst in the Sheriff's return for November 1818, six individuals were categorised as 'gentleman' and no fewer than 36 of the 96 listed (37.5 per cent) were described as 'merchant', lending some slight credence to the argument that they might be part of a ruling class,[146] this impression is belied where more detailed descriptions of the heterogeneous occupational status of individuals are provided. Thus, those called for service in November 1818 included:

auctioneer	cooper	plummer
baker (n=2)	distiller	printer
blacksmith	druggist	rope maker
boarding house keeper	farmer (n=2)	sail maker (n=2)
boatman	gardner	sausage maker
book binder	grocer (n=12)	shipmaster
bootmaker	harbour master	shoemaker
cabinet maker	innkeeper	shoe store keeper
carpenter (n=3)	inspector customs	storekeeper
clothing store	mariner	tailor (n=2)
comb maker	painter	watchmaker

Moreover, those who actually appeared and served were an equally heterogeneous group comprising:

auctioneer	carpenter	harbour master
baker (n=2)	gentleman (n=3)	merchant (n=14)
bookmaker	grocer (n=4)	painter

---

[145] See W Nelson (1975) p 154. However, the hierarchy of authority within the court, beginning with the mayor, was deeply respected in any jury deliberation, and the mayor's views regarding the law as well as those of the recorder and aldermen, should they differ, would be considered in the spirit of arriving at a result not only just to the individual but to the wider needs of the City.

[146] This is not strong evidence because 'merchant' was a broad category.

printer	shoe store keeper	watchmaker
sail maker	shoemaker	
shipmaster	tailor (n=2)	

The 1840 jury returns contained an even broader spectrum of occupations reflecting the growth of the City and the increased diversity of its manufacturing base.

CONCLUSION

In the first half of the nineteenth century, governance of a highly stratified political economy in New York City centred on a mercantile elite and originated in the Mayor's Court. The criminal justice system provided private citizens who spanned the socio-demographic spectrum with access based upon notions of deference and strict adherence to legal formalism. Defendants, who tended to be drawn from those who were of low status in the market economy, had the right to notice of the charges (through the complaint or the indictment), the right to counsel on the trial of an indictment (often by a prominent lawyer irrespective of the defendant's standing in society), the right to confront and cross-examine witnesses, and the right to a jury trial.

In indicted cases prosecuted in General Sessions, committal proceedings were conducted and witnesses and suspects examined by Special Justices in line with legal form. Whilst these cases were most often initiated by private citizens, the private prosecutor was supported by a law enforcement system which secured the apprehension of suspects and the memorialisation of evidence. Subsequent to the bind over decision, cases were screened by a Grand Jury and prosecuted in the court of General Sessions pursuant to an indictment. The court, whose judges were prominent lawyers themselves, was serviced by a District Attorney and the private bar all of whom were experienced in the practice of criminal law. Ultimately cases were decided by a petit jury with general jurisdiction over law and fact and comprised of a broad spectrum of citizens within the mercantile economy.

Offending prosecuted in the first half of the nineteenth century was, in general, simple in terms of both execution and factual proof. Overall, prosecutions were dominated by routine property crimes involving theft from small merchants and houses. Whilst there clearly were persistent offenders and some organised criminality, most property offences resulted from behaviour which was essentially opportunistic, committed by petty offenders, those who were presented with a chance and those who were down on their luck. Whilst the prosecutor in property prosecutions was often a person of some means, our data do not support the view that access to justice was a question of class. Regardless of class, any individual could be a prosecutor and this included the initiation of prosecutions for offences which had wider public policy implications.

Crimes against the person resulted mostly in indictments for assault and battery with a residual number of homicide offences. For the most part, these were intra-class usually between people of the same occupational group and mostly involving males. They mostly involved factual rather than legal issues. Public order offences raised issues of quality of life and morality as well as a concern for mob behaviour. The accused were mostly a plebeian class, although owners of disorderly houses were certainly people of some means.

Chapter 3

Crime Detection and Investigation in General Sessions Prosecutions: 1800–1845

INTRODUCTION

In this chapter we analyse the detection and investigation of crime pertaining to prosecutions in General Sessions in early nineteenth century New York in order to understand whether citizens had to act alone or whether the official system of policing was able to assist citizens in a meaningful and purposive manner. We first consider the respective role of police and citizens in the investigation, detection, and apprehension of those accused of criminal activity. We then consider the work of the Police Office and Special Justice in the seizure of tangible evidence, and the locating, identifying and memorialising the testimony of prosecution witnesses, including the granting of immunity. Finally, we consider how the Special Justice utilised the examination process to obtain admissions from the accused.

Policing: watch and constables

Different descriptions exist in the literature of the system of night watchmen, constables and marshals which was established to apprehend suspected offenders and bring them before the Special Justice. For some, like Michael Feldberg,[1] James Richardson[2] and Robert Fogelson,[3] this earlier system which came to be replaced by the municipal police beginning in 1846 was viewed, at best, as minimally competent and, at worst, as slothful and corrupt. Typical of this line of analysis is Feldberg's statement describing the state of policing prior to police reform:[4]

---

[1] M Feldberg (1980).
[2] J F Richardson (1970).
[3] R Fogelson (1977).
[4] Feldberg (1980) pp 109–10; see further, David Johnson (1979) p 22–4.

Before the introduction of police reforms in the late 1840s and 1850s, public order in Jacksonian cities was preserved by men who were neither full-time officers nor deeply committed to keeping the peace. Responsibility for law enforcement, public safety, and public health was assigned by day to elected sheriffs, constables, aldermen, or marshals and by night to politically appointed nightwatchmen ... Many nightwatchmen literally 'moonlighted', that is, worked—or just as often slept—on their posts, after putting in a full day at another job. Often, these men took watchmen's positions only to supplement their income. The rest tended to be older men, no longer able to earn their keep through physical labor, yet without other means of support. To get a watchman's job, one's physical strength or ability to perform responsibly was less important than one's willingness to work for the political party in power, or one's personal connection with an elected official.

By contrast, others like Sydney Harring[5] argue that those critical of watch-era policing accept on face value the allegations of reformers who sought to 'professionalise' the policing system by advancing allegations of corruption and inefficiency. On this view, the idea of reform of policing was as much a struggle for control of the police, as in New York from local to state authority, in which reform meant little more than the triumph of ideologies of social discipline, the real object of which at a time of pre-industrialisation was an emergent labour class. In this context, Harring contends, inefficiency and corruption did not disappear with the coming of the 'new' police: instead, it increased as police departments grew in size.[6]

Without attempting to bring resolution to the dispute over inefficiency and corruption, our analysis of the case files seeks to determine what it is that the watch, constables and marshals did preparatory to a case being prosecuted in General Sessions in the first half of the century,[7] what policing methodologies were employed, how these impacted upon the capacity to prosecute individual suspected offenders and whether, as we will later analyse, there was significant change in the capacity to produce reliable evidence of guilt upon the introduction of the municipal police after 1846. Our analysis also sheds light on whether enforcement of the criminal law mainly furthered the interests of the ruling elite, or whether the system of detection and investigation was so organised as to offer a measure of protection for victims of crime.

PROPERTY OFFENCES

We made a qualitative assessment of the respective roles of citizens and police in the investigation of property offences to see the extent to which prosecution

---

[5] S Harring (1983). See also S Spitzer and A Scull (1977).

[6] The general debate over police efficiency and corruption is mirrored in England: C Reith (1952); T A Critchley (1978); D Ascoli (1979); and R Storch (1975).

[7] Accounts in the Nominative Reports accord with our analysis of the District Attorney's files.

depended upon the efforts of citizen-amateurs thereby rendering evidence and proof unreliable, haphazard and contingent. Whilst our research shows that in the reporting of committal proceedings there was a systematic under-recording of police involvement, criminal prosecutions being viewed as essentially *private*,[8] citizen-prosecutors could nevertheless rely upon the fruits of police action without the need for the officer to provide sworn testimony. Hence, a private prosecutor's complaint would be based not only upon what prosecutors knew, but also upon what they had been told were the results of police action. In this way, reasonable or probable cause was commonly founded on the prosecutor's information and belief that the defendant had been found in possession of the articles said to have been stolen without any police officers attesting to the fruits of their investigative activities which formed the basis of the prosecutor's assertions.

Against this background, our overall conclusion is that, whilst citizens had, as today, a major role in the identification and arrest of suspected offenders, the police played a much more prominent role than traditionally assumed. Our general evaluation of the roles of citizens and police in the investigation of property offences and the apprehension of offenders is set out in Table 3.1:

TABLE 3.1: *General Sessions, District Attorney's Files: The Contributions of Citizens and Police to the Investigation of Property Offences over a Thirty Day Period for One Court Part, 1800–1845*

	N	%
Dominant role played by citizen	208	39.3
Dominant role played by police	123	23.2
Joint citizen-police role	76	14.3
Probable dominance of citizen	42	7.9
Probable dominance of police	81	15.3
Inadequate information	196	0.0
Total	726	100.0

Dominant role played by citizen

Our sample of case files shows that, of property prosecutions for which clear information survives (n=530), although police officers were doubtless involved in some capacity, in almost forty per cent the principal factor leading to the apprehension of the suspected offender was the action of a citizen, usually the private prosecutor. Citizens had a prominent role because they initiated the arrest of the defendant, identified the location of stolen goods, or claimed to have actually witnessed the crime. In this context, the detection of crime or the apprehension of offenders was an act of individual citizens, as complainants or bystanders, or

[8] In *Winfort Van,* District Attorney's Files, 16 April, 1830, for example, a case involving theft of calico from Temperance Jones, Temperance is described as the 'Prosecutrix'.

of groups of citizens who combined spontaneously to pursue a criminal in the act of flight. Although the merchant and propertied classes might employ private watch to secure their premises, unlike in England, associations were not formed charged with the detection, management and prosecution of crime. For the most part, efforts of individual citizen-prosecutors were generally un-coordinated outside of the official system of constables and watch.[9]

In our sample of case files, no fewer than 25 per cent of defendants in property prosecutions (where good information is available) were actually detained and/or arrested by the complainant-prosecutor or some other civilian acting on the prosecutor's behalf. In some citizen-arrest cases, the act of taking the property was blatant and the defendant made little or no attempt to escape, as in the following example:

> *Thomas Hollaway*[10]
> Hollaway, a laborer, was charged with theft of a pick-axe, the property of Peter Yerick, a blacksmith who stated that he saw Hollaway put the pick-axe 'under his jacket and walk off with it from [his] shop' and stopped Hollaway with the pick-axe in his possession.

Typical cases where the defendant was caught in the act in addition to shoplifting, were pick pocketing offences, thefts from people in the same household, and burglary,[11] as illustrated in the prosecution of George Williams:[12]

> James Russell was disturbed when his dwelling-house and store was broken in the early hours of the morning, and, as he told the Special Justice, he 'arrested [George Williams] as he was attempting to make his escape out of front door of the store ...' On his examination, George, 'a Black boy', stated that Russell 'discovered and took him before he got out of the store ...'

Our sample shows that in two per cent of cases where the defendant was not caught in the act, the private prosecutor engaged in more extended acts of detection by, for example, personally tracing the stolen goods, as in James Wilson:[13]

> Here a grocer's wagon valued at $75.00 was taken from the street in front of John Meyer's store at 122 Washington Street on 20 June, 1845. According to John McKimmin, the defendant James Wilson then sold him the wagon on 21 June for $28.00. McKimmin further said that on the same day Meyer

---

[9] For the position in England see: J M Beattie (1986) pp 48ff; D Phillips (1989); and P King (1989).
[10] District Attorney's Files, 8 August, 1805.
[11] For similar examples in the nominative reports see: *Mary Maxwell* (1816) Rogers, vol 1, 32; *John W Bingham* (1816) Rogers, vol 1, 30; *Thomas Smith* (1816) Rogers, vol 1, 52; and *Terry Scandlin* (1816) Rogers, vol 1, 108.
[12] District Attorney's Files, 12 July, 1815.
[13] District Attorney's Files, 17 July, 1845.

came to him and claimed the wagon stating: Meyer 'went to the Police office made his affidavit that the waggon was stolen from him and [McKimmin] then delivererd … Meyer the said waggon'. Wilson was in the habit of stealing wagons. He had approached David Scott of Jersey City earlier in the month of June and asked him to sell a wagon at auction on Monday 9 June. Scott said that he told Wilson that he could not sell the wagon without 'some recommendation' and that Wilson produced one signed by James Harrison. On this basis, Scott sold the wagon at auction on 9 June for some $30.00 which amount, 'deducting one dollar and fifty cents expenses', he paid over to Wilson. The next day, however, Hendrick Meirs came and claimed the wagon as his own and, Scott stated, the recommendation supplied by Wilson was a forgery. This account was confirmed by Meirs who told the Special Justice that, after the theft, he 'looked around for the waggon and found [it] at an auction store in Jersey City, claimed the property as stolen from me. I then went to court and took an affidavit of the fact and received my waggon …'

Citizens also employed private watchmen[14] and used reward notices, as in the case of Richard B Hildreth[15] in which the private prosecutor, William H Maxwell advertised for the return of a clock stolen from his office, as depicted in Illustration 3.1:

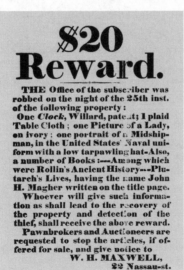

ILLUSTRATION 3.1: Richard Hildreth, District Attorney's Files, 12 March, 1835.

---

[14] As in *Patrick Lane*, District Attorney's Files, 22 October, 1845.
[15] District Attorney's Files, 12 March, 1835. See also: *Mary Riley's Cases* (1816) Rogers, vol 1, 23; *John Brannan* (1816) Rogers, vol 1, 50; and *John Francis and John Jones' Cases* (1816) Rogers, vol 1, 121.

In a further fifteen cases, prosecutors swore out a complaint which was the basis for a search warrant, as did Isaac Simonson, in respect of tools stolen by persons unknown which he believed to be concealed at John Green's[16] address, as shown in Illustration 3.2:

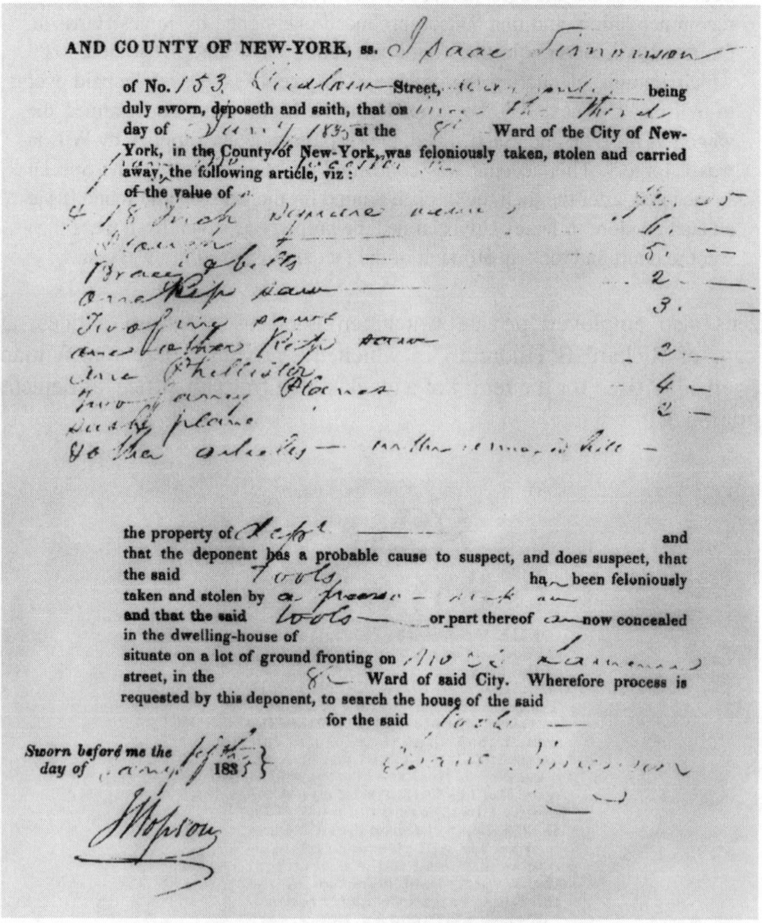

AND COUNTY OF NEW-YORK, ss. Isaac Simonson

of No. 153 ______ Street, ______ being duly sworn, deposeth and saith, that on ______ day of ______ 1835 at the 8th Ward of the City of New-York, in the County of New-York, was feloniously taken, stolen and carried away, the following article, viz: of the value of

the property of ______ and that the deponent has a probable cause to suspect, and does suspect, that the said tools ha__ been feloniously taken and stolen by ______ and that the said tools ______ or part thereof ______ now concealed in the dwelling-house of ______ situate on a lot of ground fronting on ______ street, in the 8th Ward of said City. Wherefore process is requested by this deponent, to search the house of the said ______ for the said tools

Sworn before me the ______ *day of* ______ 1835

ILLUSTRATION 3.2: John Green, District Attorney's Files, 15 January, 1835.

Dominant role played by police officers

Whilst the role of the private prosecutor/citizen was crucial in many cases, it would be wrong to conclude that the police played an insignificant role in the

[16] District Attorney's Files, 15 January, 1835.

detection and investigation of property prosecutions. Whilst the full extent of their contribution cannot be discovered from our sample in which files were concerned principally with court documents, witness statements and briefs essential to advancing the prosecution, nevertheless, over the entire period 1800–1845, 11 per cent of defendants are recorded as having been stopped[17] and arrested[18] by police officers, although officers' statements were recorded more frequently from 1839 onwards,[19] and there is enough other evidence to demonstrate the importance of constables, marshals and watch in the detection and resolution of property offences.[20]

Commonly, the indication of the involvement of the police in the discovery of the apprehension of the offender appears in the examination of the accused or the prosecutor. Thus, in the prosecution of Pegel Warren[21] involving theft of sheets of copper and augers, the accused stated that 'between seven and eight o'clock on the same evening he was taken up by the watch with the said copper and augers …' Similarly, in the prosecution of Samuel McFarland,[22] the prosecutor, Joseph Williams, a carpenter, complained that on or about 11 January 1810 a moving plane, two saws, a side fillister (plane) and other articles were stolen from him which he contended were in McFarland's possession and 'said to have been found by a Mr Concklin a watch man.'[23] Greater insight is provided into police practices where civilian witnesses gave more extended accounts to the Special Justice, as in John Frisby and Charles Lawrence:[24]

> The case arose out of the burglary of the store of George B Pomeroy. Isaac Kirkland, a clerk in the store, told the Special Justice that he had fastened the store securely before leaving it at night and in the morning found that the front window shutter had been forced open during the night and marks of candle grease had been left on the shutter and window sill. Isaac added that …

---

[17] There are also many examples provided in the Nominative Reports in which officers stopped suspicious persons in the street. See eg *Bartram Galbrant's case* (1816) Rogers, vol 1, 109 and *Thomas McKee* (1816) Rogers, vol 1, 110.

[18] The Nominative Reports provide strong evidence that the police were instrumental in many street arrests. See eg *Bryant Jepson* (1816) Rogers, vol 1, 32; *Samuel De Witt* (1816) Rogers, vol 1, 134; *Peter Dempsey* (1816) Rogers, vol 1, 172; and *John Canton and Charles Redding* (1817) Rogers, vol 2, 149.

[19] It is clear from the Nominative Reporters that police officers might be called to give evidence once the case went to trial in General Sessions. See eg *Mary Riley's Cases* (1816) Rogers, vol 1, 23; *Lyman Rowley* (1816) Rogers, vol 1, 121; and *Jesse Hopkins and Benjamin Gannon* (1816) Rogers, vol 1, 173.

[20] In addition to rewards that the loser of stolen goods might offer, the Common Council also administered a reward system for which constables and watch were frequent claimants: Michael Millender (1996) pp 114–15.

[21] District Attorney's Files, 9 February, 1805.

[22] District Attorney's Files, 14 February, 1810.

[23] The list of witnesses on the bill of complaint includes 'Concklin' and that on the indictment 'Joseph Concklin' without in either case any designation attributed.

[24] District Attorney's Files, 8 February, 1839.

'he is informed by Mr Henry Van Houton now present one of the City Watchmen that he last night found a colored man calling his name *John Frisby* and a man calling his name *Charles Lawrence* near said premises, when from the suspicious appearance and movements he suspected they intended to commit a burglary upon some of the stores in the neighborhood, several of them having been lately entered, whereupon with assistance of Mr Charles S Booth a private watchman arrested said men & upon the way to the Watch House the colored man Frisby dropped an iron Prig or Bar & that upon their arrival at the Watch House there was found upon their persons & upon and under the seats where they were sitting various Iron Instruments for the purpose of forcing doors, windows etc ...' (emphasis in original)[25]

Kirkland's examination illustrates the reasons for arrest in terms of both the alleged 'suspicious appearance' of the defendants and their suspicious 'movements' in an area subject to burglaries—the classic hallmarks of many modern day stops and arrests.

In ten cases in our sample, police officers tendered statements in their own right, as in the prosecution of Peter Heaton:[26]

Heaton was charged with petit larceny in stealing four lobsters valued at eighteen cents each the property of Jonathan Crocker of the Fly Market. He was arrested after being stopped while out at night by Joseph Ayers, a watchman. The principal evidence against him consisted of sworn statements given before the Special Justice on 15 July 1805 by Ayers, a statement by the owner of the lobsters, and Heaton's own confession. The statements of Ayers and Crocker were taken together:

City of New York SS:

Joseph Ayers, one of the City Watch, being sworn saith that on the fourteenth Inst. in the Second Ward of said City at twelve o'clock in the night while on duty he took Peter Eaton[27] with four lobsters, the said Peter Eaton then confessed to this deponent that he had stolen them out of a Car and went with this Deponent and showed him the Car, at the same time Jonathan Crocker being sworn who saith that the Car said Eaton says he took the lobsters out of his property and that said lobsters is worth about six shillings and eight pence.

For his part, Peter Heaton admitted that he had stolen the lobsters, adding that 'he was discharged from the State Prison on the eleventh of June inst.'

---

[25] John Frisby, a 48 year old man from Delaware, admitted at his examination that he knew Lawrence 'by sight' having served time with him in State Prison but claimed that they had not been together on the night in question.

[26] District Attorney's Files, 6 August, 1805.

[27] The spelling of Heaton's name as given in the examination record.

ILLUSTRATION 3.3: Peter Heaton, Complaint Jacket, District Attorney's Files, 6 August, 1805.

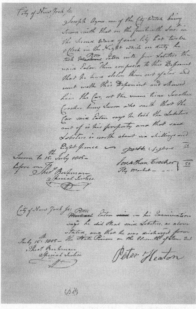

ILLUSTRATION 3.4: Peter Heaton, Witnesses' and Defendant's Statement, District Attorney's Files, 6 August, 1805.

In all probability, police officers who served for an extended period acquired considerable knowledge of the criminal underworld. For example, constables like Henry Abell, Abner Curtis and George Raymond served in this capacity for many years and became knowledgeable about local criminal intelligence. Most notable of all was Jacob Hays who became high constable in 1802, a post he held for almost fifty years. Paul Gilje offers this description of Hays:[28]

> Hays had an eye for the main chance and concentrated most of his efforts on capturing thieves, collecting rewards, and serving summonses and writs, thereby making himself a rich man. He also claimed to know every criminal in the city. To keep track of them he maintained a record of all the inmates in the state prison, their crimes, their age, their description, and the date of their release. He may even have had some corrupt dealings with the underworld.

Contrary to the views advanced by some commentators, moreover, the policing system clearly had the capacity to address 'professional'[29] crime in a coordinated manner, as illustrated in the prosecution of William Fowley:[30]

> Fowley occupied the lower part of the house at No 12 Front Street letting other rooms to boarders, some of whom were clearly involved in crime. Fowley, on being charged with two separate offences of receiving stolen goods, sought to exonerate himself before the Special Justice by claiming to have bought various articles from one of his boarders John McQuaid and 'a boy now in Bridewell said to be named Jon. Lockwood.' However, John Lockwood, produced from the Bridewell, told the Special Justice that:
>
> 'Mr Fowley of Front St is in the habit of recg. stolen goods [John Lockwood] has been in there when he has brought stolen goods viz. a surtout coat—a frock & shawl.'

Thus, others associated with Fowley were also prosecuted in a concerted drive against a house of thieves: John McQuaid was convicted on two charges of petit larceny and sent to the penitentiary;[31] John McCarty who boarded at Fowley's was convicted of petit larceny having come out of the penitentiary only two weeks earlier;[32] James Graham 'who had staid at Fowleys in Front Street some days' was convicted of petit larceny;[33] and William Hall, an associate of John McQuaid, was convicted of burglary.[34]

---

[28] (1987) p 270 (footnote omitted).
[29] There were repeat offenders involved in crime though probably few full time career criminals.
[30] District Attorney's Files, 7 May, 1825.
[31] *John McQuaid*, District Attorney's Files, 13 May, 1825.
[32] *John McCarty*, District Attorney's Files, 10 May, 1825.
[33] *James Graham*, District Attorney's Files, 13 May, 1825.
[34] *William Hall*, District Attorney's Files, 13 May and 14 June, 1825.

Joint citizen-police role

Whilst citizens and police both took a lead role in many prosecutions in our sample, in others it is difficult to distinguish the importance of their respective contributions. A number of these cases involved searches of the person or property undertaken at the behest of the citizen but requiring the authoritative intervention of the police. In other instances, the collaboration occurred in advance of the commission of a crime with the object of thwarting the crime or apprehending the offenders in the course of its commission.[35]

Although many property disputes were doubtless settled without court action by the taker surrendering the goods on being challenged by the loser, others were not solved by the citizen unaided. The latter cases resulted in prosecutions when the citizen called for assistance from the watch or constables.[36] In a few prosecutions, it is clear that a police search of the suspect premises was conducted in the presence of the prosecutor as in the case of Mary Gilmartin:[37]

> The prosecution arose out of the theft of muslin valued at $2.50 from the store of Pomeroy, Wilson and Butler by four boys who admitted to the theft and claimed to have sold the muslin to Mary Gilmartin:[38]
>
> > Oliver Hicks, who worked at the store, stated that the boys had sold the muslin to Mary at 41 City Hall Place 'where [he] this day accompanied officers Sparks and Pick and found the [muslin].'[39]

In another group of prosecutions, citizen-prosecutors called for the intervention of the police whilst the crime was in progress, as in the case of Richard Parsells and John Devoe:[40]

> The defendants were charged and convicted of the theft of a coat and other items from a merchant, Thaddeus Sherman, as a result of the initiative of John Lavis of Banker Street.

---

[35] See eg *William Pierce* (1816) Rogers, vol 1, 2; *Joseph Nichol* (1816) Rogers, vol 1, 5; *Jeremiah Totten* (1816) Rogers, vol 1, 32; *Isaac Traux* (1816) Rogers, vol 1, 44; *Christian Wall* (1816) Rogers, vol 1, 88; *John Alexander* (1816) Rogers, vol 1, 98; and *Phebe Jarvis* (1816) Rogers, vol 1, 105.

[36] See eg *Manuel Jose Degante*, District Attorney's Files, 3 April, 1805.

[37] District Attorney's Files, 11 January, 1839.

[38] A note on the file records that: 'The knowledge of the muslin being at Mrs Gilmartin was obtained from the Boys themselves who on the night following that on which they sold it went to the same store and there stole ten pieces, when they were caught in the act, upon which arrest it was that they made the confessions...'

[39] A note on the file states: 'When officers Sparks & Pick went to the premises of Mary Gilmartin she denied all knowledge of the Boys and also of the muslin when on their thinking to search she gave the muslin up'.

[40] District Attorney's Files, 6 March, 1820.

John Lavis described the events leading to the arrest of two of the three individuals[41] said to have been involved in the burglary in the following terms: '... last evening John Devoe and Jas. Farrington the two young men now here came in his place & offered to sell him the Blue surtout coat which is now here for three dollars—That [he] made an excuse to go out & get a Bill changed but instead of which he went & got a Watchman & had the said Farrington & Devoe taken ...'

There is also evidence of citizen-police coordination *prior* to the commission of any crime. At least on occasions, citizens acted in police-supervised undercover operations to forestall criminality and capture criminals in the act,[42] as in the case of Abel Smith and Henry Holmes:[43]

The defendants faced two separate indictments charging them with the possession of counterfeit money found on Smith at the time of his arrest. The case involved a classic 'sting' operation the nature of which emerges from the account of John Parks, an engraver and plater of William Street, given at his examination before the Special Justice on 18 November 1810, the substance of which is reproduced below:

[A]bout three or four weeks ago ... Abel Smith came to his House in William Street and came into his shop and asked [him] if his name was Parks and being informed that it was, he told [him] that he wanted to speak to him—[Parks] then took ... Abel Smith who was then an entire stranger to him into a back place and there he told [Parks] that he wanted some thing of a machine made to mill anything in, a dollar or any thing else ... According to Parks, he told Smith he could make such a machine and Smith told him that he would be well paid for his work. Parks encouraged Smith by showing him several kinds of metals and talking freely with him about the nature and process of coloring metals. When the machine had not been made in the time agreed, Parks said that Smith, who was with Henry Holmes, became quite angry but Parks placated him by telling him that he did not know whether Smith wanted a machine to mill Spanish dollars or American dollars.

Parks, after recounting further exchanges between the parties, took up the story:

[Parks] procured an old milling machine for Spanish Dollars out of the Police Office and then concluded the bargain with ... Smith for

---

[41] James Farrington was not charged. He told the court when examined that he, together with Parsells and Devoe, had committed the burglary, adding 'this information is given by him not to be used against him.'

[42] See also *Joseph Manetti and Andrew Ferguson* (1818) Rogers, vol 3, 60 in which police officers were stationed inside a house after receiving reports that the defendants intended to set fire to it and commit other criminal acts; *Peter Mitchell* (1821) Rogers, vol 6, 1; *Timothy Sands* (1821) Rogers, vol 6, 1.

[43] District Attorney's Files, 15 December, 1809.

the ... milling machine which [Parks] pledged himself would be ready at 4 o'clock on Wednesday afternoon the 15 [November 1809]— accordingly [Parks] filed up the old machine & made it look some thing like a new one and carried it to the House of John Anderson in Henry Street where ... Holmes and Smith lodged and there sold it to ... Smith for six dollars and one half and while [Parks] was shewing Smith how the machine opperated (sic) Holmes was peeping from behind a door to see likewise ... Once the deal had been concluded, the trap was sprung:[Parks] after making sale of the ... machine ... went out and met the officers according to appointment who went into Andersons house and arrested ... Smith and Holmes.[44]

CRIMES AGAINST THE PERSON

Because assault and battery prosecutions in the first half of the nineteenth century tended to involve persons known to each other, the prosecution of the defendant rested primarily upon the alleged victim bringing a complaint, identifying the defendant, giving a statement to the Special Justice and, in the absence of a settlement, giving evidence at General Sessions. Thus, whilst we can be confident that, in most assault and battery cases, the citizen-prosecutor was the principal instrument through which the case was prosecuted, the overall role of the police is less clear.

From an analysis of our case sample it appears that the police played the key role in the apprehension of the accused and investigation of the offence in 7.0 per cent (n=23) of assault prosecutions in our sample over the 1800–1845. However, in 22 of these cases, police officers were said to be victims of the assault in the course of their duties and in the remaining case[45] one of the City's Marshals filed the complaint having been a witness to the acts of the defendant. Whatever other witnesses might have been available, therefore, it is clear that in these cases the prosecution rested primarily on police evidence.[46]

The relative dearth of documentation in allegations of assault and battery between citizens makes it impossible to chart with any degree of confidence the extent of police involvement in the apprehension and prosecution of such cases. In the usual assault prosecution, the District Attorney's case files consist of the

---

[44] Abel Smith confirmed the general account of Parks saying that he had commissioned the making of the machine 'for a man in the country'.

[45] *Peter Kifer*, District Attorney's Files, 11 December, 1804.

[46] See eg *Pender Webb*, District Attorney's Files, 5 April, 1805; *Eleanor Downing*, District Attorney's Files, 12 August, 1805; and *Mary Saunders*, District Attorney's Files, 3 May, 1825. Assaults on police officers are also occasionally reported in the Nominative Reports. See eg: *Cornelius Lynsen* (1816) Rogers, vol 1, 151; *James Cummings* (1816) Rogers, vol 1, 151; and *Anoria Roy* (1817) Rogers, vol 2, 165.

complaint sworn by the private prosecutor in which the means by which the defendant was produced at court is not revealed. Even where police involvement is disclosed, it tends to emerge indirectly, as in the prosecution of John Kerwin[47] where police are mentioned only in the affidavit submitted to the Special Justice by the son of the alleged victim who stated that he saw the assault and 'some watchmen came & arrested Kerwin'.

When the allegations are not limited to simple assault and battery, police involvement in the investigation of crimes against the person were apparent and appeared in three ways. First, officers might be involved as witnesses to a civilian assault[48] or, as in the prosecution of Lawrence Farrell,[49] witnesses to some events related to the incident:

> Farrell was charged with assault and battery with intent to rape Sarah Hockman, aged 'about fifteen years', the daughter of Caspar Hockman of 86th Street on Sixth Avenue.[50] According to Sarah the incident happened at about 10 o'clock in the morning on the south side of the Upper Reservoir as she was driving her father's cows from off the common towards his home. She said that Farrell apprehended her and asked to kiss her; that when she refused he caught hold of her and attempted to forcibly kiss her; and that he threw her down on the ground and attempted to pull up her clothing. Sarah struggled and got away from Farrell who then exposed himself to her. As she made her way home, frightened and crying aloud, she saw a man on the rock inside the reservoir enclosure who asked her what had happened to make her cry. The man in question was William Hancock a policeman who lived at the five mile house kept by Andrew Howe on Third Avenue and was stationed at the Upper Reservoir. According to Hancock he saw Sarah
>
> '... crying and going towards her house, and a short distance from her the man now here who calls himself Lawrence Farrell who was running in the opposite direction to the one Sarah Hockman was going—[I] asked ... Sarah what was the matter with her, upon which she told [me] that the man Farrell had grossly insulted her, that he had thrown her down. [Hancock] says that he then pursued the man and after a long chase overtook and arrested him ...'

Second, officers might supply evidence of an unsolicited confession, as in the prosecution of Daniel Bowdowine:[51]

---

[47] District Attorney's Files, 16 October, 1845.
[48] See eg, *Henry Caldwell*, District Attorney's Files, 14 January, 1839.
[49] District Attorney's Files, 23 October, 1845.
[50] Young girls appear to have been a particular target for predatory males. See T Gilfoyle (1992).
[51] District Attorney's Files, 4 February, 1839.

The defendant was charged with assault and battery with intent to kill his wife Margaret who said that he had stabbed her 'on the right side of her back near the shoulder with a knife or some other sharp instrument'. Samuel Watson, a watchman, swore in an affidavit before the Special Justice that

'... while he was on his post at the corner of 3rd Avenue & 28th Street—about half past 10 oclock—Daniel Bowdowine—came to [him]—and said he wished to be taken to the Watch-house—that he had hurt his wife—and that he expected he had killed her.'

Third, police might report on some matter relevant to the prosecution, by offering evidence seized once the defendant was in their custody, as in the prosecution of William Durban:[52]

The defendant was charged with assault and battery with intent to kill Aaron Jacob by attempting to discharge a pistol loaded with powder and leaden shot. According to Aaron, the defendant drew a loaded pistol on him, attempted to discharge it but only the cap exploded. Whilst there is no record of officers being formally examined by the Special Justice, a note on the file records that Captain Knapp of the Watch examined the pistol and 'found it loaded with two balls'. Another watchman, John Tilley, is also mentioned to whom the defendant is said to have 'declared that he wished he had killed the Negroe'. Durban said that he had 'no explanation to give' except that he was drunk at the time.

POLICE OFFICE INVESTIGATION

Private prosecutors, who often initiated the responses of policing officials through a 'hue and cry,'[53] responded to their immediate concerns which often involved the need to achieve a remedy for personally invasive behaviour—theft or physical injury—without any long term view of prosecution or prosecution policy. It was here that members of the Police Office would interface with the event leading to the apprehension of the accused and the obtaining of criminal evidence in order that a case for the prosecution could be constructed.

Whilst much of the investigative work was carried out by police officers alone, under the authority of a warrant or in response to an immediate policing imperative, the police often liaised with the Special Justice in executing searches or in other investigative acts. In some instances, however, the Special Justice himself

---

[52] District Attorney's Files, 7 March, 1835.
[53] The old common law process of pursuing felons with horns and shouts: vol 4 Blackstone's Commentaries 293.

conducted the investigation, perhaps supported by police officers, as in the case of Noah M Hauxhurst:[54]

> On the first trial, on the indictment for grand larceny, it appeared, by the tes-
> timony of Venable, that he kept a shop at No 64 Fourth-street, and the pris-
> oner, with several others, worked therein. He missed the shoes on the 26th
> day of December, and made inquiry in the shop, when the prisoner and the
> others belonging to the shop were present, when the prisoner *swore a solemn
> oath, by all the Evangelists*, that he *was not guilty*. Venable, from that time,
> suspected the prisoner, by reason of his guilty looks.
>
> On the Sunday following, while the prisoner was absent from the house, and,
> as the witness believed, gone to the Methodist meeting, of which he was
> either a member or a steady attendant, the witness went to the police office
> and made a complaint, and James Hopson, one of the police magistrates,
> came to the house where the prisoner kept his trunk, which was in a garret
> chamber of the house near or adjoining the shop. The prisoner being present,
> denied that he had the property stolen, in the trunk, but admitted that he
> had one pair of shoes therein, which he had taken to make the witness more
> careful of his property. Justice Hopson then asked the prisoner for the key of
> the trunk, but he said that he had left the key belonging to the trunk with his
> uncle. There was a key, however, which he had in his possession, which was
> tried to the lock, but not suiting it, Justice Hopson broke open the trunk, and
> found therein the shoes and uppers stolen, with a quantity of other uppers,
> and other materials, among which were the *foreparts of a pair of boots*, not
> belonging to Venable. The prisoner, on being questioned where he had
> obtained the uppers, answered, that he had them of a Mr Ammerman, of
> New-Brunswick, for a debt which the latter owed him. It further appeared,
> that the prisoner calculated to carry his trunk away from the house of
> Venable, on a visit to his friends, on Long-Island, about the time of the dis-
> covery, as above related, occurred. (original emphasis)

Joint investigatory activities by the police and Special Justice also occurred following the examination of the prosecutor at the Police Office, as depicted in the
case of Hester Knapp[55] where the defendant was indicted for having in her possession a counterfeit note of the Montreal Bank, with the intention of passing it.
Once Hillyer, to whom the defendant had given counterfeit notes, had implicated
Knapp, Special Justice Abel supervised the search of the prisoner's house conducted by constables Hays and Montgomery, as detailed by the nominative
reporter:

> Montgomery, a police officer, testified, that on the 12th of March, he went
> up to Knapp's with Hays and Abel, and while he was in the room where the

---

[54] (1817) Rogers, vol 2, p 33.
[55] (1821) Rogers, vol 6, pp 18, 20.

prisoner was, she took a loaf of bread, and went into the pantry, and he followed her, and in a desk in that room he found two twenty dollar counterfeit bills, on the Montreal Bank, and several other counterfeit $2 bills on banks in this city.

Henry Abel, a police magistrate, testified that he was present during the search; and that the prisoner was very anxious to get into the pantry where the bills were found, and attempted it several times, but was prevented.

In assembling the case, the Special Justice would preserve any real evidence relevant to proof of the crime, the role of the defendant in it or the state of mind of the accused. For example, on a charge of possession of counterfeit gold coins, the file contained a list of items of real evidence: eg, 'one pair of speck tickels', 'one pen knife' 'one nest of crewsables', 'potash', 'salmonick' and 'asnick'.[56] In counterfeiting cases, the notes in question were preserved and retained by the Police Office. Thus, when John Roberts obtained a loan of two dollars from Anthony Schuyler by falsely pretending that he was E Reid of Fish Grinnell & Co., the false bill of exchange relied upon by Roberts, was preserved by the Police Office, is shown below:

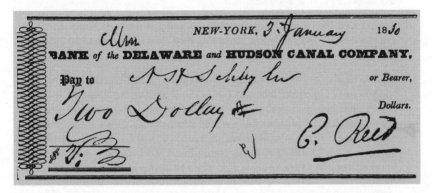

ILLUSTRATION 3.5: John Roberts, District Attorney's Files, 12 March, 1830.

Locating and questioning of prosecution witnesses

The locating and questioning of witnesses was a staple of the Police Office's work. The Special Justice and Clerk played a central role in coordinating criminal intelligence obtained as a result of the examination of the accused and witnesses and investigative activities which followed therefrom. This enabled the Justice to assemble the evidence to prosecute complex cases, including arrangements to systematically steal and fence stolen property, the external evidence of

---

[56] *Abel Smith and Henry Holmes*, District Attorney's Files, 15 December, 1809.

which might only be an isolated act which otherwise would have been viewed as limited in value.

Typical of the labour employed by the Special Justice in constructing the case file, with the assistance of the watch and police, is the evidence amassed in the case of Lewis van Dyke, charged with grand larceny of a gold watch, chain and seal to the value of $95.00, the property of John T B Ketcham, on 12 December 1834.[57] Ketcham swore a complaint on 13 December stating that the watch had been stolen from the privy of No 30 Front Street by 'two blacks', van Dyke and Wm Turner, as he has been told that the watch was 'seen in van Dykes possession':

> William Turner, 'a Black man of Cherry near Walnut', was examined on 13 December. He stated that 'he knows nothing at all about the watch, only that he heard it was lost and he was working in the store at the time, says he knows nothing about the other man Lewis van Dyke's having the watch but that a woman named Susan Hobbs who lives in [his] house told [him] this morning that a young man who attends at Mr Moses' store Corner of Cherry & Walnut told him that he had seen Lewis van Dyke have a Gold Watch last night in Mr Moses' store, and that Lewis van Dyke showed him the watch & this is all [he] says & knows about it ...'

> David Floyd and George Clawson, two boys living near Cherry Street, were examined on 13 December and stated that they 'saw Lewis van Dyke have a watch with a chain yesterday that looked like gold.'

> Frances Harris: 'a coloured woman' was examined on 15 December and stated that, on 12 December, 'she saw Lewis van Dyke have a gold watch with linked chain also gold', and shortly afterwards saw him and Frank Johnson 'go off together and in about one hour and a half afterwards saw them come back & have a plenty of money' and she stated she saw Lewis show 'David the clerk in Mr Moses' store the aforementioned watch and also had David the clerk ask him where he got it from when he answered that he had had it for some time.'

Thus, in addition to the private prosecutor's statement, the examination yielded the testimony of three witnesses, each of whom (Floyd, Clowson and Harris) added important circumstantial evidence establishing van Dyke's culpability and connecting him to the theft of Ketcham's watch.

Similarly, when the police moved against receivers this would commonly be the culmination of the Special Justice's examination followed by a coordinated investigation undertaken by the Police Office, as detailed below in the case of James Brown[58] where the real object of concern was the fence William Ward:

---

[57] District Attorney's Files, 8 January, 1835.
[58] District Attorney's Files, 23 February, 1810.

Brown was arrested when putting a bag of stolen coffee in the cellar of William Ward whom the magistrate also bound over for the action of the Grand Jury and trial at General Sessions. The clerk of the justice, Mr Bernard O'Blenis, informed the Grand Jury of the circumstances surrounding the arrest of James Brown, telling them that Ward had been the subject of previously unsuccessful prosecutions for receiving stolen property in similar circumstances where thieves named him as the 'fence' who suggested the theft and agreed to act as receiver thereby making the theft profitable. O'Blenis also gave the names of potential witnesses in addition to those already examined by the magistrate, stating:

> I wish to state to you some circumstances concerning a Mr William Ward who keeps a Grocery Store and Tavern in Front Street near the Coffee House Slip—This man has several times been found in the possession of stolen property but under such circumstances that he could not be convicted of having accrued such property knowing the same to be stolen altho there was the Testimony of the thief that Ward had actually engaged him to steal & bring to his House—Now another circumstance of the kind has turned up and Ward with his usual boldness braves all that can be said against him and having amassed a considerable fortune probably by the practice of receiving stolen goods feels himself very secure—The circumstances are these—a yellow man by the name of *James Brown* was seen by a Mr Gale a Clk to Mr Hezekiah Lord to take a bag of coffee out of Lords store and arrested the said *Brown* just as he got into Ward's Cellar with the bag—Mr Lord within a few minutes previous to Brown's being taken as above stated had lost two other bags of coffee—Brown was committed to prison and on his examination yesterday by myself he says that Ward did engage him and one *Harman Allen* a Black man to steal the said coffee and states further that he Brown went and stole one bag of coffee out of the said Lord's Store and carried it to *Ward's* House and there in the presence of a boy who attends Ward's Barr (*sic*) and an elderly woman a servant in *Ward's* House, Ward cut one end of the bag open and looked at the coffee—That he Brown went immediately out for another Bag and got one out of said Lord's Store and brought it into Ward's cellar and just as he came into the cellar he was taken with the bag by the said Gale—He also states that just as he came to the Door of Lord's Store for his second bag he saw Harman Allen come out with a bag and go also with it to Ward's, as he thinks, that being their agreement —

> Mr Gale has since told me that he was told by the Ferry Master that the said *William Ward* on the same evening on which Mr Lord's coffee was stolen, and but a short time after, was seen taking two bags of coffee to Brooklin where the said Ward keeps another store —If all these circumstances are proved I expect it will pave the way for Ward's conviction—Mr Gale can inform the name of the

> ferry master—Ward is bound to the present sessions—on this occasion.[59]
>
> Yours etc.
>
> B Oblenis
>
> To the Hon. The Grand Inquest   9 Feby 1810

The criminal intelligence obtained by the Police Office also proved valuable in enabling the District Attorney and the Grand Jury to assess the probity of any assertions made by witnesses and/or the accused during the examination process and to determine how to proceed thereafter, as in the prosecution of Jane Jones,[60] who was accused of stealing a hat and other articles:

> On her examination, Jane informed the Justice that she had 'arrived in this City yesterday in a sloop from up the river somewhere—she left Philadelphia about six weeks ago—never was in New York before in her life—she has no friends here ...'

A note in the case file based upon intelligence provided by the Police Office gave an altogether different picture:

> About six weeks ago this woman lived at Mr Burnhams Tavern by the name of Jane Crawford, stole his articles & ran away & the Hat she stole was taken off her Head in Bridewell.

Selection of cooperating defendants

To assure that sufficient and persuasive evidence would be later available, the Special Justice had the discretion to select co-operating witnesses from among those accused of criminal activity—putative defendants who would agree to testify against their compatriots in exchange for immunity from prosecution. As a matter of practice, the exercise of discretion in the selection of putative defendants as prosecution witnesses frequently occurred at the Police Office, upon consideration by the Special Justice, and prior to the transference of the case to the Grand Jury. Multiple-defendant cases presented the opportunity to obtain co-operation from putative defendants where more than one criminal suspect had knowledge of the whereabouts and activities of the others, as illustrated in the prosecution of Charles Hayden and John McDonald,[61] a case involving four putative defendants charged with a series of burglaries:

> The defendants were prosecuted for burglary of the store of Edward Pitcher with the assistance of key testimony supplied by one of their accomplices, James Medlar. The latter, when examined by the Special Justice as a

---

[59] Emphasis in the original.
[60] District Attorney's Files, 16 June, 1825.
[61] District Attorney's Files, 15 January, 1835.

possible defendant, acknowledged his own involvement and implicated the others 'on condition it is not to operate against him'. Subsequently, upon examination as a putative witness, Medlar gave a *sworn* statement against one Owen O'Connor who Medlar explained to the Special Justice was 'a receiver of stolen goods' to whom another accomplice, Richard Pell, had fenced part of the proceeds, namely a stolen watch. Subsequent to Medlar's examination, John McDonald, one of Medlar's associates, upon examination by the Special Justice implicated himself, Richard Pell and Charles Hayden in a burglary of the store of Ebenezer Fisk 'on condition it shall not be used against himself'. Following the examination of Medlar, McDonald was examined by the Justice, after which Richard Pell, who having the day before denied any involvement in the burglary, on examination admitted having participated with Medlar, McDonald and Hayden in the burglary of the premises of Fisk. Thus, the efforts by the Special Justice to obtain co-operation resulted in eye-witness accounts of the acts of each of the per-petrators with one perpetrator, Medlar, having escaped prosecution and con-viction as a result of the co-operation.

Examination of the accused

Questions that the Special Justice placed to defendants were supposed to be coin-cident with the theoretical purpose of the examination—to permit accused per-sons the opportunity to provide an explanation of their conduct and to enable them to exonerate themselves.[62] Such questioning was unlikely to provide more than general criminal intelligence, as in the examination of John Smith for steal-ing muslin from the door of Nathaniel and Harvey Weed the previous afternoon:

Q: What is your age, business and residence
A: I am 24 follow nothing-belong at New Lots on Long Island but have been in New York this last time about a month and live No.16. Mulberry St. with Peter Morris-
Q: Where were you yesterday afternoon
A: Up town on the five points all day till about 4 oclock when I went alone to the Battery and from there came up Pearl St. alone to Cedar Street up Cedar St. near William Street I was taken & charged with stealing muslin
Q: Did you take or had you any
A: I neither took nor had any. I saw none till the Gentleman brought three pieces in the store —
Q: Did you see any men black or white after leaving the points with whom you were acquainted
A: No sir

---

[62] *People v John Robinson* (1824) Wheeler 2, p 240 Editor's note.

Q: How do you support yourself
A: I calculate to pay the man who keeps me after I get well after bad disor-
     der and dissentary (sic)
Q: Is the statement made true
A: It is true

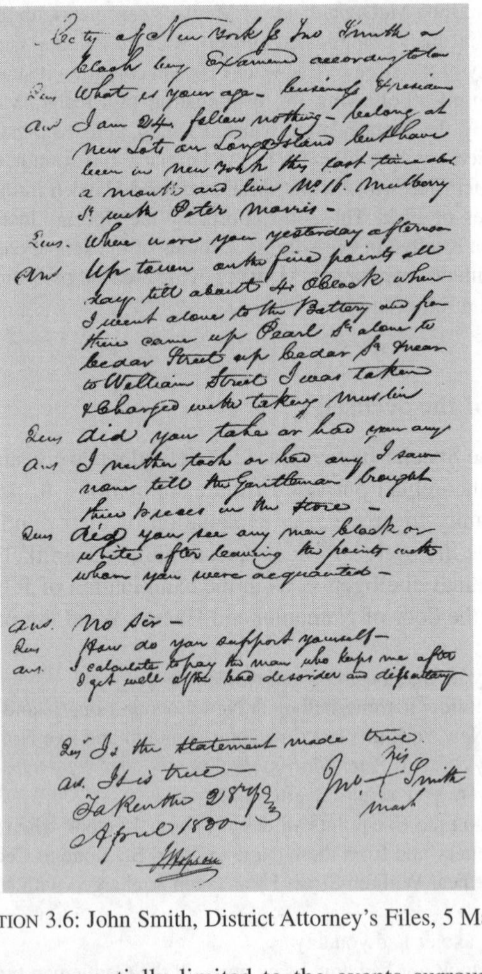

ILLUSTRATION 3.6: John Smith, District Attorney's Files, 5 May, 1830.

The examination was essentially limited to the events surrounding the instant offence and was not to include attempts to elicit admissions of prior bad acts, although spontaneous statements made by the defendant during the examination about prior behaviour and not in response to the Special Justice or Clerk's questions were later admissible at General Sessions.[63] Despite these qualifications,

---

[63] (1823) Wheeler 1, p 54.

Special Justices used both leading and non-leading questions to pin down what it was that the accused was saying had occurred, as shown in the grand larceny prosecution of Caty (a Black), the examination being recorded as a single narrative with the location of unstated questions indicated by short pen strokes as detailed below and in Illustration 3.7:[64]

> Caty a Black girl within named says that she does not know how long ago
> it was that she took the within mentioned bag and snuff box with money
> but this she knows that she took it off a shelf over a window in Mr Paul

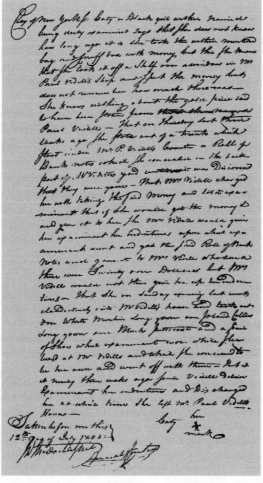

ILLUSTRATION 3.7: Caty (a Black), District Attorney's Files, 6 August, 1805.

[64] District Attorney's Files, 6 August, 1805.

Videll's Shop and spent the money but does not remember how much there was—She knows nothing about the gold piece said to have been stolen from the within named Paul Videll—That on Thursday last three weeks ago she stole out of a trunk which stood under Mr P Videll's Counter a Roll of Bank notes which she concealed in the back part of Mr Videll's yard until it was discovered that they were gone—That Mrs Videll charged her with taking the said money and told examinant that if she would get the money and give it to her she Mrs Videll would give examinant her indentures upon which examinant went and got the said Roll of Bank notes and gave it to Mrs Videll who said there were Twenty one Dollars but Mrs Videll would not then give up her indentures—That She on Sunday evening last went clandestinely into Mr Videll's house and took out one White Muslin long gown and plaid Callico long gown, one Black petticoat and a pair of shoes which examinant wore while she was at Mr Vidells and which she conceived to be her own and went off with them—That it is nearly three weeks ago since Videll Deliver examinant her indentures and Discharged her at which time she left Mr Paul Videll's House.

Moreover, our review of the sample of case files and the nominative reports of trials in General Sessions showed that commonly, upon examination, the defendant was confronted with a searching and aggressive inquiry regarding the prosecutor's allegations. It became accepted that tactics to uncover incriminating evidence were a major purpose of the examination of the accused employed at the Police Office. The underlying philosophy was captured by District Attorney Pierre van Wyck who stated in 1815, '[m]any offenders would escape if the magistrate did not extract from the evidence to aid their conviction.'[65] Such an approach would increase the likelihood of obtaining admissions to certain facts that were against the penal interests of the accused which would then be introduced at trial.

Where the Special Justice knew of the actions of the accused from speaking with the private prosecutor, watch or other witnesses or through personal knowledge acquired at the scene of searches and arrests, leading and pointed questions could be put to elicit these and pin down an admission, as in the prosecution of John Brown, Samuel Hillman and William Rider:[66]

It was alleged that a showcase containing watches, rings, jewellery and pencil cases was stolen by the defendants from the door of Allen S Wightman's shop at 15 Fulton Street. The only detailed information about property was that given to the magistrate by the keeper of a house in Chatham Market in which Brown and Hillman stayed who stated that Brown and Hillman had a watch and pencil cases in their possession 'some of which', he said 'were

---

[65] *Hiram Maxwell's case.*
[66] District Attorney's Files, 10 February, 1835.

last evening taken by the officers when they were arrested ...' It is clear, however, that the magistrate must have been given more precise information about the search, probably by the officers, because Brown was asked on his examination: 'who put the pencil cases etc. into the pot of victuals'.

In seeking to pin down an admission, the Special Justice often employed a similar assumption of guilt derived from the examination of the prosecution witnesses and the magistrate's own knowledge of the event leading to the arrest of the accused. This is evident in the entire examination of Charles Cozzens Jnr.[67] on theft of thirty four dollars from the pocket of Daniel Avery who slept in the same room as Cozzens, as set out below:

Q: What is your age—residence & business
A: I am 23—Newport Rhode Island is my home & I follow the sea
Q: When and where did you take Averys' money
A: I took Averys money viz twenty nine dollars yesterday afternoon as he
    lay in bed in Mr Holts house and the money is now here

In the prosecution of William Hunn (a black boy),[68] the examination of the accused occurred, following the prosecutor's assertion that William had 'acknowledged' that he had stolen money from him, with the following question: 'Can you tell how often you have taken money in Bank notes out of Thomas McGlade's chest'. To assure that the defendant's previous admissions which the Special Justice learned from the examination of the private prosecutor would be admissible at trial, the examination of Hunn also included the following pointed questions directed towards establishing the voluntariness of these statements:

Q: How come you to acknowledge to have stolen the said money etc.
A: They asked me about it —
Q: Did you confess it before you was whipped
A: Yes sir —

Our data show that the Special Justice or Clerk after extracting an admission or confession from an accused would frequently offer trial testimony introducing and/or authenticating these statements. Such statements were either obtained from an accused in the course of an examination or uttered by the accused when initially produced at the Police Office. Thus, in our 1804–1805 and 1809–1810 samples, Bernard O'Blenis, often the Clerk to the Special Justice and the person who was present and may have conducted some examinations under the authority of the Special Justice, was listed in 17 cases as a potential witness to the defendant's statement made at the examination.

---

[67] District Attorney's Files, 5 May, 1830.
[68] District Attorney's Files, 11 August, 1815.

Whilst the knowledge gap between the Special Justice and the accused favoured the eliciting of incriminating information it did not necessarily result in admissions. Even at the height of the Special Justice's power prior to 1830 when the advice of rights to the accused was not regularly recorded, no more than about 35 per cent of indicted defendants in our sample of cases made admissions in response to the questioning of the Special Justice. Some, when cornered by the questions of the Special Justice, resorted to denials or refused to co-operate in the process, as where the defendant told the Special Justice: 'Cant tell where he lodged last night, eat his breakfast and dinner in a cook shop but cant tell where ...',[69] and where another defendant: '... *on being asked where he was the night that* he was out *'answers'* that is my business' (emphasis in the original).[70] Others who made admissions upon examination might refuse to authenticate the statement even after admitting that the substance of the examination was true by stating 'that he does not know that he is under any obligation to sign any writing.'[71]

In a few cases, the accused had consulted with counsel who was either present or who it appeared had earlier advised the accused to decline to respond, as illustrated in the prosecution of Alexander B Atherton.[72] The defendant was indicted for forgery of notes or bills in imitation of Corporation notes of the City of New York ordinarily signed by Daniel E Tyler. At the trial, Jacob F Cisco, who had been employed by the high constable Jacob Hays to arrest the defendant, after first describing the circumstances, then recounted Atherton's examination:

> The several examinations of the defendant in the Police [Office], taken down by way of question and answer, were then read in evidence. To the first interrogatory, 'where was you born, and what your age,' he replied, 'Not at present having access to my legal adviser, nor the opportunity of conversing with Mr Tyler, I beg to avail myself of the privilege of the laws of America to remain silent.'

After 1830, examinations of defendants began to routinely refer to the notice of the various rights and entitlements enjoyed by the suspected person.[73] Thus, for example, our sample of case files showed that the defendant had 'the charge and his rights explained',[74] was 'informed of his rights',[75] and was informed that 'he was not bound to answer any questions that would criminate himself ...'[76] Yet, even by 1835, despite the providing of notice of the right to counsel,[77] lawyers did not appear routinely at the Special Justice's examination.

[69] See eg, *James Shaw*, District Attorney's Files, 9 July, 1825.
[70] *William Hall*, District Attorney's Files, 13 May, 1825.
[71] *William Clark and Moses Phips*, District Attorney's Files, 7 August, 1805.
[72] (1816) Rogers, vol 1, p 159.
[73] 1829 *Revised Statutes of the State of New York*, Part IV, Chapter II, Title II, Sections 14–15, p 708.
[74] *William Greenhough*, District Attorney's Files, 10 March, 1830.
[75] *Hiram Gardner*, District Attorney's Files, 10 March, 1830.
[76] *Edward P Mitchell*, District Attorney's Files, 10 March, 1830.
[77] 1829 *Revised Statutes of the State of New York*, Part IV, Title II, Section 14, p 708.

CONCLUSION

The foregoing analysis shows that the image of the policing and evidence-acquisition system as disorganised, unresponsive, unengaged and dependent entirely on lay people in the detection and investigation of criminal activity is not sustainable in New York City prior to mid-century. Time and again the case files and the nominative reports showed how the system of constable and watch engaged proactively and reactively both alone and in conjunction with private citizens. Thereafter, the over-arching fabric of evidence which constituted the case for the prosecution—including those facts and statements which tended to exculpate or be favourable to the accused—was knitted together at the various Police Offices. Without this co-ordinated process, it would have been very difficult for cases to be successfully prosecuted or to have achieved the high rate of conviction which, as we will document, preceded the rise of the guilty plea system.[78]

Moreover, the detection, arrest and investigatory processes demonstrate that police and magistrates responded to a wide range of victims and thus provided a public service that could not be, in New York City, characterized simply as a concern for social control by a privileged class. Nightwatchmen and constables in conjunction with Special Justices effectively supported any private prosecutor in an effort to secure the apprehension and conviction of the transgressor. This system of criminal justice was participatory at both the grass roots level and in the method by which the case for the prosecution was assembled.

Prior to mid-century, in New York City, crime detection was, in a real sense, responsive to the individualised concerns of everyday citizen-prosecutors.[79] It was on the basis of these concerns that warrants were sworn out, police and Special Justices mounted searches or engaged in surveillance operations. In addition, testimony of witnesses from a broad spectrum of society was significant in many prosecutions. Of course, those with property such as store keepers were most likely to invoke the protection of the law; but the justice system was, as in England, *accessible* to those with little means and no property. Whilst this remained formally a system of private prosecution, that term is misleading because it does not account for the broad range of activities and factual-legal determinations made by a wide group of people concerned with law and order.

---

[78] See Figure 9.2 in Chapter 9.

[79] Other writers have found the same broad prosecution representation in English research. See eg J Langbein (1983); P King (1984) and (2000).

Chapter 4

Preparation for Trial in the Mercantile Era

INTRODUCTION

In this chapter we consider to what extent trials in General Sessions were spontaneous happenings without a lawyer's forethought or reference to the components of proof essential to sustain conviction in a rational legal system. Overall, this chapter asks whether a lawyer's concern regarding evidence and proof predated the onset of the trial so as to tailor that event in a purposive way toward the elements of the offence. In this regard, we analysed our sample of District Attorney's case files for examples of pre-trial preparation beyond that already undertaken by the Special Justice leading to the bind over decision. Our inquiry includes preparation on behalf of the accused in terms of establishing an affirmative defence with any force or clarity beyond the mere presentation of character witnesses.

We begin with the Grand Jury screening process leading to an indictment and then turn to the briefs prepared by lawyers for the prosecution detailing the testimony of potential witnesses. After this, we consider the District Attorney's use of *nolles prosequi* and *subpoenas* as well as the proceeding convened to perpetuate testimony where prosecution witnesses were likely to become unavailable at trial. Thereafter, we focus on the investigative preparation by the defence followed by the legal research of both parties prior to trial.

Grand Jury indictment

Indictments in New York were drawn in line with precedent for all routine offences, as exemplified in the illustrations below relating to prosecutions for larceny, assault and battery and the keeping of a disorderly house:

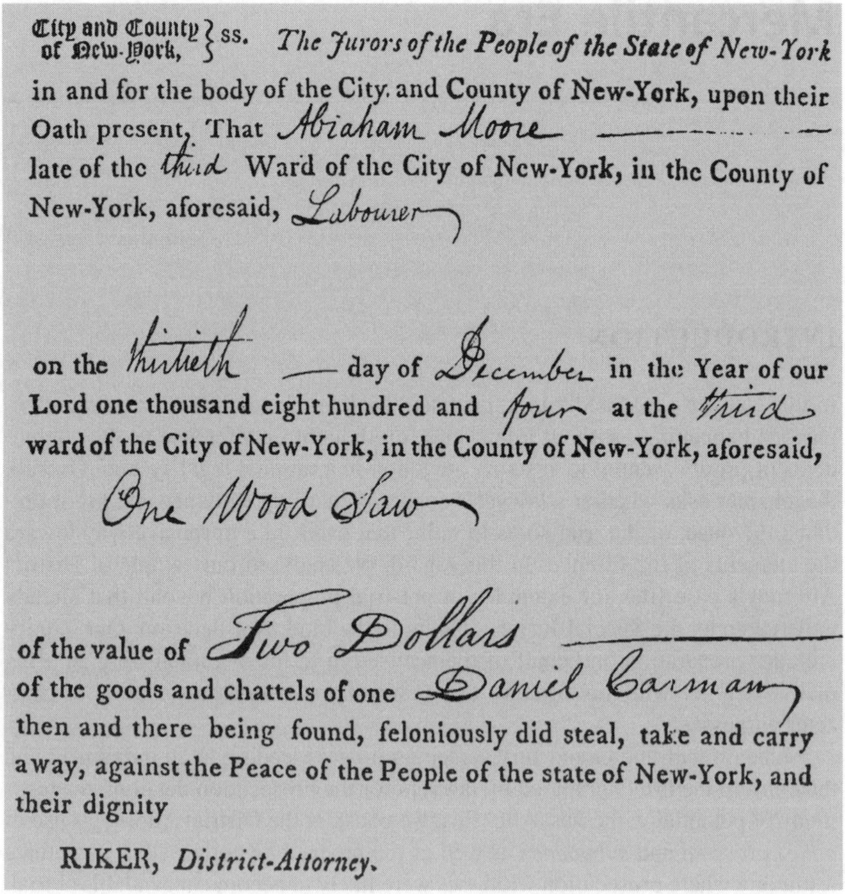

City and County of New-York, ss. *The Jurors of the People of the State of New-York* in and for the body of the City and County of New-York, upon their Oath present, That *Abraham Moore* _____ late of the *third* Ward of the City of New-York, in the County of New-York, aforesaid, *Labourer*

on the *thirtieth* —— day of *December* in the Year of our Lord one thousand eight hundred and *four* at the *third* ward of the City of New-York, in the County of New-York, aforesaid,

One Wood Saw

of the value of *Two Dollars* _____ of the goods and chattels of one *Daniel Carman* then and there being found, feloniously did steal, take and carry away, against the Peace of the People of the state of New-York, and their dignity

RIKER, *District-Attorney.*

ILLUSTRATION 4.1: Abraham Moore, District Attorney's Files, 7 February, 1805.

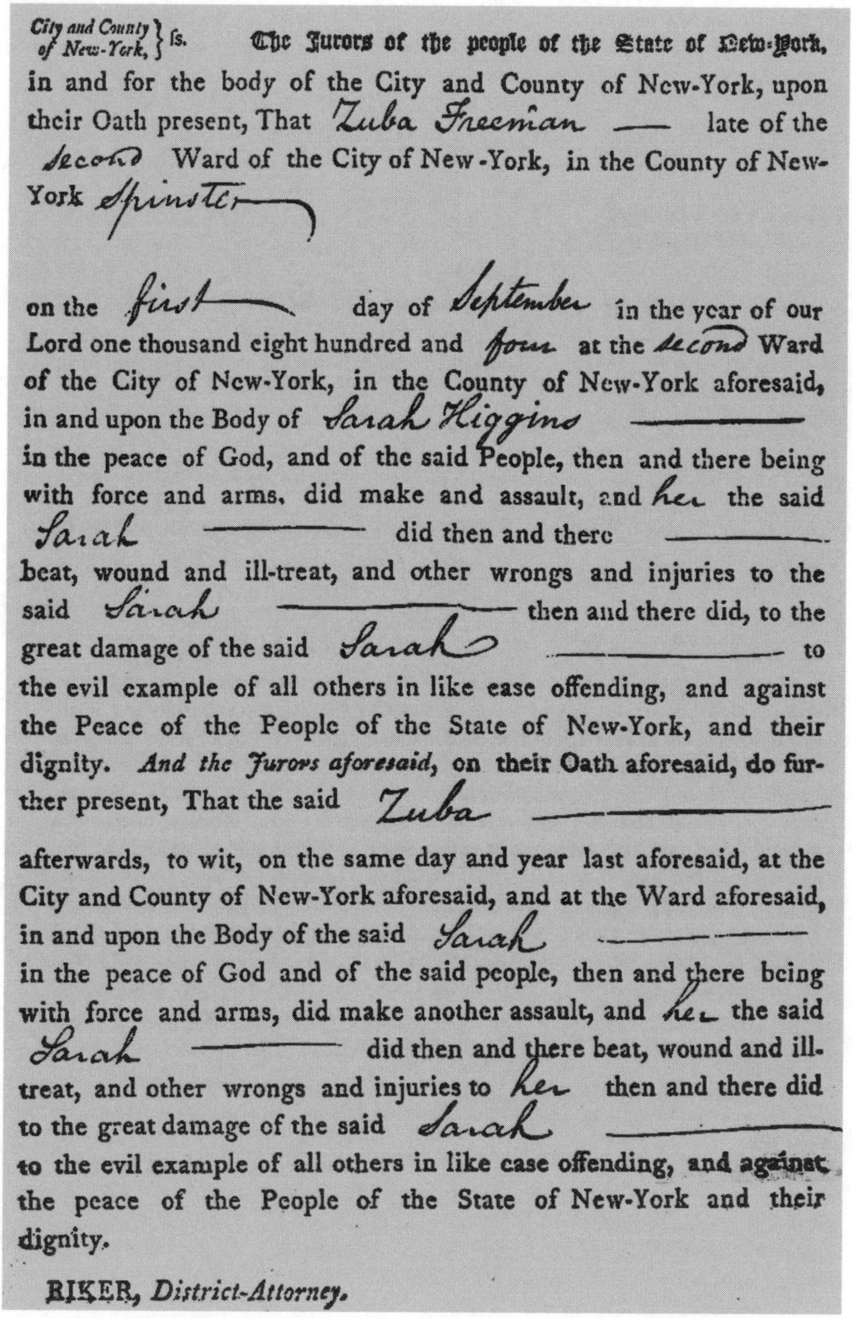

City and County of New-York, } ſs. **The Jurors of the people of the State of New-York,** in and for the body of the City and County of New-York, upon their Oath present, That *Zuba Freeman* —— late of the *second* Ward of the City of New-York, in the County of New-York *Spinster*

on the *first* —— day of *September* in the year of our Lord one thousand eight hundred and *four* at the *second* Ward of the City of New-York, in the County of New-York aforesaid, in and upon the Body of *Sarah Higgins* ————

in the peace of God, and of the said People, then and there being with force and arms, did make and assault, and *her* the said *Sarah* ———— did then and there ————. beat, wound and ill-treat, and other wrongs and injuries to the said *Sarah* ———— then and there did, to the great damage of the said *Sarah* ———— to the evil example of all others in like case offending, and against the Peace of the People of the State of New-York, and their dignity. *And the Jurors aforesaid,* on their Oath aforesaid, do further present, That the said *Zuba* ————

afterwards, to wit, on the same day and year last aforesaid, at the City and County of New-York aforesaid, and at the Ward aforesaid, in and upon the Body of the said *Sarah* ———— in the peace of God and of the said people, then and there being with force and arms, did make another assault, and *her* the said *Sarah* ———— did then and there beat, wound and ill-treat, and other wrongs and injuries to *her* then and there did to the great damage of the said *Sarah* ———— to the evil example of all others in like case offending, and against the peace of the People of the State of New-York and their dignity.

RIKER, *District-Attorney.*

ILLUSTRATION 4.2: Zuba Freeman, District Attorney's Files, 11 December, 1804.

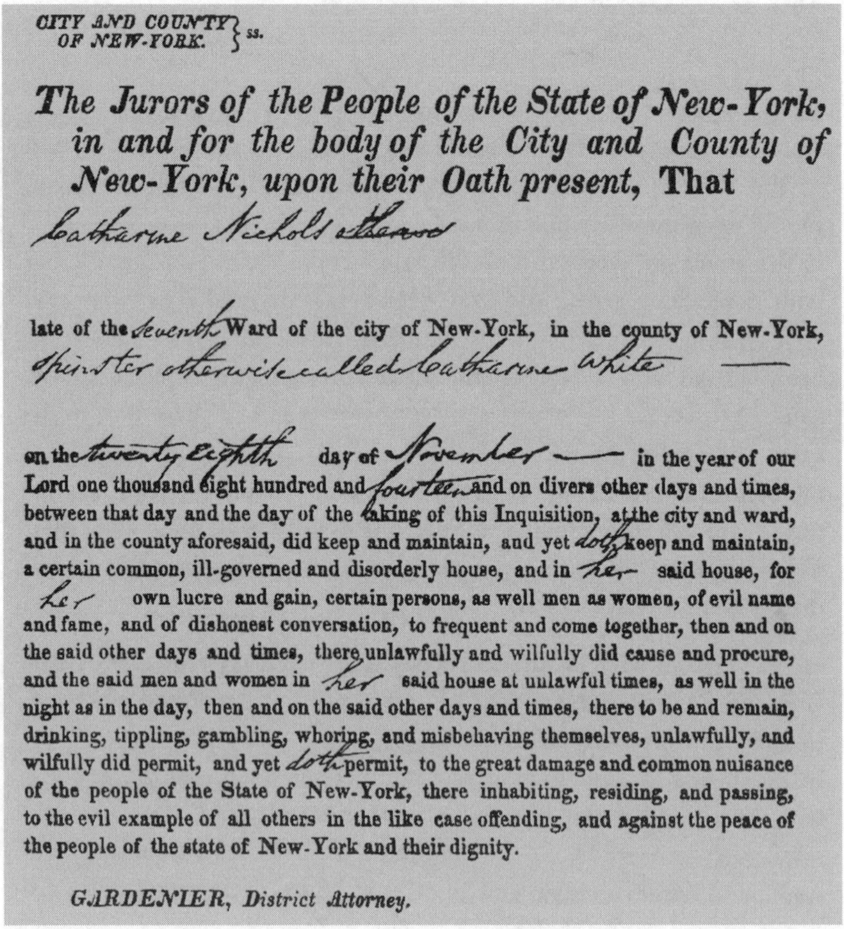

CITY AND COUNTY
OF NEW-YORK.   ss.

*The Jurors of the People of the State of New-York,
in and for the body of the City and County of
New-York, upon their Oath present, That*

Catharine Nichols otherwise

late of the *seventh* Ward of the city of New-York, in the county of New-York,
spinster otherwise called Catharine White ——

on the *twenty eighth* day of *November* —— in the year of our
Lord one thousand eight hundred and *fourteen* and on divers other days and times,
between that day and the day of the taking of this Inquisition, at the city and ward,
and in the county aforesaid, did keep and maintain, and yet *doth* keep and maintain,
a certain common, ill-governed and disorderly house, and in *her* said house, for
her own lucre and gain, certain persons, as well men as women, of evil name
and fame, and of dishonest conversation, to frequent and come together, then and on
the said other days and times, there unlawfully and wilfully did cause and procure,
and the said men and women in *her* said house at unlawful times, as well in the
night as in the day, then and on the said other days and times, there to be and remain,
drinking, tippling, gambling, whoring, and misbehaving themselves, unlawfully, and
wilfully did permit, and yet *doth* permit, to the great damage and common nuisance
of the people of the State of New-York, there inhabiting, residing, and passing,
to the evil example of all others in the like case offending, and against the peace of
the people of the state of New-York and their dignity.

GARDENIER, District Attorney.

ILLUSTRATION 4.3: Catherine Nichols, District Attorney's Files, 11 January, 1815.

In addition, the District Attorney's presence in the Grand Jury enabled him to make an assessment of the probity and persuasiveness of the prosecution's witnesses, beyond that contained in the Special Justice's examination. Thus, the form of the indictment coupled with direct knowledge of the witnesses' evidence enabled the District Attorney to prepare for trial.

Lawyers' brief

Briefs cataloguing the prosecution's evidence and the anticipated testimony of witnesses were prepared for the attorney who would try the case by either the District Attorney or private lawyer, as in the case of William Clark and Moses Phips as set out in Illustration 4.4 and transcribed below:[1]

> The defendants Clark (alias Collins) and Phips were charged with grand larceny from the store of Ignatius Longchamp, adjacent to the river. After Clark and Phips had suggested to George Shaffer that the store should be robbed, Shaffer agreed to participate but secretly informed the Watch of the plan with the result that the defendants were caught red-handed. It appears that the District Attorney prepared a comprehensive brief for Long, a private attorney, who appeared on behalf of the private prosecutor. The brief included the following attributions:
>
> > George Shaffer will swear that he and Moses Phips and William Clark als. Collins on the afternoon of Saturday the 29th July 1805 agreed to rob Longchamp's Store and that Phips was to be in the street near the store and pretend that he had lost $300 in Bank notes and that he was walking about there all night for fear some one might pick it up in the morning before him and by this means was to engage the attention of the watchman who should chance to come there while Clark and Schaffer were to go in the store & bring out the goods which were to be put in trunks prepared for that purpose which were on board a small boat lying at the wharf near the store
> >
> > —That when they were ready to go into the store Schaffer ran to the Watch House and told the Capt. of the Watch all the circumstances & showed him the store.
> >
> > George Raymond will swear that he saw Schaffer & Phips hire the boat at fly market the trunks were found in.
> >
> > Joseph Hasket will swear that he made the trunks for Phips and Clark and put the initials of their names on with nails.
> >
> > Robert Cronk and James Graft[2] will swear that Phips came as Schaffer had said & pretended to have lost $300.
> >
> > John Concklin, Richard Smith and Wm. Van Wart will swear that they caught Clark & Schaffer with the goods coming out of the yard—

---

[1] District Attorney's Files, 7 August, 1805.
[2] Cronk and Graft were described in the indictments as 'two of Capt Van Wart's Watchmen'.

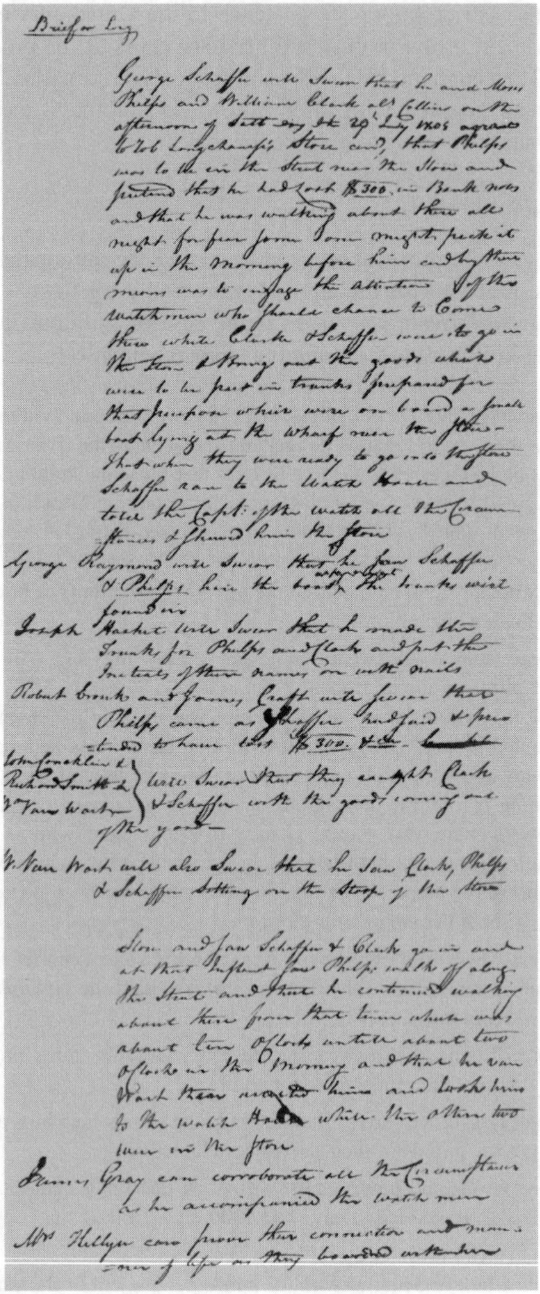

ILLUSTRATION 4.4: William Clarke and Moses Phips, District Attorney's Files, 7 August, 1805.

W Van Wart will also swear that he saw Clark, Phips and Schaffer sitting on the stoop of the store and saw Schaffer & Clark go in and that instant saw Phips walk off along the street and that he continued walking about there from that time which was about ten o'clock until about two o'clock in the morning and that W Van Wart then arrested him and took him to the Watch House while the other two were in the store.

James Gray can corroborate all the circumstances as he accompanied the watch men.

Mrs Hilyer can prove their connection and manner of life as they boarded with her.

As the foregoing shows, such briefs explained the interrelationship of witnesses to facts and the meaning of the available documentary evidence. Another example of a prosecution brief is contained in the case of Lewis Berry *et al*,[3] set out in Illustration 4.5 and transcribed below:

Lawyer's brief in *Lewis Berry et al*:

The defendants were indicted for grand larceny of tortoise shell from the store of William Stevens, 157 South Street who swore out a complaint as the basis for a search warrant stating his belief that part of the stolen shell was concealed in the house of one, Charlotte Smith. On the same day, Rebecca Smith, 'a Black', and Lewis Berry, 'born on the Eastern Shore of Maryland a slave to Joseph Payne' were brought before Special Justice James Warner. Rebecca Smith implicated Lewis Berry who had, she said, together with Jacob Cannon and Joseph Nichols, brought a bag 'somewhat larger than a pillow case' filled with tortoise shell and had asked her to take some to combmakers to see whether they would buy it. She told Justice Warner that a combmaker, Mr Littleboys in Chatham Street, had said that he would take the shell 'if it was good' and that Berry and the others then took the bag away. On a subsequent occasion, she went with Berry to Mr Littleboys and sold a dozen pieces of shell.

The prosecution case was given coherence in a brief listing the witnesses the prosecution proposed calling and the evidence they would offer at trial, extracts from which are set out below:

William Stevens will testify as to the property being stolen etc.

William Curtis (clerk) will testify that the store was found open twice—the first time in Novr & last Dec last and also that Jacob Cannon assisted in taking the shell into the store & asked him what was in the Barrels—

Gedney (combmaker) will prove that he bought of Cannon & another Black (supposed since to have died) about 31lbs of

---

[3] District Attorney's Files, 11 and 13 March, 1820.

William Stevens, will testify as to the property having been
stolen &c —

(William Beckter - (clerk) will testify that the iron was
found often twice — the first first time in Moor & last
in Lear bath as also that Jacob Cannon assisted in
taking the shell into the store & asked him what was
in the Barrels —

— Stoney — (comb-maker) will prove that he bought
of Cannon & another Black, (Stafford) said to have
died) about 31 #s of Shell — he has a receipt for
the shell money paid therefor, witnessed by Cannon
in a fictitious name — Cannon observed that he
was satisfied to take his (that is Stoney's) oath
as he had sold to him before

— Littleboy (comb-maker) will testify that
he purchased shell of Jacob Cannon several
times — & also once or twice of a man about
answering a friends description to Lewis
Berry, tho he thinks (having seen him since
his arrest) that he is not the man —
& also that he purchased of Isaac (Mulatto
Girl of a very black man supposed to
be Joseph Nicholls, now away, as mentioned
before — & Stewart — Tho there is no doubt
that Littleboy actually bought from
Berry the Shell — yet as the inducements
are so strong it is thought probable that
he will deny & it is therefore a question
if it will be best to examine him over
— If examining — ask Littleboy what ~~kind of~~ coat
the man wore he bot shell of —

— Betts — combmaker, will admit that he
purchased 20th of shea from said Cannon at
one time, about the 1st of Sept & some months
before another parcel — The ~~Cotton~~ parcel was
taken from Stewart's store at the time that
Cannon opened their store — They will further
certify that purchased 1st on the 14 day from
a man answering in description to Lewis Berry
— He says he ~~thinks~~ Berry is not the man —
He may not remember him from the circumstance of Berry's not having been but once
in the store or he may be actuated by ~~improper~~
motives —

Mrs Smith (Sleak) will testify that the four Prisoners
were frequently in the ~~to~~ at her house, together
that Lewis Berry boarded with her — that at two
different times previous to Christmas or his
going out at night he requested that the Front
door might be left open, that 2 or 3 o'clock in
the morning of different nights she heard the Prisoners bringing at
something & depositing them in the back room — that
she at about 6 o'clock of one these mornings the
Prisoners came to her house & from the circumstance of her hearing something rub against the
partition of her room she looked out of the
Front window — & saw Sandy Cameron with
a large bag — full, on his back — & that on
Lewis Berry's coming into the room, where
she was, she asked him what that was she
had — he laughed & told her that it was none
of her business but afterwards said it was
something they had stole, but it would not

Rebecca Smith from Bridewell will testify
to most of the above facts — Also that she
accompanied Lewis Berry to Mr Littleboys after
he purchased 19th of Shell at £4 profit that
at another time she sold another parcel there
herself, receiving the Money & gave it to Lewis
Berry —

Hannah Vincent — 37 Mulberry St will prove
another division of money at her store, her Brothers
stolen by the Prisoners — & Jacob Nicholls deceased —
Jacob Cannon brought the money — & counting it
out — Mrs Vincent the Mother with proven that
Lewis Berry secreted himself there & left
her store last Saturday night —

—— Mollens will testify his having purchased
a "Monkey-coat" similar to the one that
Little boy of Shells will testify the man
wore they bought the Shell from —

Thomas Tonguss — will prove that Berry came to
Brady about the 4th Inst at the store, where
he boards — that he develops himself — that he
confessed to him the Theft of the Shell — &
that the Prisoners were with him — & offered
to sell him a parcel at £3 — Stating the
value to be £6 — & that Mrs Smith had
the two parcels, which parcels he (Tonguss)
afterwards Mr Stevens obtained for him from
Mrs Smith —

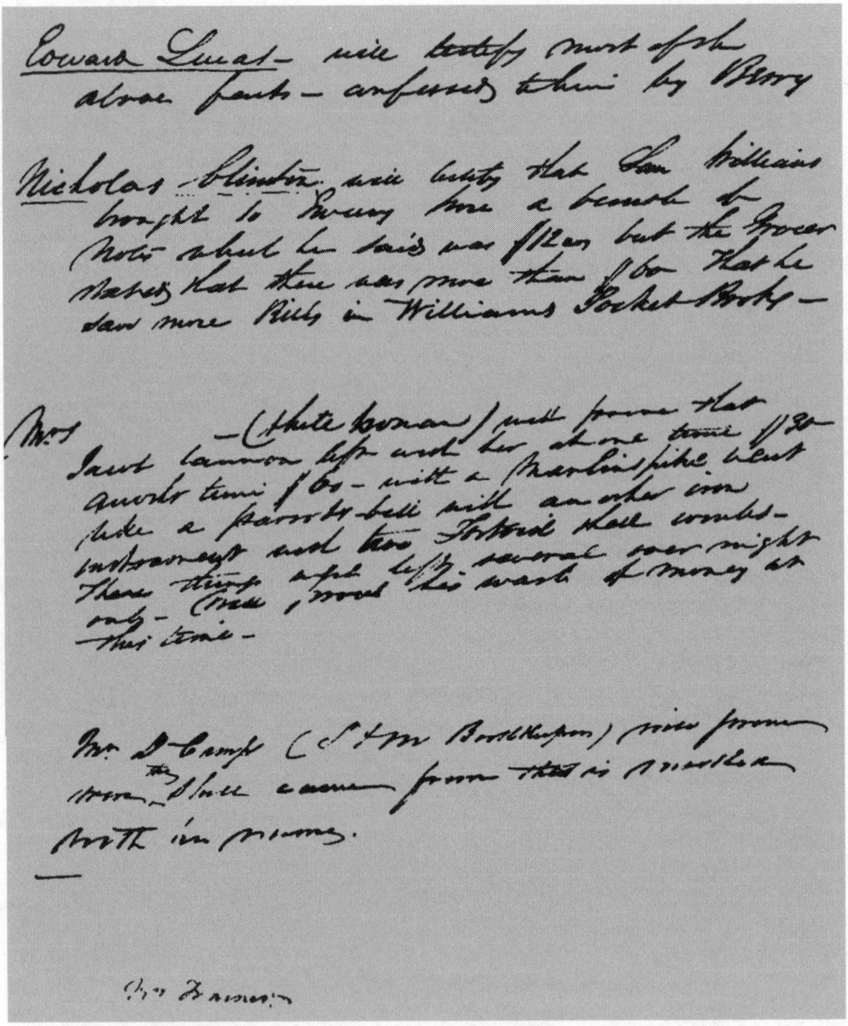

Edward Lucas – will testify most of the above facts – confessed to him by Berry

Nicholas Clinton will testify that Geo Williams brought to Berry here a bundle of Notes which he said was $1200 but the Grocer stated that there was more than $800 that he saw more Bills in Williams Pocket Book –

Mrs — (white woman) will prove that Janet Cannon left with her at one time $130 another time $80 – with a Marlin spike, what like a parrots bill with another iron instrument and two Tortoise shell combs – These things after left several over night only – Cannon proved his want of money at that time –

Mr D Camp (S & M Bookkeeper) will prove that the Shell came from there is a market worth in money.

ILLUSTRATION 4.5: Lewis Berry *et al.*

Shell—He has a receipt for the money paid therefor, witnessed by Cannon in a fictitious name—Cannon observed that he was satisfied to take his (that is Gedney's) check as he had sold to him before.

Littleboy (combmaker) will testify that he purchased shell of Joseph Cannon several times—& also once or twice of a man about answering in description to Lewis Berry, tho' he thinks (having seen him since his arrest) that he is not the man—& also that he purchased of Mulatto Girl of a very black man supposed to be Joseph Nicholls, now dead, and mentioned before—*Remark*—Tho there is no doubt that Littleboy actually bought from Berry the Shell—yet as the inducements are so strong it is thought that he will deny & it is therefore a question if it will be best to examine him. If examining—ask Littleboy what kind of *over coat* the man wore he bot shell of—

Betts—Combmaker will admit that he purchased 20 lbs of shell from Jacob Cannon at one time, about the 18th of Decr & some months before another parcel was taken from Martins Store at the time that Cannon opened their Store—He will further certify that purchased 18 lbs on the 19 Decr from a man answering in description to Lewis Berry—tho' he *says he thinks* Berry is not the man— He may not remember him from the circumstances of Berry's not having been back over in the store or he may be actuated *by improper motives.*

Mrs Smith (Black) will testify that the four Prisoners were frequently at her House together—that Lewis Berry boarded with her—that at two different times previous to Christmas on his going out at night he requested that her Front door might be left open— That 2 or 3 o'clock in the morning of different nights she heard the Prisoners bringing out some things & depositing them in the back room—that at about 8 o'clock of one these mornings the Prisoners came to her house & from the circumstances of her hearing some thing rub against the Partition of her Room she looked out of the front window—& saw Jacob Cannon with a large bag—full, on his back—& that on Lewis Berry's coming into the room where she was, she asked him what was Jacob had—he laughed & told her that it was none of her business—but afterwards said it was something they had stolen, but it would not bring her into trouble—also that they all presently supped at her house together at night & on one occasion divided a very large sum of money amongst themselves—The division took place in the Front Room—She asked them where they money came from—they told her they had found a Mine—that they dug it & intended to play *Boss*—Lewis Berry gave her two parcels of shell to keep—which she sent by her daughter Rebecca to a black woman by the name of Sparks—& a few evenings since on Mr Stevens calling at her house, went out with Thomas Youngs who accompanied Mr Stevens & brought the two parcels & delivered them up. She will testify as to the extravagance of the men.

Eliza Smith (daughter of the above) will testify to all the above in substance & to some additional ones—particularly to another division of money in the back room which was seen by her herself & sister thro a hole in the partition. From her accounts the parcel of Bank notes was large with considerable silver—abt. this division,

Sam Williams was dissatisfied saying that his share was short three dollars—when the money was counted again—The next day when the witness mentioned to Lewis Berry what she had seen he threatened her if she was not silent. This witness will identify all the Prisoners. She saw or heard them when they brot. the shell in & heard it rattle when put on the floor—The next morning they all called & Jake Cannon & Wm Trusty each took a large bag with something that showed thro' the Bag like tin (This was not the same night mentioned before the mother being asleep during this occurrence but in the morning). She also went with her sister Rebecca when they took a parcel of shell to Littleboys.

Rebecca Smith from Bridewell will testify to most of the above facts. Also that she accompanied Lewis Berry to Mr Littleboys when he purchased 19 lbs of shell at $ per lb. That at another time she sold another parcel there herself, received the money & gave it to Lewis Berry.

Hannah Vincent—37 Mulberry St—will prove another division of money at her mother's house by the prisoners & Jacob Nicholls deceased—Jacob Cannon brought the money & counted it out— Mrs Vincent her mother will prove that Lewis Berry secreted himself there & left her house last Saturday night.

Mokens will testify his having purchased 'monkey-coat' similar to the one that Littleboy & Betts will testify the man wore they bought the shell from

Thomas Youngs will prove that Berry came to Board about the 4th Inst. at the House where he boards—that he secreted himself—that he confessed to him the theft of the shell & that the Prisoners were with him & offered to sell him a parcel at $3 stating the same to be $4—That Mrs Smith had the two parcels, which parcels he (Youngs) informed Mr Stevens & obtained for him from Mrs Smith—

Edward Lucas—will testify most of the above facts—confessed to him by Berry.

Nicholas Clinton will testify that Sam Williams brought to Grocery store a bundle of notes which he said was $12 but the Grocer noted that there was more than $60. That he saw more Bills in Williams Pocket Book—

Mrs—(White woman) will prove that Jacob Cannon left with her at one time $30. Another time $60—with a Marlin spike bent like a parrott-bill with another iron instrument with two tortoise shell combs ...

It is clear from the above example that not only was detailed information available to the lawyer for the prosecution about the movements and actions of the

various defendants but also that there was a lawyer's awareness of the vulnera-
bilities of potential witnesses and their motivations from which lines of questioning most likely to develop the prosecution case might be prepared.

Another illustration is found in the case of Barbara Tuomy,[4] on a charge of
grand larceny from Patrick Shea, on 16 December 1838. In addition to Shea's
complaint sworn on 28 December 1838, the District Attorney's files contain a
lengthy 'statement of Patrick Shea' dated February 4, 1839 specifically prepared
to assist the District Attorney in the presentation of the prosecution. Since the
statement was drafted with an understanding of legal principles and since Shea
did not sign his examination but made a mark, it seems clear that this brief had
been prepared by a private lawyer acting on Shea's behalf. Following a detailed
account of Shea's knowledge of the character and habits of Tuomy and Barbara
Muldoon (an accomplice said to have absconded after gaining release from
Bridewell on a false plea of approaching confinement) and the available witness
evidence, the statement concludes:

> These are the principal matters to which said Shea can testify in detail—they
> seem to afford sufficient ground on which to base a moral conclusion of the
> guilt of the accused, and are given in this form for the purpose of informa-
> tion for the public prosecutor that he may better know in advance of exami-
> nation, to what points to call the attention of said Shea, when sworn, as well
> as that of any other person having knowledge of the facts and circumstances
> of the case.

Further evidence of pre-trial preparation is found in annotations entered onto the
file jacket of the indictment or other case papers in our sample. These aides-
memoire appear to be typical jottings of a trial lawyer concerned with detailing
the main issues which arose at the magistrate's examination and were likely to be
relevant at trial. In the aforementioned prosecution of Lewis Berry *et al*,[5] for
example, as seen in Illustration 4.6, the lawyer made notes regarding the theory
of defence and the responsive evidence available to the prosecution, including
points that might be pursued in cross examination:

The lawyer's notes in the Berry case include the following observations:

3 Divisions of money—

They deny being together & deny dividing the money

Berry = fled—secreted himself—sold shell—confided with Young & told
him where he got it— & the manner of the felony

Williams—in the Company—divided money—complained of the division

[4] District Attorney's Files, 8 February, 1839.
[5] See n 3. See also *Mary Fenton*, District Attorney's Files, 9 February, 1805; *Williams and Roberts*,
District Attorney's Files, 8 August, 1805; *James Smith and Catherine Smith*, District Attorney's Files,
7 April, 1820.

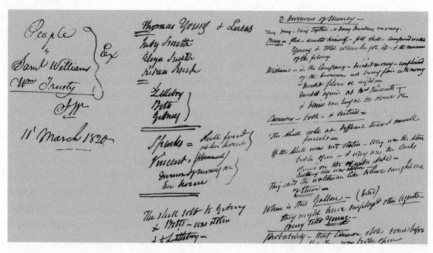

ILLUSTRATION 4.6: Lewis Berry *et al*, District Attorney's Files, 11–13 March, 1820.

not being fair in the morning

= divided silver at night =

divided again at Mrs Vincents—

& denies ever being at the house

The shell sold at different times & small parcels =

If the shell was not stolen—why was the store broke open— & why was the casks opened on the *under* side =

nothing else was stolen—

They said the watchman like to have caught one of them—

Where is this *Gallon*— (dead)

they might have employed other agents—

Berry tried Young.—

Probability that Cannon stole some before the store was broke open.

Nolles prosequi

Once the District Attorney had familiarised himself with the Police Office file, additional evidence could be sought beyond that obtained by the examining magistrate. For example, choices could be made in co-defendant cases involving the need to prove concerted action among each of the actors and whether to give immunity to one of those accused in return for testimony against the others. Thus, it was not uncommon for the District Attorney, intent upon proving culpability to supplement the decision-making of the Special Justice in this regard, by exercising his authority to enter a *nolle prosequi* in cases in which one prisoner testified against the others, as in the prosecution of James Malone, indicted with John G Welsh:[6]

> Malone, a man of about twenty six years of age and Welsh, aged about twenty one years, and described as 'both of decent appearance' were indicted for conspiracy to forge and alter bank bills from a lower to a higher denomination. The District Attorney, Hugh Maxwell decided that the prosecution would benefit by having Welsh as a co-operating witness; accordingly, as reported by the nominative reporter:
>
>> Maxwell entered a *nolle prosequi* on the indictment, in favour of Walsh, for the purpose of introducing him as a witness on behalf of the prosecution.
>
>> Welsh was subsequently sworn as a witness for the prosecution and testified that Malone had proposed having a plate struck by an engraver for the purpose of pasting a five on a one dollar bill and confirmed the evidence of John Ridley the engraver that this had been done whilst asserting, under cross-examination, that no agreement or understanding existed between himself and Malone to alter bank bills or to pass such altered bills.[7]

Subpoenas

When the appearance of witnesses was considered essential and a question arose as to whether the witness would appear voluntarily at trial, the District Attorney could exercise his authority to issue *subpoenas* to obtain the witnesses' testimony at trial,[8] as in the prosecution of Samuel Clews for assault and battery on John Duberay:[9]

Subpoenas could also be issued in respect of witnesses from out of state and whilst the timing of this was often not perfect, the District Attorney could re-open the case upon the appearance of the witness and upon demonstrating to the court that an effort had been made to produce the witness in a timely fashion.[10]

---

[6] (1817) Rogers, vol 2, 22.

[7] Clearly, the District Attorney had also decided to use the engraver John Ridley as a prosecution witness rather than joining him in the indictment. In evidence, Ridley said that the engraving had been made for the purpose of making labels to put on vials in an apothecary's shop as represented to him by Malone and Welsh who were then 'utter strangers to him'.

[8] See O L Barbour (1852) p 315. 1829 *Revised Statutes of the State of New York*, Part IV, Chapter II, Title IV, Sections 59–62, p 729. The Statute adopted existing practice enabling the District Attorney to issue *subpoenas*. Otherwise, on application of the defendant, the clerk of the court in which the indictment was filed would be authorised to issue the *subpoena* under seal of the court, a practice derived from the 1801 *Compilation of the Laws of the State of New York*, Acts of the 24th Session, Chapter LX, Section xi, p 261.

[9] *Samuel Clews*, District Attorney's Case files, 11 February, 1805. The drawings in the file have nothing to do with the case and indicate the clerk's dark sense of humour.

[10] See eg, *Joel Sturdivant* (1816) Rogers, vol 1, 110. The court reiterated the basic rule that, whilst the prisoner had a right to introduce new and additional testimony at any stage prior to the retirement of the jury, new evidence could be introduced by the prosecution only at the discretion of the court.

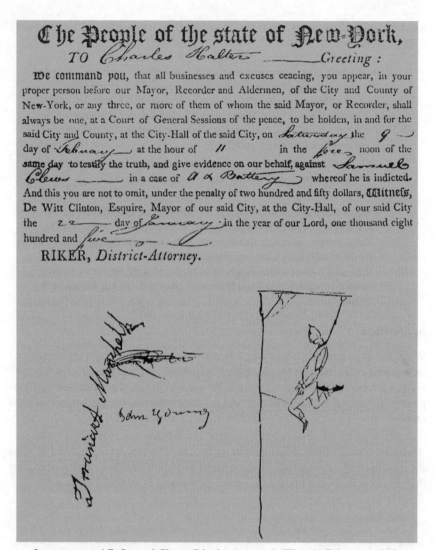

ILLUSTRATION 4.7: Samuel Clews, District Attorney's Files, 11 February, 1805.

Perpetuation of testimony

By 1844 statutory authority existed whereby the District Attorney could apply to a superior court judge,[11] for permission to perpetuate the witness's testimony so as to secure its admissibility at trial, after having been alerted by the Special Justice or others that a witness would leave the jurisdiction following the

---

[11] 1844 *Laws of the State of New York*, p 476; O L Barbour (1852) p 410.

examination at the Police Office. This involved the staging of a formal hearing at which time the witness would be deposed and in which both parties were represented.

The procedure that had to be followed in a perpetuation proceeding is illustrated in our case files in the grand larceny prosecution of Mary Wood,[12] before a judge of the Common Pleas:

> This case involved a complaint dated August 1st 1845 by Alexander Crook, a resident of Kingston, Ulster County who stated that he intended to return there almost immediately after reporting the offense. The complaint alleged that Crook had met Wood in the street late at night, gone to her apartment, given her $1.00 for sex, that she had persuaded him to put his clothes on a chair, they had gone to bed, when almost immediately there was a rapping on the door, she got up and whispered to someone, told Crook a visitor had arrived, he got up, dressed, found his money gone; she denied knowledge of the theft; he got officers who came and eventually secured entry.
>
> Because Crook intended to leave the city and return home, the District Attorney obtained an 'order to examine non-resident witness' which deposition was conducted before an Associate Judge of the Court of Common Pleas, the Hon D P Ingraham at his Chambers in the City Hall on 2nd August 1845. Mary Wood was not present. As a result, her counsel James McGay Esq., objected to the taking of the testimony from Alexander Crook contending that Wood's presence was required by the statute.[13] However, Judge Ingraham overruled the objection, 'proof having been made that the witness had been personally served with copies of the affidavit & order to take the same ...' The proof in question was a deposition by George E Walter that he had served copies of the affidavit and order on Mary Wood 'by delivering the same to her personally & at the same time exhibited to her the originals thereof.'
>
> Following the direct and cross examination of Crook which was transcribed and signed by the witness, the following certification appeared:
>
> > Sworn before me
> >
> > this 2nd day of August 1845
> >
> > D P Ingraham
> >
> > Judge of New York Com Pleas
> >
> > I certify that the foregoing deposition was taken before me in pursuance of the previous order on due proof of service personally of the said order on the Defendant. The witness having been first sworn in the cause and the counsel for the people and the defendant both attending before me on such examination—

---

[12] District Attorney's Files, 22 October, 1845.

[13] 1829 *Revised Statutes of the State of New York*, Part IV, Chapter II, Title V, Section 15, p 735 states that no person indicted for a felony can be tried if not present during such trial.

Dated 2nd day Aug 1845 [signed D P Ingraham, Associate Judge of New York Com Pleas]

Whilst the availability of this procedure benefited the prosecution in that it enabled the witness's testimony to be presented at trial, it could also work to the advantage of the defendant who, through the process itself could impeach or discredit the witness while obtaining advance disclosure of the witness's detailed allegations thus enabling the defendant to prepare in advance of trial appropriate refutation evidence.

The defence investigation

Whilst accused persons brought before the Special Justice would sometimes indicate that they had consulted with a lawyer prior to the examination, the involvement of counsel in the case was more likely to occur between the committal proceeding and prior to or shortly thereafter arraignment in General Sessions.

Most defendants charged with a felony were detained at Bridewell, the local gaol which serviced the criminal courts and a procedure existed whereby lawyers were provided the opportunity to speak with the accused in private. At the outset this involved the keepers or turnkeys arranging for counsel to visit the accused in his 'apartment' at Bridewell where the lawyer would be locked in with the accused until completion of the conference. Indeed, those accused who were known to the keeper to be unrepresented would be disclosed to lawyers who were regulars in General Sessions and who would have the opportunity to visit the accused to see if an arrangement could be made for representation. The practice of jail-house interviews was vividly described by the nominative reporter in the trial of James Lent, jun[14] in which Dr Graham, one of the City's prominent criminal practitioners, complained that he had been falsely imprisoned by the defendant, an under-turnkey, who had not heeded his call upon completion of the interview with his client, despite Dr Graham's efforts at 'halloing' at the window. On direct examination, Graham testified that he had been let into the Bridewell by Lent, who, he said, before they arrived at the door of the prisoner's room, asked Graham if he had five dollars for him. According to Graham, no money was given to Lent who later deliberately ignored his calls and abused him when he finally gained his release. Thereafter, Graham was cross-examined by Mr Maxwell, the lawyer for Lent as detailed in the nominative report:

Q Is it not usual for gentlemen of the profession who have frequent occasion to visit the apartments of prisoners in the Bridewell, to give money to those persons, the turnkeys?

A I have myself sometimes, for sixteen years past, when they have been uncommonly attentive, given them something, supposing them to be in an unpleasant situation.

[14] D Bacon (1818) p 124.

> Q Will you give the jury some information about a quantity of gold pieces
>   you saw in the Bridewell which had been taken from one of the prison-
>   ers?
> A Yes, sir, I saw a number of gold pieces there of that description, and
>   remarked that they would make a handsome fee, and believe I told Lent
>   I would give him half if he would get them for me as a fee, or something
>   like it.

Mr Dunsmore, one of the other turnkeys called by the prosecution, testified on
direct examination that there were three hours set aside every day for lawyers to
visit their clients and that it was common to laugh and joke with the lawyers
about their fees. In charging the jury, the Mayor made clear both the importance
of access to counsel of prisoners in the Bridewell and of the objectionable character of any demand for a fee by the turnkey:

> Every man there imprisoned on criminal accusation is, in the eyes of the law,
> innocent, and is to be treated with tenderness and humanity. —Counsel must
> visit them, that they may receive the full immunity of the laws; and they
> must visit them as often as they please; and the doors must open for their
> entrance at their approach; and, though perhaps it may not be proper to exact
> the attendance of a turnkey at the door of an apartment every moment a
> counsellor is tarrying in consultation, yet that apartment must be opened
> promptly and speedily when he wishes to retire, and without the formality of
> negotiating a *doceur*!

Access to the defendant prior to trial is also evidenced in other General Sessions'
cases described by the nominative reporters which demonstrate that the lawyer
had, on the basis of the accused's instructions, prepared particular lines of
defence, as in Joseph De Costa:[15]

> Following prosecution evidence in a false bills of exchange case, J T Irving
> counsel for the defendant, admitted to the court that he had been led to
> believe that the state of facts was different from what they now appeared to
> be. He had believed that the defendant had been created an agent to purchase
> the disputed bill and had, therefore, 'brought authorities to show, that where
> there was merely *a breach of trust*, an indictment for obtaining money or
> goods could not be supported.' (*ibid*, p 35, original emphasis)

Case preparation extended beyond interviewing the defendant and included an
investigation into the testimony of potential defence witnesses. The nominative
reports disclose instances in which defence counsel had interviewed and later produced at trial, witnesses to the event, witnesses to whom impeaching statements
had been made by the prosecutor, witnesses who would support an alibi, and

---

[15] (1816) Rogers, vol 1, p 83.

witnesses who would either offer character evidence to impeach the prosecution's witnesses or to accredit the defendant. Should a witness be unavailable at the time the case was calendared for trial in General Sessions, defence counsel could request an adjournment by submitting a sworn affidavit attesting to the materiality of the witness's evidence.[16] The following cases detailed in the nominative reports are indicative of the fruits of the defence lawyer's own investigations:

Philip McNiff [17]
On a charge of receiving stolen goods, a prosecution witness called McDonald swore that McNiff had often advised him to steal goods for which he would give him two thirds the value. He said that when the constables first came for McNiff at his lodgings, McNiff had told him that he had stolen goods with him and offered him $5 to help him out of the city with the goods. In an effort to impeach McDonald, the defence called several witnesses 'from whom it appeared, in substance, that there had been a quarrel between McDonald and the prisoner; and that McDonald declared he would be revenged on the prisoner, for he had him in his power'.

Edward Latham [18]
The prisoner, 'a black man', was indicted for burglary and grand larceny of the dwelling-house and grocery store of Thomas Sexton on the night of 4 March 1816. Sexton gave evidence that on the evening before the burglary, Latham had come there and got something to drink. Latham was arrested the day following the burglary and was found in possession of bills identified by Sexton as his and as stolen in the burglary. The nominative reporter added that following this evidence:

> The prisoner introduced two black boys as witnesses, who proved, that during the night in which this felony was proved to have been committed, the prisoner was with them at a house in Bancker-Street, and that he did not leave that house from about nine in the evening until five o'clock the next morning ...

Mary Rothbone [19]
Mary Rothbone was indicted for keeping a disorderly house in Banckerstreet where, according to prosecution witnesses, men and women of lewd character often resorted for the purposes of prostitution. In rebuttal, 'Hull, a son-in-law of the defendant, and several women, were called on her behalf' to establish that she occupied only the lower part of the house as a cook-shop and that she had nothing to do with the chamber occupied by girls and let to them by the house owner, Mr Newton.

---

[16] See eg John W Brigham (1816) Rogers, vol 1, p 30.
[17] (1816) Rogers, vol 1, p 8.
[18] (1816) Rogers, vol 1, p 45.
[19] (1816) Rogers, vol 1, p 26.

Legal research

Legal research was also part of the pre-trial preparation particularly where a lawyer could reasonably anticipate an objection to either the admissibility of evidence or its legal sufficiency or because of a defect in the institution of the prosecution. Research on legal authorities required the lawyer to have familiarity with both English common law and American common law and statutory law. In practice, it appears that lawyers exchanged legal authorities to be relied upon in support of or against any contention of law, and thus it was not uncommon for both parties in the dispute to cite legal precedents in response to disputed issues in the case. Should one side attempt to take advantage of the other by not revealing in advance of trial the authorities it intended to rely upon the opponent would call this to the court's attention and indicate that the lack of notice had affected the ability to prepare a full response. When legal issues were raised, therefore, the nominative reports showed that lawyers evidenced preparation and thought which enabled them to argue the various points with detailed reference to cases, statutes and treatises, as indicated in the following examples:

> *George Wellington and Abel S Franklin*[20]
> The prisoners were jointly indicted for forgery and possession of false bills with intent to utter and pass them. Wilson, one of the three counsel engaged for the defendants, made a severance motion at the outset of the trial, as described by the reporter:
>
>> Before any evidence was introduced, Wilson applied to the court, that the prisoners be tried separately, and cited the case of Howell (Johns Re 296) as an authority directly in point. He argued, that as this was an offence for which the prisoners might be punished with imprisonment in the state prison for life, they were each entitled to their peremptory challenge (1 vol N R L p 496, ix). Should, therefore, one of the prisoners be compelled to be tried with an associate, who had a right to a peremptory challenge; the rights of the prisoner thus compelled, would be directly infringed by the other, who might reject jurors whom the other might choose to retain.
>
> *Charles Jones and William Honeywell*[21]
> One of the counts in the indictment involved an allegation, which was admitted by the defence, that the prisoners broke open the store of William S Hick at No 129 Water Street and stole watches, jewellry and other articles, having been seized by Watchmen before they could escape. The only question was whether their offence amounted to burglary, as charged, or the lesser offence of grand larceny. The building in which the offence was committed was owned by Daniel Sullivan and let separately to two tenants, Catherine Jones and William Hick. Hick's store, located in the lower part of the building, had

---

[20] (1818) Rogers, vol 1, p 144.
[21] (1816) Rogers, vol 1, p 183.

a front door leading directly onto Water Street but the doors from the store to a side entry shared in common with Mrs Jones were no longer in use, goods having been placed against them prior to the time of the break in. Hick himself lived at another building. Accordingly, defence counsel (Wilson and Price) argued, with reference to the English common law reports, Hale's *Pleas of the Crown* and East's *Crown Law*, that because of the layout of the building and the arrangements within it, there could be no burglary as a matter of law:

> ... There was no communication from the store to the entry, and there was a separate entrance for each of the tenants. The store was wholly unconnected with the other parts of the building. The counsel, in support of their argument, cited 1 Hale's P C 287, and read from 2d East's C L p 500 ...

The District Attorney, John Rodman, argued that the indictment was properly drawn and that the offence disclosed was burglary:

> The several parts of the building were connected, and all under the same roof. Even had this offence been committed in an out-house ... the indictment under the testimony would have been sufficiently supported; much more so, when it appeared that the place where the felony was committed, was a part of the building, and under the same roof. The counsel cited 2d East's C L p 491, 2 & 4.[22]

Defence lawyers seeking to challenge the facial sufficiency of the indictment were encouraged to raise these issues in advance so that should the indictment be defective it could be corrected without prejudice. Furthermore, the presiding judge was apt to inquire of counsel regarding appropriate legal authorities during the course of trials that required anticipation by the lawyers because it might be dispositive of a substantive issue in dispute, as in the case of William Davis:[23]

> The defendant was indicted for obtaining $2000 by false pretences from John Hitchcock and Uriah R Scrivner by falsely pretending that a bill of exchange for $3000 drawn in his favour had been accepted and that he would shortly receive payment on it. It appeared in the evidence of John Hitchcock, however, that the $2000 had not been advanced solely on the basis of the representation regarding the bill of exchange but also because Davis had given Hitchcock a check for $1500. As detailed by the nominative report, this testimony raised an issue of substance and not merely of form:

---

[22] The Mayor advised the jury to find the prisoners guilty of grand larceny only: 'No authority, directly in point, had been cited on behalf of the prosecution; and those authorities cited by the counsel for the prisoner, seemed to support the doctrine for which they contended' (1816) Rogers, vol 1, p 184.

[23] (1819) Rogers, vol 4, p 61.

After the production of this testimony ... the mayor inquired of the public prosecutor, whether, in cases of this description, the inducement to part with the money or goods should not be the false pretence *solely* charged in the indictment; and whether any other thing, in conjunction with the false pretence so charged, could legally form the inducement.

His honour having called on the counsel for some authority on this point, and none being produced, after the introduction of some further testimony on behalf of the prosecution ... the mayor charged the jury in favour of the defendant, on the principle above laid down, and he was immediately acquitted.

CONCLUSION

It is clear from grand jury indictments, perpetuation of testimony, lawyers' briefs and legal research that trials were planned events whereby actors knowledgeable in legal rationality sought to assemble evidence and proof in a manner that would assure a desired outcome. Thus, litigation at trial was not a 'spontaneous' event 'cobbled together' without forethought nor devoid of legal content. Pretrial lpreparation regularly occurred on behalf of the prosecution and defence to assure compliance with legal precedent established through common law cases and, to the extent the actors were able, witness examination itself became choreographed set-pieces in which the role and function of each of the participants was considered and known in advance of the trial itself, through a shared understanding of evidence and proof.

Chapter 5

Litigation Practice at Trial 1800–1845: Prosecution and Defence

INTRODUCTION

In this chapter, we seek to encapsulate the litigation practices at trial in the first half of the nineteenth century, at a time when the overwhelming majority of General Sessions' cases were adjudicated through the testimony of witnesses, introduction of tangible evidence and arguments of counsel. Our principal data source is the nominative reports prepared by lawyers who acted in a semi-official capacity and whose case reports were later cited as authoritative in General Sessions and other courts of record. What follows is an illustration of an extract from the case report of the prosecution of Jerimiah Hill contained in the New York City Hall Recorder, the reporter of which was Daniel Rogers, a lawyer himself:

ILLUSTRATION 5.1: Extract from the Nominative Reporter, Daniel Rogers.

The illustration shows the date on which the case appeared in General Sessions, the composition of the Bench, counsel for the prosecution and defence as well as the listing of the grand jurors who returned the indictment. What is important to note is that, as the illustration demonstrates, these are trial level reports which focused upon the actual statements and arguments of the lawyers, the testimony of witnesses and, as we will see the charge given to the jury by the judge.

After providing an overview of General Sessions trials detailed in the nominative reports, we consider the actions and behaviour of courtroom lawyers to see whether there was any code of conduct which gave coherence and meaning to criminal law practice. Thereafter, we describe trial procedure and practice beginning with empanellment of the jury. We then trace the forensic process: the presentation of the prosecution's case, the rules relating to the admissibility of evidence and the adduction of evidence through the examination and cross examination of witnesses; the procedure by which the defence presented its witnesses, legal arguments and theories; before turning in chapter 6 to the role of the judge and jury in the decision making process.

The structure and nature of trial litigation

Whether the case was publicly or privately prosecuted, trials were conducted within a framework of legality and due process, animated by a barrister class culture of the courts. The eminence and authority of the bench of General Sessions, the mayor, recorder and aldermen, was in itself a guarantee that trials would be an orderly, even solemn, affair. The hallmark of justice was fidelity to the rule of law; the native experiences of the country in the pre-revolutionary period melded with more positive inheritances from the colonial regime to give pre-eminence to legal form, adherence to criminal procedures and to rules of evidence.[1]

The desire to restrain governmental power manifested itself in what David Bodenhamer[2] described as 'the form of justice' embodied, as it were, in the constitutional, statutory and common law rights of the accused: technical correctness served as the touchstone of due process and related to the indictment, jury selection and the conduct of the trial. Filed indictments served as notice of the charge, live witness testimony facilitated confrontation, cross examination and the right to subpoena witnesses, while retained and court-assigned lawyers satisfied the right to counsel.

At the outset of the trial, legal issues might arise in the form of motions (applications by lawyers) regarding such matters as the facial sufficiency of the indictment. Upon resolution of these issues the trial continued to be an orderly process involving opening statements followed by witness testimony adduced through

---

[1] See William E Nelson (1975) pp 97–8.

[2] David J Bodenhamer (1992) pp 48, 50. For accounts of the gradual lawyerisation of the criminal trial in England, see Stephan Landsman (1990); Langbein (2003).

direct and cross-examination. The prosecution's evidence was directed at the offences charged in the indictment and often raised evidentiary issues regarding admissibility. However, broader legal issues, both procedural and substantive, could arise at any stage which counsel would be expected to address through reference to statutes and case law precedent. Rebuttal evidence by the prosecution would follow the defence evidence and this would be followed by argument to the jury.

The examples of the form of practice which follow are presented to provide the reader with an understanding of the typicality of practice in General Sessions and the underlying concern with an orderly and formalistic system of justice rather than as a comprehensive account of the individual rules and legal principles.

The ethics of advocacy

The trial was viewed by the courtroom actors as the quintessentially fair and reliable means of deciding issues of guilt and innocence. Whilst in a few cases adjudication by trial was avoided through a guilty plea, this method of disposition was not encouraged and, for the most part, trials were the staple diet of General Sessions in the first half of the century. The ethics of advocacy—the behaviour of lawyers at trial—is illustrative of these concerns.

Trials were not viewed by the actors as what Wigmore later characterized as 'sporting events' whereby one side or the other attempted to 'get over', employing heightened adversariness simply to accord the party greater likelihood of a favourable outcome.[3] Lawyers saw themselves as 'officers of the court' whose task it was to assure a reliable outcome within a due process framework,[4] while guarding against a miscarriage of justice associated with what they saw as either an improper conviction or acquittal. Thus, lawyers felt able to represent the prosecution and defence in different cases because their overarching loyalty was not to 'winning' as such but to what they considered a fair and just proceeding.

Whilst procedural 'formalism' was insisted upon in broad terms as an adjunct of the requirement that the prosecutor discharge the burden of proof, it was not interpreted in ways that would routinely obfuscate the search for the truth. This point is reflected in the argument detailed in the nominative report and made by defence counsel in the trial of James Dalton:[5]

> [T]he statute in question is highly penal, and is of course to be strictly construed. I do not insist on the frivolous and ridiculous distinctions which have sometimes been urged, and even sustained, in relation to this subject. I do not allege that a statute enacted to punish stealers of 'horses', would not apply to a man who should steal a single horse; nor that an act mentioning

---

[3] See R Pound (1906) at p 404, citing 1 Wigmore, *Evidence* 127 (1904).
[4] See Michael Millender (1996).
[5] (1823) Wheeler, vol 2, 161, p 175.

dogs, could with propriety be confined, by the technical scruples of grave and learned expositors of the law, to the masculine gender alone. But I do contend, that counsel for the people is bound to bring his case, substantially and strictly, within the provisions of the act and the allegations of the indictment. These requisitions are not complied with in the present instance, as I shall endeavour to show conclusively to the court.

The independence from partisanship that lawyers demonstrated was evident when the District Attorney, either because the defendants were unrepresented or having heard the evidence, no longer chose 'to press for conviction.' Similarly defence counsel, having heard and considered the persuasiveness of the evidence of the prosecution's witnesses, might pursue only a qualified defence or 'withdraw' a defence believed to be hopeless or specious. Acts of withdrawal demonstrated the culture of the barrister class in relation to the extent of reliance on adversarial advocacy, as evident in the following trials:

William Hamilton and James Latham[6]
The defendants, two 'coloured' men, of 'sober, industrious habits', were charged with nuisance arising out of the use of their carpenter's business. The business was operating from an old wooden building in ruinous condition, in and around which was considerable lumber, and next to which were a number of buildings of great value. The actions of the District Attorney, Rodman, are reported:

'As no counsel was employed, Rodman did not press for a conviction.'

Peter Buck, Joseph Palmer and Avery Reed[7]
On a charge of grand larceny, the complainant gave evidence that implicated all three defendants in stealing money from his person. Hawkins, counsel for the prisoners, put forward a limited defence for Buck and Palmer, that they were guilty of petit larceny only because, as stated in the nominative report, 'candour forbid an attempt to exculpate the two prisoners first named in the indictment, from the charge of Larceny.'

Peter Mitchell[8]
Mitchell was indicted for grand larceny in stealing a shawl from a store in Broadway. The chief prosecution witness was a fourteen year old clerk in the store, Oliver E Cobb, who, according to the nominative report, gave evidence in a clear and convincing manner after which Mitchell's 'counsel abandoned his defence, and the jurors found him guilty'.[9]

---

[6] (1817) Rogers, vol 2, p 46.
[7] (1816) Rogers, vol 1, p 4.
[8] (1816) Rogers, vol 1, p 5.
[9] The practice of withdrawal was not confined to New York: see eg, *Ann Carson* (1823) Wheeler 1 p 487, a case of passing counterfeit money heard in the Philadelphia Mayor's Court.

The ethics of advocacy of General Sessions' lawyers was the glue that enabled the process to retain its structure without fear that the professional behaviour of lawyers would manipulate the system so as to render more likely miscarriages of justice and the concomitant lack of public faith in the importance and integrity of the process. For these lawyers there appears to have been no higher calling than to present the case for the prosecution and defence with eloquence, legal argument and passion. Both prosecutor and defence attorney were deemed equally worthy of this reputation and the opportunity, as they saw it, for a just determination.

Empanelling the jury

Trials began with the delivery by the Sheriff of twenty four 'good and lawful men' to serve as impartial jurors.[10] Thereafter a process of selection occurred whereby jurors could be challenged for favour or peremptorily, with the defendant entitled to twenty peremptory challenges for any crime punishable with death or with life imprisonment[11] and the prosecuting attorney, after 1829, entitled to the same number, as in civil cases.[12]

Challenges for favour or cause alleged that the prospective juror could not serve impartially either because the juror had formed an opinion or because of some predisposition or state of mind. The 'voir dire' or trial of the principal challenges for favour would be tried by the two first sworn jurors.[13] Once sworn the presiding judge would inquire of the juror first whether he had formed an opinion or made any declaration which would be inconsistent with his serving impartially. Should the juror deny any basis for impartiality then either the prosecution or defence could challenge the juror for cause by examining the juror and by calling witnesses to confront the juror's assertions. Such inquiries would include questions relevant to pre-trial publicity and relationships bearing on the case, as in the report of the trial of Edward Milligan and Hugh Welchman[14] involving embezzlement and theft from the Phenix Bank:

> While the jurors were about being called, several questions were raised as to
> the competency of several. The two principal points decided will be noticed.
> One called as a juror, was inquired of whether he was a stockholder in
> an insurance company; and it was urged to the court, by the counsel for the

[10] 1801 *Compilation of Laws of State of New York*, 24th Session, Chapter VIII, Section XI, p 175. Fines were imposed on jurors who failed to appear for service and had not been excused; see Abrahmson (1994) pp 38–45.

[11] 1801 *Compilation, ibid*, Chapter LX, Section IX, p 261. This was revised in 1829 as the penal law was amended to include imprisonment of 10 years or more: 1829 *Revised Statutes of the State of New York*, Title V, Sections 9–17, p 734.

[12] *Revised Statutes, ibid,* Title V, Sections 9–11, p 734. Special provision was made for foreigners. See *Joseph De Costa* (1816) Rogers, vol 1, p 83. When a foreigner was to be tried, counsel for the defendant could apply to the court for a jury *de medietate linguae* by virtue of which procedure the sheriff would return a competent number of aliens competent in the English language.

[13] See eg *Diana Sellick's Case* (1816) Rogers, vol 1, p 185. See also *William Coleman's Case* (1817) Rogers, vol 2, p 89; *Clarissa Davis* (1818) Rogers, vol 3, p 45.

[14] (1821) Rogers, vol 6, p 69 p 71.

prisoners, that if he answered this question in the affirmative, he was incompetent. They cited 2d Caines 129.

The Recorder pronounced the opinion of the court, that an answer in the affirmative would not render the juror incompetent. This was but a *general* interest which he might have in common with others, and was not that particular interest which would operate to disqualify him.

Another question was raised: as several of the jurors were called to be sworn; they were inquired of by the prisoner's counsel, whether, from any thing they had heard or read, they did not, at any time, believe the prisoners guilty. The jurors had answered, that they read a statement in the newspapers, relative to the robbery committed on the Phenix bank; and that at the time of reading it, and now, they believed the prisoners guilty, *if that statement were true*; and as to a prior or present belief, several called as jurors, would answer in no other manner than by saying they believed the prisoners guilty, *if the account they read was true*.

It was strenuously urged by Messrs Emmet and Price [counsel for the defendant] that persons answering in that manner were not competent as jurors; and that a direct answer, without the *if*, should be required; and they farther urged that the same mode should be adopted by the court, in testing the competency of jurors, as was adopted in the several cases of Goodwin.[15]

Maxwell and Jones, for the prosecution, argued that it was not every loose impression or opinion, which one might form from a newspaper paragraph, which would disqualify him as a juror; it was that fixed and settled belief which was not to be changed by evidence. And it was manifest, that on the broad ground assumed by the opposite counsel, every man of intelligence in the community, who had read a newspaper, would be disqualified.

After much desultory discussion, the court framed the following interrogatories which were put to each of the jurors, with such further enquiries as the court might consider as falling within the range of such interrogatories:

1 Have you, at any time, formed, or expressed an opinion, or even entertained an impression, which may influence your conduct as a juror?
2 Have you any bias or prejudice on your mind, for or against the prisoner?
3 Do you in every respect, according to the best of your knowledge or belief, stand perfectly indifferent between the people and the prisoner?

And on the two first interrogatories, the same jurors who had been inquired of by the counsel for the prisoners, as before stated, answered in the negative, and to the last in the affirmative; and, on the suggestion of Price, the following interrogatory was added: are you a stockholder in the Phenix

---

[15] *Trial of Robert M Goodwin*, see below, nn 35, 36–40.

bank? Those who answered as aforesaid, unequivocally, and also this inquiry in the negative, were declared competent jurors.

In the case of *John W Thorn et al*,[16] involving an embezzlement conspiracy by the first teller and others of the Merchant's Bank, the nominative reporter indicated that the Mayor, while presiding over the prosecutor's challenge for favour, marshaled the evidence adduced by the parties and distinguished the burden of proof at the trial of the general issue from that needed to successfully recuse a prospective juror.

...[T]he mayor said that the question was whether in a challenge to the favour it was necessary for the party, interposing the challenge, to specify the cause previous to the trial. The court think this is not the case. We believe this from the general words contained in the authorities which speak of a challenge to the favour; and this opinion is strengthened by the consideration, that the oath administered to the triors, renders it incumbent on them to try, whether the party challenged stands indifferent between the prosecution and the party accused. If the person challenged be an intimate friend of the party, this constitutes a sufficient ground of a challenge to the favour; and we do not think that a logical precision in assigning cause in this species of challenge would, in general, be practicable; and, in the opinion of the court, it is unnecessary.

...[T]he mayor charged the triors that the question for them to decide was, whether Richard Allen stood indifferent between the prosecution and the accused.

He was accused of no crime; and, in the opinion of the court, the triors ought to be governed by a principle different from that which prevails where a jury are to decide on a question of innocence or guilt. *There*, whenever the jury entertain a rational doubt, they are bound to acquit; *here*, should the triors, from all the circumstances produced, believe that the challenge is not wholly indifferent and free from all exception, or should they entertain a doubt on the subject, in either case, it would be their duty to decide in favour of the challenge.

In the species of challenge now under consideration, nor relationship alone forms a sufficient cause of challenge: but if the party on trial is an intimate acquaintance of the juror called and challenged, he is incompetent.

If, in this instance, relationship is proved to the satisfaction of the triors, there could be no doubt of their verdict. On this head we have the positive declaration of Thorn, testified to by Richard Varick. Generally, a confession is the highest evidence; but even a confession may be rebutted or explained by other testimony. For this purpose, William W Thorn, a brother of one of

[16] (1819) Rogers, vol 4, 81 pp 83–4.

the defendants, has been produced, who swears that Richard Allen is not a relation; and in this he is corroborated by Isaac Burr.

If, from the facts, the triors should believe that Richard Allen is a relation to Thorn, one of the defendants, then, it will be their duty to decide in favour of the challenge.

But in this case relationship is not the only cause of challenge; and should the triors believe that there is, and had been, a peculiar intimacy subsisting between Thorn and the party challenged, this is equally a sufficient cause for his rejection as a juror …

THE PROSECUTION'S CASE

Opening statements

Once the jury had been empanelled, the trial proper began with opening statements made by the District Attorney or private lawyer for the prosecutor followed by the introduction of the prosecution's evidence in the form of witnesses, documents and tangible evidence.[17] If the proof offered varied substantively from the allegations contained in the indictment, or if the indictment was defective, the prosecution would fail. In most cases, the prosecutor's opening was a brief proffer of the evidence in support of the elements of the offence, and to the point as exemplified by the opening statement by Price, the private lawyer for the prosecution, in the trial of Charles Carpenter,[18] for rape of Ellen Carson, a person of colour:

> It would appear in evidence, that Sunday evening, the 8th November last, while the man and woman with whom the prosecutrix lived, had gone out at an early hour to church, leaving only the prosecutrix, their servant, to take care of the house in their absence, the prisoner entered the house and finding the girl alone, commenced some indecent familiarities with her which she instantly repelled; but when she found he was determined to persist in his purpose of having connection with her, she fled out of the house, with a view to escape from him; that he, however, followed her out and finally seized her, and, with violence and superior strength, dragged her into a dark alley, or back yard, and there consummated his abominable design. We shall prove, Mr Price continued, that first to last, the prosecutrix resisted his design, and by screams and outcries, for near an hour, whenever she could get his hand off her mouth, with which he partially suppressed her cries, endeavoured to alarm the watch and procure assistance.

---

[17] It appears prosecution witnesses were not permitted to be in court or could be excluded from the courtroom until they were called to give evidence. See eg *Isaac Roget* (1817) Rogers, vol 2, 61 p 63fn.

[18] (1818) Bacon, p 293.

Competence of witnesses

Common law decisions in English cases frequently governed the competency of any witness and whether the witness was qualified to give evidence.[19] Defendants prior to 1869 were not competent to testify under oath because of the presumption that 'interest' in the outcome alone would eliminate the accused's capacity to provide reliable evidence.[20] Additional disqualifications arose from the fact that an individual was a slave or married to the accused or because of age, prior criminal record or mental infirmity lacked adequate capacity to testify truthfully, to recall and to speak. Thus, in a homicide prosecution, Benjamin Johnson, 'a black', was called and sworn as a witness for the prosecution and his competence as a witness was tested:[21]

> *By the counsel for the prisoner.* Have you even been a slave?
>
> *Johnson* Yes, but I am now free.
>
> *Counsel* How did you become free?
>
> *Johnson* Mrs Alexander purchased me of Mr Curtis, and I lived with this lady after her marriage with Mr Jaques. She always told me that after her death I should be free, and that Mr Jaques had nothing to do with me.— After her death I became free, and left the house. I have often seen Mr Jaques since, and he spoke very friendly to me, and has never made any claim of me.
>
> *By the counsel for the prisoner* Have you any manumission paper?
>
> *Johnson* I have not.
>
> *Emmet* [defence counsel] May it please the Court, we object to the testimony of Johnson: he is the slave of Jaques.
>
> *By the Court, to the lawyer for the prosecutor* Mr Maxwell, you had better go on with other testimony, and let this witness stand aside for the present.[22]

Similarly, convictions of crimes of moral turpitude which rendered a witness 'infamous' were a basis for disqualification, as illustrated in the trial of Gilbert B

---

[19] O L Barbour (1852) pp 420 *et seq.*

[20] *Ibid,* p 422; see also Wigmore, *Evidence in Trials at Common Law* (Chadbourn. Rev, Boston, Little Brown & Co, 1970) p 684. The practice of disqualifying the accused continued until defendants were given the right to testify on their own by statute: 1869 *Revised Laws of the State of New York,* Chapter 678, Section 43, p 1032.

[21] *Diana Sellick* (1816) Rogers, vol 1, p 185.

[22] The court later ruled that Johnson was not a competent witness because, in law, he was owned by Jaques who had a legal right to dispose of him or his ownership of him following the death of Mrs Alexander.

Hutchins,[23] when Van Wyck for the prosecution sought to call one John Neafie, defence counsel, Wilson, objected:[24]

> Wilson produced the record of three several convictions of Neafie, at the court of oyer and terminer, holden at Goshen, in Orange county, in June, 1806, before the honourable Daniel D Tompkins (then judge,) and others. The first conviction was on the 5th of June, 1806, for grand larceny, in stealing the cattle of Joseph B Hasbrouck; the second on the 6th of the same month, for the same offence, in stealing a horse, the property of Jacobus Jansen; and the third for the same offence, in stealing the cattle of Catharine Banks. On the 7th of the same month, he was sentenced on the first conviction to the state prison for two years, on the second for one year, and on the third for two years.
>
> Van Wyck hereupon produced a pardon of Neafie, by his excellency Daniel D Tompkins, on the 3d of September, 1808. This pardon recited a conviction for grand larceny in the month of June, 1806, at the court before mentioned, and a sentence to the state prison *for five years*, and proceeded to release the prisoner from further imprisonment, in the usual form.
>
> The counsel for the prisoner contended, that the several convictions for grand larceny, which they had produced, or either of them, rendered Neafie infamous, and disqualified him from being a witness, notwithstanding the pardon.—This recited but *one* conviction, whereas the record showed there were *three*; and it by no means followed, that because the sentences on the three several convictions amounted to five years, the time contained in the pardon, the conviction for the grand larceny recited in the pardon, and the several distinct larcenies in the record were the same.
>
> *Van Wyck, contra.*
>
> The court decided, that the pardon was of no avail, and the witness offered was therefore incompetent. It appeared from the record produced, that there were three several convictions for grand larceny, on each of which the prisoner was sentenced for a term less than five years, and the offence was the same, yet, it cannot be justly inferred that the pardon was intended to apply to the whole or either of those convictions: and, for aught that appears, the prisoner may have been convicted of some other grand larceny, at the same court, during the same month; and the pardon may have been granted for that offence. A pardon should recite truly, and with a certainty to a common intent, the conviction to which it is intended to apply.

The prosecution could call a former defendant or accomplice as a prosecution witness upon the grant of a *nolle prosequi* thus rendering the witness competent

---

[23] (1819) Rogers, vol 4, p 119.
[24] *Ibid,* pp 119–20.

and eliminating the impediment which the witness might claim of the privilege against self-incrimination.[25]

Hearsay

Nuanced case law and English common law rules related to the admissibility of evidence determined what the lawyer would be able to adduce from any given witness.[26] The constraints that these rules imposed was an essential part of the idea of legal formalism and restricted the evidence that could be adduced from the whimsical, whereby disputants and their witnesses would simply have their say, to a content-scrutinised presentation with limited scope and breadth. Thus, the trial of George Kelly's case,[27] on an indictment for grand larceny, shows how the relationship of the hearsay rule to the admissibility of out of court statements of the victim testified to by another witness became the subject of the District Attorney's objection. The prosecution's witnesses testified that they observed the defendant, a hackney coachman, pick the pocket of John Westcott, an intoxicated passenger, and steal a silver watch of the value of $40 by 'put[ting] it in his own'. The passenger did not appear and testify at trial. To controvert the claim of theft, the defendant on cross examination sought to introduce, from the same witnesses, the passenger's statement, made shortly after the alleged observation, '... that he was well satisfied; for that on the way he found the watch in his waistcoat pocket':

> Van Wyck objected to the testimony offered; inasmuch as Westcott was absent; and his declarations were but hearsay testimony, which is ever inadmissible.
>
> *Price and Wilson, contra.*
>
> The mayor decided that the prisoner was entitled to the benefit of the declarations of Westcott, made at the time, as part of the *res gesta*.

Similarly, out of court statements by co-conspirators or accomplices made in furtherance of the offence were admissible as a recognised hearsay exception and included as part of the prosecution's case-in-chief despite the absence of the declarant and the lack of cross examination.[28] By contrast, out of court statements that did not fall within an exception to the hearsay rule were inadmissible, as exemplified in the trial of Pienovi,[29] in which the court stopped the prosecution's

---

[25] See eg *James Malone and John Welsh* (1817) Rogers, vol 2, p 22.
[26] See O L Barbour (1852) p 456.
[27] (1818) Rogers, vol 3, p 153.
[28] See eg *John Duprey* (1819) Rogers, vol 4, p 121.
[29] (1818) Bacon, p 14.

medical expert, Doctor Francis Berger, when he was about to testify what
Madame Pienovi said to him about the criminal incident:

> *Doctor Francis Berger, sworn*
> Said he was called to Madame Pienovi early in the morning, immediately
> after the wound was inflicted. That the cartilege, which he described to be
> only the end and fleshy part of the nose, was taken off and seemed to be torn
> away and mangled, as with a bite of the teeth. The wound was healed in
> about three weeks, *leaving her face somewhat disfigured.*
>
> Doct B was beginning to relate what Madame P told him of the affair, but
> was stopped by the court, and retired.

Voluntariness of statements

Common law rules of voluntariness governed the admissibility of statements
made by the accused. Any confession made as a result of threats or promises of
favour would be subject to legal challenge.[30] The principal exclusionary rule of
the period, as in England, required that before an accused's statement could be
admitted in evidence it must be shown to have been made freely and voluntarily.
Although a confession made under the influence of promises or threats was not
to be received in evidence, property found as a result of such a confession (deriv-
ative evidence) could be, as in England today, admitted.[31] The voluntariness rules
applied both to the admissibility of statements made to police officers, private
prosecutors and lay people, at the time of apprehension as well as to those made
to the Special Justice in the Police Office, at the time of examination. The trial of
John W Thorn *et al*[32] shows how a violation of these rules would result in their
exclusion:

> Thorn and others were indicted for conspiracy to obtain money by fraudu-
> lent means from a Bank, the President of which, Richard Varick, first caus-
> ing the arrest of Thorn, a teller at the bank. Thorn was then effectively
> imprisoned in Varick's house, assured that the object was to apprehend the
> accomplices, and confessed following a promise by Varick that Thorn would
> be used as a prosecution witness. Varick himself candidly told the court that
> he believed that his promise to Thorn influenced the confession. Counsel for
> Thorn objected to the admission of the confession on the basis that no con-
> fession could be received if induced by a threat, promise or misrepresenta-
> tion, supporting the submission with citations to established authority. The
> mayor, in rejecting evidence of the confession, re-stated the general rule:
>
> > ... [I]t made no difference whether a party, making a confession, was
> > under arrest on criminal process or not; or whether such confession was

---

[30] O L Barbour (1852) p 459.
[31] *Berthina Tucker* (1821) Rogers, vol 5, p 164; *Charity Jackson* (1816) Rogers, vol 1, p 28.
[32] (1819) Rogers, vol 4, p 81.

made before a private person or one concerned in the administration of justice. If a promise of favour, made by or before any person, influences a confession, it is well settled, that it cannot be received in evidence.[33]

As time went on the Special Justice's examination of the accused came to contain the refrain that the statement was made 'freely and voluntarily'. However, the question of the admissibility of defendants' statements made at the Special Justice's examination was a continuing source of debate in which defence lawyers sought to exclude inculpatory statements or sought the admissibility of exculpatory statements as essential evidence of innocence. Lawyers would argue that incriminating statements taken by the Special Justice in the absence of defence counsel or without caution violated the common law right to silence as well as the constitutional privilege against self-incrimination, as illustrated in the argument made by Dr David Graham, a prominent trial lawyer, in the trial of Hiram Maxwell[34] when objecting to the reading of the defendant's examination taken before the Special Justice, as detailed in the nominative report:

> He contended that it was the duty of the magistrate, who took the examination, to caution the prisoner that he was not bound to confess: 2 That his confession should be free and voluntary: 3 That the magistrate should inform him that his confession might be read against him on his trial: and lastly, that all this ought to appear on the face of the depositions. The Doctor went into an argument of great length and ability in support of each position.

> The court observed that Mr Colden, in the case of *Goodwin*,[35] before the examination was taken, cautioned him that it should be free and voluntary, but that they knew of no law to compel the magistrate to caution the prisoner that his examination ought to be free, or that it would be read in evidence against him, or that it ought to appear on the face of the depositions.

Witnesses to defendants' post arrest statements included the Special Justice and Police Clerk (to the contents of the examination of the accused), as well as constables and watch involved in the apprehension of the accused. Proof of the magistrate's examination would take the form of written and oral testimony. Thus, in the case of Lawrence Pienovi,[36] the prosecution relied upon the Special Justice, Charles Christian, and a police officer to authenticate Pienovi's inculpatory statements:[37]

> Charles Christian, esq. one of the Police Magistrates, was then sent for into court, sworn and examined; he attested to the examination as offered in evidence, and stated, that the reason of its not having been signed by the

---

[33] See also *John Williams* (1816) Rogers, vol 1, p 189; and *Robert W Steele* (1820) Rogers, vol 5, p 5.

[34] (1823) Wheeler 1, p 162.

[35] *Robert Goodwin's* Case (1820) Rogers, vol 5, pp 11, 97 and 131.

[36] (1818) Bacon, p 14.

[37] *Ibid*, pp 15, 17.

prisoner, as also of its being so brief, was the interference of a friend of his who cautioned him not to sign it, nor to say any thing more—It was then read as follows, to wit:—

City of New York   } ss. July, 11th 1818.

Lawrence Pienovi, being brought, charged with having on the 29th July, 1818 (1817 meant, and so explained by witness,) bit of his wife, Elizabeth Pienovi's, nose; on examination says, 'that he only bit off the end of said Elizabeth's nose',—that he did it because he was jealous of her.

Taken by, and admitted

Before me, Charles Christian,   (Refuses to sign the above.)

Special Justice.

Mr Christian further remarked, that while prisoner was on his examination before the police, every thing was fairly explained to him in French, although it appeared he could speak English; and that on confession of having bit off a part only of the nose, he attempted to show, by motion with his finger, more precisely, how much he had bitten off. From the confession alone it would appear that whatever was the degree of the mental alienation, which was set up as his defence, he had at all events a clear conception and memory of the transaction.

Charles Raymond, Police Officer, sworn.

Said that he arrested Pienovi, on a bench warrant the 11th July last, and took him to the Police Office; that when he told Pienovi what he arrested him for, he replied, that he might have been taken at any time; and while they were on their way to the Police Office he talked freely about the matter, not pretending at all to disguise or deny the fact; and appealed to witness whether any man would not have done the same under such provocation;—that he then went on to relate the immediate circumstances which inflamed his jealousy to such a pitch at that time.

He said that Sunday morning, the day before his attack upon his wife, he went with her to the bath—that she went into the bath, and was there alone, as he thought; for that he, considering it indecent to go in with her, staid waiting for her without;—that she staid so long in the bath that he grew impatient, and a little anxious about her, and asked permission of the black girl who attended the bath to go in himself, which she refused;—that after waiting a while longer, he demanded permission to go in, and told the black girl he was the lady's husband, and must go in; to which the black girl replied, that's impossible; for her husband is in there with her now.

Similar fact evidence

In line with common law rules, evidence of prior bad acts was not necessarily admissible at trial in General Sessions, as today, without a showing of probative significance which outweighed its prejudicial value. Such evidence had to tend to

prove an element of the indicted offence and could not be offered in an effort simply to prove that the accused had a propensity to commit criminal activity. An
example of the concern for probative value over prejudice occurred in the cheque
forgery trial of William Coffey:[38]

> The *District Attorney* here proposed to prove that the prisoner has offered to
> pass other checks, besides those stated in the indictment, which were spuri-
> ous. That a number of spurious checks had been taken from the prisoner's
> possession by the officers of the police, which he would produce in evi-
> dence.
>
> Mr *Scott* objected to this evidence on two grounds; 1st, that it was not com-
> petent for the counsel for the prosecution to support one charge by estab-
> lishing another of the like kind; and 2ndly, on the ground that the prisoner
> came prepared to meet the offences only which were specified in the indict-
> ment; and had no notion that evidence would be given in relation to other
> checks than those upon which the indictment was framed; and such evidence
> as was offered would, therefore, be a surprise upon him. Mr S. admitted that
> upon an indictment for uttering counterfeit coins, or forged bank notes,
> knowing them to be forged, it was admissible on the part of the prosecution,
> to prove that the prisoner had upon him when arrested, or had attempted to
> pass other counterfeit money, or forged notes of the same kind, as evidence
> that he knew that the notes or coins, specified in the indictment, were forged;
> yet this, he said, was an exception to the general rule of evidence in analo-
> gy to an existing exception, in which way the rule itself might be destroyed,
> as no limits to such exceptions could be established.
>
> After much discussion by the counsel upon both sides, *his honor the Mayor*
> suggested that this testimony is as proper as to prove that a man has coun-
> terfeit bank notes in his possession. The object is to get at the *scienter*, which
> must be made out, in order to support the indictment. *His honor* declared that
> he had doubts upon the subject, that if he decided against the prisoner on this
> point, and if he should be convicted, the opinion might be renewed before
> the supreme court. His honor remarked that this opinion might deviate from
> the strict rules of law. The jury must decide upon the mind of the prisoner. If
> there is a circumstance from which the jury can rationally draw an inference,
> ought it to be excluded? He thought not. The counsel may avail themselves
> of their objections.

Direct examination

Direct examination had its own rules derived from case law and common law
practices. Typically the examination was non-leading[39] and began with a general

---

[38] (1818) Bacon, p 298.
[39] See O L Barbour (1852) p 437.

narrative question—'Will you please state Mr—what you know of this incident?'—which provided the witness the opportunity to detail the occurrence
in the witness' own words, without suggesting any particular response.
Thereafter, a follow up examination would occur utilising a few closed questions
that sought to clarify or emphasise information omitted from the initial response.
An example of this practice occurred in the trial of Charles Carpenter,[40] when the
prosecutrix and rape victim gave the following response to a narrative question,
followed by a clarifying closed question by Price, counsel for the prosecution.

Ellen Carsen, Sworn.
Says she lives with Mr Garniss, No. 63 Mott-street; is bound to him as an
apprentice until the age of twenty-three, when she is to have her freedom.
That Sunday evening, about four weeks ago, she was left alone by her master and mistress to take care of the house, and tend their child while they
were gone to church. That as she parted with them at the door she saw the
prisoner standing by the gate a little way off, and directly after they were
gone he came in; that he waited until she put the child to bed, and she then
asked him what he wanted? he replied, nothing. She presently asked him
again, and being alarmed by his manner, ran down into the basement story,
where another family lives, who she found were also out that evening; in her
way she jumped and fell, and at that moment the prisoner seized her, and
said he would then tell her what he wanted; that he wanted to stay all night
and sleep with her, but she told him she would not do it. That by this time
she had got out into the yard, and told him to go about his business; that there
was company in the house, and she would call the watch, which she actually did, and screamed and rushed to the gate which opened into the street, and
got it partly open in order to get out, when he seized her, pulled her back,
and shut the gate; she still kept hallooing, until he put his hand over her
mouth, and made her promise not to halloo any more; that as soon, however, as he took his hand off she began to halloo again; that he then pulled her
clothes up, put one of her feet up on a barrel, turned her clothes over her
head, and did as he was a mind to her; she trying to halloo all the time.

To the question, pointedly put, whether he actually had connection with her?
she answered, that he had, and that the time he kept her in the position last
mentioned was as much as three minutes, that she extricated herself as quick
as possible, and as soon as she could get away, went into the street; that she
did not consent, and struggled with all her might while she was on the barrel; that she shut the gate as soon as she came out of the alley and called for
the *watch*; that the prisoner, however, came out after her with his breeches
down, struck her, and called her *a bitch*, and made off; that Mr Duffie who
had been attracted by her cries, caught her when she came out, and asked her
what was the matter? That she told him the man had abused her very much;
had thrown her clothes over her head, and done what he was a mind to. The

---

[40] (1819) Bacon, p 165.

man was then in sight, and Mr Duffie went after him and brought him back
to her, and then took him to the Police-office. That she saw the prisoner the
next morning, and certain he is the man.

Price.
To whom did you tell of the affair besides Mr Duffie?
I told an old woman, who lived in a cellar near by; she came to our house
when she heard the disturbance and stayed with me until Mr Garniss and his
wife came home from church; and when they came home, I told them what
had happened: I also told Mrs Pine

Another example of this style of direct examination occurred in the perpetuation
proceeding described in chapter 4 regarding the prosecution of Mary Wood.[41]
There, after a brief introductory question the District Attorney asked a narrative
question for which the private prosecutor, Alexander Crook, needed little prompt-
ing to give his account in detail:

Q What is your age, where do your reside and what is your occupation.
A I am thirty three years of age. I reside in Kingston County and am a
   house carpenter.
Q Do you know Mary Wood the defendant: when & where and under
   what circumstances did you first become acquainted with her.
A I know her by sight. I met her on the evening of the 31 of July last in
   Church near Anthony St. between ten & eleven o clock. She hailed me,
   and asked me which way I was travelling. I told her I was travelling out
   to see how many women I could discover on the route. She turned about
   and was going the other way; she then came along behind me, until I got
   near the corner of Anthony St. She there asked me if I was going across
   the town. I replied to her that I was going until I found a woman or something to that purpose. She then asked me if I would go along to where she
   lived. I asked here where she lived; she said she lived close by or right
   by; she said she had as good accommodations in her house as in any place
   that could be found around town; I told her I would go in and see it; she
   took me to a door of a house in Anthony Street, near the Station house,
   we went in the house, she opening the door; we went up stairs, into a
   room, and there was a female, who when we went in took up her bonnet.
   Mary Wood told her she was much obliged to her for keeping house for
   her while she had gone out; the woman then left. There was her bed room
   adjoining this room. After the woman out [*sic*] Mary Wood locked the
   door of the room we first entered. She then threw the key on the table
   where the light stood opposite the bed room door & told me if I wanted
   the key I could take it & put it in my pocket. I told her I had keys enough
   of my own; she then said let's go to bed; she then asked me to settle the
   bill & asked me if I was going to stay all night. I told her no. I asked her

[41] District Attorney's Files, 22 October, 1845.

what she charged & she said she ought to have two dollars. I said I would
not give that to a better looking woman than you are. I took out my pocket book & gave her a dollar, & then returned my pocket book to my pantaloons pocket. It contained between twenty three and thirty dollars in
money. [Crook then itemised the bills he had]. I pulled off my clothes,
and put them on a chair which stood in the front room, near the door of
my bed room just out of my sight. She took the chair & placed it there &
told me to put my clothes on it, that my coat would not crumble if I hung
it on the back of the chair. We both then went to bed, the bed room door
was left open. We were in bed about a minute—there came a rap at the
door of the front room—she jumped out of bed, & went to the door where
the knock was. I then got up & looked out of the door of the bed room to
see where she was; she stood in the room whispering to some person out
of the room—She then said to that unknown person, she would come
down in a moment. She then came back and said that her cousin or uncle
(I don't know which) had come & I must be quick and get my clothes on.
She told me when I came down to the front door if any body should be
there as she would come down with me that she would say she would do
that sewing for me to morrow to give them to understand that I was the
man she did sewing for. When I was pulling on my pantaloons, a thought
struck me ... [I placed my] hand into my left pantaloons pocket to feel for
my pocket book—I found my pocket book disturbed that is turned
wrongside out—that it was not as it ought to be—I took it out of my
pocket & discovered that my money was gone. I examined it again &
found that two one dollar bills had been left in it which was all that was
left except my papers. I then told her that my money was gone & that she
had taken it. She then said she hadnt it & hurried me to go off—& said
that there would be a man or men there directly & there would be trouble. I then made my way out, she coming down stairs with me to the front
door. I told her then I would go and get an officer & see if I could not get
my rights unless she would pay me back the money I had been robbed.
She then told me 'to go to hell or something to that effect'. I then went to
Hudson Street and met two officers—I told them the circumstance—
described the house—the situation of the house & the woman—told them
she was pock broken in the face rather fleshy woman & between 4 and 5
feet high as near as I could judge. The officers & myself then went to the
house & demanded admission. A woman stuck her head out of the window. I believed it to be Mary Wood, who said they should not come in—
the officers then told her they must come in—they did not tell her they
were officers; then one or two more officers came up, upon being rapped
for by the others. They then demanded admittance & told her they were
officers. She said 'they could not come in that night'—An officer then
went to the Assistant Alderman of the 5 Ward I believe who came to the
door & demanded admittance—She called who was there—he then said
'Mary let me in' & she then came down & unlocked the door and the
Alderman another officer & myself went in. The Alderman asked me if

that was the woman & I said it was & she said I was a liar. She said she had never been out as late as 9 or 10 o clock—I then told her she was the very woman that I had been with ... She said 'D-n you—you havn't lost any money, clear out of this—I wont be disturbed of my rest'. She was then arrested & taken to the watch house, & the next morning I went & made my affidavit at the Police ...

Q   Are you positive that the woman Mary Wood who you saw at the Police Office when you made your affidavit, is the same female you met & with whom the circumstances you have related took place.

A   Yes sir. I cannot be mistaken. I examined her countenance particularly both before and after her arrest.

Q   When you paid her the one dollar did you then see the rest of your money in your pocket book.

A   I did and she did too—I took the dollar bill from out the roll of money & put the rest back in her presence.

Q   How was she dressed that evening.

A   She had on a kind of light dress. I wont be confident that it was a loose dress, there might have been a drawing string around.

Q   When do you intend returning to Kingston.

A   In this afternoons 4 oclock boat.

[Alexander D Crook signs]

Here again, the narrative response was followed by a limited number of closed questions placed by the District Attorney to eliminate ambiguity and emphasise certain details which were omitted from the initial narrative account. Overall, the style of the examination limited the proceeding itself which was then followed by cross examination.

Cross-examination

Cross-examination, as with direct examination, was informed by case law and common law rules and practices.[42] The focus of cross examination included discovering information regarding the subject matter elicited from the witness on direct examination as well as issues which went to the reliability of the witness's testimony, including intoxication, failure of recollection and such traditional impeachment evidence as prior inconsistent statements and prior bad acts which tended to discredit the witness's character.

These issues were raised to some degree in the perpetuated cross examination of Alexander Crook in case of Mary Wood (above):

Being cross-examined by Mr McGay the counsel for the Defendant—the witness answers as follows

---

[42]   O L Barbour (1852) p 438.

Q Are you a married man?

A No sir. I never have been.

Q When did you leave Kingston.

A I left Kingston on the 30th July.

Question objected to:

Q What was your object in coming down here.

A I had special business with Judge Soper for my father & also for a visit. I had not been in this city for about three years before.

Objected to:

Q Are you in the habit of frequenting houses of ill fame.

A No sir—I had not been in one before that night to my knowledge for something like four years.

Q Where had you pass'd the evening on the 31st of July.

A In walking through the city to see how it looked it was so long since I had been here—part of the time with gentleman & part of the time alone.

Q How much had you drank in the course of the evening.

A I had not tasted any liquor stronger than cider or beer in two years. I don't know how much beer I drank in the course of that evening. I might have drunk 2 or 3 glasses—not more.

Q When did you see your money last previous to going to that house.

A I saw it at the corner of Anthony Street & Broadway—not exceeding 25 minutes before I went to the house with the woman & saw it afterwards in her house when I gave her the dollar bill.

Q How large was the bed room in which you went.

A About seven feet one way and about five feet the other as nigh as I can tell.

Q When you got into bed where was Mary Wood.

A She was standing by the table in the front room near the bed room door. When in bed I could only see the corner of the table in the front room. I could not see the chair, upon which she told me to put my clothes.

Q Who took your money.

A I cannot say who took but I have no doubt it was taken while I was in bed in that house.

Q How tall was the woman?

A I have said between 4 & 5 feet. I may be deceived in her height as she is fleshy. She is a middling sized woman.

Q At what hour did you meet her in Church Street.

A Between ten & eleven as near as I can tell.

Objected to:

Q Did you ever swear it was at a different hour?

A I stated before it might have been eleven.

Q Was the woman you went to bed with the same woman you met in Church Street.

A Yes sir.

Objected:

Q Can you identify every woman you have every had carnal intercourse with.

A I do not know that I can.

Q Had you carnal intercourse with Mary Wood?

A I had not.

Q Was the woman you saw in the front room the same one as Mary Wood.

A She may have been—she went out so suddenly I am not able to say.

Q Did you see a man in the house.

A No sir—not before I saw the officers there.

[Alexander D Crook signs]

Again, as in direct examination, the questioning was limited although it was more pointed and relied predominantly upon closed—ended questions.

An illustration of cross-examination technique which included the hallmark of modern adversarial advocacy—the leading question—is provided in the trial of Hugh Flinn,[43] in which the defendant was charged with assault and battery with intent to rape Mary Ann Kamieson, a young girl who lived next door to Flinn's grocery store, between one and two o'clock on the afternoon of 28 July, 1822. In support of an alibi defence, John Monahan was called, gave evidence and was subject to cross-examination by Hugh Maxwell, the District Attorney, regarding the reliability of his recollection

> *John Monahan* was called and sworn. He testified that he was sitting at dinner, between one and two o'clock, on the 28th of July, and that the prisoner came into his house and remained there until near 2 o'clock, when he went away, saying he was going to Vespers. He further testified that the prisoner was regular at church every Sunday, and was a man of good character.
>
> Upon being cross-examined by *Maxwell*, he said he recollected the day by referring back, after he had heard of the charge: he was certain as to the hour, because he always dines on Sunday between one and two o'clock.
>
> Questions by *Maxwell*.
>
> Do you recollect what kind of dress the prisoner wore?
>
> A No.
>
> Q Where do you live?
>
> A No 69, Pike-street.
>
> A How far from your house is it to the church?
>
> A About three minutes' walk.
>
> Q What coloured pantaloons did the prisoner wear?
>
> A Can't tell.
>
> Q What coloured vest?
>
> A I don't know.
>
> Q Why do you remember so well the day and hour he was at your house, and forget his dress?
>
> A I cannot tell.

---

[43] (1823) Wheeler 1, p 74.

Q Have you been at Flinn's store since the charge?
A Yes.
Q Have you been there often since the charge?
A Yes.
Q Have you an account with him?
A I deal at his store.
Q Are you in debt to him?
A I cannot tell; there is an account between us: perhaps I am.
Q Have you any fact or circumstance to fix the day of the month?
A No.
Q· How do you ascertain it?
A When I heard the charge I referred back to the day.
Q Mr Monahan, you are certain of the hour and the day although it hap-
   pened in July, yet you have no recollection what kind of clothes he wore,
   or any other circumstances but the fact of his being at your house at the
   day and hour you mention. How do you account for your recollection of
   this circumstance, not calculated to make an impression upon the mind,
   and a total forgetfulness of all others?
A I do not recollect what dress he had on.
Q You have a bad memory then, Mr Monahan?
A Of some things I have.

Privilege against self incrimination

While the common law right to silence and the constitutional privilege against
self incrimination protected against questions that would incriminate or disgrace
a witness,[44] the capacity of a witness to refuse to respond to a question without
being held in contempt was limited to those questions which the court foresaw
would give rise to a clear possibility of incrimination. This is illustrated in the
trial of Henry Hagerman in which a defence witness, Abraham W Groesbeck, was
cross-examined by Griffen, the lawyer for the prosecution:[45]

> *Q* Had you seen Hagerman before this attack on that day?
> *A* That question I don't wish to answer.
> *By the Mayor* I think you are bound to answer that question: it is not
>   improper.
> *Q* Had you any conversation with him concerning the attack on Mr.
>   Coleman before it was made?
> *A* I don't think proper to answer that question.
> *By the Mayor* Mr Groesbeck, you must answer, or suffer the consequence.
>   The court will take that no improper questions are put by the counsel.
> *W* (After some hesitation). I think that an answer to this question will have
>   a tendency of criminating myself.

[44] See *Rosewell Saltonstall* (1816) Rogers, vol 1, p 134.
[45] *Henry B Hagerman* (1818) Rogers, vol 3, 73 p 83.

The court hereupon instructed the witness that no such effect could follow, and directed him to proceed.

He then stated, that he had a conversation with Mr Hagerman two or three days before the affray, and he said that he intended to chastise and disgrace Mr Coleman. The occurrence took place at about five o'clock in the afternoon; about a half hour before which time the witness, at his store, saw Mr Hagerman, who from that place went down Murray-street.

Q Did you accompany Hagerman from your store into Murray-street?

A I went down Murray-street.

Q Why, at that time, did you go down Murray-street?

By the Court We think that the witness may refuse to answer that question. Whether so designed or not, an answer may clearly have a tendency of criminating himself.

Q Why did you go down Murray-street?

By the Court (To the witness) You may either answer that question, or refuse to answer it, as you think proper.

W I shall decline answering.

Q Did you see Hagerman standing behind the carriage, previous to the attack?

A I did so: the carriage stood about one hundred feet from Broadway, and the defendant went behind the carriage to let Coleman come up Murray-street.

THE DEFENCE CASE

Whilst a defendant was permitted to appear 'in proper person', undertaking his or her own defence, the normal rule was that this could not occur once an election had been made to be represented by counsel and should the defendant so elect counsel and not the defendant would conduct the defence. This rule, however, might be relaxed where the defendant was an alien. Thus, in Decosta,[46] J T Irving, defence counsel, on being confronted with evidence which contradicted the facts in the instructions of his client, suggested to the court that the defendant, 'being an alien and a stranger', might be permitted to address a few remarks to the jury.

> *By the Court*—Although the strict rules of practice will not admit a defendant, who has already elected to appear by his counsel, to undertake to manage his own defence before the jury; yet in the case of an alien stranger, we think the rule, under peculiar circumstances, may be relaxed. In this instance, therefore, the defendant may address the jury; nor can we undertake to prescribe to him the rules which govern the counsellors of this court, with regard to confining themselves to the evidence. He must, in summing up, be allowed to take his own course. (*Ibid*, p 85)[47]

[46] (1816) Rogers, vol 1, p 83.

[47] De Costa, a South American, re-examined witnesses and addressed the jury in 'very broken language'.

Opening statement

Upon the prosecution resting its case, the defence attorney would be provided the opportunity to make an opening statement on behalf of the accused. Such a statement might respond to the evidence adduced during the prosecution's case in chief by presenting an alternative perspective on the evidence which was consistent with innocence, contextualising the incident which led to the prosecution and proffering evidence on behalf of the accused and explaining its significance in terms of relevance and proof.

For example, in the trial of Moses Simon,[48] in which the defendant, a person of colour and a lawyer admitted to practice before General Sessions, was charged with assault on Charles Berault after Berault had requested that Simon leave a public ball room at Washington Hall, it appeared on account of his race, following objection to his presence by members of a dancing school, Fay, one of the lawyers for Simon, sought both to show that Berault was the aggressor and also that discrimination was contrary to the constitution:[49]

> Fay opened the case on behalf of the defendant. The counsel stated, that the defendant would show that he is an accredited gentleman: that he had received a liberal education, in one of the best universities in the country, and that his connexions were wealthy and respectable.
>
> The defendant, on this occasion, having purchased a ticket, which entitled him to an admittance, was refused by the master; and, in a momentary excitement of passion, while smarting under the indignity offerred to his feelings, the defendant inflicted the blow. He would contend, that the master, by this outrage, was, in fact, the first aggressor: he thereby struck the first blow, and had no right to complaint.
>
> The defendant would further rely on the constitution, which had declared all men equal: on the constituted authorities of the country, by which he had been admitted a member of an honourable profession; and, in time, he would make his appeal to the sympathies and moral feelings of the jury: for, said the counsel, an enlightened community will be ready to sanction this philanthropic sentiment, though varied from the words of the poet:
>
> > 'Honour and shame from no "complexion" rise,
> > Act well your part, there all the honour lies.'

This being the first opportunity for counsel to address the jury, the opening statement might be used to remind the jurors that they were not only the triers of the facts, but that they had 'the duty to understand the principles of criminal law applicable to this transaction'.[50] Thus, counsel might emphasise the power that

---

[48] (1818) Rogers, vol 3, p 39.
[49] *Ibid*, p 40.
[50] See W Sampson (1820) p 74.

the jury brought to bear as 'judges of law as well as of fact' which the jurors must determine, after advice by the court as to the state of the law 'according to [their] best judgments and the dictates of [their] own consciences'.[51]

Moreover, in emphasising the policy issues inherent in the prosecution, counsel might proffer that his own observations were likely to be confirmed by the testimony, as exemplified in the opening statement in the trial of Roger Prout,[52] an ink manufacturer charged with criminal nuisance upon the testimony of several neighbours:

> Price, in opening the case, stated to the jury that he had himself been on the premises, and the manufactory was conducted with the utmost cleanliness.
>
> It would appear, in testimony, that in the process of manufacturing ink, linseed oil, and that of the purest kind, was used, and that nothing offensive resulted from the boiling, which occurred, upon an average, but once a month.
>
> It would also appear, that the defendant, an industrious, meritorious citizen, about seven years ago, and when but few buildings were erected in that quarter, at considerable expense, had built this manufactory: he had invented a process for making printing ink of a better quality, and at a less expense, than any other manufacturer in this country.
>
> The jury would recollect, that a populous city is, necessarily, a congregation of disagreeable smells: if we reside here, the many benefits and comforts we have, must have a portion of alloy.
>
> A judgment in this case affects the living of the defendant: if he is convicted, his establishment must be abated—his property become useless, and his prospects blasted.

Legal defects in the prosecution

The defence could always challenge the propriety of the prosecution on the ground that the proof was insufficient as a matter of law or at variance with the facts alleged in the indictment. The accuracy and precision of the indictment was an issue grounded in common law which sought to assure that the prosecution would not proceed under a theory at variance with what the Grand Jury had found to be the basis for the charge.[53] Challenges phrased in the form of oral motions to traverse or quash the indictment might occur at the outset of the proceedings, during the trial, or in final argument. Thus, in the trial of John I Decker and

---

[51] W Sampson (1820) p 74.
[52] (1819) Rogers, vol 4, p 87.
[53] O L Barbour (1852) p 318.

Richard Ritter,[54] a lottery case, defence counsel (Price and Phenix) attacked the facial sufficiency of the indictment during final argument:[55]

> On the traverse of the indictment against Decker and Ritter, it appeared that the defendants kept a lottery office at the corner of Warren-street and Broadway, and that Prime Marin, a black, twice purchased a policy for $5; but the particular day on which the insurance was effected, or the day on which the number was to be drawn, or the sum or sums paid, or the number insured, the witness did not know.

> The counsel for the defendant contended to the court and jury, that the indictment was defective for uncertainty and that the proof was insufficient to produce a conviction. In the indictment neither the numbers of the tickets, the sums paid for insurance nor the days for which the insurance was made were set forth. The counsel commented on the testimony and concluded.

> Maxwell [the District Attorney] read to the court and jury the section of the statute on which the indictment was founded, and contended that the provisions of the statute were sufficiently broad and extensive to embrace any violation of the act, and that it was not necessary to set forth the particular number insured, nor the day for which the insurance was effected.

> The Recorder [Richard Riker], after recurring to the second count in the indictment, to which the testimony applied, charged the jury that the indictment, in not setting forth the number insured, nor the day for which it was insured, was loose and uncertain; and his honour, therefore, advised the jury to acquit the defendants.

A typical challenge at the outset of the proceedings might involve a motion for severance when co-indicted defendants contended that they might be prejudiced by the joinder. An illustration of this process is found in the case of George Wellington and Abel Franklin,[56] where an oral application was made at the outset to sever the trials:[57]

> Before any evidence was introduced, Wilson [counsel for the defendant] applied to the court, that the prisoners be tried separately, and cited the case of Howell (4 Johns Rep 296) as an authority directly in point. He argued, that as this was an offence for which the prisoners might be punished with imprisonment in the state prison for life, they were each entitled to their peremptory challenge .... Should, therefore, one of the prisoners be compelled to be tried with an associate, who had a right to a peremptory challenge; the rights of the prisoner thus compelled, would be directly

---

54 (1818) Rogers, vol 3, p 53.
55 *Ibid*, pp. 54–5.
56 (1816) Rogers, vol 1, p 144.
57 *Ibid*, pp 144–45.

infringed by the other, who might reject jurors whom the other might choose to retain.

By the Court. The case read from Johnson, does not decide the present question. The point there decided, was, that a person indicted for an offence, punishable with imprisonment for a term of years only, had no right to a peremptory challenge; and might, therefore, be tried with another jointly; and the very point now under consideration, was left with a *query* by the Reporter. The Supreme Court, in fact, leave it questionable, whether if the party had even a right to a peremptory challenge, he is entitled to a separate trial. In this case, it is true, that the court may punish with imprisonment in the state prison for life, or, for a term of years, at discretion, would the prisoners be found guilty. But we do not think that it necessarily follows, that the prisoners are entitled to a separate trial. The right of a peremptory challenge by one of the prisoners to a juror, which his associate may choose to retain, cannot be urged with propriety in favour of the privilege for which the counsel for the prisoner contends. When a juror is challenged by a prisoner, no negative right exists on behalf of the associate to retain such juror on the panel, because the right of challenge rests on an *objection* and not on *choice*.

We, therefore, deny the motion. To consume the time of the court and jury, with a repetition of the same cause, depending on the same evidence, would be obviously a great inconvenience, and we are happy, that in preventing this inconvenience we overrule no adjudged case. The right of a peremptory challenge is given to each of the prisoners by that statute, and they are at liberty to exercise this right should they think proper.

Contrary to the assertions of twentieth century critics—'reformers' who derided legal formalism and its intricate technicalities—as the above example illustrates, those who administered justice in General Sessions were mindful of balancing, on the one hand, the need to uphold the rule of law and, on the other, the public interest in an efficient and fair system of law enforcement. Thus, in ruling on challenges to the indictment, the Court sought a balance between the practical consideration of protecting the public interest against frivolous challenges and upholding the rights of defendants where there was a material defect in the indictment or in the prosecution itself. Whilst, therefore, the Court would overrule a challenge to an indictment for 'stealing a hog' based on the fact that at the time of the felony the animal was dead and partly dressed[58] or to an indictment for stealing an 'unmade pair of trowsers' based on the argument that the description of cloth 'unmade' could not be applied to 'trowsers',[59] it would uphold a challenge to an indictment for keeping a disorderly house in the 'seventh' ward when

---

[58] *Reed Lennington et al* (1817) Rogers, vol 2, p 168.
[59] *Charles Moon* (1818) Rogers, vol 3, p 92.

it was shown to be in the 'fourth' because the location of the house constituted the very essence of the offence.[60]

Indeed, when sufficiency of the prosecution's evidence was at issue, and it turned entirely on legal interpretation, so as not to prejudice the prosecution, the presiding judges permitted the points to be preserved prior to submission to the jury while enabling the jury to return a verdict on the general issue. Should there be a conviction, additional consideration would be given to legal sufficiency at a post-trial proceeding to set aside the verdict whereby the court could discharge the defendant as a result of the points reserved by counsel at the outset of or during the trial proceedings, as in the trial of Charles Tomlinson:[61]

> At the close of the prosecution case, various objections were taken to the form of an indictment which charged the defendant with willful and corrupt perjury arising out of representations he had made as to his means when standing bail for James Finegan. Whilst David Graham, one of the counsel for the defendant, sought to support his objections as to the form of the indictment with reference to legal citations, this being an objection to form, the District Attorney said that 'he was not at present prepared with authorities' but argued that the indictment was conformable to long approved precedents. The nominative report states that:
>
> > In charging the jury, the Mayor reminded the jury that it was common for them to be governed by the court's advice on legal issues, a practice appropriate where objections to form were made because:
> >
> > > ... should the jury, believing the prisoner to be guilty from the facts, nevertheless undertake to decide the law and acquit him, should that decision be wrong, he could never be brought to answer for this offence again; whereas, on the other hand, should he be convicted, he could have the advantage of moving this court in arrest of judgment, and the whole matter then would be open for revision; and should the decision be against him he might appeal from this to a superior tribunal, by a writ of error.[62]

Refutation witnesses

Defendants were entitled by statute to 'bring in witnesses for their defence and to compel the same.'[63] Thus the defence was afforded the opportunity to challenge directly the accuracy of the testimony of prosecution witnesses by

---

[60] *Michael McDonald* (1818) Rogers, vol 3, p 128.

[61] (1819) Rogers, vol 4, p 125.

[62] On the defendant's conviction, the court suspended the sentence until the next term to give defence counsel the opportunity to bring the matter before the Supreme Court of New York or to move General Sessions in arrest of judgment. Arguments on a writ of error or in arrest of judgment were commonly replete with legal citations: see eg, *John G Scholtz* (1820) Rogers, vol 5, p 112.

[63] 1801 *Compilation of the Laws of the State of New York*, Acts of the 24th Session, Chapter LX, Section XI, p 261.

bringing forward civilian witnesses to refute prosecution accounts, as in the trial of William and Elizabeth Brown.[64] There the defendants were charged with assaulting John C Gillen, a marshal, when Gillen attempted to remove furniture belonging to William Brown in satisfaction of a judgment for legal fees, and an altercation occurred with Elizabeth, his wife. In seeking to show that the defendants' actions were in response to the marshal who had exceeded his authority and used excessive force, the defence adduced a number of witnesses to the incident:

> Several witnesses, on behalf of the defendants, concurred in showing, that when Gillen came to the house to carry away the goods, the husband was not present: that the wife requested to know by what authority the officer acted; but he would not show the execution: that he appeared to assume more authority than was necessary; and, according to the account given by one of the witnesses, actually assaulted and beat Mrs. Brown:—that when he was about taking away the table, she seized it, and there was a considerable struggle between them; the one in retaining, and the other in taking it away.
>
> While they were thus engaged, the husband came, but neither of the witnesses saw him strike the officer, as he asserted in his testimony, though several of them testified that they saw the whole affair.

Common law notions of relevance and materiality underlay the right of defence counsel to call a competent witness on the issues of guilt or innocence. Should this threshold be satisfied, the defence could even call an Alderman, a member of the trial bench, as exemplified in the trial of Roger Prout, referred to earlier, whereby the defendant was charged with a public nuisance prosecution for 'keeping and maintaining a certain ink manufactory', the furnaces of which allegedly 'emitted noisome and unhealthy smells'.

> Jacob B Taylor, an alderman, on being called from the bench, and sworn on behalf of the defendant, testified, that he had passed by the manufactory several times, and neither saw nor smelt any thing offensive; and that, on being called there by the defendant, the manufactory appeared as cleanly as the nature of the business would admit.

Police witnesses, who were not the property of the prosecution, might also be called by the defendant to adduce refutation or exculpatory evidence where they satisfied the standards of relevance and materiality. While the defendant was excluded from the category of available witnesses, this rule did not apply to co-defendants called by the accused provided they were separately charged and not tried jointly in the same indictment.

---

[64] (1818) Rogers, vol 3, p 56.

Character witnesses

Proof of good character distinguished the defence from the prosecution in that such evidence was always relevant and material to the defence of charges involving moral turpitude. Where the prosecution evidence was either equivocal or seriously in question, the good character of the defendant itself could raise a reasonable doubt.[65] This was in line with common law practice the rules of which did not apply to other witnesses either prosecution or defence whose good character could not be put in issue unless first attacked, for example, on cross examination.[66] Indeed, Michael Millender, in analysing the difference between American trials in the early decades of the nineteenth century with later trials, contended that evidence of good character was a hallmark of the defence whereby lawyers sought to have the jury identify with the defendant through appeals to notions of lenity and compassion.[67] This is illustrated in the trial of Dennis Dougherty,[68] in which the defendant was indicted for passing counterfeit money. The prosecution brought evidence that the bills were counterfeit and that they were found in possession of the defendant but also had to establish *scienter*, ie that at the time he passed the bills he knew them to be counterfeit. For this purpose, the prosecution was able to produce only weak circumstantial evidence and the testimony of an approver. Counsel for the defendant, Gardenier and Price, relied on character witnesses to raise a reasonable doubt:[69]

> The prosecution having rested, the counsel for the prisoner called on Robert McQueen, the Alderman of the fifth ward, Samuel Trumbull, Stephen Burdett, and Ezra Frost, assistant justices, John White, Patrick Benson, Paul Gallaudet, Jacob Hays, George Gardner, and Dr George Cummings, who concurred in stating from an acquaintance of a number of years, and from dealing with the prisoner in his official capacity, as constable of the fifth ward, that his character for honesty and integrity was unexceptionable.

Given the weakness of the prosecution, the testimony of the defence character witnesses took on special significance, as the charge to the jury shows:[70]

> Upon the whole, this was a case, in the view of the court, in which good character is entitled to weight in the mind of the jury in determining on the guilt or innocence of the prisoner.

---

[65] Where moral turpitude was not implicated in the charge, evidence of good character was not admissible. See eg, *Thomas Gillespie et al* (1819) Rogers, vol 4, p 154 where character evidence was held inadmissible on a charge of assault and battery.

[66] O L Barbour (1852) p 432.

[67] Michael Millender (1996) pp 4–5.

[68] (1818) Rogers, vol 3, 148.

[69] *Ibid*, p 150.

[70] *Ibid*, p 151.

Common law rules permitted defence counsel as well as the prosecution to impeach the character of witnesses and to do so by producing other witnesses to testify as to bad character. For example, in the trial of Edward Robbins and John Sheffield[71] for conspiracy to defraud, the defendants called several character witnesses to impeach the veracity of the loser, Mr Camman. The latter had asserted that he had his agent transfer $4800 in bank notes to the defendant, a money lender to whom the loser was already indebted, but had not received $3000 in return, as Mr Camman contended the defendant had promised. An extract from the direct and cross examination of witnesses by some of the prominent attorneys regularly appearing in our sample of case files is set forth below:

John Sandford sworn.

Anthon Do you know Mr Camman?

A Yes, Sir.

Q What is his general character?

Price That is not the proper question. You must ask what is his character for truth and veracity.

The Mayor No, sir. You may ask as to general characters first, and then, if you please, as to truth and veracity.

W I know nothing good of him.

Q Would you believe him on oath.

A I have no reason to.

Cross-examined.

Hamilton Were not you and Mr Camman witnesses on Lazarus's trial?

A Yes, sir.

Q The jury in that case convicted on Mr Camman's testimony; did they not: and disbelieved you?

A I can't say—they had no reason to. Witness further said he had heard Gordon S Mumford, and a Mr Ogden, speak in favour of Mr Camman; and about the time of the affair of Lazarus, Michael Paff against him; Mr Geib also before that and while he had dealings with him.

Daniel Haniland sworn.

Q Do you know Mr Camman: and what is his character?

A I knew him about six years ago, and had some dealings with him about a pair of horses; he did not act right, and we had a dispute and difficulty about the business. His character, so far as I have ever heard, is bad.

Q Would you believe him on oath?

A No, I wouldn't believe his oath, or his word.

---

[71] (1819) Bacon, p 221.

Cross-examined.

Price Where was this dispute about the horses?
A   At Brooklyn; he lived over there then. I wouldn't, as I said, believe him on his oath.

John Jeroleman sworn.

Knew Camman six years ago at Brooklyn; his character very indifferent; don't think he would believe him on oath.
Price Why not, sir?
A   Because he deceived so many persons in his dealings with them.
Q   How long have you known Mr Robbins?
A   Since last Summer, sometime.
Q   What business do you follow?
A   I farm it in the village of Brooklyn.
Q   Have you seen Mr Robbins lately?
A   I saw him at Brooklyn about a fortnight ago, at my house.
Q   Any conversation with him about Mr Camman?
A   None at all
Q   Was nothing said about Mr Camman?
A   Why, he asked me if I knew Camman, and I told him I did.
Q   Who have you ever heard give Mr Camman a bad character?
A   Two men of the name of Pillon, who lived with him.
Q   One of them in the State Prison, isn't he?
A   Yes, I believe so. I heard three or four speak against him. I have heard the people in Brooklyn generally speak ill of him.

Tunis Jeroleman, of Brooklyn, Justice of the Peace, sworn.

Says, Camman is generally spoken of unfavourably; as a man who would take advantage where he could in dealings with people. Witness is asked if he would believe him on oath? Answers that he can't say as to that.

PROSECUTION REBUTTAL EVIDENCE

The prosecution could offer contradictory evidence to the answers of defence witnesses on cross examination and it might call witnesses to swear that they would not believe the word of a defence witness or it might introduce evidence to refute any manner of affirmative defence which could not have been anticipated. The trial of Tellesphore Robetaille,[72] on a charge of grand larceny, provides an example of the common law rule permitting the prosecution the opportunity to rebut evidence introduced by the defence through evidence that would not form

---

[72] (1820) Rogers, vol 5, p 171.

part of the prosecution's case in chief.[73] There, after the defence offered an *alibi* through the testimony of Ann Tingley that at the time of the felony the defendant had been with her at various places in the city, the prosecution recalled constable Jacob Hays who testified that Ann Tingley 'was a common prostitute.'

FINAL ARGUMENT—DEFENCE

Once both sides rested, first the prosecution and then the defence was allowed to sum up which would be followed by the charge of the presiding judge to the jury. Because the jury was the trier of both fact and law, summation for both sides was the occasion to argue facts and law through characterisation of the evidence, interpretation of applicable common law principles, and emphasis placed on the standard of beyond reasonable doubt certainty which had to be satisfied by the prosecution. Jury trial was an occasion in which legal argument was permitted to flourish; indeed, cases could be argued late into the night with specific aspects commented upon at length as raising doubts.[74]

The importance of legal argument is illustrated in Layman Rowley,[75] where in summing up, defence counsel placed emphasis directly upon the burden of proof, when the principal question raised on a charge of passing counterfeit notes was the identity of the person involved, and the defence disputed that the defendant was that person by offering an alibi:

> The counsel for the prisoner argued, that from the testimony adduced, the jury could not pronounce with certainty, that the prisoner was the same person who came into the store of the prosecutor, and passed the bill laid in the indictment. One of the witnesses present in the store went no further than to state, that the person who passed the bill was about the same size of the prisoner; and although the other two were positive on that subject, yet it should be recollected, that on no subject are judicious men more liable to be mistaken than on the subject of personal identity.
>
> The counsel referred to the celebrated case of Parker, tried in this city several years ago, for bigamy, in support of their argument.

---

[73] O L Barbour (1852) p 441.

[74] As Millender observes: 'Early nineteenth-century trial oratory … offers the reminder that defence lawyers wished audiences to regard them as defenders of time-worn conventions and not as zealous procedural innovators. Formulaic language anchored these practitioners to the past and helped them link their own role with the jurors' role. By their own example in setting aside everyday concerns and coming to a prisoner's defence, they introduced jurors to their version of the traditions of the criminal trial and encouraged them to deliberate with mercy and humanity.' Millender (1996) p 44. For an insightful discussion of the history of the standard of certainty in both England and America, see Barbara Shapiro (1991).

[75] (1816) Rogers, vol 1, p 47.

But in the present case, an *alibi* had been clearly shown by the testimony of
Sebert and Smith; and unless the jury could bring their minds to the conclusion, that the prisoner was in two different places at the same time, it would
be impossible to convict him...

Final argument would commonly seek to focus the minds of the jury upon giving
the benefit of the doubt to the accused when evidence was ambiguous or the reliability of prosecution witnesses was called in question. This is illustrated in the
following cases:

Glorianna Lewis[76]

The defendant purchased three yards of bombazet from the store of Mr
Fountain at No. 231 Broadway and gave in payment a note. The note was
put into the drawer by one of the clerks. Soon after the defendant left the
store, doubts arose as to the genuineness of the note and, after being taken
to several brokers' officers, it was pronounced bad. Jacob Wheeler reports:

> *Price*, her counsel, contended that the evidence against her was too
> uncertain; that the bill was out of the possession of Mr Fountain and his
> clerks, that it did not appear, with sufficient certainty, that it was the
> same bill passed upon the prosecutor (if any was passed), that it lay in
> the drawer, and was subject to be taken out, or even changed by one of
> the clerks: he contended there was a chasm in the evidence, an uncer-
> tainty not admitted in prosecutions of this nature...
>
> The Court were of the same opinion, and so instructed the jury.

William Pierce's Case[77]

This was an indictment for having in his possession forged notes with the
intent to pass them knowing them to be forged. When the defendant was
arrested by Conklin, one of the City's constables, he is said to have attempted to conceal the notes by grasping them in his hand 'from which they were
with some difficulty wrested.' Counsel for the defendant, in addressing the
jury, sought to undermine the evidence of Conklin as to the key question
whether the defendant knew the bills to be bad. In doing so, counsel sought
to question the reliability of such evidence from constables in general, as set
out in the nominative report:

> The Counsel adverted to the anxiety displayed by Conklin, the witness
> on behalf of the prosecution; and although said the Counsel, the vigi-
> lance of the Police officers is praiseworthy, yet the situation in which
> they are so frequently placed, is necessarily calculated to give their
> minds an imperceptible bias against the offender, unfavourable to the
> development of truth.

---

[76] (1823) Wheeler 1, p 181.
[77] (1816) Rogers, vol 1, p 2.

Defence counsel might urge the jury that a reasonable doubt existed because the defendant was a victim of entrapment or that some other affirmative defence applied, as illustrated in the trial of Ichabod Ward[78] in which questions put to the prosecution witnesses by defence counsel attempted to show that an 'artifice had been resorted to on the part of the police, to induce the prisoner to come to the city, for the purpose of arresting him ...' Based on the cross-examination, defence counsel argued that the defendant was a victim of entrapment:[79]

> ... the circumstances in this case forbid the conclusion that the prisoner had this money in his possession with the felonious intent laid in the indictment. It had been in his possession a long time, and he had not attempted to pass it. He had been decoyed by a stratagem into the city, where he came in search of Burroughs, merely to deliver it into his hands; and there is reason to believe that the police was instrumental in alluring him from his residence in New-Jersey, into this city. The counsel contended, from these circumstances, that this was at the least a case of doubt, and that the excellent character of the prisoner entitled him to an acquittal.

If more than one counsel represented the accused, final argument might be divided according to the two tasks confronting the jury—to decide the issue of fact and law. Thus the initial submission might confront directly the testimony given by each of the witnesses testing it against the burden of proof or some over-arching theory of innocence, while the second submission might be a detailed summation of the applicable principles of criminal law. This doctrinal summation often referred to American case law as well as the common law of England and introduced English authorities as relevant to the legal decision-making process in New York as exemplified by Price's summation in the aforementioned trial of *Roger Prout*[80] in keeping an ink manufactory:

> The counsel further urged to the jury, that to constitute a public nuisance in conducting a lawful business, it was not sufficient for the prosecution to show that the annoyance was disagreeable merely; it must appear, that it was unreasonably so. It is not sufficient for him to show that a few individuals are incommoded; it must appear that it is a *common and public nuisance*.
>
> The counsel, in support of his argument, read to the jury a case from 1 Peake's Rep p 91, Rex vs Neville.
>
> The defendant having been indicted for a nuisance in carrying on the business of a melter of kitchen stuff and other grease, and it appearing that there had been manufactories which emitted disagreeable and noxious

---

[78] (1817) Rogers, vol 2, p 56.
[79] *Ibid*, p 56.
[80] (1819) Rogers, vol 4, p 87.

smells carried on in this neighbourhood for many years; and that the defendant came into the neighbourhood about four years ago, Lord Kenyon instructed the jury, 'that a man setting up a noxious business in a neighbourhood where such business has long been carried on, is not indictable for a nuisance, unless such noxious vapour is much increased by his manufacture.'

The counsel also read the case of The King vs Lloyd, 4 Esp Rep p 200.

This was an indictment for a nuisance against a tinman, prosecuted by the Society of *Clifford's Inn*.

The prosecutors, attorneys, proved, 'that in carrying on such part of their business as required particular attention, in perusing abstracts, and other necessary parts of their profession, the noise was so considerable, that they were prevented from attending to it.'

Lord Ellenborough said, 'that upon this evidence the indictment could not be sustained; and that it was, if any thing, a private nuisance. It was confined to the inhabitants of three numbers of Clifford's Inn only; it did not even extend to the rest of the society, and could be avoided by shutting the windows: it was therefore not of sufficient general extent to support this indictment. The defendant was acquitted.'

Final arguments might be marked by rhetorical flourishes that sought to invoke the jurors' respect for the solemnity of the process and the certainty by which a decision should be reached. This could occur through metaphorical invocation describing the plight of the accused and the need for the jurors as the guardians of humanity to assure that some miscarriage did not occur, as illustrated in the trial of Thomas Ward,[81] a manslaughter prosecution,[82] in which the defence argued self-defence. Mr Anthon and Mr Price summed up the evidence and the law for the defence, leaving Dr Graham to deliver a speech in the classical rhetorical tradition, extracts of which are reproduced below:

The learned counsel associated with me have read to you the law from *Black. Com.*, *Hale's Pleas of the Crown*, *East's Crown Law*, *Lovet's case*, *Harcourt's case*, *Goodwin's case*, and some other authorities which ought to govern in this case ... Let me call your attention to the *two* great laws of human society, from whence *all the rest* derive their force, and obligation; they are those of EQUITY and SELF-PRESERVATION; by the first, all men are bound alike not to hurt one another; by the second, all men have a right to defend themselves... All the laws of society are entirely reciprocal, and no man ought to be exempt from their force; and whoever violates

---

[81] (1823) Wheeler 2, p 122.

[82] The argument itself suggests that jurors, whilst not necessarily members of a propertied elite, were sufficiently educated to be persuaded by references and analogies drawn from the classical literature.

this primary law of nature, ought by the law of nature to be destroyed. He who observes no law forfeits all title to the protection of law. It is wickedness not to destroy a destroyer, and all the ill consequences of *self defence* are chargeable upon him *only* who occasioned them. To allow a license to any man to do evil, with impunity, is to make vice triumph over virtue, and innocence the prey to the guilty. The law of nature does not only allow us, but obliges us to defend ourselves. It is our duty, not only to ourselves, but to society ... And Cicero says, 'He who does not resist *mischief* when he may, is guilty of the same crime, as if he had deserted his *parents*, his friends, and his country'. So that the conduct of my client, in *defending his person* and *his property* against the unlawful and wicked attack of the deceased, is, I contend, *excusable homicide in self defence*, by all laws human and divine ... The prisoner deeply laments the death of the deceased; but he feels no remorse—no disquieting dread of God or man, because his conscience whispers to him, that what he did on that occasion was only in *self defence* ... If the authorities and arguments my learned associates and I have used, have not been convincing, you would not be convinced though one should arise from the dead. Justice and humanity revolt at the idea of a verdict of guilty against the prisoner; and should you, by your verdict, pronounce the horrible word *guilty*, I should blush over this departure from those characteristic features of moral rectitude in the gentlemen who fill the panel, and tremble at the impending vengeance which awaits your future destiny.

Thus every effort might be made by defence counsel to enable the jurors to empathise with the accused who would commonly (although not entirely) be drawn from the lowest substratum of New York's society and whose ways and manners might be foreign to those of the jurors. This was particularly important where the appearance of the accused or his witnesses was disconcerting, dissimilar from that of the private prosecutor and not in keeping with the style and mores of those who comprised the jury. By contrast, as illustrated in the aforementioned trial of Jerimiah Hill,[83] when the prosecution depended on the testimony of an approver to establish the defendant's knowledge, an essential element of the crime of receiving stolen property, the defence summation compared the character and status of the accused, a pawn broker, with that of the approver, an admitted thief, after a number of character witnesses were called on behalf of the defendant:

> *Wilson* said, that with the Counsel on behalf of the prosecution he was equally ready to deprecate the existence of any class of men in this city, calculated to seduce and lead astray from the paths of rectitude the young and inexperienced; but the case presented did not, in his mind, assume that aspect. His client, a gentleman, whose good name was of itself sufficient to give the lie to every syllable uttered by the principal witness, was selected by the public prosecutor as a victim; while that witness, with infamy itself

[83] (1816) Rogers, vol 1, p 57.

stamped on his visage, was suffered to escape with impunity. The Jurors were required, by the public prosecutor, on the bare uncorroborated assertion of that wretch, to find that the defendant *knew* these goods to be stolen!—Is there, then, to be no distinction between virtue and vice? Was it possible that all the future hopes and prospects of his client—all his well-earned fame— nay, all that can render life itself desirable to an honest man, should, at once, be blasted by the foul breath of contagion itself?

Look, gentlemen of the Jury, at the foul character of the principal witness, established by his own showing. Having squandered his wages by living beyond his income, he imposed on the defendant by false names, false pretences, and expended the property of his employer, in taverns and brothels! He was a thief from choice, not from necessity. His was not the situation of the poor houseless wanderer, destitute of bread and employment, or that of the poor friendless outcast, begging from door to door, and depending on the mercy of a merciless world. No—his external appearance forbids the conclusion. Fortune smiled on him—friends surrounded him—he was placed in a situation of trust and responsibility: and, Oh! What an opportunity presented itself for him to become an ornament to society—an honor to his friends, had he not in an evil hour been allured by the gilded bait of temptation; From that moment his guardian genius fled forever—the radiant sun of his prosperity was overcast with black clouds, and now fallen, disgraced and ruined, the meanest reptile in the creation is an Angel of light compared with this abandoned profligate. And yet he appears against a respectable citizen, and you are shortly to be called upon, gentlemen, to pronounce the defendant guilty from such testimony! Is there, then, any safety in society? Could either of the Jurors be safe, if credence, for a moment, should be given by twelve men to such a witness? This is to be an important decision in the annals of this Court, and the important question was to be decided by the Jury, whether a man stained with the blackest crimes, shall have the power to destroy the reputation of an honest man, and subject him to punishment to screen himself, or to gratify the malignity of others.

No, said the Counsel, I speak not as the advocate, but in the proud triumph, the confidence of truth, that the Jury will immediately exculpate the defendant from the thraldom in which he has been placed by the barefaced villany of this witness, and restore him, as he ever has shown himself, a worthy member of society.

FINAL ARGUMENT—PROSECUTION

Whilst private lawyers for the prosecution might employ the same rhetorical skills in final argument that they had enlisted on behalf of the defence,[84] our

---

[84] See eg, Graham's summation, as private lawyer for the prosecution in *Mary Rothbone* (1816) Rogers, vol 1, p 26.

research shows that District Attorneys' summations tended to be measured, focusing upon the gravamen of the charge as it related to the law and facts. Thus, for example, in William R Thompson,[85] where the defence rested on the argument that the offence was a mere larceny rather than highway robbery because the prosecutor had not been put in fear until after the money was taken, the District Attorney made his final argument to the jury in these terms:

> Maxwell contended, that if the jury should believe, from all the circumstances in the case, that there was sufficient *violence* used by the prisoner on the occasion to induce a well-grounded fear, it would be their duty to convict him. The jury must judge from the whole; and are not to be confined to the threats used as the means of depriving the prosecutor of his money. The counsel, in support of his argument, cited 4th Black. Com. p 243, to show that, 'though it is usual to lay in the indictment that the robbery was committed *by putting in fear*; it is sufficient, if laid to be done by *violence*. And when it is laid to be done by putting in fear, this does not imply any great degree of terror or affright in the party robbed: it is enough that so much force or threatening, by word or gesture, be used, as might create an apprehension of danger, or induce a man to part with his property, without or against his consent'.

Nonetheless, on occasion, when the prosecution involved wider policy issues, final arguments of District Attorneys would employ moral force as in James H Thompson and Royal A Bowen,[86] for kidnapping slaves, where powerful declamations appealing to community values were employed:

> *Thompson and Bowen*
>
> *Maxwell* [District Attorney], in an eloquent appeal to the jury, expatiated on the peculiar enormity of the crime of which the prisoner at the bar was guilty. We live, said the counsel, in a country boasting of its civil and religious freedom. Our institutions are purely republican; and the principles of genuine liberty are here cherished. In such a country and before this tribunal, in the very sanctuary of justice, we are assembled; and we are called upon to extend protection to a forlorn, miserable race of men.
>
> Manstealing is an offence, so atrocious in its nature, so appalling to the feelings, so disgusting to the moral sense of mankind, that language is inadequate to express its turpitude. Its cruelty can hardly be conceived; and, before it, every other species of theft sink into insignificance. The prisoner at the bar comes among us for this abominable purpose. He selects his instruments; and he ransacks the country, far and near, for his victims. He collects them; and at the dead of night, and in a secret manner, he transports them on board of this vessel, in a remote and solitary part of our city. When

[85] (1818) Rogers, vol 3, p 10.
[86] (1817) Rogers, vol 2, p 120.

detected in his infamous career, what is his conduct? He resorts to subterfuge and lies. He tells the witness that no other persons are on board. This poor, degraded set of men, confined in the vessel, inform their deliverers that other persons are on board. Forlorn, wretched and miserable, they assume the dignity of our nature: they rise in the majesty of innocence, and proclaim their wrongs; while he, trembling and confused, sinks appalled, into the insignificance of conscious guilt. His counsel have not denied his criminality; and it will remain for you, gentlemen of the jury, to provide the most efficacious means for its punishment.

CONCLUSION

At a time when jury trials were the dominant method of case disposition, litigation practice was characterized by rational legal events which occurred in a professional setting. Lawyers were present throughout and their purpose was more than mere window-dressing. While the ethics of advocacy eliminated the sharp edges of adversariness later ascribed to trials in the latter part of the nineteenth century, lawyering activities created substantial symmetry between the formal canopy of legal rules and their implementation in everyday trials.

The litigation practices in the first half of the nineteenth century refute the contention that these proceedings were unprofessional, haphazard and largely unrelated to rules of evidence, procedure and proof. Whilst the length of witness examination meant that trials were not as protracted as those of the twentieth century, this does not mean that the actual legal disputes when they existed were not probatively and rationally addressed. Motions and arguments were based upon case precedent, frequently derived from the common law with which the lawyers and bench were familiar. Perhaps of greatest importance was the orderly manner in which the proceedings were undertaken. These were not haphazard events; from jury selection to the conduct of the trial itself, lawyers sought to adhere to established procedures which enabled their reasoning to be examined and considered by the bench so as to enable what went forward to be in conformity to case precedent. Final argument itself was a demonstration of lawyers' eloquence as well as knowledge of law as it applied to the facts in dispute and legal issues raised.

Chapter 6
Adjudication by Trial 1800–1845: Judge and Jury

INTRODUCTION

As is evident from the preceding chapter, the presiding judge's involvement remained close throughout the trial. It was the judge's responsibility to oversee the way in which cases were presented and to rule on all questions relating to the admissibility of evidence. Whilst the adduction of evidence was generally left to counsel, the Mayor or Recorder would directly involve themselves in the questioning of witnesses where issues raised required further clarification or to avoid duplication and unnecessary argument. In this setting we consider the importance and role of the judge in charging the jury and its effect upon the process of jury deliberation and verdict. We first turn, however, to the autonomy of the jury with an analysis of the broad general power of the jury to decide issues of law and fact.

THE PROMINENCE OF THE JURY

The rationale for the authority of the jury and its constitutive importance in law-making and its application can be seen in the Mayor's charge to the jury in Mordecai Noah's case,[1] where on a motion to set aside a jury verdict convicting the defendant of 'intercepting, opening and reading a private letter' the Mayor stated:

> As to the general power of jurors to decide both the law and the fact in a criminal case, subject to the qualifications which I shall endeavour briefly to state, I never before heard it questioned in the courts of this state. It has been constantly claimed by counsel for defendants at this bar, when they thought it might be beneficial to their clients, and ... one of the counsel for this defendant, urged it on the trial of the present case.

[1] (1818) Rogers, vol 3, 13 pp 24–5.

In England the same doctrine is maintained, and the power of jurors in this respect, has there been frequently exercised in favour of parties—prosecuted on the part of the crown. The right of a jury to return a *general verdict*, and the privilege of not being questioned as to the grounds of their verdict, are founded upon this doctrine. Of this right and privilege there can be no doubt, and it is a necessary consequence from the right of rendering a general verdict, and the privilege of not being questioned as to their reasons for it, that the jury must pass on *the whole matter in issue*, and decide both the law and the fact. It is a power established and maintained as an additional security to the party accused. In England it is considered to afford a great protection against the undue influence of the crown. To us this reason does not apply, but independent of the constitutional provision that the trial by jury shall remain inviolate for ever, there are, in my view, other cogent reasons which ought to induce the people of this country for ever to cherish this mode of trial, especially in criminal cases, and to support the power of juries in their fullest extent.

In times of turbulence and faction, *the spirit of violence* and persecution may become very extensive and dangerous. If unfortunately this spirit should ever reach any of our courts, it would be found that the trial by jurors drawn and balloted as the law provides, would afford a higher security to the citizen than any other mode of trial that can be devised. Although it cannot be expected that jurors should be versed in the science of the law, I think it vastly more important for the protection of innocence, that they should be *impartial and independent*. Drawn and balloted as the law directs, it can rarely happen that some of them at least should not be so, and with the aid of counsel, whatever may be the disposition of a court, they furnish a stronger shield against oppression than is known in the institution of any other country.

In some respects however the decision of legal questions necessarily belongs to the court. In relation to the evidence on a trial, it must be so. The jury have nothing to do with the admission or rejection of evidence. These are always preliminary questions, and however important in their consequences, must of necessity belong exclusively to the court...

Again, in the course of a public prosecution a number of applications may be made to the court on questions of law, with which a jury can have nothing to do. If the indictment be informal or insufficient, the defendant may move to quash it, or he may demur to it, or he may, after a trial and verdict against him, move in arrest of judgment, and in these several ways appeal to the court for its judgment, whether the charge as alleged against him amounts to a legal offence. So, also ... he may move for a new trial on a variety of grounds, according to the merits of his case. On all these applications the court acts independently of a jury, and is governed solely by its own opinion. But it is important to observe that all such applications *proceed from the defendant himself*, and are made wholly for his benefit. The power of the court is applied to, either to save him from the necessity of submitting to a trial, or to relieve him from its effects after a verdict is found against him. If he be acquitted, a new trial is never awarded, although the court should be of opinion that he ought to have *been convicted*. Thus it is that the power of the court can be exercised in his favour only, but can never be exerted against him.

In addition to this, the jury have legally the right to differ from the court, both as to law and the effect of evidence, and their verdict can never be *disturbed*, except for the purpose of favouring a defendant, by granting a new trial in case of a conviction.[2]

The jury thus was given considerable autonomy over substantive criminal law issues including but not limited to questions of legal sufficiency, and in effect could render a verdict which represented a consensus on communitarian values. Procedural and evidentiary matters, on the other hand, were the province of the court[3] although the symbolism of a jury verdict was so important that, while being advised to defer to the opinion of the court on such issues, the jury was still required to return a verdict to enable a final judgment to be entered.

Charging the jury

Following final arguments, the presiding judge would charge the jury, although additional charges could be given *seriatim* by the other judges on the bench in the event of a difference of opinion over interpretation of the law. Charges[4] would vary dependent on the presiding judge's perceived need to intervene in the process to emphasise to jurors the policy implications of their decision, the legal rules implicated by the case, and the need to settle the law particularly when the case involved actions which had relevance to the wider mercantile economy. By contrast with modern American practice, presiding judges frequently marshaled the evidence and explained its significance to the jury in a manner which extended beyond an enumeration of the elements of the offence charged and the burden of proof. In so doing, the presiding judge might express an opinion as to the veracity of any witness or the importance of their testimony. Furthermore, where the judge found that the case had been proven without doubt or where the prosecution had not sustained its burden, he would not hesitate to direct a verdict by informing the jurors that they should either convict or acquit.

An example of a court directing a verdict of acquittal where it believed the prosecution failed to discharge the burden of producing legally sufficient evidence occurred in Anthony V Bartow,[5] where the defendant faced two indictments

---

[2] *Ibid*, p 25.

[3] *Frederick Johnson* (1816) Rogers, vol 1, pp 21–2. See Nelson (1975) pp 170–71.

[4] Whilst in everyday cases the charge would be *extempore*, in more complex or difficult cases the judge might reduce the principal points to writing so that the defendant would have the full benefit of any errors for the purposes of appeal. See eg *Robert Goodwin* (1820) William Sampson, p 178.

[5] (1818) Rogers, vol 3, p 143.

for forgery arising out of his possession of forged cheques. After producing two witnesses, one of whom stated that he had received a cheque from Bartow in return for cash to that amount, and another (the brother of the defendant) who stated the cheque to be a forgery, the prosecution rested and the Mayor intervened:

> The mayor said there was not sufficient evidence to put the prisoner on his defence. In addition to the fact of passing a forged instrument, there should be some fact or circumstance of suspicion that the prisoner had a felonious intent in the transaction, to throw on him the burden of proof. Otherwise, an honest man, who might innocently come into the possession of a forged instrument, which he had reason to believe genuine, might be subjected to the punishment, because he might not be able to account satisfactorily for its possession.

Whilst these 'directed verdicts' were not binding upon the jurors, control of the jury, while certainly not absolute, was considerable given the prestige attached to the mayor or recorder as presiding judge who, along with the aldermen, were considered pillars of the community as well as their authority in legal matters.[6] This is apparent in the trial of James Ridgway[7] where the verdict of guilty was certainly heavily influenced by the Mayor's charge in which he said that, 'there were singular circumstances in this case, inconsistent with the innocence of the prisoner'.

The Court was particularly sensitive to arguments about legal sufficiency— whether the specified conduct of the defendant fell within the provisions of a statute—that raised important issues involving the public interest. The care with which the Court approached the task of instructing the jury on matters of legal sufficiency is illustrated in the case of George Lynch,[8] where, on a charge of fraud, the Court, of its own motion, directed counsel for the defendant to relevant statutory law and stated it was inclined to think that the conduct complained of was not within the statute. The District Attorney, John Rodman, contended that the indictment was valid and that the statute applied:

> Rodman contended to the court, that the statute was enacted to protect the weaker part of mankind against the artifices practised by the designing. The defendant, on this occasion, had resorted to such false pretences as were calculated to deceive the most prudent and vigilant persons in the community. He argued, that this offence came directly in contemplation of the statute; and to support his argument, cited the case of Rex vs. Jackson (2 Leach's Crown Law, p 656.) In that case the indictment was under the 30th George

---

[6] Very occasionally, the jury would disregard the view of the court where a settled point of law arose for discussion. Thus, in *Lewis Smith* (1818) Rogers, vol 3, p 2 the mayor indicated to the jury that there was a fatal variation between the proof and the indictment. The report of the case indicates that 'the jury notwithstanding the opinion of the court, found the prisoner guilty'. On a motion for a new trial, a new indictment conformable to the proof was found to which the prisoner pleaded guilty.

[7] (1816) Rogers, vol 1, p 3.

[8] (1816) Rogers, vol 1, p 138.

2d C 24 of which the statute on which this prosecution is founded is a transcript, and it appeared in evidence, that the prisoner had obtained money from another, to a considerable amount, by pretending he had money in the hands of a banker, and by giving a draft for the amount, whereas he had no money in the hands of such banker. The court held, on solemn argument, that the offence was within the statute.

Rodman contended, this case was perfectly analogous to that under consideration, and that unless the court were inclined to overrule adjudged cases, the prisoner must be convicted.

In a considered response, the Mayor put the opposite conclusion to the jury:[9]

> The question before us, is, whether the offence of the defendant, as disclosed in the testimony, falls within the statute? The decision of this question is important, inasmuch as it will furnish a precedent, applicable to all cases of this description which may hereafter come before us. We are aware of the decision established in the English courts, to which the counsel on the behalf of the prosecution has averted. The case cited, is directly in point, and goes the full length of the doctrine for which he contends. But we think, that in England the courts have strained the principle, on which this prosecution is attempted to be supported, too far. Where a man makes use of a false token, or any deceit or artifice, calculated to gain credit beyond his own assertion, or his act predicated on his own responsibility, and by such means obtains money or goods, this offence falls within the statute, and the defendant is liable to its penalty; but, in a case like the present, where the defendant merely makes use of his own name, and draws his own check on a bank, where in truth he had no money, as a security for money then already advanced, and further sums are advanced on the promise to give further checks; we think, that although this is a fraud for which the defendant is answerable in a civil action, his offence does not fall within the provisions of the statute. This case can hardly be distinguished from that where a man, by representing that there is a fund from which there is a certainty of obtaining a sum of money, at a given time, obtains money or goods from another, and gives his own promissory note, whereas, in truth, he had no reasonable prospect of obtaining such sum at the time. To contend, that in such case the defendant would be liable to a criminal prosecution would be preposterous; and yet there is little difference in principle, between a check drawn by a man on a bank and his own note. Besides, it is well known among men of business in the city, that to answer commercial purposes, checks are frequently drawn on banks by merchants, who have no funds therein, and such checks are passed from hand to hand as cash. But should the present prosecution be supported, a door would be opened to numerous prosecutions against persons engaged in practices innocent within themselves, and calculated to promote the interests of commerce. The court for these reasons advise the jury to acquit the defendant.

[9] See also *Mordecai Noah* (1818) Rogers, vol 3, p 13, pp 19–21.

The centrality of the burden of proof might prove especially decisive where a case rested upon circumstantial evidence and the defendant was drawn from a section of society that would not ordinarily attract the sympathy of jurors. Thus, in the trial of Plunkett and Truax on a charge of grand larceny,[10] theft of a watch could be inferred from the hue and cry of the loser and testimony that the defendant offered the loser $50 to appear and not testify. However, since the loser did not testify at the trial and witnesses testified that he had voluntarily spent the evening with the defendant, the prosecution's evidence raised the issue addressed by the mayor's charge regarding the sufficiency of the proof:

> Before all the testimony had been introduced, the mayor expressed a strong intimation to the counsel that this prosecution was not supported and that he should so charge the jury. For this reason the counsel for the prisoner declined summing up, and the case was left to the charge of the court, after a single remark from District Attorney Van Wyck. He said that if ever there was a case in which the commission of a felony was established by strong circumstantial proof, this was one.

> The mayor in his charge instructed the jury, that whatever might be their opinion relative to the prisoner's guilt, still, it would never do to depart from the established rules of evidence. Before a conviction for a felony could take place, it was incumbent on the public prosecutor to show *that a felony had been committed.* In the opinion of the court, on this occasion, he had failed in this important particular.

> The ordinary mode in establishing a felony of this description was *to show that the property was stolen*, and found in possession of the prisoner, on whom the burden would then be cast of accounting for such possession. That the property was in the possession of the prisoner at the bar admits of no doubt and the counsel for the prosecution, in the absence of direct testimony, has resorted to circumstantial proof for the purpose of showing that this property was stolen. The most satisfactory proof, to this point, is from the mouth of the person who has lost the goods; and testimony from that source is generally produced. Here Dimmick, the only person who, according to the circumstances, could positively swear whether the property was stolen or not, is absent; and the extraordinary fact of his having invited the prisoner, an utter stranger, to lodge with him, and of their having drank together at a late hour of the night, is well worthy of the consideration of the jury. Not that it is absolutely necessary, for the purpose of proving that the goods were stolen, to produce the owner, for cases frequently occur where the production of such proof cannot be obtained; but where circumstances are resorted to for this purpose, they should be such as are reconcileable only with the guilt, and are wholly inconsistent with the innocence, of the prisoner. He might have offered Dimmick $50 not to appear against him, and he might have endeavoured to escape from the officer, for the purpose of avoiding the

[10] (1818) Rogers, vol 3, p 187.

odium of a public prosecution, and this might have been from a conscious-
ness of guilt; and these circumstances, relied on by the prosecution, are as
well reconcileable with innocence as guilt.

For these, with other reasons stated in the charge, the court advised the jury
to acquit the prisoner...

A similar charge where the sufficiency of circumstantial evidence was in issue
occurred in the trial of Charles Davis:[11]

Charles Davis, a young negro lad, about 16 years of age, was put to the bar,
charged with arson in setting fire to the barn of Mr William Good, at the
corner of 3rd Avenue and Stuyvesant-lane, on the 12th of February, 1823.

The circumstances of the case ... were as follows: - The prisoner had been
hired as a labourer by Mr Good, and had served him faithfully since
September last: that on the 12th of February, in the morning between 7 and
8 oclock, he told Mr Good that his brother had died the night before, and
asked leave to attend his funeral. Mr Good gave him money, and he went
away and returned early in the evening; went out again for a few minutes,
and came in and went to bed.

In a very short time after, the fire broke out in the stables; the negro was
waked up, and assisted to put out the fire: they were successful in extin-
guishing it, and Mr Good and his family retired to bed, leaving the negro in
the barn, and requested the watchman who was stationed in the neighbourhood to pay particular attention to the premises. In about one half an hour
the barn was again discovered to be on fire, and was entirely consumed.

It was proved by Mr Good and others that Charles was an industrious boy:
that during his service with him he had behaved himself very well; had had
no quarrel with Mr Good, or with any of his family; was temperate in his
life, and orderly in his conduct.

It was also proved that at the first fire he carried water and assisted in putting it out; and that, after it was extinguished, he remained in the barn after
the family had retired to bed, and until the barn was again on fire.

It was also proved that after Mr Good and the people thought they had extinguished the fire, it was found still burning under some bags of cut straw that
lay in the barn, and this occurred two or three times before the fire was finally put out...

The Court observed to the jury that the crime charged upon the prisoner
was one of a very serious nature; the punishment was very penal by our
statute, and required satisfactory proof. In this case the evidence was of the
kind denominated in law presumptive evidence; and they intimated their
opinion, that the circumstances were of two (sic) slight a nature to warrant a

[11] (1823) Wheeler 1, p 235.

conviction: that in cases where the penalty was so very severe, the proof ought to be satisfactory. It may be probable that some third person threw combustible materials into the barn; and that after Mr Good and his people supposed they had put the fire out, there were some sparks left that shortly after lighted up into a flame. This is the most charitable conclusion. Inferences from facts are always to be taken in favour of the prisoner; and in matters of doubt presumptions of law and fact are to operate in his favour; and in this case they are violent: he had no quarrel with Mr Good, no difference with any of the family: he was not intemperate, or addicted to any vicious habits, etc. In such cases, the absence of positive proof, or strong presumptive testimony, is material and indispensible.

When there was a challenge to the charge by either the prosecution or defence, the court might incorporate counsel's contentions into its charge in the context of what the court thought appropriate. Thus, in the trial of James Gordon,[12] the defendant was charged with assault and battery with intent to ravish having allegedly mistaken the house of the prosecutrix for a house of ill fame and then pretended to be her husband. The defence produced character witnesses to show that James Gordon was industrious and religious and argued that there was no intent to ravish because no act of violence towards the prosecutrix was asserted. The Mayor reminded the jury that whilst good character was beneficial in cases of doubt, it was not in a case of clear guilt. Pouring scorn on the 'very extraordinary' defence attempted, the Mayor concluded that the prisoner's behaviour destroyed any presumption in his favour arising from his character, however fair it might be. This triggered the following exchange with one of the defendant's counsel, Mr Price:

> After the mayor had finished his charge, Mr Price requested to know of his honour whether he intended, in his charge, to instruct the jury that they *could not* find the defendant guilty of the assault and battery, and acquit him of that offence with an intent to ravish.
>
> *By the Mayor.* Mr Price, I intended to charge the jury, and I now wish them to understand, that *they have the power* of finding the verdict for which you contend; but that *they ought not to do so*, according to the facts of the case. (original emphasis)[13]

However, in most instances the Mayor or Recorder would put to the jury the factors tending towards conviction and those operating in favour of the accused, without expressing an opinion one way or the other, leaving the resolution of the conflicting evidence entirely to the jury, as illustrated in the trial of Robert McCollister:[14]

---

[12] (1818) Rogers, vol 3, p 91.
[13] *Ibid*, p 92.
[14] (1823) Wheeler 1, p 391.

The defendant, who lived in the upper part of the town, came to the store of Mr Simonson, 47 Greenwich-street, on the 27 May 1823 in the evening and purchased a few trifling articles, amounting to three shillings, and gave in payment a five dollar counterfeit note of the Ontario Bank. On 30 May 1823, he again went to the store and offered another note of the same amount and description for payment for a quarter of tea. On being told by Mr Simonson that the note was counterfeit, McCollister said that he knew from whom he had received the note. He was taken by Mr Simonson to the police and denied being in possession of any other money. He was searched at the police office, found to be in possession another counterfeit note of the same Bank and of the same description, and gave a false account of his residence, connections, conduct etc. to the police officer.

The prosecution case was supported by a number of separate strands of evidence. The prisoner had made a confession to Mr Simonson at the time of the initial arrest and when being taken to the police office which, against the objection of the defence, was admitted in evidence. The bills were proved to be counterfeit and McCollister's statements that he lived in Spring-street, was a married man, and obtained the bills in New Orleans were proved false by the testimony of respectable witnesses. Additionally, police-officers gave evidence of finding a trunk in McCollister's brother's house containing small quantities of tea and sugar, allegedly bought for the purpose of affording an opportunity of changing money at the places at which they had been purchased.

On the defendant's part, evidence was given that he was illiterate and a hard working and industrious man. There was also evidence that he had visited New Orleans about a year earlier, was a man of good character and had never been charged with a crime before. The defence contended that the evidence against him was not sufficient; that the best men were actually deceived by counterfeit money; and that it was hardly strange that an illiterate man, unacquainted with bank notes, should have them by accident in his possession.

Against this background, Recorder Richard Riker's charge to the jury was evenly balanced. Whilst setting out the strong community interest in the suppression of counterfeiting, he put the case for and against McCollister as it appeared from the evidence:

The Court observed to the jury, that it was of the greatest consequence to free the community of offences of this description: the frequency of the crime, of late, demanded the most serious attention of courts of justice. No man's property is safe while he is subject every day to be defrauded of it by means of this spurious paper. In the case now before the Court, it appears the prisoner lives in the upper part of the town, and came a great distance to purchase of the prosecutor small quantities of tea and sugar, for which he passed upon his clerk a counterfeit note, and returned in two or three days and

offered another note, of the same bank and description, for another trifling
article, when he was arrested; and upon examining his person, another counterfeit note was found upon him of the same bank and description, after having denied being in possession of any more money. His honour observed, the
identity of the bills, and the person of the prisoner had been proved, and that
it was the province of the jury to say whether the prisoner had these bills in
his possession with an intention to pass, and actually passing them, as laid
in the indictment; and proceeded to note some circumstances in favour of the
prisoner, that it appeared by the testimony that he was a hard working, industrious man, and had, heretofore, sustained a good character, and that in cases
where the intent was in issue before the jury, the prisoner ought, and had a
right, to have the benefit of it on his trial. It was also proved, that he was illiterate—this circumstance, although no excuse for the crime, might be an
argument, in favour of his ignorance of the quality of the bills etc.

The Court left it to the jury to say whether the prisoner was guilty, from all
the circumstances of the case or not.

Whilst for the most part the aldermen as members of the bench would bow to the
legal acumen of the presiding judge, this did not preclude separate opinions
occasionally being rendered *seriatim* on issues of law. This, in turn, meant that
the jurors (and they were so instructed) had the right to select from among the
opinions offered by the different judges as well as by the lawyers in their clos-
ing arguments.

An illustration of the practice in dealing with a division of opinion within the
court is provided by the trial of John Weeks,[15] which concerned the extent to
which the confession of a prisoner should be taken against him. Although the
owner of three tumblers was able to testify to their theft from his house, he knew
nothing of the prisoner and had never seen the tumblers in the possession of the
prisoner. In support of an indictment for petit larceny, the District Attorney sought
to rely upon the examination of the prisoner in which he denied that he had stolen
the property but admitted that he had had possession of one of the tumblers stating that it had been given to him by a black man. There being no other evidence,
there was discussion as to legal sufficiency:

The *Mayor* expressed an opinion, that the testimony was not sufficient to
convict the prisoner.

The two aldermen on the bench dissented, and said they thought the prisoner's confession that he had had a part of the stolen property in his possession, would warrant the jury in finding him guilty.

The district attorney addressed the jury in support of the opinion expressed
by the aldermen; after which the mayor said, that unfortunately there was a

---

[15] (1818) Bacon, p 138.

difference in the opinion of the bench, as to the law which applied to this case. That when it so happened it was the duty of the judges to give their opinion *seriatim*; and the jury, who in this, as in every other criminal case, were judges of the law as well as of the fact, were to render their verdict as their judgments should be influenced by the reasoning that might be offered to them.

After giving a set of reasons for his opinion which rested in principles he had followed in twenty five years of practice at the bar, a great part of which time he said, he had acted as public prosecutor, the Mayor enjoined the jury to listen 'with great respect and attention' to the opinions of the other judges.[16]

Jury deliberation and verdict

On completion of the court's charge, the issue of guilt or innocence was left for decision by the jury who had the right to return a general verdict and the privilege of not being questioned as to the grounds for their verdict.[17] Whilst legally the jury had the right to differ from the court both as to the law and the effect of evidence and their verdicts could not generally be disturbed,[18] given the deference toward the court, with few exceptions, the jury's verdict followed the instruction of the court. Indeed, it is this deference of the jury or control by the court that in large measure explains the nature and extent of the jury's deliberation patterns.

In a clear majority of trials (64.0 per cent) contained in the nominative reports in which the deliberation process is recorded, the jury decided upon their verdict without retiring.[19] In the vast majority of trials in which there was an immediate verdict (83.0 per cent) the evidence of guilt or innocence appears to have been overwhelming. In these cases, the decision of the jury followed the direction of the court's charge which oftentimes amounted to an instruction to convict or acquit the defendant or the withdrawal of the prosecution or the abandonment of the defence.[20] The following trials illustrate the context of such verdicts of acquittal or conviction:

[16] Only one other member of the court, Justice Warner, gave reasons in support of his opinion. In exceptional cases where there was a dispute as to the state of the law, it was open to the jury to find a special verdict in which the detailed findings of fact would be submitted to the court for judgment, as in *Daniel K Allen* (1818) Rogers, vol 3, p 118 and *Tobias McClure* (1818) Rogers, vol 3, p 154.

[17] When the general verdict was returned, counsel for the prisoner could make a motion that each juror be polled to ensure that the verdict was the verdict of all of the jury. In such cases, each juror was bound to answer the question but counsel had no right to interrogate a jury as to the reasons or grounds for the verdict: *Mordecai M Noah* (1818) Rogers, vol 3, p 13.

[18] *Augustus M Stone et al* (1818) Rogers, vol 3, pp 2, 6. The court always had power to grant a new trial in the event of a conviction felt to be wrongly founded and, in very exceptional cases, could order a new trial on an acquittal if satisfied that the jury were mistaken either as to law or as to the evidence: *Mordecai M Noah* (1816) Rogers, vol 3, 13 p 25.

[19] This is variously recorded as 'immediately pronounced ...', 'without leaving their seats ...', 'without leaving the box ...' and occurred in 65 out of the 101 reported General Sessions cases in which the jury's deliberation pattern was recorded.

[20] In the residue of cases of immediate retirement (11.0 per cent) there was inadequate detail in the report of the cases to establish any link between the charge and the verdict.

John Connor,[21]

On a charge of forgery, in which the defendant had been apprehended in possession of counterfeit bills, Counsel for the prisoner raised a point of law concerning the validity of the prosecution:

> The mayor said that on the facts in the case there was no doubt of the guilt of the prisoner; but though he was in some doubt on the question of law raised by the counsel for the prisoner, yet he was inclined to believe it substantial. He, therefore, advised the jury to acquit the prisoner; and, without leaving their seats, they did so.

Mary A Turrell,[22]

On an indictment for petit larceny, in which the prisoner had been found wearing stolen clothes and had offered an innocent but unsupported explanation, the Recorder charged the jury:

> That from all the circumstances of the case, the safest way would be for the jury to acquit: The articles, it is true, were found upon her, and it is equally true, that the explanation she has given how she came by them, is not entirely satisfactory to the Court; we believe before this charge her character was good, and she ought certainly to have the benefit of it at this time, and in such a case; the case, to say the least of it, is very doubtful from the evidence in support of the indictment, and which is made still more doubtful by the good character of the prisoner.

The Jury acquitted her without retiring from the box.

Robert S Watts,[23]

The defendant was charged with passing a counterfeit $3 note of the Bank of Morris, upon Mr Molahan, a respectable grocery store-keeper. Subsequently, further notes were passed to Mr Molahan by Susan Brown, who, it was said, had been set to work in the counterfeit business by Watts. As reported by Jacob Wheeler, on her arrest and confession, Watts was arrested:

> *Price*, counsel for the prisoner, declined any remarks to the jury.
>
> *By the Court*—'It appears absolutely certain, from the evidence offered, that the prisoner is one of those gang of counterfeiters and venders of counterfeit money, that infest the City with loads of spurious paper: he employed a young artless girl, to whom he was paying his addresses at the very time, to assist him in his criminal pursuits, and who is ruined by his arts'.

The jury found him guilty without leaving the box.

John Degey,[24]

The defendant was charged with disturbing a divine service at the Ebenezer Baptist Church after interrupting a service of pastor Vanvelser to argue that

---

[21] (1818) Rogers, vol 3, p 59.
[22] (1822) Wheeler 1, p 34.
[23] (1822) Wheeler 1, p 52.
[24] (1823) Wheeler 2, p 135.

the pastor was contradicting what he himself had said at a service the previous Sunday. Counsel for Degey argued that the conduct of the defendant was not indictable at common law and that it was the duty of worshippers to oppose publicly services at which doctrines derogatory of Christianity were taught provided this was done decently and with decorum. As reported by Jacob Wheeler, the jury immediately convicted after receiving the following charge:

> His Honour the Recorder observed, that the court was of opinion that this was a good indictment at common law, and could be sustained. That if the law was as contended for by counsel for the defendant, the important provision in the constitution which guaranteed the free enjoyment of religious principles and worship to every person, would become nugatory. No man had a right to disturb another in the exercise of that important privilege. If he did, he might be indicted, and if convicted, suffer a penalty of fine or imprisonment, or both.

> By the evidence in this case, it appeared the defendant had disturbed the worshippers in the Ebenezer Baptist Church by an indecorous controversy with the officiating minister of that church, during divine service; the motive of his attendance at the church appeared by the evidence if not bad, very suspicious: he was not a member, and had no right to interfere at all in the mode and manner of that worship; or at least, not by disturbing the congregation during service.

> The court was, therefore, clearly of opinion, that the offence charged in the indictment was an offence at common law, and that the evidence against the defendant fully proved the charges set forth in it.

> The jury immediately returned a verdict of guilty.

Further, we found no evidence of compromise verdicts. The nominative reports, our own sample of case files and Minute Book entries showed that juries returned verdicts according to the charge in the indictment rather than, for example, returning a verdict of guilty to uncharged lesser included offences unless, as happened occasionally, there was guidance from the court to the contrary. The practice under which English juries manipulated the value placed on stolen goods in order to moderate the effects of capital punishment at the time of the Bloody Code found no counterpart in our sample. Thus, in William Taylor,[25] the defendant was indicted for grand larceny of a watch, gold seal, and gold keys. After a witness for the prosecution under cross examination stated that the intrinsic value of the materials of which the property was made was less than the market value, counsel for the defence urged the jury to convict of petit larceny on the basis that the proper criterion of value of goods was the intrinsic value. However, the court intervened:

> *By the Court.*—There is no other criterion of the value of goods, with which the court is acquainted, except that of their value in the market.

> The jury immediately found the prisoner *Guilty*.

[25] (1816) Rogers, vol 1, p 28.

Retirements in trials where the nominative reporters provide details[26] tended to be brief. Where the jury did retire to consider their verdict (n=36 or 36.0 per cent of cases in the nominative reports) deliberations were concluded within what the reporters themselves described as a 'short time' in eleven cases,[27] and in eight further cases within at most fifteen minutes of retirement.[28] More extended deliberations were reported as taking between thirty minutes and six hours.[29] At the other extreme were a few cases in which the jury engaged in very extended deliberations despite structural disincentives to do so by withholding food and water from the jury from the moment of retirement until verdict. Where the court anticipated a long retirement, however, arrangements were made to ensure that the jurors would not have to begin the deliberation process immediately and could first break for lunch or dinner upon the completion of a morning or afternoon listening to evidence.

CONCLUSION

Whilst it was clear that the Mayor and Recorder represented a classically-educated elite with strong ties to the mercantile class, aldermen and jurors (sometimes without either of these antecedents) had a significant contributory effect in the deliberative process and could act independently where there was a disagreement with the mayor or recorder's charge. Indeed, the broad authority which the jury had over both law and fact and their right to issue a general verdict, without interrogation, assured their autonomy and contributed to General Sessions being a forum of consensus on community norms. Moreover, the constrained and rule-bound nature of the process which evolved betweeen the presiding judges and the jury guarded against miscarriages of justice within an expeditious framework and without protracted delay. Judges commonly marshalled the evidence to the jury, often expressing their views as to what appeared to be probative and credible and did not hesitate to direct verdicts of acquittal or conviction to avoid what the court considered to be an outcome contrary to the evidence. This in turn facilitated juries returning verdicts without retirement and when retiring being able to complete deliberation in a timely manner and before their next meal.

---

[26] In one in five cases where the jury was known to have retired, the period of retirement is indeterminate being described, for example, as for 'some time': *Joseph Rhodes* (1816), Rogers, vol 1, p 1; *Lyman Rowley* (1816) Rogers, vol 1, p 47.

[27] See eg *James Martine* (1821) Rogers, vol 6, p 27; *Hugh Flinn* (1822) Wheeler 1, p 76; and *John H Osborn* (1822) Wheeler 1, p 96.

[28] See eg *Joseph Decosta* (1816) Rogers, vol 1, p 83 'about five minutes'; and *Michael Romaine* (1823) Wheeler 1, p 369 ('about fifteen minutes').

[29] See eg *Martha Coold* (1817) Rogers, vol 2, p 171 (in which the verdict was arrived at 'in about two hours'; *John Byrd* (1820) Wheeler 1, p 242 ('The Jury retired, and in about three hours returned with a verdict ...'); and *Noel M Hauxhurst* (1817) Rogers, vol 2, p 33 (where the original trial jury failed to agree following a six hour retirement).

Chapter 7

Adjudication by Guilty Plea

INTRODUCTION

Whilst trials were the principal means by which adjudication occurred in the Court of General Sessions, in a minority of cases throughout the first half of the nineteenth century the method of disposition was achieved through the entry of a guilty plea. In this chapter, we seek to identify the factors that may have animated defendants, either individually or in discrete groups, to enter guilty pleas at a time when jury trial was the normal method of case disposition. We consider first the guilty plea process itself and whether charge bargaining emerged with the advent of the 1829 Code containing enumerated lesser included offences. We then consider to what extent exogenous factors entered into the decision to plead guilty and whether the plea represented an acceptance of responsibility, fear of publicity or inchoate protestations of innocence. Before concluding we consider under what circumstances the private parties were able to engage in an informal settlement of the dispute without an adjudication of guilt.[1]

THE PLEA PROCESS

It would appear from the case files and reports that guilty pleas were almost invariably entered personally by defendants themselves. The entry of a guilty plea was usually inscribed on the jacket of the indictment, as in the prosecution of Thomas Shearer below.

Exceptionally, it seems to have been possible for the plea to be entered on the defendant's behalf by the defendant's counsel, as illustrated in the prosecution of Margaret McClure:[2]

---

[1] We were able to trace case papers in the District Attorney's files in only 97 of 118 guilty plea cases and there were no records of magistrates' examinations in assault and battery cases.

[2] District Attorney's Case Files, 11 February, 1815. *McClure* is an example of where the defendant's initial plea of not guilty or *nolle contendere* (NC) was entered by her counsel Peter De Witt after which a guilty plea was entered by counsel as endorsed on the papers.

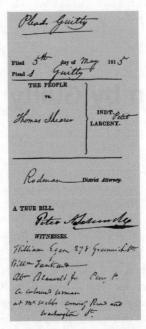

ILLUSTRATION 7.1: Thomas Shearer, District Attorney's Files, 5 May, 1815.

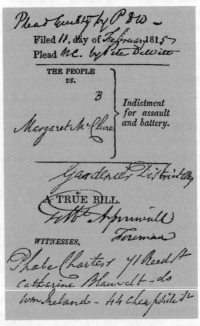

ILLUSTRATION 7.2: Margaret McClure, District Attorney's Files, 11 February, 1815.

However infrequent and whatever method used to enter the plea itself, there is no indication in the case files or nominative reports that this method of disposition was in any other respect regarded as problematic or aberrational: on the contrary, the few discussions of the guilty plea that are found in the nominative reports indicate that disposition by guilty plea was a normal part of criminal procedure for which there was specific legal practice, for example, in terms of adducing evidence of the defendant's motive and degree of culpability.[3]

What follows is an analysis of the principal structural factors that socio-legal researchers have identified as motivating guilty pleas or creating the opportunity for them. However, the reasons animating a guilty plea rather than a not guilty plea and trial are difficult to discern in the mass of cases. Indeed, a review of our sample of case files shows that, in those prosecutions where the information was known (n=88), no fewer than 73 per cent (n=64) of guilty pleas were offered on the filing of the indictment without any further endorsement or description in the case files of the circumstances underlying the plea.

Recipe formula

The relative infrequency of guilty plea dispositions[4] reflects a culture of jury trials which continued throughout the period 1800–1845 that is in stark contrast to the opportunity created by the adoption of the 1829 Penal Code and its gradation of offences by degrees. The 1829 Code, on its face, could enable courtroom actors to induce guilty pleas based upon lesser included offences which broadened considerably the range of offences arising out of a single criminal act thereby creating a formula for plea bargaining.[5] Thus, after 1829, in exchange for a guilty plea to a lesser offence, the District Attorney had the discretion to *nolle* any greater offence charged and thereby had the capacity to engage in charge bargaining.[6] While under the 1829 Statute the legislature had precluded prosecutors from entering a *nolle prosequi* to the entire indictment or to discontinue or abandon the indictment without permission of the court,[7] as Fisher explains, it did not limit the prosecutor's authority to *nolle prosequi* a single (greater) count within the indictment.[8] The statutory incentive for the defence would be to limit the maximum sentence through the acceptance of a lesser charge that would also

---

[3] Thus, in the course of the trial of *The People v John Moore and others* (1824) Wheeler 3, 82 p 90, after an exchange between counsel as to the admissibility of evidence tending to show the reasons behind the actions of the defendants, the court ruled as follows: 'When the party pleads guilty, the motive then comes up by affidavit, but where there is a trial, that is the proper time to show the *intent* of the parties' (original emphasis).

[4] See Chapter 9 below, Figures 9.1–9.4.

[5] 1829 *Revised Statutes of the State of New York*, Part IV, Title II, pp 662 *et seq*.

[6] See also for a discussion of prosecutorial charging discretion, *People v McLeod* 1 Hill 377 (1841).

[7] 1829 *Revised Statutes of the State of New York*, Part IV, Chapter II, Title IV, Section 54, p 726.

[8] *Ibid*, p 609. See Fisher (2000) pp 1034–35.

significantly alter the minimum sentence to which defendants who were second offenders would be exposed.[9]

Yet, in practice, our sample of District Attorney's case files showed that no concerted effort was made to utilise these new-found offences as a way to induce defendants to forego their right to a jury trial on the top charges. Throughout the period, single count indictments amounted to more than ninety per cent of all prosecutions[10] while jury trial outcomes almost invariably involved convictions of the top count or acquittals, with little desire manifested on the part of the jury to return compromise verdicts of lesser included offences. More importantly by 1846, 80 per cent of guilty pleas were to the top charge.

This is of particular importance given the arguments advanced by the functionalists regarding the variables of professionalism necessary for the rise of guilty pleas. Between 1800 and 1845 the rate of guilty pleas to total dispositions oscillated within a broad band anywhere between close to zero and twenty per cent under conditions that, after the revisions of the 1829 Penal Code, gave the District Attorney greatly enhanced charging discretion by enabling the prosecutor to choose from among several degrees of offences.[11] For example, a prosecution for forgery subsequent to 1829 enabled the District Attorney to draft an indictment charging the defendant in any one of four degrees, each a lesser-included offence of the greater, with the first degree carrying a sentence of not less than 10 years in state prison while the fourth degree carried a sentence of not more than two years in state prison or more than one year in County jail. Moreover, since the Court of General Sessions was a lawyered court, with lawyers recorded as appearing in over 60 per cent of all trials in 1830 and in 1839–1850 between 80–100 per cent, there was no lack of awareness on the part of courtroom actors of the nuanced differences between the degrees of offences when contrasted with the available evidence and the opportunities these differences created for charge bargaining. Hence, there was motive, opportunity and a recipe formula in place that could facilitate plea bargaining, yet by the middle of the century guilty pleas to lesser offences and attempts were only infrequently entered.

Absence of exogenous factors

Looking across the samples as a whole, we could find no generic factor to explain the pattern of guilty pleas. To the contrary, it is clear that variables such as race

[9] 1829 *Revised Statutes of the State of New York*, Part IV, Chapter 1, Title 7, Sections 8–9, pp 699–700.

[10] See Chapter 14 below, Fig 14.8.

[11] See Chapter 9 below, Figure 9.4. For his part, George Fisher contends that our data show 'a strong increase in the rate of guilty pleas beginning by the late 1830s' (Fisher (2000) p 1035, citing McConville and Mirsky (1995)). However, while there was an increase in the rate of guilty pleas between 1830 and 1839, the rate never exceeded that which occurred in 1800 or 1810. Where the changeover occurs is by 1850, as Figure 9.4 shows. More important, however, is the reason for change and the absence of any causal relation to the 1829 Penal Code.

and sex were not linked to the kind of pleas defendants entered.[12] We can state with confidence that, as attested to by both our sample of cases drawn from the District Attorney's file and those prosecutions described in the nominative reports, guilty pleas were entered on behalf of defendants whose cases seem indistinguishable from those of other defendants who went to trial.

Whatever the motivation to plead, however, defendants were exposed either to mandatory punishment or sentences meted out by the court which were as harsh as or might exceed in severity those given to defendants convicted after trial. A vivid example of a defendant pleading guilty in circumstances where, because of mandatory provisions provided by statute,[13] there could be no sentencing advantage occurred in the prosecution of William Henry, Thomas Smith and Edward McColgan,[14] drawn from the account of the nominative reporter:

> The prisoners, who were described as 'foreigners', were indicted for highway robbery committed on Jacob Dayton an old man from Horseneck in Connecticut. Having arrived in the City by boat, Dayton, 'not one of the most intelligent men of his age', met Henry and asked him whether he knew a friend he was seeking who lived in John Street. Henry told him that he would take him to this man, he himself having a house in John Street. In the course of conversation, Henry also claimed to come from Horseneck. They were then joined by the other two prisoners. By purchasing something from a grocery, Jacob Dayton revealed to the prisoners that he was carrying about $47 in bills. They then took him to the upper part of the City near Stuyversant's Green where he was attacked for his money at the head of the rope-walks, near the house of Whitfield Case. By good fortune, Mrs Case happened to be looking for one of her children and came upon one of the prisoners keeping look-out while the other two attacked Dayton. When the others joined the look out, Mrs Case told them that they were villains and that she would mark them. They ran and she called murder; and they were captured in a hue and cry.

> When arraigned with the other prisoners, Edward McColgan said, 'I took the money, but the other two knew nothing about it'. When all three were brought up for trial, McColgan, repeating his assertion concerning the two others, pleaded guilty.

> After the introduction of the testimony of Jacob Dayton and that concerning their apprehension, the prosecution rested its case and Price, as counsel for the prisoners, abandoned their defence.

[12] A specific illustration of the general position is provided by the District Attorney's Files for 10 February, 1815 on which day eight defendants, of whom six were black and one further was a servant, had their cases disposed of by way of trial rather than by means of guilty pleas.

[13] 1813 *New York Laws*, Chapter xxix, Section 3i, p 408.

[14] (1816) Rogers, vol 1, p 128. See also *Benjamin Hampton* (1821) Rogers, vol 6, p 31 who was sentenced to life imprisonment after pleading guilty to burglary.

All three prisoners were sentenced to the State Prison for the terms of their lives.

The absence of any incentive to plead guilty in the hope or expectation of a lesser sentence is illustrated in four separate prosecutions which were reported together in the nominative reports for 1816, involving larceny of an almost identical character, punishable by indeterminate sentences up to fourteen years' imprisonment,[15] in which items of property varying in value from $16 to $33 were stolen from ships in the city. Two of the prosecutions, that of Manuel Bedis and George Spencer, went to trial and resulted in convictions, the other defendants, Andrew Smith and George Collins, pleaded guilty. Notwithstanding the different modes of disposition, all four defendants were sentenced to the state prison, each for the minimum term permitted by statute of three years and a day.[16]

In the few prosecutions where different sentences were imposed on jointly-charged defendants, there is no clear evidence that the entry of a guilty plea by one or more of the accused was causally linked to sentencing. In several of these cases, other factors, particularly prior criminal record, appear to have been of most significance.

Overall, therefore, the entry of a guilty plea in and of itself did not serve as an 'implied bargaining tool' resulting in defendants avoiding long terms of imprisonment or being made a public example,[17] and we could find no firm evidence of any sentence differential dependent upon plea. What follows is our effort to analyse data contained in our sample of case files and the nominative reports to determine what factors unique to the defendant's case may have motivated the individual to enter a plea of guilty.

Acceptance of responsibility

In the normal case, the entry of the guilty plea was entirely consistent with the way in which the defendant had responded to the allegation from the inception of the case, notwithstanding the fact that in other seemingly identical cases the defendant chose to go to trial. Our sample disclosed that in two-thirds of prosecutions containing magistrate's examinations of the defendant at which the defendant admitted to the crime, a guilty plea followed in General Sessions.[18] In some,

[15] 1813 *Laws of the State of New York*, 36th Session, Chapter xxix, p 409.

[16] See Rogers, vol 1, pp 178–79; and 1813 *Laws of the State of New York*, 36th Session, Chapter xxix, Section x, p 410.

[17] Thus, a recidivist who had recently escaped from state prison and had stolen watches and jewellry was sentenced to fourteen years' imprisonment to commence from the expiry of his former term: *Jacob Johnson* (1817) Rogers, vol 2, p 160; and guilty pleas were entered in cases where the mandatory sentence was life imprisonment: *William Henry, Thomas Smith and Edward McColgan* (1816) Rogers, vol 1, p 128 (highway robbery); *Benjamin Hampton* (1821) Rogers, vol 6, p 31 (burglary). Exemplary sentences were given out on guilty pleas in several cases: *William Goldsby* (1816) Rogers, vol 1, p 81; *John Alexander Kennedy and Richard B Swim* (1816) Rogers, vol 1, p 170.

[18] In total, information was available as to the defendant's response at Examination in 55 cases, in 67 per cent of which (n=37) a full confession was made.

the defendant proffered poverty as the explanation for the offence; in some partial reparation was proffered in mitigation; and in others the defendant asked for mercy and another chance as illustrated by the following examples:

Samuel Burt,[19]
When Ebenezer P Ward, a mariner on board the Schooner Nancy, went ashore because of sickness, his chest on board the schooner was opened up and gold coins taken from it by the defendant, a cook and cabin boy on the Schooner. When examined, Samuel made a full confession telling Special Justice Buckman that he had taken the money and that 'he has spent the whole of the said money except five dollars and said guinea which he has returned to the said Ebenezer P Ward ...' Ward confirmed that he had received the money as stated by the defendant.

Christopher Donlevy,[20]
Christopher Donlevy was accused of stealing one piece of linen and cotton check from Richard Berrian's shop at the corner of Roosevelt and Catharine Streets, Berrian telling Justice Buckman that Christopher Donlevy had confessed the theft to him. On his examination by the same Special Justice, Donlevy repeated the confession, stating that he took the linen from Mr Berrian's door 'with an intent to make him shirts as he had not any shirt to wear.'

William Dickson,[21]
Dickson stole a bundle of fine combs from the store of Charles Christian and Samuel Paxton whose clerk, John Alexander, shortly afterwards arrested Dickson and found the combs in his pocket. Dickson made no attempt at denying the offence, stating at his examination that he had committed the theft in order 'to get him some victuals, having eaten nothing in two days ...'

Jacob Wanderly,[22]
The defendant was charged with stealing a side of leather of the value of three dollars the property of John Sandford from whose stable it was taken. When taken before Special Justice Hopson, Wanderly admitted his culpability, stating that 'he did take the Leather as charged' but that he would 'never do so again if he can be let go.'

Guilty pleas might also be entered in the course of a trial after defendants came to realise that further resistance would be pointless and that a conviction was certain. An illustration of this is drawn from the nominative report of the prosecution of Lewis Smith[23] who was charged with obtaining $10, the money of Joseph

---

[19] District Attorney's files, 5 February, 1805.
[20] District Attorney's files, 5 February, 1805.
[21] District Attorney's files, 8 April, 1805.
[22] District Attorney's files, 9 June, 1825.
[23] (1818) Rogers, vol 3, p 4.

Cutler, by false pretences. Smith purported to make an arrangement to lodge at Cutler's boarding house and was loaned ten dollars in bank bills after appearing to count out one hundred dollars in bills and placing them in his pocket book that he then gave to Cutler for safe custody. In fact, Smith had deceived Cutler by counting out several fives for $20 bills and then 'palmed' the lot into the sleeve of his coat, leaving Cutler with an empty pocket book.

> Defense counsel, Gardenier, moved to dismiss the indictment on two grounds challenging its facial validity; that it alleged obtaining money from Joseph Cutler when the evidence showed that bank bills were obtained;[24] and that the indictment ought to have stated that Smith had resorted to artifice.[25] The Mayor, whilst of the view that Smith was undoubtedly guilty of the crime and ought to be punished, conceded the correctness of the objections to the indictment. However, notwithstanding the opinion of the court, the jury found Smith guilty upon which Gardinier moved for a new trial in arrest of judgment. It soon became apparent that a further trial would be futile:[26]
>
>> The mayor said that as the guilt of the prisoner was manifest on the state of facts disclosed in the testimony, the better course would be to have a new indictment framed, conformable to such statement.
>>
>> On the following day, the mayor, on this motion for a new trial, remarked, that the court could not depart from legal forms. They ought to be preserved, for they had been established for a series of ages, and were in their origin designed to guard the rights of the citizen against oppression.
>>
>> The motion was granted: a new indictment was found, to which the prisoner pleaded guilty, and on the last day of the term was sentenced to the penitentiary three years.

A similar result appears in Lewis Weaver:[27]

> Weaver was indicted, tried and convicted of robbery after stealing a hat from Samuel Healy. He then faced a second indictment in which he was jointly charged with John Collins for robbing John Barry of watches and money. According to John Barry, he had been robbed at knifepoint by Weaver and Antonio[28] acting in collusion with Collins whom they had purportedly come

---

[24] Bank bills, as choses in action, had no intrinsic value and should have been so described in the indictment. As the law then stood, 'money' did not include bills.

[25] Where a person had simply been told a lie, the law required that there was a duty to guard against it by the use of ordinary caution. As the indictment was drafted in this case, it appeared that Cutler might have guarded against the lie simply by examining the pocket book.

[26] (1818) Rogers, vol 3, pp 6–7.

[27] (1812) Rogers, vol 6, pp 101–04.

[28] Antonio is described in the report as 'an old offender' and Collins had recently come out of the state prison.

to arrest whilst pretending to be police officers. His account was detailed and highly persuasive. Just as his wife, Margaret, began to give evidence implicating Collins, counsel for Collins withdrew, telling the court, 'I abandon the defence'. When this happened, it became clear to Weaver that he, too, would not escape.[29] As reported by Daniel Rogers:

> Weaver, having pleaded not guilty to this indictment, *now* withdrew his plea, and pleaded guilty ... (original emphasis).

Whilst the abandonment of defence by counsel, as in Weaver, effectively condemned the defendant to conviction, in such circumstances this was normally achieved by the verdict of the jury rather than through the entry of a guilty plea.[30]

Fear of publicity

Fear of publicity drove some individuals to seek the shelter of the guilty plea.[31] We can see this in the prosecution of John Clarke,[32] for example, in which the defendant stated on his examination before the magistrate that his real name was John Bamber and that 'he gave the name Clark because he did not want his name in the Sun ...' In line with this, the nominative reports contain clear examples in which people with means or reputation might plead guilty in General Sessions to avoid the embarrassment or humiliation flowing from a public trial or even to avoid an appearance in court altogether:

> *Marcus Tully,*[33]
> Marcus Tully is ... a young Englishman, whether of *respectable connexions* or not, he did not stay long enough in the prisoner's box to inform us. During the term of June, he pleaded guilty to an indictment for petit larceny in stealing a pocket-book of the value of three shillings, the property of Loring Palmer, and hurried from the bar, ashamed to stand a public trial ... (original emphasis).

> *George Lingan,*[34]
> Lingan was indicted for grand larceny in stealing a pocket-book containing more than $100 in promissory notes, the property of William Robertson. Considerable efforts were evidently made to shield the defendant from

---

[29] Weaver's sentence was suspended on this charge in case he should be pardoned for robbing Healy for which offence he was sentenced to state prison for life along with John Collins. The report does not mention any charge against Antonio who, presumably, was not apprehended at that time.

[30] See eg *Augustus M Stone* (1818) Rogers, vol 3, p 2.

[31] For a general account of the City's press over this period see Burrows and Wallace (1999) pp 522 ff.

[32] District Attorney's files, 7 February, 1835. The *New York Sun*, launched in 1833, was a mass circulation paper aimed at artisans with an emphasis upon sensational stories and a diet of crime: see Burrows and Wallace (1999) pp 523 ff.

[33] (1816) Rogers, vol 1, p 114.

[34] *Ibid.*

publicity which reporting of the case would create—a device always resisted by the nominative reporter, Daniel Rogers, as his account of the case makes clear:

The prisoner having been brought to the bar, the jury and the prosecutor being sworn, and the latter being about to give evidence, the counsel for the prisoner put this question to Robertson—'Is not the prisoner the son of the late general Lingan?'

Robertson 'I have understood so.'

Counsel The prisoner now pleads guilty.

By the Court We do not think that his being the son of general Lingan is much of a palliation of the offence.

Counsel (speaking low to the Reporter) You do not publish the *name* of every criminal brought before the court.

Reporter The *name* of such a criminal as this, with all the circumstances of his guilt, which the *Record* can furnish, I shall publish.

Counsel Why? He has very respectable friends.

Reporter His offence is therefore the greater; he has not only committed an offence against the *public*, but has abused his *friends*. The public have a right to know the contents of their own *records*—his friends have no right to complain. (original emphasis)

The efforts made to shield Peter Kettletas[35] from publicity were even greater. Kettletas was indicted in April 1816 for grand larceny in stealing treasury notes in the sum of $3,400.00 and four gold coins, the property of William Goelet Bucknor. In his account of cases dealt within the July Term, the nominative reporter Daniel Rogers, explained why the case of Kettletas had not been earlier reported:

We did not, at any time, see him in court, and we understand he was not publicly arraigned; but we did see and the people have a right and ought to see the *Record*. It is their property. He pleaded guilty.

Clearly, in an attempt to shield Kettletas from public shame, undue influence, no doubt linked in some way to the guilty plea, had been exercised. Such cases did not, however, predictably lead to the desired outcome. In his account of the case of Kettletas, for example, Daniel Rogers saw the defendant's background as aggravating rather than as mitigating his offence and as an opportunity to restate the principle of equality before the law, in language which the contextualists

---

[35] (1816) Rogers, vol 1, p 113.

might contend legitimated a system of criminal justice which was directed primarily at controlling the underclass of New York society:

> This young man, if we are correctly informed, had every inducement, which could operate on an ingenuous mind, to deter him from engaging in the business which he undertook. *He had respectable friends.* This circumstance, we allow, should prompt the feeling mind to commiserate *their* misfortune; but to *him*, it furnishes no excuse, no palliation; but, on the contrary, enhances his crime. What! Shall it be said, because a man, in addition to his other horrible crimes, has done all in his power to entail disgrace on worthy and respectable friends, that he is less a felon? Because, from an elevated situation, he has voluntarily degraded himself to the rank of a common negro-malefactor, who had ignorance, poverty and starvation, perhaps, to allege in extenuation of his crime—shall *he, the white, delicate, soft-handed thief,* who was, or ought to have been, taught better, not be amenable, at least, to an equal punishment?

> ... We meddle not with, we express no opinion concerning politics: it is foreign to our business; but, when speaking of the public administration of justice, our opinion, our language shall ever be decided. We do profess ourselves at open war with aristocracy; and we shall as inflexibly adhere to the maxim, that *all thieves are equal*, as the murderers of Lewis the XVI did to that which is similar but less true ... (original emphasis).

Court reporters were not alone in their distaste for giving a sentence reduction to those who pleaded guilty. An illustration of the contrarian attitude of the General Sessions' judges to differential sentences for guilty pleas, even those involving 'respectable gentlemen', is provided by the nominative reporter's description of the prosecution of John Alexander Kennedy and Richard B Swim:[36]

> The defendants, young men of about twenty one years of age and being 'of good external appearance' pleaded guilty to an indictment for conspiracy to steal from a store-house. A petition, signed by several 'respectable gentlemen', was presented to the court for the purpose of obtaining a suspension of the sentence of the defendants, that mercy might be extended to them. In pronouncing sentence, the Mayor made clear that they should suffer the full authority of the law and gave no indication of any credit being given for the guilty plea even though it was coupled with respectable character:
>
> > Had this been a dwelling-house instead of a store, your offence would have been burglary, which would have subjected you to imprisonment in the state prison for life.
> >
> > Under the peculiar circumstances of your case, the offence of which you have been convicted is of a very serious nature, and requires a punishment adequate to its enormity.

[36] (1816) Daniel Rogers, vol 1, p 170.

You are young men just entering on life, and the court is informed that your connexions are respectable. That you should stand at this bar in the awful situation of convicts, awaiting the sentence of the law, is much to be lamented. On this occasion, public expectation is excited, and it is hoped, that the example about to be made in your case, will be a salutary lesson, to young men of your age, in deterring them from the commission of similar offences. One of the principal objects of punishment is public example; and when young men in the situation in life wherein you have been placed and might have stood, with the advantage of respectable friends, become the objects of punishment, the example is more impressive than in those cases of punishment inflicted on common offenders.

Every criminal, whatever his situation in life, or connexions may have been, when convicted, is placed on an equal footing; and it would be a stigma on our system of jurisprudence, should the guilty be suffered to go unpunished, because his friends are respectable.

It now remains for the court to discharge the painful, but imperious duty of passing sentence on you. The sentence of the court is, that you John Alexander Kennedy and Richard B Swim, be imprisoned in the city penitentiary, each for a term of three years.

Another example of the court's contrarian attitude towards discounts for 'respectable' individuals who pleaded guilty occurred when a defendant sought to obtain the testimony of witnesses and was able to persuade the court to adjourn the matter for this purpose, after which it became clear that no such testimony was available and no other defences existed, as in the following prosecutions:

William Goldsby and James Covert,[37]
On a charge of possessing bills knowing them to be forged, Covert was tried and found guilty whilst Goldsby secured several adjournments on the ground of the absence of material witnesses. When the evidence in question could not be produced, Goldsby, a man of respectable background who kept a boarding house at No 172 Reed Street,[38] pleaded guilty to three indictments.

His efforts to forestall justice were to no avail. As reported by Daniel Rogers, in pronouncing sentence, the Mayor Jacob Radcliff said:

You, William Goldsby, have for several terms on divers pretences, applied to the court for a postponement of your trial, and the court has granted you every reasonable indulgence. Finding that you could delay it no longer, you have at length pleaded guilty to *three indictments* for

[37] (1816) Rogers, vol 1, p 81.
[38] This is disclosed in the case of *Lyman Rowley* (1816) Rogers, vol 1, 47 p 48. Elsewhere, Rogers describes Goldsby as among the 'most illustrious' seen in the courts: (1816) Rogers, vol 1, p 114.

> forgery, and having in your possession, with an intention of knowingly passing it, counterfeit money to a large amount.
>
> Considering the enormity of your offence, the court consider it a duty, in your case, to make a signal public example. You are now a man considerably advanced in years; and the term to which you are now about to be consigned to the State Prison, will be equal to imprisonment for life. The court sentence you to the State Prison *seven years on each indictment.* (original emphasis)

Even if fear of publicity induced some defendants to plead guilty and avoid the full glare of a trial, however, this is unlikely to have relevance for the mass of guilty pleas which involved people not drawn from the ranks of 'respectable' society. Thus, of those in our sample of case files who pleaded guilty (n=118), seven are recorded as having previous convictions, a further five are described as 'slaves', four more as 'boys'; three as being in a state of destitution; and a further fourteen are described as 'blacks' or 'yellow,' descriptors which indicate the disapprobrium that 'respectable' (white) society exercised in general towards members of minority groups. Although biographical information is scarce in most of the accounts of guilty pleas contained in the nominative reports, similar examples occur there, as in the prosecution of Jacob Johnson[39] a 'mulatto' who pleaded guilty having been 'brought to the bar in his state prison dress, having recently escaped from that place' and who was 'immediately sentenced to the State Prison for fourteen years.'

Protestations of innocence or excuse

Prosecutions where assertions of innocence were made in the face of substantial evidence of guilt illustrated dilemmas that confronted defendants and their legal advisers when considering whether to enter a guilty plea. We cannot fully evaluate decisions by counsel to withdraw when defendants sought to continue with the trial. However, we found one prosecution, Richard Chew,[40] where the defendant, having assessed the evidence, sought to plead guilty rather than proceed to trial, in which the Court itself appears to have departed from its fidelity to formalism, the facts of which appear in the following account of the nominative reporter:

> Richard Chew pleaded guilty to an indictment for an assault and battery, committed on Naphtali Phillips, in Fly-market. This assault, we understand, was wanton and unprovoked. The defendant, when arrested, denied that he was the man who committed the offence, and persisted in the denial until he found the proof against him would be conclusive. Even in court, when called

[39] (1817) Rogers, vol 2, p 60.
[40] (1815) Rogers, vol 1, p 152.

on for his plea, he said, 'I plead guilty, although I am not guilty'. He was ashamed, no doubt, to stand a public trial. The court imposed on him a fine of $25.

Because of the paucity of detail in this report, it would be unwise to set great store by this occurrence; but it appears on the face of it that the Court exceptionally accepted what is today known in the United States as an *Alford* plea, under which the court can accept a plea of guilty from a defendant who, with knowledge of the prosecution's evidence against him, continues to maintain in court that he is not guilty of the crime charged.[41]

In other cases, it was even more unexpected that a guilty plea would follow a flat denial by the defendant, given that the normal course of events in such prosecutions was a full trial rather than a guilty plea. Even so, in certain circumstances, it was occasionally possible to ascertain some factors that might have persuaded the defendant to accept responsibility, notwithstanding an earlier denial, as where the defendant was a predicate felon (repeat offender), arrested in compromising circumstances and unable to offer a convincing account to explain his or her possession of the stolen property, as illustrated by the following prosecutions from our sample of case files:

William McFeat,[42]

McFeat was charged with theft of the pocket-book of Charles Colyer which was taken at about seven o'clock in the afternoon in the fly market. Charles Colyer swore that he shortly afterwards found the pocket book in the possession of the defendant. McFeat's posture throughout his examination by Special Justice Montague was defiant and unforthcoming rather than convincing, a picture enhanced by his criminal background:

> 'William McFeat being examined says that he was Discharged from the State Prison on the ninth of February last—lodges with his wife at a Boarding House in Greenwich Street near the New Albany Basin—He knows nothing at all about ... Charles Collier's pocket book—he neither had nor took it—He came to Town yesterday from Albany in a vessel Commanded by a man he does not know—was married about four months ago to a woman by the name of Elizabeth Cutting in New Jersey—It makes no difference what name he went by the time he married the said woman—Examinant after admitting the above to be true refuses to sign his examination.'

---

[41] See *North Carolina v Alford* 400 US 25 (1970). The report in Chew's case does appear to indicate that the defendant's assertion of innocence was made at the point of entering the guilty plea rather than subsequent to it at the *allocutus* when defendants were asked whether they had anything they wished to say prior to sentence being passed.

[42] District Attorney's files, 8 August, 1805.

John Campbell,[43]

Two guages were stolen from the shop of Josiah Ward, a cabinet maker living at No. 40 Lumber Street who told the Special Justice that the guages
were later found in the possession of the defendant. John Campbell, a predicate felon,[44] could say only that the guages were his property and that he
'bought them about two months ago at Norwich about 14 miles from New
London ...'

In another group of prosecutions, the guilty plea was entered at General Sessions
following the defendant's examination before the Special Justice at which the
conduct complained of was admitted but with some explanation or excuse. Given
that the explanation or excuse was at best unsupported, the subsequent entry of a
guilty plea appeared quite provident and it was little more than the formal abandonment of a forlorn hope of escape. Thus, when caught stealing property or with
stolen property in his or her possession, the defendant might typically admit the
act of taking but claim that another unknown person had asked for the property
to be collected or that the property had been given to the defendant by a person
unknown. We set out below, some illustrations of such prosecutions taken from
our sample of case files:

David Marshall,[45]

David Marshall was indicted for the theft of a piece of smoked beef from
the store of John H Frederick, a grocer on the corner of Warren and Chapple
Streets, who witnessed the taking. David's excuse given at his examination
was partial and unconvincing, telling Special Justice Buckman that 'one John
Murphy whose place of abode [he] does not know last night sent him for the
said piece of smoked beef which the said Murphy said, he had purchased, and
gave [him] six pence to buy some liquor for the trouble of going after the said
piece of beef & on account of getting work for the said Murphy.'

John Campbell,[46]

While at an auction, John Layman had his pocket book and contents stolen
and shortly afterwards recovered it, except for one dollar, from John Campbell.
When examined, John Campbell did not dispute having possession of the
articles, telling Special Justice Montague that the items had been 'given to him
by a person whose name nor place of abode' he knew.

William Tryon, William Kingston and Peter Williams,[47]

The defendants were charged with theft of the contents of the money drawer of the grocery store belonging to Benjamin Green at the corner of Orchard

[43] District Attorney's files, 3 April, 1805.
[44] This was revealed at his examination when he was arrested a few months later: District
Attorney's files, 8 August, 1805.
[45] District Attorney's files, 4 April, 1805.
[46] District Attorney's files, 8 August, 1805.
[47] District Attorney's files, 15 March, 1820.

and Division Streets. At his examination, William Tryon, a fourteen year old boy, stated that William Kingston, who gave his age as fifteen, had 'got some liquor & made [Tryon] drunk' and that, in that condition, he had entered the grocery store and taken money from the drawer at Kingston's suggestion and that the three defendants had thereafter divided the proceeds of the crime. In large measure, Peter Williams and William Kingston corroborated this account, although Kingston claimed that the theft was entirely Tryon's idea.

Settlements

Statutory authority authorised, in assault and battery cases and in certain misdemeanour offences that, where there was injury, the citizen-prosecutor and accused could settle the matter by restitution and payment of damages.[48] These were the only clear cases in which the non-trial disposition resulted from negotiation between the parties rather than a unilateral act by one of the parties to terminate the adjudicatory process.

An example of such settlements occurred in the prosecution of Richard Chew,[49] Chew, a Boarding House Keeper, was charged with assault and battery on Joseph Dorset, a cordwainer, and an indictment to this effect was filed on 14 October 1809. Prior to that, however, there are indications that the parties were close to settling their differences, an endorsement on the complaint, subsequently cancelled, recording: 'Let the prosecution be Discontinued Oct. 3rd 1809.' No doubt, discussions continued and the matter was eventually 'Settled by parties' on 7 December, 1809 and recorded on the jacket of the indictment.

The practice of settling assault and battery cases in this way was, however, infrequent and normally limited to disputes of a *personal* character. By contrast, assaults which involved more general disorder—such as affray or riot—were not susceptible to settlement by the private parties and such cases had to go through the full adjudicatory process resulting in a trial or guilty plea. An exceptional course, however, was taken in the prosecution of Amos Broad,[50] whose activities as a minister of religion were the focus of persistent unrest in the City:[51]

> According to his own account, Amos Broad had purchased a church at 51 Rose Street in about 1810 and had officiated there as a minister of the baptist denomination until 1817 with the exception of about a year. The sermons of Broad, a self-appointed evangelical who portrayed himself as a messiah,

---

[48] 1801 *Laws of the State of New York*, Chapter LX, Sections xviii and xix, p 264. In such cases, the District Attorney would enter a *nolle prosequi* upon appearance of the complainant before the court with acknowledgement that he or she had received satisfaction for the injuries inflicted. The provision for settlement did not extend to any assault and battery or other misdemeanour committed by or on any officer or minister of justice: *ibid*, p 264.

[49] District Attorney's files, 7 December, 1809.

[50] (1819) Rogers, vol 3, p 7.

[51] See also an earlier case of riot and assault and battery which took place in the Church of Broad at Rose Street: *John Scott et al* (1817) Rogers, vol 2, p 25.

continually attracted riotous opposition such that his church was often the scene of disorder.[52] In an earlier case centered on the church, it appeared that 'much noise and disturbance' had been made during divine worship, that boys had 'fired crackers', and that the church had been damaged by rioters. Whereas Amos Broad had been the complainant in the previous court case, he now faced an indictment containing four counts in which he was charged with keeping a disorderly and ill-governed house ('meaning his pretended church in Rose-street'); being a common sabbath breaker and profaner of the Lord's day; having caused and procured divers disorderly persons to meet and assemble together at the same place; and assaulting John W Jarvis.

At Broad's trial, the Recorder presided, the Mayor declining to sit because, having been frequently called out with other magistrates to suppress riots in Broad's church and having expressed his opinions so freely to Mr Broad, he felt that Broad would consider him biased and, in any event, he might be called as a witness in the case. More than one hundred witnesses for the prosecution were said to have left their business in order to be in court. On behalf of Amos Broad, however, counsel successfully moved for the postponement of the trial because of the absence of material witnesses, and he was bound over to be of good behavior for thirty days or until his trial on condition that he furnished personal recognizance of $2,000 and two sureties of $1,000 each.[53]

Subsequent to this undertaking, an affidavit was filed in the court by counsel for Broad stating, in effect, that on the advice of his friends, he had decided not to preach in his Church in the future and to dispose of it as soon as possible. In furtherance of this undertaking, Mr Broad delivered the key of the church to one of his counsel, Dr Graham, and executed a bond, in the penal sum of $5,000, promising not to preach in his church again and that he would dispose of it within six months. It was this set of voluntary undertakings by Amos Broad which put into question the appropriate way of disposing of the case.

Prosecution counsel argued that, in these circumstances, the trial should proceed unless Amos Broad would consent to plead guilty to the several indictments. However, the court was not happy to require this, particularly in a case involving delicate issues of religion.

... [T]he court expressed a decided disapprobation of proceeding in that manner, stating that they considered the object of the prosecution attained, by the voluntary submission and engagements on the part of the defendant, that the subject, involving the right of religious worship, was delicate in its nature, and ought not unnecessarily to be brought in question; and if the

---

[52] For a more detailed account of Broad's activities, see P Gilje (1987b) pp 214–20.

[53] The two sureties who stood for Mr Broad were his counsel, Dr Graham, and his associate counsel, Mr Pike: see (1818) Rogers, vol 3, p 9.

defendant should not comply with his engagements, the indictments would remain, and he might afterwards be brought to trial.

In this way, the court effectively approved of the settlement of the case not on an agreement between the parties but on the basis of Broad's undertaking and by deferring or suspending the prosecution and leaving the indictment on the file to be reactivated in the event of future breach.[54]

Exceptionally, the court might give its imprimatur to agreements between the parties in cases other than assault and battery. Whilst the court was generally hostile to any suggestion that there should be a compromise of any kind between the private prosecutor and the defendant we did find one case, Matthew R Lewis, John Thompson and John R Turner,[55] in which a private arrangement involving restitution was taken into account by the court in imposing sentence, although it did not displace the entry of a formal guilty plea in court. In that case, the defendants were indicted for conspiracy to obtain goods and chattels by fraudulent means. At the first trial, the jury failed to agree and were discharged. It is clear from the nominative report of the case that prior to the re-trial a settlement had been reached involving those who were the object of the fraud:

> On Tuesday the 12th of October, the prisoners were again brought to trial; and after Van Wyck [the District Attorney] had opened the case, and called one witness, they pleaded guilty to the indictment.
>
> An arrangement, as we understand, had been entered into, by which the prisoners agreed, as far as might be in their powers, to satisfy the creditors.
> The prisoners were each fined $100, and the costs.

The outcome here reflected the overall principle that once a prosecution had been initiated, justice should result in a trial or guilty plea regardless of any settlement or bargain. Where a bargain of any kind had been made, the courts were quick to voice their disapproval, as appears from the account drawn from in the nominative report of the prosecution of John Collins:[56]

> John Collins, 'a foreigner of good appearance', was indicted for stealing watches and articles of jewellery, from the store of Joseph Burjeau, an auctioneer in the city.

---

[54] 'On file' dispositions were discussed at length by George Fisher (2000) who found that in Sussex County, Massachusetts, this process, in effect, was a method of non-trial disposition equivalent to plea bargaining. However, our analysis of the District Attorney's case files, the Minute Book of the Court of General Sessions and the nominative reports showed no indication that this practice was regularly employed in New York City, as Fisher found in Sussex County. Indeed, as we indicated above, the case of Broad was an exceptional manner of settling assault and battery cases which extended beyond disputes between individuals to those which confronted the wider society.

[55] (1820) Rogers, vol 5, p 129.

[56] (1819) Rogers, vol 4, p 139.

When first arrested, Collins was brought to the Police Office where a large chest in his possession was searched in the presence of Special Justice Hopson. None of the property of Burjeau was found on Collins or in his chest and he was accordingly discharged.

Afterwards, Lucretia Woolsey entered a fresh complaint against him for having, while a boarder, stolen from her $300. He was arrested and committed as a vagrant by Special Justice Christian. Mrs Woolsey then brought into the Police Office a gold watch and a coral which Collins had given to Mrs Woolsey's daughter. These items were known to belong to Burjeau; and Collins, on being brought from the Bridewell, admitted that he did give them to Miss Woolsey. On this, he was committed as a felon by Justice Christian after which a bargain was then struck between Collins and Joseph Burjeau, as described by the nominative reporter:

> It was deemed desirable that Burjeau should recover the residue of the property; and to that end, he came to the police office, and made a bargain with Messrs Gardenier and Simons, the counsel for the prisoner, that if a clue was given by which the property could be recovered, that the disclosure should not operate to the prejudice of the prisoner on the trial.

In fact, though Collins did direct Abner Curtis, a marshal, Joseph Burjeau and others to a trunk, none of the stolen items was recovered and the jury was left to decide whether Collins had stolen everything on the basis of the evidence supplied by Mrs Woolsey.

In summing up for a conviction, the Mayor spoke out strongly against the discussion that had taken place between Collins and counsel for Burjeau:

> In the conclusion, the mayor took occasion to protest against the practice of bargaining between a prosecutor and prisoner, as in this case. It was obviously wrong, and would never be tolerated by the court. It was the duty from one whom property has been stolen to prosecute the felon to conviction; and never, through motives of interest or compassion, suffer him to elude the arm of justice.[57]

CONCLUSION

Whilst a trial was the expected method to be followed in deciding criminal cases in the first half of the nineteenth century, disposition by way of a guilty plea was an entirely normal aspect of the criminal justice process, albeit in a minority of cases. The guilty pleas that were entered were for the most part to the top count in the indictment and thus the explanation for the avoidance of trial must be sought in factors personal to each case. There is evidence that some defendants

---

[57] Following conviction, Collins received seven years imprisonment in State prison.

sought to avoid a trial because of the shame that attendant publicity would bring to themselves or their family, whilst others appear to have entered guilty pleas after abandoning hope of escaping justice or after being abandoned by their own lawyers. Whatever the underlying motivations, once guilty pleas were entered most defendants were exposed to sentences which were as harsh as those that would have followed conviction at trial. Explicit or implicit bargaining over plea was not, in short, a feature of criminal justice in the first half of the nineteenth century in New York City and was explicity deprecated by the Court.

Chapter 8
Sentencing in General Sessions

INTRODUCTION

In this chapter, we examine the sentencing practices of General Sessions in the early decades of the nineteenth century in order to understand whether the sentencing of offenders in the pre-modern era was unreflective and, to that extent, primitive or to what extent it related to the individual offender, degree of culpability as well as the offence charged. We also examine to what extent sentences tended to fall within standardised ranges and whether the court engaged in episodic leniency as part of a process of legitimation.

We begin with a discussion of the ambit of sentencing followed by an analysis of the framework of penality employed by judges in the imposition of sentence. We then consider the role of such factors as culpability, character of the defendant, race, gender and ethnicity in the sentencing decision. Thereafter, we consider the procedure employed at the sentencing stage including evidence in mitigation, the defendant's statement, the court's own investigation and the exercise of discretion.

THE AMBIT OF SENTENCING

Commentators have asserted that pre-modern penal systems were heavily focused upon gradations of offence in which punishment was a function mostly of the seriousness of the infraction itself. By contrast, they argue, as the modern system of penality gained ascendancy by the early years of the twentieth century it became characterized by its focus upon the offender. As David Garland put it in his analysis of the transformation of British penality at the end of the nineteenth century:[1]

> [T]here was a qualitative change in the criteria of assessment in so far as many of the new sanctions directed attention towards the type of character and antecedents possessed by the offender, rather than the gravity of the offence.

[1] D Garland (1985) p 24 (footnote omitted).

Garland adds that, whilst judges had no doubt taken some account of 'character' when sentencing in the pre-modern era, the twentieth century saw the introduction of a formalised and across-the-board system of character assessment and classification, qualitatively different from the traditional practices.[2]

Our analysis of sentencing practices in General Sessions shows that in deciding upon a particular sentence, the court was not limited to the gravity of the offence alone but could take into account a range of sources of information: the verdict of the jury; affidavits submitted in mitigation; a personal statement of the convicted person; and background information on the offender obtained by the court through its own investigations or through review of the Special Justice's file. Given that in the first half of the nineteenth century most penal statutes prosecuted in General Sessions authorised sentencing within a range of years and/or a fine, individual factors had the potential to influence final sentence except in those cases where the sentence was mandatory (usually involving second offenders).[3] Thus, the court had considerable sentencing discretion enabling it to hand out token punishments to the least culpable or to pass exemplary sentences on those deemed incorrigible.[4]

The framework of penality

The sentencing of offenders took place within a framework of penality that was seen both as distinctively American and, through the lens of General Sessions' judges, as uniquely able to calibrate punishments in order to achieve the objectives of retribution, deterrence and reformation. The general philosophical background of the system prevailing in the post-revolutionary period, with its intellectual origins significantly influenced by the philosophy of Cesare Beccaria,[5] was set out by the nominative reporter, Jacob Wheeler, in the preface to his criminal case reports of 1823 and 1824. The concern was that, as nations progressed in civilisation and science, their laws, once harsh and cruel, would be replaced by more humane and enlightened criminal codes. This tempering process was felt to be at its most advanced state in America:

---

[2] D Garland (1985) p 34.

[3] Prior to 1829, sentences authorised by statute for felonies above petit larceny were up to fourteen years, while petit larceny and felonies under petit larceny were for terms of not more than three years. See 1807 *Compilation of Laws of the State of New York* (*Acts of 1783–1801*), Session 24, Chapter LVIII, Act of March 21, 1807; 1813 *Laws of the State of New York*, Session 36, Chapter XXIX, Act of March 19, 1813. Beginning with the Revised Statutes of 1829, the sentence range authorised for petit larceny was not more than six months in the County Gaol and/or a fine of $100, while offences above petit larceny extended from not more than one year in County Gaol to between not more than two and ten years in State Prison or, where mandatory, not less than between two and ten years or life: 1829 *New York Revised Statutes*, Part IV, Chapter 1. For certain offences, the sentence was prescribed by statute.

[4] Not only did the court have discretion as to whether to imprison or not, and as to the term of years to which a person might be sentenced, but it could also impose particular types of imprisonment such as hard labour, imprisonment in chains, or solitary confinement. See L Masur (1987) 8:21.

[5] Beccaria's treatise, *Essays on Crime and Punishment* (1764) was the inspiration for reformers in New York, like Thomas Eddy, as well as for those in England such as John Howard.

In Modern Europe ... the several criminal codes are marked with many shades of cruelty and barbarity, that have gradually been becoming lighter, but will take many changes to become a perfect colour.

A comparison between the laws of the different States of Europe and the United States of America, cannot fail to strike the most inattentive observer: not only as it respects the quantum of punishment to a specific crime, for it is confessedly notorious that the sanguinary and cruel nature of the criminal laws of the United States bears no proportion to those of the different States of Europe: but also the *manner* in which they are administered.[6]

The merciless structure of European criminal codes[7] was seen to be a cause of increased crime and offensive to moral sentiments,[8] while the rejection of cruel and unusual punishments by the Eighth Amendment of the Constitution of the United States was considered as one of the glories of the revolution:[9]

The cruel and barbarous punishments of burning, beheading, quartering, impaling, burning in the hand, corruption of blood, etc. do not exist in the United States. The imperfection and cruelty of former systems were known and considered by those great and good men, who laid the foundation upon which has been erected the superstructure of our criminal code. Here, the punishment is tempered with mercy, but, at the same time, graduated by the enormity of the crime.

Drawing upon the principles set forth by writers such as Bentham, Beccaria, Montesquieu and Pufendorf, the claim was that America stood foremost in its adoption of a system of penality that was modern and moderate:[10]

America, yet in her infancy, in the improvement she has made in her criminal code, has all the knowledge, discretion and vigour of the most ripened age. Her codes of criminal law have become models to many of the ancient States. America has not only already felt, and still feels, justice tempered by mercy: but this sensation has been spread abroad by her influence and her example. The bright example has been set, and it has already been partially followed, and will be followed as long as truth shall prevail over error.

Celebrated as a model of the frugality of punishment, the sentencing system had to be applied to individual offenders and in this regard it reproduced the broader ideology of deterrence. The right to punish was based on the construction of the

[6] Wheeler, vol 1 Preface p 7.
[7] For a discussion of the 'Bloody Code' of England see D Hay (1977). See also P Linebaugh (1991); R McGowen (1987); and V Gatrell (1994).
[8] The concept of the proportionality of punishment was justified through reliance upon the reasoning of Jeremy Bentham, 'Theorie des Peines et des Recompense' published in the *Edinburgh Review*, vol 43.
[9] Wheeler, vol 2 Preface p xiii.
[10] Wheeler, vol 1 Preface p 10.

offender as a juridical personality, both a rational being and a moral agent. As a social animal, man was seen as accountable to himself and to others:[11]

> He finds new relations constantly springing up around him, new responsibilities imperceptibly attaching him to more numerous objects: family, kindred, and all mankind pass in succession before him, and all those thousands and tens of thousands of complicated and important relations that grow out of property, liberty, and life. Man is not only a social but a reasonable being, not only rational, but moral, and, therefore, accountable.

The application of these general principles to the imposition of sentence was articulated by the court in a case of possession of counterfeit bank bills, conviction for which often attracted long terms in state prison. After reporting the sentencing of six defendants each to seven-year terms for such offences in 1816, for example, the nominative reporter, Daniel Rogers, added this note:[12]

> The Court, in pronouncing sentence on the criminals convicted for passing money, observed that some time ago, they had hoped that a check was put to the commission of that offence. It was, however, a subject of regret that the evil had increased to an alarming degree. To exercise lenity and forbearance in such cases, they deemed inconsistent with the general good, and they were determined, for the purpose of repressing the crime, to make examples of such as might hereafter be convicted.

By admonishing, restraining and punishing the foolish, the rash, and the wicked, the system of penality was therefore claimed to bind society together in one bond of equal justice, despite the socio-economic inequalities in society.[13] And those who fell by the wayside, whether individually or in aggregate, were seen as lacking moral virtue and, temporarily, immune to the threat of sanction. Thus, in seeking to explain the disproportionate involvement in crime of 'young boys and coloured people,' the nominative reporter, Jacob Wheeler, emphasised a lack of moral principle and a failure to transmit moral values:[14]

> It must be apparent to the most superficial observer, ... that the proportion of young boys and coloured people charged with crimes is far too great in proportion to the whole.

> It has already furnished matter of complaint to the citizen, and it can only be accounted for by supposing (as the fact is) the absence of moral discipline, and a hardened contempt of punishment among this class of people. Considering the limited number of the black population, it is a matter of regret and astonishment that so great a proportion should furnish business

---

[11] *Ibid*, pp 5–6.
[12] (1816) Rogers, vol 1, p 134.
[13] Wheeler, vol 1 Preface p 6.
[14] *Ibid*, pp 11–2.

to our courts of justice, and can only be accounted for by supposing a neglect of them by the more respectable part of the community.

Additionally, as in England, mercy towards wrongdoers considered artless and lacking in guile remained a feature of criminal justice in republican America.[15]

SENTENCING FACTORS

Culpability

Our research revealed that General Sessions' judges recognised degrees of culpability among offenders that might be reflected in sentencing practice. In reaching a determination as to the respective involvements in the offence, the court would often look at the evidence in its entirety including, where considered relevant, those matters that the jury had been instructed to ignore in considering liability. Thus, for example, though the jury would be instructed to disregard any portion of a confession of one defendant before the Special Justice in so far as it incriminated the co-accused, the court, in apportioning punishment, would look at the totality of the examination.[16]

At a more general level, the court sought to identify the independent roles played by co-defendants and reflect their involvement both in the sentence and in the sentencing homily that ordinarily sought to justify the varying levels of punishment. An example of the process at work is the case of James Wyms, Patrick Wyms and John Martin,[17] who were jointly charged with committing assault and battery on James Stuart.

> A few days before the offence, James Wyms went to a store in Brooklyn where James Stuart was at work measuring corn and provoked a fight with Stuart. On the day of the offence, Stuart came over from Brooklyn in a boat to Crane-warf where he was set upon by the defendants. When he ran into Mott and Williams' store for protection, he was followed by James Wyms who struck at him with a club. When the club was taken from James, Patrick Wyms gave him an axhelve. After the defendants were detained at the scene, they were taken to the police office where James Wyms was found to have a cocked pistol upon him, and three large clubs and another weapon with a large iron on the end of it were recovered from the defendants. As described by the court reporter, in passing sentence, the Mayor drew a distinction between the defendants in terms of their respective involvements in the crime:

[15] For English practice, see P King (1984); and C Conley (1991). For an account of the role of defence lawyers in constructing defendants as deserving of mercy to attract the sympathy of juries and judges, see Michael Millender (1996) pp 121 ff.

[16] See eg, *Peter Bowerhan et al* (1819) Rogers, vol 4, p 136.

[17] (1818) Bacon, p 62. Another co-defendant, John Rooney, failed to appear at trial.

You, James Wyms, if the full desert of your offence had been understood, must have been brought here this day for an assault and battery
with intent to murder, and have met your punishment accordingly. You
threatened to kill the prosecutor, and had the means to kill him on your
person. As it is, we must do what justice we can, under the indictment
for assault and battery. The court sentence you to two years hard labour
in the penitentiary.

You, Patrick Wyms, are but little behind in guilt. On seeing James
stopped in his murderous purpose and his club taken from him, and an
uproar already excited among the citizens; so far from relenting or
thinking at all of the savage business you were upon, you volunteered
to furnish him another weapon to complete his design. You, Patrick
Wyms, the court sentence to eighteen months in the Penitentiary.

As to you, John Martin, though not implicated to the full extent of
either of the Wyms, it is necessary for us to inflict on you a sufficient
measure of punishment, to teach you to beware of similar undertakings
in the future. Foreigners must be taught, when they come to this country to avoid the oppression of the laws of their own, or whatever may
be their inducement, that our laws must be respected; and they are not
to calculate, that because this is a free country, they shall be allowed to
indulge in whatever wantonness of outrage their turbulent passions
may inspire. We sentence you to imprisonment in the Penitentiary for
a term of one year.

Character of the defendant

Whilst differing degrees of involvement in an offence affected final sentence,
'character' also had an impact upon sentence outcome and was an animating feature that governed punishment tailored to the individual. As a juridical subject in
a laissez-faire society, each citizen was inscribed with rationality and free choice.
In so far as individuals fell foul of the rules of society, the strength of condem-
nation would vary according to the degree of moral turpitude exhibited by the
offender, so that those who repeatedly offended or who had deliberately chosen
a lawless lifestyle deserved the greatest censure, whilst those who were first
offenders, or whose infraction was the result of mistake or artlessness rather than
wickedness, deserved the least. The symmetry between the market economy and
the legal economy of punishment thus rested upon the legislature's and the
court's estimate of the offender's moral culpability and capacity to become inte-
grated into the market economy as measured by the offender's character.

The clearest indication of the relevance of character at sentencing was the concern voiced by the judges with the criminal record of the defendant, in so far as
it demonstrated a propensity to persistently commit crimes, that the individual
had not reformed and was, if not incorrigible, in need of additional punishment to

correct the character defect that was evidenced by repeated transgressions of the law. Indeed, the court might even construe the acquittal of a person without a criminal record as an opportunity to warn the defendant of the enhanced punishment which would follow from any future successful prosecution, as illustrated in the case of Lemuel H Mitchell.[18]

> Mitchell, a man said by the court reporter to be of respectable background and who had been a lieutenant in the recruiting services, was acquitted on two indictments for grand larceny. The nominative reporter's account states that, after thanking the jury, Mitchell was about to leave the prisoner's box when he was addressed by the court:
>
>> Mitchell—You have had a very narrow escape. The court much regret to see a young man of your appearance in this awful situation. We know of your relations, and their respectability, and we cannot but feel for them. On this occasion, although we do not say you are guilty, yet we deem it incumbent on us solemnly to admonish you to amend your past life, to refrain from evil, and endeavor to retrieve your character. Above all, remember, that if ever hereafter you are arraigned in this court, it will not then be said, 'this is the first time;' but it will be known you had been here before, and you will be dealt with accordingly. You may now depart.

Sentencing of defendants with a prior criminal record was not an uncommon experience for judges of General Sessions given the liberal pardoning power exercised by the Governor in response to prison overcrowding.[19] However, where defendants with prior criminal records and a history of imprisonment reappeared, their bad character would aggravate the sentence, as exemplified in the reporter's account of John McEvoy:[20]

> The *Mayor* remarked to *McEvoy*, that he was an old offender—that he had been convicted three times—(Prisoner, interrupting, *My dear sir, if I transgressed I suffered for it, and I don't think I ought to be punished again for what I did.*) The Mayor.—In 1795, when you were quite a boy, you were sent to the State Prison—in 1805, when I was district attorney, I tried you for grand larceny, and you were sentenced to the State Prison again for three years. Either your *name* or your *countenance* was familiar to me, as soon as you were now put to the bar. Since 1805, you have been in the Penitentiary; you ought to set a better example. These are reasons for severity of punishment against you. The court have a large discretion, they can sentence you for one day or three years—Penitentiary two years, at hard labor on the roads in chains.

[18] (1816) Rogers, vol 1, p 43.

[19] The nominative reports criticised the pardoning practices which led to predicate felons coming again before the courts. See eg (1820) Rogers, vol v, p 170. See generally, W David Lewis (1965) pp 41–5.

[20] (1819) Bacon, p 325.

Although lacking in such rich detail, accounts of cases in the nominative reports commonly explain differential sentencing of co-defendants, otherwise not distinguished in their involvement in the crime, in terms of the predicate status of the individual given the highest sentence.[21] Thus, for example, on their joint conviction for grand larceny in 1816, Benjamin Gannon was sentenced to five years in the state prison whereas his co-defendant, Jesse Hopkins, received seven years in the state prison the reporter adding, 'from which place (where he had been sentenced before for passing counterfeit money) he had lately been liberated';[22] and Sarah Peterson received seven years in state prison 'in which place [she] had been before', whereas her confederate, Hannah Johnson, who had never been to state prison, received only five years.[23]

Character was not simply a function of prior criminal record but directly linked to the defendant's status as a rational, legal subject possessed of a free will which enabled a choice between good and evil to be exercised. As such, and contrary to the argument of some commentators,[24] the fact that the defendant came from a respectable background, far from mitigating the offence, might be seen as an aggravating factor demonstrating a propensity to commit crimes out of choice or guile as opposed to necessity or naivety. Daniel Rogers, discussing the cases of individuals from respectable backgrounds heard in 1816, justified reporting such cases and explained the sentencing rationale:[25]

> The crime, rather than the criminal should ever be the subject of public recrimination. At the same time we must be permitted to say, that where the influence of education, and the good example of respectable friends, have been lost and contemned by a young man, who, notwithstanding these powerful incentives in the ingenuous mind to virtuous actions, has become depraved in principle, and by his villany has disgraced his friends, and fixed a stigma on his name, justice demands a tenfold punishment on his devoted head.

> The low, worthless, abandoned offender, consigned by the unerring sentence of the law to the State-prison, till his *'foul crimes are purged away'* had not the example, the reproof and admonition of a virtuous, respectable father ... His was not that mother who, even while in his infancy, watched with a tender solicitude over the dawning reason of her smiling progeny,

---

[21] See also: *William Allen and William Pettinger* (1817) Rogers, vol 2, p 24; *Jacob Shourt, Thomas Davis and Joseph-Noel Fowler* (1817) Rogers, vol 2, p 37; *John Brandon and Elizabeth Griffiths* (1819) Rogers, vol 4, p 140; *John Smith, Washington Taylor and William McMurray* (1820) Rogers, vol 5, p 167.

[22] (1816) Rogers, vol 1, p 174.

[23] (1817) Rogers, vol 2, p 24.

[24] See eg, Hay (1977). Our findings in this regard accord with King's account of sentencing criteria operative in England in the eighteenth century. King's data are discussed in Langbein (1993) pp 113–14. King found that the most important factors in mitigating sentence were: good character, youth, the circumstances of the crime, poverty of the defendant or his family, with respectability of the defendant or his family being the least important.

[25] (1816) Rogers, vol 1, p 41.

and taught his stammering tongue to articulate the name of Him who dwelleth in the heavens—who taught him, that to be happy here and hereafter, he must 'remember his Creator in the days of his youth ...' (original emphasis)

The sentiments expressed by Rogers found an echo in General Sessions where judges were affronted by having to deal with those who had thrown away the advantages of respectable background and chosen instead a life of crime. Such a case was that of Solomon Valentine[26] who appeared to be about twenty-two years of age and of 'handsome address'. Valentine was convicted on a series of indictments for stealing and obtaining goods by false representations and sentenced in the following terms as described by the nominative reporter, Daniel Bacon:

> The *Mayro* (sic), in pronouncing sentence, remarked that he was found guilty of several acts of petit larceny, and obtaining goods under false pretences; that the amount stolen was not sufficient, in either case, to constitute the crime of grand larceny; that he was more guilty than the wretch who is induced to steal to gratify his hunger: that he had adopted swindling as a *system of living*; that no ordinary caution could have guarded against him; that at one time he represented himself as a merchant in Broad-way, at another time as a wholesale merchant from the country; that he talked of his children; that no ordinary caution, not even the greatest prudence, could have guarded against him; that he might have entered any store in the city and obtained goods.

> The court sentenced this accomplished villain to the penitentiary for three years, on the first indictment; six months on the second, the same on the third, the same on the fourth, in succession, each term to commence after the termination of the preceding.[27]

In a similar way, the maturity of a defendant might be a cause for an increment in punishment since the defendant had had the opportunity to learn the rules of society and the need for them to be observed. The prosecution of Peter Bowerhan, Samuel Hopkins and William Vanderburgh[28] is an example in point. Here, Vanderburgh was an adult and his confederates boys, a point strongly emphasised by the Mayor in his summation to the jury. Should the jury convict, the Mayor believed that they would agree with him that Vanderburgh, 'in a moral point of view, was doubly guilty', because of his position in respect to his co-defendants:[29]

[26] (1819) Bacon, p 326.

[27] The 'respectable' background of the defendant is further confirmed by an addendum to the report of the case: 'After the prisoner had been sentenced, at the request of his counsel and some respectable acquaintances of his friends, Mr Hays, the high-constable of the city, very politely granted permission for the prisoner to be conveyed to the Penitentiary in a carriage': (1819) Bacon, p 328.

[28] (1819) Rogers, vol 4, p 136.

[29] (1819) Rogers, vol 4, p 136 138. Those who were unrepentant also attracted the wrath of the court, as in *Smith and Kingston* (1819) Bacon, p 255 where the defendants were sentenced to hard labour for

He was a man; the others were but boys: and, if guilty, he was the master-
spirit who directed every operation in this atrocious transaction.

It was for this reason that Vanderburgh received a sentence of five years in State
Prison alongside Bowerhan, a predicate felon who had been pardoned out of the
penitentiary only six months earlier,[30] whereas Hopkins received a term of only
three years.

While few factors were allowed to mitigate punishment, judges understood the
temptations of a market economy[31] and might be more forgiving to those who
were young and inexperienced in life, for whom imprisonment could sully character and prospects.[32] And where the court concluded that the offence had been
committed under an honest mistake of law, it might exceptionally impose a nominal sentence.[33]

Sentencing tariffs: race, gender and ethnicity

We could find no evidence that sentencing was routinely influenced by external-
ities such as race and sex, even where defendants made restitution, confessed or
pleaded guilty rather than having been convicted after trial. Whilst caution needs
to be exercised because of deficiencies in recording practices, an exhaustive
analysis of cases reported by the nominative reporters failed to uncover evidence
that race and gender had any systemic impact upon sentencing.[34] Defendants
convicted of the same or of similar offences tended to be sentenced within well-
defined bands with, as we shall see differentials according to the culpability and
character of the accused. For example, sentences of grand larceny convictions
recorded in our Minute Book sample showed that some 26 per cent received one
day to three years, 43 per cent between three years one day and five years, and
the remaining 31 per cent were given over five years. An illustration of the sentencing tariff appears in the cases of thirteen defendants involved in ten separate

---

the period of their natural lives after conviction for highway robbery committed in circumstances
which were not of 'a very outrageous description' but where, at trial, the defendants 'continued laugh-
ing' at something in the appearance of a poor wretch who was placed between them and the bar thereby evincing 'an advancement in depravity, and a rare proficiency in guilt' rarely seen in young men.

[30] Whilst the pardoning practices of Governors was viewed as problematic, the court reminded
gaolers that the validity of any pardon of a defendant with a case now pending before General
Sessions was a matter within its province rather than that of correctional authorities: *John Merrit*
(1819) Rogers, vol 4, p 58.

[31] See Millender (1996) p 110.

[32] *The People v Judah* (1823) Wheeler 2, p 26.

[33] *The People v Melvin et al* (1810) Wheeler 2, p 262. This was a case charged as a conspiracy under
which the defendant cordwainers had established themselves as a union ('club') with the purpose of
bettering their working conditions and, through strikes, forcing employers to employ only members
of the union. The court decided that the defendants had 'erred from a mistake of law' and should be
fined one dollar each plus costs in 'order to admonish than to punish'.

[34] Very occasionally, the court might impose a nominal penalty where the defendant had made full
satisfaction to the complainant in property cases, as in *Neal G Malcolm* (1816) Rogers, vol 1, p 60.

property indictments in the April Term, 1816, each of whom was sentenced to a term of three years and one day in State Prison.[35] Of these, three men and two women were described as 'black'.[36] In some of these cases, the property the subject of the crime was fully restored,[37] in others it was not recovered.[38] In some the defendant made a confession when apprehended,[39] was convicted on confession[40] or pleaded guilty in court,[41] whereas in others the defendant denied the offence and was convicted after trial.[42] Similar sentencing practice is reported elsewhere.[43]

This outcome is perhaps less surprising than might at first appear. The fact that people of colour, for example, were treated little differently as a group than their white counterparts for sentencing purposes, should not be taken as evidence that racial stereotypes did not permeate the thinking of General Sessions judges as it did elsewhere in American society. Rather, the racial representation of 'black' people—as criminogenic or as more susceptible to temptation by reason of their reduced circumstances and failure to adopt beneficial values—worked not only paternalistically against sentence enhancement, but also against mitigation of sentencing for those who had begun life with every advantage that the 'good' society could offer.

The approach of the judges to 'foreigners' similarly began with an idealised representation of the 'American' citizen who provided the standard against which everyone was to be judged. In this understanding, American-born citizens lived under a set of laws which maximised human freedom whilst removing the tyranny of colonial oppression and which established a framework of governance both deserving and attracting respect and compliance by reason of its humanity and

[35] See (1816) Rogers, vol 1, p 57.

[36] One of the black women, Mary Williams, was found guilty of stealing from Moses Richards, 'another black'.

[37] As in *John Halliday* (1816) Rogers, vol 1, p 70 in which the stolen items were then redeemed from a pawnbroker's shop where the defendant had pledged them.

[38] *Miles McDonald* (1816) Rogers, vol 1, pp 69–70 who stole a silver watch: 'He was found a short time afterwards, but the watch has not yet been found.'

[39] *William Disley* (1816) Rogers, vol 1, p 70. The defendant, on being apprehended by Disbrow, a Watchman, made a voluntary confession which 'was read in evidence, and was conclusive against him'.

[40] *James Jackson* (1816) Rogers, vol 1, p 70 is reported to have been 'convicted on confession of stealing a firkin of butter'.

[41] *Lucas Segretier* (1816) Rogers, vol 1, p 70. According to the report, Segretier, 'a young foreigner of good appearance (we judge a Frenchman) at the time of his arraignment and on trial and on receiving his sentence, exhibited a striking spectacle of grief, shame and remorse. He hid his faee (*sic*), which was bathed in tears, and when arraigned pleaded guilty ... The Court humanely put him on trial ...'

[42] *John Paine* (1816) Rogers, vol 1, p 64, and *John Ferguson, John Hatten and Thomas Smith* (1816) Rogers, vol 1, p 65.

[43] See eg the cases in the summary for September 1816, reported in Rogers, vol 1, pp 151–52 in which the defendants received sentences of three years and a day for offences of grand larceny and where two (one 'a Dutchman') 'confessed the felony', where the property was returned in some cases but not others, where two of the defendants were women, where two were 'black' and one 'a mulatto', and where two of the victims were black.

enlightenment. This implied both respect for the law and benevolence to those whose circumstances had temporarily placed them in a position of social disadvantage. Whilst for an American-born citizen to commit crime or to exploit those who were vulnerable was a betrayal of their heritage and below the standards set by native citizens, similar conduct by foreigners might be explicable in terms of the values and practices in their countries of origin.[44] In either event, the function of the judges was to deter such practices and to uphold the American ideal, as indicative of the court's remarks in the passing of sentences in the following prosecutions described by the nominative reporters:

George Hughes[45]

According to the nominative reporter, George Hughes, a young man probably not passing seventeen years of age, was one of a group of rogues who preyed on ignorant and unsuspecting foreigners just landed in New York, deceiving them of their money by various artifices. On conviction of two separate offences of grand larceny, the Mayor, in pronouncing sentence, commented on the aggravating features of the case in these terms:

> You say you are an American. We could hope, and have reason to think, it is not so. At any rate you have violated not only every feeling and principle that you ought to cherish as a man, but every sentiment you ought to entertain as a citizen of this country. You have fallen upon the poor stranger, the rigours of whose condition in his own land have urged him to encounter the perils and vicissitudes of emigration to our more favoured country, and robbed him of the little all, of the scanted pittance he had been able to scrape together by every means on his departure, to save himself and his family from suffering and beggary, a little while on his arrival, till he could engage himself in honest labour ...[46]

John Wyms, Patrick Wyms, John Martin and John Rooney[47]

This case involved an assault and battery on the victim with clubs and other implements. In sentencing the first three named defendants, the Mayor scathingly spoke of the unprovoked, vengeful and egregious character of the attack made upon the victim before adding:

> I know not what country you are of, nor will it at all affect the measure of your punishment; but so much I will venture to declare, that you can-

---

[44] See eg, *John Williams and Edward Gilgar* (1816) Rogers, vol 1, p 130. The defendants, described by the court reporter as 'Irishmen', were convicted of assault and battery with intent to rob and were put in the prisoners' box together with three other 'foreigners' (Palmer, Smith and M'Colgan) convicted of highway robbery: '... the court observed ... that until a short time past, their crimes were almost unheard of in this country. And it was a just subject of felicitation, and reflected much honor on our countrymen, that the commission of such heinous offences was confined principally to foreigners.'

[45] (1818) Bacon, p 57.

[46] (1818) Bacon, p 60.

[47] (1818) Bacon, p 62.

not have been native citizens of this country, brought up under our mild and enlightened system of laws, and in a community where outrages of this kind so seldom occur, and are so pointedly discountenanced.[48]

SENTENCING PROCEDURE

Public proceedings

The sentencing proceeding in General Sessions was an important event, taking place on the last day of each judicial term, when all prisoners convicted over the term were produced from Bridewell to be brought to the bar of the court often occurring in a crowded courtroom. Sentencing day was a public event deliberately infused with drama: like all proceedings from charge to verdict, sentencing was handed down both as a rejection of the private character of aspects of criminal procedure in some European states and as a cautionary example to others who might be tempted into criminal activity.

Evidence in mitigation

The verdict of the jury was the starting point for the sentencing process both in the sense that it fixed the offence for which punishment could be lawfully imposed and also because the jury could indicate to the court whether any mitigation in their view existed. In particular, the jury might attach a recommendation of mercy to their verdict. When this occurred, the court would seek to give effect to the recommendation even if it could see no basis for the jury's view.[49] An example in point is the prosecution of John Francis[50] who procured an acquittal on a charge of receiving stolen goods by producing two witnesses who committed perjury on his behalf. He was then tried and found guilty of suborning those witnesses despite persuading a further witness to commit perjury on his behalf and also forging a document to assist his defence. In convicting him, the jury recommended Francis to the mercy of the court, a recommendation to which the court gave weight even though it could see no basis for the view of the jury:[51]

> The offence of which you have been convicted, although unusual in our courts, is one of the most corrupt and diabolical that can be perpetrated in society, and calls loud for exemplary punishment.

---

[48] (1818) Bacon, p 64.

[49] The case of *Lawrence Pienovi* (1818) Rogers, vol 3, p 123 might be an exception. Pienovi was convicted of assault and battery by biting off the end of his wife's nose. In sentencing Pienovi to two years in the penitentiary, the mayor remarked that 'he was unable to see the reason of that recommendation: for surely none was afforded by the evidence.'

[50] (1816) Rogers, vol 1, p 121.

[51] (1816) Rogers, vol 1, pp 127–28. see also *Jane Bibbin* (1817) Rogers, vol 2, p 58.

> We know not the reason for which the jury recommended you to mercy. The
> court has seen nothing in your case which requires a mitigation of punish-
> ment. We have the power to sentence you to the State Prison ten years, and
> no other reason has induced the court to sentence you for a shorter period,
> except the recommendation of the jury.
>
> The sentence of the court is, that you, John Francis, be imprisoned in the
> State Prison seven years.

In an effort to persuade the court to be lenient, affidavits in mitigation could be
laid prior to sentencing. These were normally introduced by defence counsel but
might be expressly advised or invited by the court.[52] Strict rules governed the
admissibility of such affidavits that had to be directed towards mitigation without, however, challenging the facts that formed the basis of the conviction.[53]
Attempts to by-pass this rule were rebuffed by the court, as in the case of
Alexander Ball.[54] The defendant was indicted for grand larceny in stealing various bags of gold coin from the trunk of James Sanford with whom he had travelled from England on the ship *Elizabeth*. The money was discovered in a bed in
Ball's apartment in Cherry-street. Following his conviction, the defendant was
brought to the bar on the last day of term to receive sentence when his counsel,
Hawkins, introduced an affidavit in mitigation from Mary Ball, the defendant's
wife:

> He proceeded to read, that the deponent herself put the three bags of gold
> in the bed, etc.
>
> The mayor hereupon apprised the counsel, that the court had established a
> rule with regard to affidavits in mitigation: that they would never regard an
> affidavit which contradicted any of the facts on which the verdict was
> founded.
>
> In this case, it would be a manifest perversion of justice to suffer the affi-
> davit of the wife to be read, controverting the facts upon which the verdict
> was founded. The toleration of this practice would be a great temptation to
> commit perjury. The court admits affidavits in *mitigation*; not in *contradic-
> tion*. (original emphasis)

Affidavits in mitigation would, in any event, be viewed within the context of the
case itself and would not be permitted to displace what had been established in
the course of evidence. Thus, applications submitted on behalf of the defendants

---

[52] See eg *The People v Adam Pentz* (1823) Wheeler 1, p 240 where, after directing the jury to convict the defendant of assault and battery as charged, the Recorder recommended that affidavits in mitigation should be laid before the Court.
[53] See *The People v James Wyms et al* (1818) Bacon, p 62.
[54] (1819) Rogers, vol 4, p 113.

convicted of conspiracy to defraud in Edward Robbins and John Sheffield[55] fell on stony ground, the Mayor observing in sentencing both to imprisonment:[56]

> Nor is there, in the judgment of the court, any single fact, proved by the testimony on either side, that mitigates the character of the transaction. So far from any thing having appeared to induce a belief that either of the defendants thought Robbins had a right to these checks, their whole conduct shows that they well knew that no such right existed. And, therefore, they resorted to fraud, artifice, deception, and violence to obtain them.

The defendant's statement

The court also had the benefit of hearing from the defendant who, having been silenced during the trial itself by reason of incompetence, was accorded an opportunity to address the court prior to sentence. At this point in the procedure, known as the *allocutus*, the defendant would be asked a standard question: 'Have you anything to say why sentence should not be pronounced pursuant to conviction?'[57] How frequently defendants responded and what they said in answer, for the most part, cannot be discovered from the nominative reports. In a few reported instances, however, the defendant used the *allocutus* to advance some claim of innocence. Such protestations of innocence were peremptorily dismissed. The authentic voice of the defendant does, however, emerge in a few case reports. A tantalising insight into the clash of cultures which such exchanges involved is provided by the prosecution of James Robinson,[58] who was indicted for burglary, the sentence for which was life imprisonment. Having entered a house by scaling down a chimney, he gathered various articles to take away before being disturbed by the occupants. In his efforts to escape, Robinson attempted to get away by ascending a different chimney but could get up only a few feet before he was stopped by an iron bar that was embedded in the bricks across the flue. He was arrested by the house owner, Henry P Haven, handed over to the police, tried and convicted of burglary. The nominative reporter described the sentencing stage in the following terms:

> When brought to the bar the last day of term, to receive sentence, and the ordinary question put by the court, have you any thing to say why sentence should not be pronounced pursuant to conviction? He addressed the court with a great deal of audacity and bitterness.—'Hitherto,' he said 'he had considered this court the sanctuary of truth; but at present he didn't hardly know what to think of it. I am not guilty, I am wickedly condemned;' and added other rude and insolent expressions, calculated to produce in the breast

---

[55] (1819) Rogers, vol 4, p 1.
[56] *Ibid*, p 12.
[57] *People v James Robinson* (1819) Bacon, 256 p 257.
[58] *Ibid*. Robinson was represented by J R Scott, whose involvement in this part of the procedure is not revealed.

of the court every other sentiment of feeling, rather than tenderness and commiseration for him.

The *Mayor* addressing the prisoner. It is the law which pronounces your sentence; you have had a fair and impartial trial by a jury of your country, they have pronounced you guilty; and there is no doubt in the mind of the court of the correctness of their verdict. You broke into the house of a citizen in the dead of night, and were apprehended in the act.

Prisoner No, that is not right, they catch'd me when I was trying to get out.

The *Mayor* You must be silent, you have had an opportunity to speak; there is no question of your guilt; you entered the house with an intent to steal, and we have considered the point, and find no reasons to view the singular mode you adopted to make your way in, as varying your case from an ordinary burglary.

Prisoner I did not go down the chimney to steal, and I can prove it. I made a bet that I would go down one of the chimneys and come up the other; if that wasn't so, why did I not go up the same chimney that I came down.

The *Mayor* I tell you again you must be silent; if your representations are true, you should have brought your witness forward on the trial. The court sentence you to confinement at hard labour in the State Prison of the Southern District of the state of New York, for the term of your natural life.

Whilst, in most cases, similar assertions of innocence were summarily dismissed by the court, the request of the defendant occasionally was received with sympathetic consideration, as illustrated by the prosecution of Frederick Johnson.[59] Johnson was convicted of perjury committed in the Marine Court in an action brought by a seaman for his wages against the captain of a schooner. Upon his conviction by the jury in General Sessions, the nominative report gave the following account:

> *Prisoner* May it please the court,
>
> These men have wickedly combined against me, and I stand convicted before this tribunal: I am innocent, and shall not dread to meet them before the last tribunal, where they as well as myself must be judged. The favour I have to implore of your honors is, that I may be sent back to my native country, rather than to the State Prison.
>
> *By the Court* Where is your native country?
>
> *Prisoner* In Egypt, about 600 miles from Jerusalem.
>
> *By the Court* We will take the matter into consideration.[60]

---

[59] (1816) Rogers, vol 1, p 21.
[60] The sentence was suspended and the defendant deported.

Court investigation

In addition to information provided by the defendant, the Court could undertake its own enquiries into the background and character of the defendant prior to sentence. For this purpose, the Court could order a search of its own trial records, make similar enquiries in other states and consult other, unspecified, sources, prominent among which, no doubt, were the Special Justice's file and data known to the Police Office. The sources were not necessarily identified in court nor were the data subject to a contested hearing in open court. Some examples of these enquiries are set out below:

Joseph DeCosta[61]

Decosta, an 'inhabitant of Spanish America,' was indicted and convicted of obtaining $366 from Ernest Sandoz by false pretences. On conviction, he was sentenced to imprisonment for one year in the City Prison, 'the court observing, on pronouncing sentence, that they had satisfactorily ascertained that he had been engaged before in practices of a similar nature.'

John Storm[62]

Storm was indicted and convicted of conspiring to defraud and rob George W Hallick of his money. In sentencing Storm to three years imprisonment in the city penitentiary, the court observed, 'that from previous trials in this court, and from other sources, the court had satisfactorily ascertained, that the house of the defendant, was a general resort for many who had been concerned in the commission of crimes, and that the defendant had been in the habit of aiding, abetting and assisting those persons in their unlawful conduct.'

Simeon Van Houton[63]

Van Houton was convicted of counterfeiting having been found in possession of a forged bill. In rejecting an application to suspend sentence, the court stated that they 'had made inquiry concerning Van Houton and his character, and regretted to say, the account was very unfavourable. He had been sentenced to the State-Prison in New-Jersey for the same offence, and the court saw no reason for delaying his sentence.'

Discretion

For most offences, the judges of General Sessions had discretion whether to imprison or not.[64] Token punishment of the convicted defendant, as a discretionary act, could be achieved in many ways, each fashioned to the case before the court.

[61] (1816) Rogers, vol 1, p 83.
[62] (1816) Rogers, vol 1, p 169.
[63] (1817) Rogers, vol 2, p 73.
[64] When imprisonment was the sentence, in most cases the judges had discretion as to the term of years up to the statutory maximum in addition to the type of imprisonment such as hard labour, in chains or in solitary confinement.

At its lowest, the court could elect to impose no punishment, giving the defendant the equivalent of an absolute discharge, as in the prosecution of James Fox.[65] Fox, a young apprentice of about 16 or 17, on being threatened with being bound with a rope and corrected for some transgression, resisted and seized his master by the throat. His master, Mr Mathews, complained to the Grand Jury who found an indictment against the apprentice for assault and battery. The trial jury, however, convicted Fox only of assault:

> His *Honor* [The Mayor], thereupon, after briefly recapitulating the facts of
> the case, and remarking that his trial would probably operate on the defen-
> dant as a serious and effectual admonition to guide his future behaviour; and
> that the jury had only found him guilty of an *assault*; pronounced the opin-
> ion of the court, that any further punishment would be unnecessary.

In other cases, sentence might be suspended (postponed) in order to allow the defendant to engage in some course of action that would render further punishment unnecessary. This might occur where the defendant was to leave the jurisdiction or where the defendant was to be given an opportunity to reform. Thus, this course was taken in the prosecution of John Rowe *et al*,[66] in which eight crew from the British packet *Princess Elizabeth* were convicted of petit larceny after stealing a quantity of boards from a public wharf at Albany Basin:

> The jury found the prisoners guilty; and as the court had received the assur-
> ance of the officers of the ship, that the vessel to which the prisoners be-
> longed, was about to sail for England, and that they should be taken out of
> the country, fined the prisoners $5 each, and discharged them.

Sometimes, sentence was suspended in order to provide the prisoner an opportunity to reform, as in the prosecution of John Gamble,[67] convicted of assault and battery on Mary, his wife of five years. At the time of the marriage, Gamble was a sober, industrious man but, several years before his trial, he had fallen into the habit of gambling and drinking, had assaulted Mary violently on several occasions and afforded her no means of support. The court's aim, though unavailing, was reformative:

> His sentence was suspended for several terms, for the purpose of giving him
> an opportunity of returning to his family, or affording it support.

---

[65] (1819) Bacon, p 289.

[66] (1817) Rogers, vol 2, p 86. see also *Charles Willis* (1816) Rogers, vol 1, p 165; *George Harrison* (1817) Rogers, vol 2, p 112, and the reports relating to *Marcellan and James Lucas,* 'both foreigners' and both of whom, having been sentenced to six months each in the city's penitentiary, 'in lieu of the punishment inflicted by the court, have the privilege of leaving this country forever, should an opportunity of sending them away be found': (1816) Rogers, vol 1, p 136.

[67] (1817) Rogers, vol 2, p 44. In like manner, on a prosecution for nuisance, the court could suspend sentence to enable the defendant to remove the nuisance, as illustrated in *John Deitz* (1818) Rogers, vol 3, p 9.

> The court, after the verdict, intimated that the court suspended the sentence for that purpose.

> Several terms elapsed, and on the representation of the counsel for the prosecution, that the defendant refused to comply with any terms, or afford support to his family, the court imposed on him a fine of $300.

Occasionally, the court expressly took into account the reduced social circumstances of the offender, as illustrated in John Gilmore.[68] The defendant threw some strong acid substance on the clothes of Letitia Smith and Susan Hotchkiss, 'two women of the town', as they stood one evening in Duane Street and was heard to say that 'it was above half gone, but that he had enough left yet, to burn up every—in Duane-street':

> The jury found the defendant guilty, and he was fined $50; the court, on that occasion, observing, that the offence of which he had been convicted was atrocious in its nature, and that his poverty alone had exempted him from a heavier fine.

Similarly, the court might select a nominal penalty in order to ensure that the impact of the sentence was felt only by the defendant and not those who might otherwise suffer. This happened, for example, in the prosecution of Eleanor Cleary.[69] The defendant was convicted of assault and battery upon the prosecutrix, Mary Tailor. Once it appeared that Eleanor was a married woman, the wife of a decent, sober, industrious man, the court sought to contrive a sentence that would not also punish the defendant's husband:

> The court in passing *sentence*, admonished her, that in consideration of her husband's being an industrious and inoffensive man, and that the punishment would rather fall on him, should they set a heavy fine on her, they should only fine her one dollar, and the costs of both sides, and order her to find *sureties for the peace* towards the prosecutrix, and all persons, in the sum of $100, for the term of *six months*, and to stand committed till the sentence was complied with; so that her husband would be able to relieve her, or not, as he thought she deserved, without distressing himself.

> The court intimated that they should adopt a similar discretion in other cases of the kind (original emphasis).

The court also occasionally voiced the view that the true 'sentence' might flow from the fact of conviction itself, rather than from any penalty that the court itself might impose, thereby reducing the need for any separate punishment. A good

---

[68] (1817) Rogers, vol 2, p 29.
[69] (1818) Bacon, p 87; see also *Judah* (1823) Wheeler 2, p 26.

illustration of this was the prosecution of John Wood,[70] in which the defendant was convicted on an indictment for challenging another to fight a duel. In sentencing the defendant, the court took into account the provisions of the statute passed to suppress duelling by virtue of which convicted persons were held to be 'incapable of holding or being elected to any post of profit, trust or emolument, civil or military', in the state,[71] telling the defendant that:

> '... a consideration of the severity of the punishment, incident to a conviction for this offence, by the provisions of the statute, had induced the court to superadd a nominal punishment only. The defendant must hereafter be contented to live in the country which gave him birth, as a proscribed citizen; for whatever may be his merit and qualifications in this state he could never hold any office; not even that of a subaltern in the militia ...'

> In consequence of the circumstances attendant on conviction, the defendant was fined $1.00 and costs and bound to keep the peace for two years in the sum of $200.00.

CONCLUSION

As is clear from the above, sentencing in General Sessions was a reflective and orderly procedure undertaken with specific sentencing objectives in mind. In carrying out this task, judges had both considerable discretion and access to a wide variety of information that could be used in mitigation or aggravation of sentence. Whilst judges viewed particular types of offence as falling within broad sentencing bands, it is clear that, as today, the circumstances of each defendant were considered relevant and could displace any tariff. What ultimately held the sentencing system together, therefore, was the individual juridical person, possessed of free will and reason, as affected by life's chances in a changing market economy but accountable and subject to the deterrence of the law. In this way, the ideology of punishment reflected an understanding of an imperfect laissez-faire political economy.

---

[70] (1818) Rogers, vol 3, p 139.
[71] 4 Vol *Laws New York*, p 3 (1816).

Chapter 9

The Mid-Century Political Economy of Justice and Transformation in Method of Case Disposition

INTRODUCTION

In this chapter, we first provide an overview of the changes in the political economy of New York City after mid-century, including growth in population, reorganisation of city government, the widening electoral process and the emergence of an entrenched political party system. We describe the effects of politicisation on the office of the District Attorney, judges in General Sessions and police magistrates. We then set forth graphically the concomitant and dramatic transformation in the method of case disposition in General Sessions from jury trials to guilty pleas, the increase in the overall rate of conviction contrasted with jury verdicts and the consequent reduction in the public airing of evidence and proof at trial.

We consider the offences and offending which were subject to prosecutions in General Sessions. We compare the type of indicted offences and offenders with the earlier period to determine whether the nature of offending changed such that indicted cases increased in complexity thereby limiting and discouraging the opportunity for trial in everyday cases. Thereafter, we analyse the extent to which there are significant causal links between the caseload of General Sessions and the rise of guilty pleas against the commonly advanced contention that guilty pleas are necessitated in order to enable courtroom actors to respond to dramatic rises in workload.[1] The argument is that plea bargaining naturally occurs when lawyers appear on the scene and, concerned with everyday workload pressure,

---

[1] There have, however, been attacks on the workload hypothesis, the most important of which show a lack of correlation between case load and overall guilty plea rates: M Heumann (1978); M Feeley (1979).

create or utilise procedural loopholes or mechanisms so as to manipulate the charge, induce a plea and quickly dispose of the vast majority of all cases. As Fisher states:[2]

> Once prosecutors felt a general incentive to lighten their workload, they struck plea bargains whenever they had the power to do so—that is when- ever rigid penalty schemes permitted them to manipulate sentences by manipulating charges.

Although a small percentage of case dispositions by guilty plea did occur in the earlier period when lawyer trials predominated and as caseload increased, the strong and dramatic transformation to guilty pleas occurred, as we will demon- strate, only after mid-century,[3] negating to this degree the functionalist con- tention.

In our workload analysis, we engage in a rank order of total dispositions to guilty pleas to determine the extent of the correlation. We subsequently analyse the capacity of the court to dispose of these cases entirely by trial or whether guilty pleas became necessary to maintain a constant rate of disposition. We then proceed to analyse the ability of General Sessions and of its judges and District Attorney to respond to increases in caseload without a substantial decrease in the number and frequency of jury trials as the principal method of case disposition.

This chapter will serve to presage subsequent chapters in which we examine the construction and litigation of indicted cases in order to determine whether the explanation for the sudden emergence of the guilty plea system is to be found in changes in crime detection and evidence acquisition or in the complexity and adversariness of the trial process itself. Having made that assessment in chapters 10–11, we will then analyse the structure and nature of guilty pleas themselves to determine to what degree they were a product of the sufficiency of evidence and proof or were explicable only in terms of exogenous factors unrelated to the courtroom itself.

THE CITY AT MID-CENTURY

By 1850, New York City had grown to become the largest city in the United States, with a population that exceeded half a million people.[4] Between the early 1830s and the middle of the century, the composition of the population shifted from one in which most of the citizens were native-born (from the City, New England, and Long Island) to another where the majority was foreign-born (from

---

[2] Fisher (2000) p 903.
[3] See above Chapters 2, 8, and below Chapter 14.
[4] Rosenwaike (1972) p 42.

Ireland, Germany, England and France).[5] A disproportionate share of the new immigrants was poverty-stricken 'huddled together in teeming tenements, in squalid alleys and courtyards'.[6] Poverty gave rise to stealing; although theft often involved needed goods rather than money.[7] Estrangement from the wider society and lack of employment led to alcoholism that, in turn, became associated with crimes of violence such as assault and robbery.[8]

The growth of population alone and the concomitant demands of citizens for public services led over time to a reorganisation of city government involving greater delegation, separation of powers and accountability without regard to the form and style that city politics came to acquire. For example, the Mayor became an executive branch officer whose qualifications were unrelated to those of his predecessors, steeped as they were, in legal formalism. Furthermore, as suffrage was extended, the number of elected officials expanded concomitant with the emergence of professional politicians.[9] These politicians banded together as members of the Tammany Society which, at the outset of the nineteenth century, was a fraternal organisation comprised of artisans and journeymen dedicated to expanding the right of suffrage, assuring workingmen's liens, and reducing reliance on state prison labour.[10] With the emergence of professional politics, the Tammany Society became Tammany Hall, a party dedicated to electing city and state officials that legitimated itself as representatives of the working class and immigrant poor.[11] This inaugurated the era of machine politics which, through corruption and 'ward heeling'—the distribution of patronage and 'pork'—had a formative effect upon New York City government for years to come. As Mark Haller put it, describing the more general trend in the United States:[12]

> [T]he late nineteenth century cities were noted for the rise of local political organisations, often called political machines, organised from the grassroots up and based upon the exchange of favors for votes. Many of the positions in the criminal justice system were bestowed as rewards for political service, while politically influential fixers, saloonkeepers, bailbondsmen, and others influenced the outcome of cases to reward political activity or provide favors to constituents. In many cities, for instance, courts closed on election day while judges and court officials performed political duties in the neighborhoods; policemen sold tickets to political picnics and banquets, put up political posters, collected campaign money for local politicians, protected criminal activities linked to influential politicians, and accepted money from

---

[5] Rosenwaike (1972) p 39; Ernst (1979) p 338.
[6] Ernst (1979) p 29; E Homberger (1994). See also T Anbinder (2002) Chapters 2–4.
[7] Ernst (1979) p 57.
[8] Ernst (1979) p 57. See also Edward Crapsey (1872).
[9] C Williamson (1960) p 260.
[10] S Wilentz (1984) p 70.
[11] S Wilentz (1984) p 47.
[12] Haller (1979) p 277 (citations omitted).

gamblers, prostitutes, and other law-breakers; and prosecution officials were generally expected to protect the interests of their political sponsors.

At first, the new professional politicians in New York City established an amicable relationship with the propertied and mercantile class upon whom they were dependent for financial support. These politicians continued the paternalistic paradigm that had been so successful for their predecessors, by befriending the poor and establishing themselves as leaders through courage in fighting fires.[13] By 1855, however, divisions between elected politicians, the wealthy elite and the mercantile class about the conduct of politics and those whose interests were to be served thereby, resulted in the paradigm of bosses and reformers that was to continue for the balance of the century.[14]

During the 1840s and 1850s a number of new humanitarian associations emerged,[15] a principal example of which in criminal justice was the reformist Prison Association. These organisations were distinguishable from the benevolent societies which had been a prominent feature of the City's life from the Revolution to the 1830s. Whereas those earlier societies had been dominated by a mercantile-patrician class that was willing to be involved directly in ministering to the poor, the activities of the new benevolent associations were directed and carried out by salaried employees,[16] albeit with an elite board of trustees.[17] Whereas the earlier societies symbolised the indivisibility of governance in public or private institutions, the new associations, driven by a strong evangelical spirit, stood apart from a political order dominated by Tammany's bosses. And whereas the earlier societies were part of a seamless merging of politics and charity, the new associations had a potentially antagonistic relationship with the political structure.[18]

Indeed, the 1865 Annual Report of the reformist Board of Police Commissioners described the failure of the City's criminal justice system to be even-handedly administered and to adequately protect people and their property:

> In no other such city does the machinery of criminal justice so signally fail
> to restrain or punish serious and capital offenses ... Property is fearfully
> menaced by fire and robberies; and persons are in startling peril from crim-
> inal violence. This lamentable state of things is due, in a great measure, to a
> tardy and inefficient administration of justice. ... As our laws and institu-
> tions are administered, they do not afford adequate protection to persons of

---

[13]　A Bridges (1984) pp 17, 74.

[14]　A Bridges (1984) pp 17, 74.

[15]　Other associations included the New York Association for Improving the Condition of the Poor, the New York Juvenile Asylum, the Children's Aid Society and the Five Points House of Industry.

[16]　Among the most famous of these were Charles Loring Brace of the Children's Aid Society and Robert M Hartley of the Association for Improving the Condition of the Poor. See further: E Homberger (1994); C Rosenburg (1971); C Griffin (1960).

[17]　Among the officers of the Prison Association were some of New York's leading luminaries, such as John H Griscom, J Stanton Gould and James H Titus.

[18]　See M Heale (1976).

property. Some remedy must be found and applied, or life in the metropolis
will drift rapidly towards the condition of barbarism.[19]

THE POLITICISATION OF COURTROOM ACTORS

The District Attorney as political operative

Perhaps the greatest impact of the new politicisation of City government, however, was its effect on the role of the District Attorney and the character of the
individuals inhabiting the office.[20] In 1846, the District Attorney became an elected official,[21] closely aligned with party politics, who thereafter controlled almost
all criminal prosecutions in General Sessions.[22] Whilst at the outset of the period,
distinguished lawyers like Nathaniel Blunt continued in office, by 1855 the position became tied to Tammany Hall. Indeed, between 1853 and 1869, with the
exception of three years, the office of District Attorney was held by one person,
Oakey Hall,[23] whose political aspirations led him later to become Mayor. Closely
identified with Tammany's ward-heeling policies, he exercised discretion to
further those objectives and was a leading member of the Tweed Ring, described
by many as 'the model of civic corruption in American municipal history.'[24]
Tammany depended upon an electorate for its bedrock support many of whom
were regular violators of the law, and it sought to accommodate its constituents
through a wide variety of discretionary practices which, in criminal justice
administration, sought to avoid the discontent that harsh terms of imprisonment
would engender among the immigrant underclass, who, under the movement for
universal suffrage, had become part of the newly formed electorate.

An expression of the infusion of Tammany's politics occurred in the discretionary practices of the District Attorney who displaced the private prosecutor in
determining whether and by what means to prosecute a felony case. For example,
by 1850, the District Attorney had 'the keys' of the grand jury room. Even when
a complaint had been dismissed by an examining magistrate, complainants could
'avai[l] themselves of the privilege of the subpoena of the District Attorney, to

---

[19] *The North Atlantic Review*, vol CCXVI, July 1867, pp 171–72.

[20] As Carolyn Ramsey (2002, p 1328) points out, the change in the prosecutor's role was part of a
wider process: 'The election of District Attorneys represented a small part of the move to subject a
variety of local officials, including sheriffs and coroners, to the vote. The change ostensibly arose
from a desire to increase accountability to the voters' (citations omitted). The impact of the change,
however, in respect of the role of the District Attorney was, as the reader will see far from small.

[21] A Chester (1925) Vol 11, 886–7; J F Richardson (1970) p 80.

[22] Even after the creation of the elected office of district attorney, a handful of prosecutions continued to be privately prosecuted. See eg Robert M Ireland (1995), especially pp 53–4.

[23] In fact, Hall earlier held the post of Assistant District Attorney for three and a half years until the
death of Nathaniel Blunt, at which point he resigned his post to return to private practice.

[24] See A Callow (1966) p vii. see also Griffith (1974) pp 69ff.

present themselves before the grand jury ...'[25] By contrast, should the grand jury return an indictment which may have offended a substantial portion of the newly enfranchised electorate (such as indicting Irish tavern owners and proprietors of German beer gardens for a violation of liquor laws), the District Attorney could 'pigeon-hole' the case, without prosecuting it in General Sessions.[26]

Judges

After 1846, the Recorder became an elected official.[27] In 1850, the Recorder was joined by an elected City Judge, after which the Aldermen ceased to sit as associate judges.[28] Whilst at the outset elected judges were men of character and legal learning, by 1855 the office had become a political plum of Tammany Hall with some judges ignorant of the law or acting in a manner that favoured individuals accused of criminal activity with political connections. The emergent political boss system had an adverse impact on the types of individuals who inhabited this office and their attitudes towards law enforcement generally. Thus, the Recorder between 1858–1861, George C Bernard, a close political ally of Tammany Boss William Tweed,[29] was impeached and removed from office based upon a series of these misdeeds, as was City Judge, John H McCunn who served 1861–1864.[30] Bribery was reported in cases involving indictments where, despite the evidence, the judge directed an acquittal[31] and judges were found to have cashed cheques received from defendants whose indictments were dismissed on technicalities. Aside from overt corruption, as judges became linked to Tammany's constituents, sentencing became generally ameliorative. For example, our Minute Book sample showed, in contrast to the earlier period, that there were dramatic changes in the tariffs for grand larceny convictions with 70 per cent of defendants now sentenced to one day to three years and only 12 per cent of defendants receiving three years one day to five years.

Police magistrates

In 1848, the Special Justices became elected police magistrates.[32] These Police Justices, as they were now called, were also firmly connected to the system of political party patronage. Whilst in the earlier period magistrates were men with a career interest in law enforcement who were chosen by the Governor's Council

---

[25] The Code of Criminal Procedure for the State of New York: Reported Complete by the Commissioners on Practice and Pleading (Albany, Weed, Parsons & Co, 1850; appearing as New York State Assembly Document 150, pp 126–27).

[26] See below.

[27] H W Scott (1909) p 232; Wilson (1893).

[28] H W Scott (1909); I N Phelps (1967) vol v.

[29] See A Callow (1966) p 24.

[30] For a discussion of how McCunn came to be elected by Tammany leaders rigging the returns from Five Points, see Anbinder (2002) pp 322–23.

[31] Thomas Shearman, 'The Judiciary of New York City' *The North American Review*, vol cv, July 1867, p 148.

[32] *Laws of New York*, 1848, Chapter 153.

of Appointment, by 1850 the position had become an elective appendage of Tammany Hall, whereby unlettered individuals without any background or interest in law enforcement could be nominated for the salaried position of Police Justice, as a brief stepping stone to further their political careers.[33]

Unschooled amateurs appointed to the Bench not only lacked technical competence for the job but were also susceptible to influence from political party operatives.[34] Richardson, in his study of the origins of policing in New York City, sums up the impact of the election of police magistrates on the quality of justice they administered:[35]

> These enactments tied the magistrates even more firmly to those who controlled the party nominations, often ward heelers, saloon keepers, gamblers and gang leaders. These men needed a friendly judiciary to conduct their operations, and in the 1850s they definitely had one. As one former police justice put it, the 'shoulder hitters, gamblers, mock auctioneers, policy dealers and thieves' who controlled the primaries could be counted on to retaliate against any magistrate who 'fearlessly dealt out the law to them'.

In discharging their responsibilities, Police Justices had considerable latitude given the discretion they exercised in the committal process, whether to bind over the defendant to the Grand Jury or to dismiss the complaint, and the absence of any systematic oversight. Contemporaneously, there appears to have been little accountability between Police Justices, on the one hand, and the Grand Jury and office of the District Attorney on the other. This enabled the 'pigeon-holing' of cases to occur, by which magistrates discharged the accused and let allegations lie fallow. And there were often no records of the proceedings other than in the papers which the clerk stuffed somewhere in the office of the Police Justice, as was openly acknowledged in testimony of magistrates in the legislative hearings of 1855:[36]

Testimony of Daniel Clark (magistrate):
Q What is done with the papers in dismissed cases?
A They are generally put away in the pigeon holes
Q They are not returned to the District Attorney's office at all?
A Not that I am aware of ...

Testimony of James H Welch (police magistrate):
Q I think the general statute requires that examining magistrates shall make returns to the district attorney of all cases whether dismissed or not?
A I think that is not the case in this city ...

---

[33] Amy Bridges (1984).

[34] An aldermanic report of 1844 spoke of 'the want of independence and competency of many of the most important officers, owing to the fact of political influence, and not real merit, being the great recommendation for the appointments ...': Board of Aldermen, *Report on the Reorganisation of the Police Department* (1844) 691, cited in Smith (1996) p 517.

[35] J Richardson (1970) p 74. See also Hill (1993).

[36] Assembly Documents (1855) p 40 and pp 49–50.

By 1867, the background and character of many of those who became Police Justices in New York City and their impact upon Police Court became emblematic of the office, as described in the *North American Review*:[37]

> [I]t is indisputable that most of the Justices in charge of criminal business in New York are coarse, profane, uneducated men, knowing nothing of law except what they have picked up in their experience on the bench. One of the best of them was a butcher until he became a police justice; another was formerly a bar-keeper. As a rule, they are excessively conceited and overbearing, and in some cases positively brutal in their demeanour. The officers in attendance naturally take their tone from their superiors, and treat everyone who enters the court room with a roughness which makes attendance upon such places ineffably disgusting.

THE TRANSFORMATION IN METHOD OF DISPOSITION

Over the fifteen year period leading up to 1865, the process and method by which indicted cases were disposed of in General Sessions were uniformly turned on their head so that guilty pleas came to predominate over trials and jury verdicts. In the system extant in 1845 and prior thereto, when trials predominated, not guilty pleas accounted for between 80–100 per cent of all defendant pleas. By 1860 guilty pleas outstripped not guilty pleas accounting for 60 per cent of all defendant pleas and by 1879 over 70 per cent. The changed pattern of pleas in our sample of District Attorney's case files is set out in Figure 9.1:

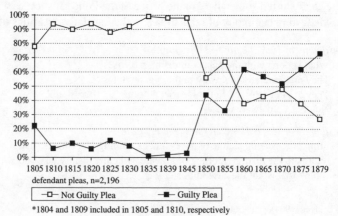

FIGURE 9.1: General Sessions, District Attorney's Files—Percentage of Not Guilty and Guilty Pleas Over a Thirty Day Period for One Court Part, 1804–1879*

[37] 'The Judiciary of New York City' *The North American Review*, vol cv, July 1867, 148–76 p 166.

The effect of the changeover in defendant pleas is readily apparent in a measure of the percentage of guilty pleas to total convictions in General Sessions over the years 1839–1865, as reported by the Secretary of State and set out in Figure 9.2:

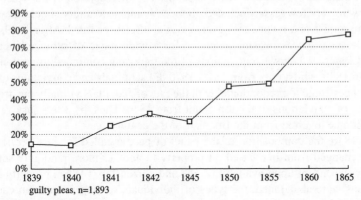

FIGURE 9.2: General Sessions, Secretary of State Reports—Percentage of Guilty Pleas to Total Convictions Over the Year, 1839–1865

These data show that, in 1839, guilty pleas amounted to no more than 15 per cent of total convictions whilst, by 1865, they represented over 75 per cent. Guilty pleas assured and, indeed, increased the rate of conviction.

This was of some significance when we analysed trial outcomes over the entire period of the research to determine whether there were any macro changes in the nature of jury verdicts, as depicted in Figure 9.3:

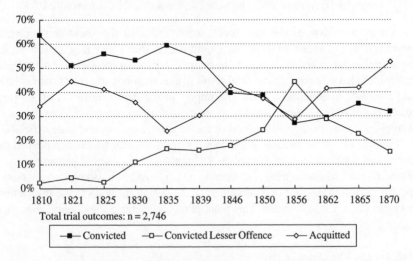

FIGURE 9.3: General Sessions Minute Book—Percentage of Trial Outcomes Over the Year, All Defence Lawyer Cases for One Court Part, 1810–1870

As Figure 9.3 shows, there was a dramatic shift in trial outcome patterns in General Sessions, through a reduction in the proportion of top count convictions, an increase in the proportion of uncharged lesser included-offence convictions and an increase in acquittals. Of course, prior to the adoption of the 1829 Code there were very few lesser-included offences available to a jury should they wish to compromise and reduce the severity of the offence charged. After 1829, however, lesser offences became available for a wide range of offence categories yet, as Figure 9.3 shows, convictions of the top count continued to predominate prior to 1839, whilst only from 1846–1870 did acquittals and convictions of lesser offences come to predominate, with the rate of acquittals virtually outstripping the rate of convictions of the top count from 1846. Thus, by 1865, jury verdicts had become inverted from the first half of the century.

By 1846, the composition of the panel of people called for jury service formally changed from one based on property to another more randomly selected largely dependent upon availability, age and citizenship.[38] When property qualifications were abandoned, the types of individuals serving as jurors broadened to include labourers and the unemployed who often, with nothing better to do, would volunteer for jury service when those called had failed to appear. In the 1846 debate over the revision of the state constitution, reformers complained that

> Very many of our courts are haunted, day after day, by dissolute loungers, waiting a chance to obtain a shilling by getting on a jury, whose integrity and judgment no man can confide in, and who are utterly unfit to decide either the law or the facts of any case...[39]

The *New York Times* also lamented the loss of respectable citizens from jury service and their replacement by 'drunks', 'crooks', and the 'unemployed'.[40]

As the composition of the jury more nearly reflected the socio-demographic characteristics of those on trial, one would expect that a jury might exercise its equitable power to acquit as well as to return compromise verdicts for uncharged lesser included offences. This would result in a reduction in top count convictions and a growth in acquittals. Thus, one impact of the democratisation of the jury might be found in verdicts contrary to the evidence and, were this to be the case, it might account for the villification of the jury by reformers and state officials.

The effect the deterioration of top count convictions after trial may have had on courtroom actors, and in particular the District Attorney towards bargaining over lesser offences without a trial, is something which must be considered when assessing the growth in reliance on guilty pleas as the overall method of case disposition over the same period of time. This point is of considerable importance given our

[38] O L Barbour (1852) p 63; J Colby (1868).

[39] Report of the Debates and Proceedings of the Convention for the Revision of the Constitution of the State of New York (1846) p 111.

[40] *New York Times*, 9 April 1859, 9 November 1859, 24 September 1867, 12 November 1867. See R M Ireland (1962) p 59.

analysis of the effect of the increased reliance on guilty pleas on the total proportion of convictions, acquittals and discharges, as depicted in Figure 9.4:

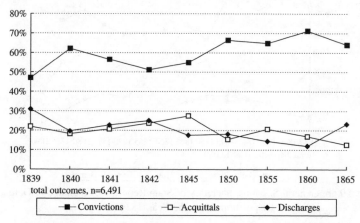

FIGURE 9.4: General Sessions, Secretary of State Reports—Percentage of Total Convictions, Acquittals, and Discharges Over the Year, 1839–1865

As Figure 9.4 shows, increased reliance on guilty pleas affected the overall rate of conviction. While between 1839 and 1845 convictions were mostly at about 50 per cent, with an acquittal rate of about 30 per cent in 1845, by 1860, after greater reliance on guilty pleas, the conviction rate extended to approximately 70 per cent of all dispositions with the overall acquittal rate dropping as low as 10 per cent by 1865.

The long-term effect of the emergence of the guilty plea system on the method of case disposition in General Sessions is starkly portrayed in Figure 9.5 which tracks defendant dispositions beginning in 1800 and ending in 1890 utilising our three data sources:

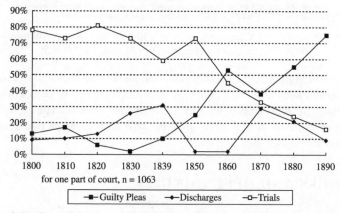

FIGURE 9.5a: General Sessions Minute Book—Percentage of Defendant Dispositions Over a Thirty Day Period, 1800–1890

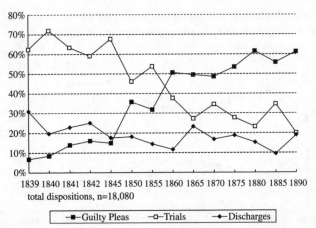

FIGURE 9.5b: General Sessions, Secretary of State Reports—Percentage of Defendant
Dispositions Over the Year, 1839–1890

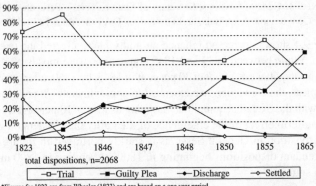

FIGURE 9.5c: General Sessions, Wheeler's Reports and District Attorney's
Files–Percentage of Defendant Dispositions, 1823–1865*

As set out in Figure 9.5, the transformation in method of disposition, inaugurated a system in which, by 1865, the overwhelming majority of convictions were
secured through admissions of guilt by the defendant rather than through the public airing of evidence at trial which met the 'beyond reasonable doubt' standard
to the satisfaction of a jury.

OFFENCES AND OFFENDING

The Secretary of State's Reports show that males continued to be the predominant indicted defendant accounting for over 90 per cent of all convictions by

1860. The Minute Book and our case files show, moreover, that there were few marked differences between the pattern of offences prosecuted over the period 1850–1865 and that in the earlier period. Indictments remained principally for property offences although, in contrast to the earlier period, their proportion increased to over eighty per cent with crimes against the person falling from thirty to fourteen per cent of our sample.

Our sample of case files similarly showed that, for the period 1850–1865 as a whole, larceny (either grand or petit) made up half the property prosecutions (50.0 per cent), though it was at its lowest level in 1850 (37.0 per cent) and rose steadily over the period so that by 1865 it consisted of 64.0 per cent of all property cases. Prosecutions for burglary, which had risen steadily throughout the earlier period, continued rising until 1850, when they comprised 47.0 per cent of all property cases, but thereafter fell away steadily so that by 1865 they made up only 20.0 per cent of all property cases.[41]

As in the earlier period, property prosecutions were mostly for theft against shops and dwelling houses,[42] and in the latter were typically carried out by a servant or lodger or opportunistic thief. There continued to be, as in the earlier period, ample outlets for off-loading stolen goods, itself evidence of people who acted regularly as receivers.[43] The most common way of tracing stolen goods remained through pawn tickets,[44] and there were plenty of pawn shops, legitimate and illegitimate, where culprits could pass off stolen property.[45]

In contrast to the earlier period, thefts from the person, mostly robbery, constituted a substantial minority of property indictments (14.0 per cent). The most common allegation was that, in the course of the theft, the prosecutor had been forcibly held or subjected to some minor assault,[46] although more serious violence was offered or alleged in some cases. As in the earlier period, other thefts from the person were grand larceny prosecutions based upon straightforward pickpocketing,[47] or an act of a sexual solicitation,[48]

[41] The choice of burglary or larceny appears to have been based primarily on whether the theft occurred at night. The residue of property prosecutions consisted of robbery, forgery, receiving, false pretences and arson.

[42] See eg *Augustus Miller*, District Attorney's Files, 23 October, 1850.

[43] The term 'fence' as referring to a receiver of stolen goods was an established part of underworld vocabulary: George W Matsell (1859) p 31.

[44] See eg, *James Smith*, District Attorney's Files, 14 October, 1850; *Andrew Gesner*, District Attorney's Files, 8 May, 1860; *Samuel McGibney*, District Attorney's Files, 8 May, 1860; *Elizabeth Haviland*, District Attorney's Files, 10 May, 1860; and *William Brown*, District Attorney's Files, 10 May, 1860.

[45] See eg, *Mary Helms*, District Attorney's Files, 13 September, 1850 where goods were pawned at Simpson's at the corner of Broome Street and the Bowery; *Charles Cook*, District Attorney's Files, 20 September, 1850 where stolen property was sold to a second-hand clothing dealer in Orange Street; and *Andrew Gesner*, District Attorney's Files, 8 May, 1860 where coats were pledged at Schlossheimer's pawn office in Houston Street.

[46] See eg, *William Bakus et al*, District Attorney's Files, 21 May, 1860; *Bernard Brennan*, District Attorney's Files, 8 March, 1865.

[47] As in *James O'Connell*, District Attorney's Files, 10 May, 1865; *Jacob Wiskowski*, District Attorney's Files, 10 September, 1855; and *John Williams*, District Attorney's Files, 28 April, 1865.

[48] See eg, *Emma Shaw*, District Attorney's Files, 12 May, 1865; *Mary O'Brien and Caroline Fletcher*, District Attorney's Files 10 April, 1865; and *Kate Dickson*, District Attorney's Files, 4 May, 1865.

or some act of fraud or deception involving counterfeit currency or false pretences.

The underlying facts in property prosecutions showed that they continued to be prosaic in nature without expertise or planning. Thus, for example, in burglary cases entry was most commonly effected by forcing a door or window[49] or by raising a window, entering through a skylight or grating.[50] Whilst the value of stolen property rose in comparison with indictments in the earlier period, this seems to have been largely a function of greater reliance on Special Sessions by 1830,[51] in which most petit larceny prosecutions occurred.[52] As in the earlier period, however, thefts of items of a low value still commonly led to sentences of imprisonment[53] and thefts involving substantial sums did not appear to attract more retributive sentences.[54]

In line with our sample for the earlier period and in contrast to prosecutions for personal offences for both periods, property offences were in general inter-class rather than intra-class.[55] Defendants were primarily drawn from the poor[56] and working class. Thus, over the period 1855–1865, the most numerous occupations listed by defendants themselves were: 'servant' (10.0 per cent of known occupations); 'sailor' or 'seaman' (6.0 per cent); 'housekeeper' (4.0 per cent); 'clerk'

---

[49] See eg, *Thomas Welsh*, District Attorney's Files, 4 September, 1850 (forcing a lock); *James Donaldson*, District Attorney's Files, 18 October, 1850 (forcing a store door); *Thomas Connors*, District Attorney's Files, 9 April, 1860 (forcing a window); and *John Liebig*, District Attorney's Files, 22 May, 1860 (forcing lock of basement door).

[50] *Augustus Müller*, District Attorney's Files, 23 October, 1850 (entering through the skylight window); and *James Williams*, District Attorney's Files, 14 November, 1850 (entered by raising the lower half of the window).

[51] The 1829 *Revised Laws of the State of New York* which regularised the Court of Special Sessions came into effect on 1 January, 1830. The history of the establishment of the Court of Special Sessions is traced by Bruce Smith (1996) pp 467 ff. The Court of Special Sessions had met prior to 1830, but only sporadically.

[52] Although these cases could be tried *de novo* in General Sessions before a jury, defendants infrequently elected this option. See Bruce Smith (1996) pp 313, 467–514.

[53] Eg, two years in state prison for theft of a watch worth $30.00: *George Harrison*, District Attorney's Files, 7 September, 1855; for theft of tools worth $45.00: *John Stewart*, District Attorney's Files, 10 September, 1855; and for a $1.50 burglary: *Philip McGuire*, District Attorney's Files, 23 May, 1860.

[54] *Peter Brennan*, District Attorney's Files, 24 March, 1865 where Brennan, who stole $3496.00 in currency from George Combs, none of which was recovered, received only two years in state prison, although the relevant statutory provision authorised a sentence of up to five years; 1863 *New York Revised Statutes*, Part IV, Chapter 1, Title iii, Sections 63–4, p 699.

[55] Prior to and including 1850 the practice had been to record the official classification of the defendant's occupation in the body of the indictment. In almost all cases, the occupation was listed as 'laborer' with defendants generally giving answers consistent with this at their examination. For the years 1855–1865, however, the practice of entering an official designation of occupational status was abandoned. Instead, defendants were asked to describe their occupations themselves and while few described themselves as 'laborers', almost all gave as their occupation a job category that would in earlier years have attracted the official classification 'laborer'.

[56] As in *Amanda Chambers*, District Attorney's Files, 5 October, 1855 ('I have got no particular occupation'); *Richard Ward*, District Attorney's Files, 15 November, 1865 ('have no occupation'); and *Michael Donohue*, District Attorney's Files, 28 April, 1860 ('I do nothing').

(3.5 per cent); 'tailor' (3.0 per cent); 'waiter' or 'baker' (2.5 per cent); with 4.0 per cent giving their occupational status as 'none'.[57]

Whilst complainants in property prosecutions tended to be people of some means, many could hardly be described as wealthy individuals. Indeed, as in the earlier part of the century, General Sessions' prosecutions were accessible to those with low status occupations and those of little means and education who were frequent victims of theft or deception.[58] Thus, for example, a number of prosecutors could only make a mark on their statement of complaint,[59] although the great majority (87.0 per cent) were able to sign their names. By contrast, almost half of defendants (45.0 per cent) made a mark instead of signing their examination.

From 1839–1865 the Secretary of State's Reports show that between 20–30 per cent of convicted defendants had previously been in prison. Whilst our sample of case files gives no systematic information on prior record of the defendant and relevant information emerges only haphazardly, the available data show that at least some of the indicted defendants over this period were repeat or habitual offenders.[60] Many repeat offenders would have been the beneficiaries of a Governor's pardon which continued throughout the entire period of the re search in response to continued prison overcrowding. Whilst for the earlier period, the overwhelming majority of offences against the person in our sample comprised charges of simple assault and battery (90.0 per cent), and a snapshot of all General Sessions' convictions reported by the Secretary of State for the years 1850 and 1865[61] shows the continued dominance of assaults, our sample of case files for 1850–1865 contained a disproportionate share of more serious charges of personal violence, with simple assault and battery comprising only 27 per cent of offences against the person (many misdemeanour assaults now being prosecuted in Special Sessions).

For contemporary commentators, serious assault was a matter of considerable concern and marked out New York as one of the most violent cities in the world. Thus, for example, in 1865, one commentator in contrasting the rise in

---

[57] The remaining designations comprise an assorted inventory of New York City's established retail businesses, its domestic and service life and its emergent manufacturing sector comprising such jobs as: 'butcher', 'hatter', 'pedlar', 'sail maker', 'hair packer', 'confectioner', 'washerwoman', 'dyer', 'engraver', 'segar maker', 'tinsmith', 'brass finisher', 'paper box maker' and 'tile cutter'.

[58] See eg, *Alexander Woolsey and Charles Wilson*, District Attorney's Files, 6 September, 1855 in which the victim John Smith was a canal boat hand; and *Margaret Crane and Mary O'Donnell*, District Attorney's Files, 21 September, 1855, a case involving grand larceny from a boatman on the ship *Active* from Connecticut.

[59] See eg, *James Sheridan*, District Attorney's Files, 11 October, 1850 where Daniel Devlin, a liquor store and dwelling house keeper, could only make his mark. See also: *Mary A Hogan*, District Attorney's Files, 7 September, 1850; *Patrick Gillespie*, District Attorney's Files, 9 November, 1855; *Jane Wright*, District Attorney's Files, 13 November, 1855.

[60] See eg, *George Hoyt*, District Attorney's Files, 16 September, 1850; *Bridget Sheridan*, District Attorney's Files, 11 April, 1865.

[61] Table E of the Secretary of State Reports.

prosecutions for violent crime in New York City with that of London observed:[62]

> Look any and *every* day in the week [in New York], at your morning paper and see what a black record of crime has been committed in your public streets the day and the night before, what *stabbings*, what shootings, what knockings down, what assaults by slung shots and otherwise; insults to women and other disgusting details of violence ...
>
> In London, from the inability of a large portion of its population to get employment, arising from its overgrown population, there is more stealing and offences against property than in New York, two to one; but in instances of violence to the *person*, and of the higher grade of crime, we far outnumber them. In acts of violence committed on the person, I believe there are more than in either London or Paris; and that there is more use of the knife in New York, more stabbing than in all the cities of Italy combined ...

Viewed as a whole, the available information suggests that, as in the period 1800–1845, personal offences were primarily intra-class in character. Disputes that were prosecuted tended to be between people of the same occupational grouping such as labourers[63] or sailors.[64] The typical assault and battery prosecution involved an allegation that the victim had been struck with a fist or had been kicked in the course of a quarrel, although in one-third of these cases in our sample, the defendant was said to have used a weapon of some kind. By contrast, in almost all of the prosecutions for aggravated assault in our sample it was alleged that a weapon of some kind was involved, generally a knife or gun, with isolated cases involving an axe, razor, club, or slingshot. The six homicide prosecutions in our sample all involved the use of some kind of weapon and most arose out of a quarrel.

One of the most remarkable features of the pattern of offences over the period 1850–1865 as disclosed in our sample of case files is the relative paucity of prosecutions outside those involving property crimes or offences against the person. Whilst a small proportion of these other prosecutions were made up of a ragbag of offences such as gambling, bigamy, libel and nuisance, over half were for keeping a disorderly house, and it is clear that, unlike the omnibus nature of the charge in the early years of the century, the mischief aimed at was houses of prostitution, whereas prostitution itself was a form of vice frequently prosecuted in Special Sessions.

---

[62] J W Gerrard (1853) pp 7, 10. However, whilst some commentators point to an increasing use of firearms from the 1840s, such observations represented an unbroken link with the very same concerns expressed by other commentators, such as Philip Hone, in the first half of the century. See Johnson (1979) p 137 who observes that this apparently arose out of political struggles in the 1830s.

[63] See eg, *Francis Kinney and Jerry Riordan*, District Attorney's Files, 20 September, 1850.

[64] See eg, *Henry Brown et al*, District Attorney's Files, 1 October, 1855.

CASELOAD

One measure of caseload is to determine the number of indictments returned over a thirty day period in General Sessions. The Court Minute Book tracks the number of new indictments filed by the grand jury in General Sessions on a monthly basis. As depicted in Figure 9.6, these data show that the number of indictments returned to one part (section) of the court was at its height at the outset of the century in 1800, diminishing thereafter and remaining broadly constant at between 100–200 indictments per month from 1810 to 1870:

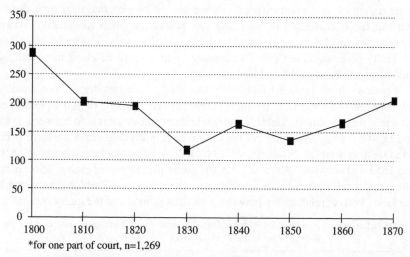

*for one part of court, n=1,269

FIGURE 9.6: General Sessions Minute Book—Number of Indictments Returned Over Thirty Day Period*, 1800–1870

As a measure of caseload, therefore, the number of indictments filed per month does not suggest an increase in case pressure such as to necessitate a new or altered method of case disposition.

Aggregate dispositions

We recognise, of course, that monthly indictments filed in one part of court over a thirty day period are but one measure of caseload and that, once filed, an indictment could remain on the court docket for more than thirty days, thus increasing the workload of the court cumulatively. Moreover, the number of sessions in which the court sat over a thirty-day period might increase exponentially thereby responding to increases in workload resulting from the ongoing and continuous filing of indictments. The court could also, by dividing into parts, expand its overall caseload capacity.

Thus, we sought another measure of caseload that would more accurately reflect the workload, taking into account all parts of the court through aggregating all trial and guilty plea dispositions on a yearly and monthly basis. To do this, we turned to the aggregate data compiled by the Secretary of State over the years 1838–1865.[65] Thus, over the period 1840–1865, as the numbers of trial and guilty plea dispositions in General Sessions increased, from 548 in 1840 to 1323 in 1865, so the rate of dispositions by guilty plea increased from 8.4 per cent in 1840 to 49.4 per cent in 1865.

Whilst focusing upon the beginning and end dates could easily suggest a causal relationship between the growth in dispositions and the rate of guilty pleas, in the way some commentators contend from equivalent data elsewhere,[66] closer examination of total court dispositions and the guilty plea rate over time shows that the facial correlates of start and end points are often misleading. When General Sessions' data are examined at five yearly intervals, it becomes clear that the guilty plea rate is not directly correlated with overall caseload measured by total dispositions, as Table 9.1 demonstrates.

It emerges from Table 9.1 that, whilst the number of cases disposed of actually fell between 1840 and 1845 by almost eight per cent, the rate of guilty pleas over the same period almost doubled; and while dispositions increased between 1845 and 1850 by only some thirty per cent, the rate of guilty pleas over the same period more than doubled. Similarly, whilst total dispositions increased between 1850 and 1855 and between 1860 and 1865, the guilty plea rate over each of these periods actually fell.[67] This can be seen graphically in Figure 9.7 which demonstrates the lack of direct relationship between total dispositions and the guilty plea rate:

TABLE 9.1: *General Sessions, Secretary of State Reports: Total Dispositions and Guilty Plea Rate for One Court Part, Over the Year, 1840–1865*

Year	Total dispositions	Guilty pleas	
	n	n	%
1840	548	46	8.4
1845	506	76	15.0
1850	654	238	36.4
1855	676	216	32.0
1860	1070	553	51.7
1865	1323	654	49.4

[65] The first Report submitted to the Senate of the State of New York in March, 1838 contains limited data in relation to convictions for criminal offences obtained in the State over the period 1830–1837.

[66] See eg Fisher's critique of the work of Vogel (1999) and Ferdinand (1992) of plea bargaining in Boston, Massachusetts. Whilst both found concurrent rises in caseload and guilty plea rates from the 1830s, Vogel concluded that caseload was not important in the growth of plea bargaining, with Ferdinand stating that the assumed link was debatable. In reviewing these studies, Fisher, by contrast, concludes that the criminal and civil (private practice) caseload pressure generally increased prosecutors' incentives to plea bargain: Fisher (2000) p 903.

[67] A similar lack of relationship between case load and guilty plea rate appears if discharges without trial are excluded from the analysis.

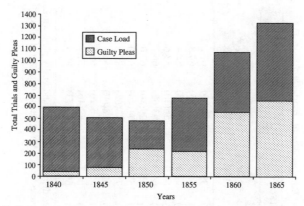

FIGURE 9.7: Secretary of State Reports: General Sessions Caseload Disposition and
Guilty Plea Rate, 1840–1865

Figure 9.7 draws attention to a significant shortcoming in the caseload hypothesis: its failure to address the question of the prosecutor's and the court's capacity to deal with fluctuations in the volume of cases (trials and pleas) without radically altering the principal method of case disposition. The caseload hypothesis assumes that courtroom actors have a finite capacity to dispose of cases through trials and that the addition of further cases beyond this capacity will demand that the actors adopt dispositional methods which allow them to get through the work load without having to try every case. What this does not adequately address, however, is what is meant by 'capacity' in a context of increased volume of cases, when the actors may wish to keep constant the normal method of disposition.

Monthly caseload capacity

The data from the Secretary of State's Reports and General Sessions' Minute Book are instructive in discerning the capacity of General Sessions to respond to an increased volume of cases, and these data demonstrate the enormous flexibility the court had to deal with fluctuations of caseload other than through reliance upon guilty pleas. Those data are particularly useful because, based on monthly returns of the clerks, they allow us to disaggregate annual disposition statistics and to gain insight into what the court's caseload capacity was at any given time. Analysis of the Secretary of State's Reports reveals that, over the whole of the period 1840–1865, there was considerable variation from month to month in General Sessions. Caseload was not, therefore, evenly distributed over the year: in some months the court would dispose of proportionately large numbers of cases; in others proportionately few. The relationship between total dispositions and guilty plea on a monthly basis is set out in Table 9.2 below.

The figures disclosed by Table 9.2 destroy any simple caseload hypothesis: the capacity of General Sessions to deal with fluctuations in caseload, expressed in terms of total dispositions, was considerable throughout the whole period

TABLE 9.2: *Secretary of State Reports: General Sessions Caseload Disposition[1] and Guilty Plea Rate per Month, 1840–1865*

Month	1840		1845		1850		1855		1860		1865	
	Case load	% Guilty pleas	Case load	% Guilty pleas	Case load	% Guilty pleas	Case load	% Guilty pleas	Case load	% Guilty pleas	Case load	% Guilty pleas
January	48(2)	4.2	57(7)	12.3	67(20)	29.9	51(15)	29.4	63(25)	39.7	58(39)	67.2
February	46(4)	8.7	22(7)	31.8	49(17)	34.7	59(22)	37.3	87(58)	66.7	54(35)	64.8
March	34(4)	11.8	37(12)	32.4	37(16)	43.2	43(9)	20.9	100(54)	54.0	63(33)	52.4
April	60(4)	6.7	55(6)	10.9	47(13)	27.7	86(41)	47.7	54(27)	50.0	56(30)	53.6
May	–	–	22(9)	40.9	23(14)	60.9	42(14)	33.3	115(75)	65.2	93(62)	66.7
June	32(3)	9.4	16(2)	12.5	56(30)	53.6	54(23)	42.6	94(53)	56.4	129(80)	62.0
July	76(13)	17.1	28(1)	3.6	33(6)	18.2	34(16)	47.1	38(22)	57.9	71(49)	69.0
August	19(0)	0.0	24(5)	20.8	21(5)	23.8	25(16)	64.0	46(36)	78.3	78(63)	80.8
September	55(9)	16.4	44(10)	22.7	55(27)	49.1	52(12)	23.1	113(71)	62.8	118(67)	56.8
October	17(1)	5.9	51(6)	11.8	39(18)	46.2	42(14)	33.3	57(29)	50.9	116(76)	65.5
November	22(3)	13.6	32(1)	3.1	37(15)	40.5	52(21)	40.4	89(59)	66.3	89(46)	51.7
December	31(3)	9.7	31(10)	32.3	71(57)	80.3	39(13)	33.3	66(44)	66.7	89(72)	80.9

Note[1]: 'Caseload' (total dispositions) throughout the Table is expressed in terms of the total number of cases disposed of by trial and guilty plea, with the number of cases dealt with by guilty pleas in parentheses; so that 48(2) represents a total of 48 cases dealt with in the month, two of which were by guilty pleas. The analysis excludes cases discharged without trial.

between 1840–1865; and there is no clear or consistent relationship between the volume of cases disposed by the court in any month and the rate of guilty pleas. Whilst, for example, the court was able to dispose of 63 cases by means of trial[68] in the month of July 1840, this alone[69] represented a higher overall caseload disposition (trials *and* pleas) than was achieved by the court in any month in 1855 except for April, and higher than that achieved in six of the months of 1860 and four of the months in 1865 during which period dispositions by guilty plea, both in absolute and relative terms, was increasing markedly.

Guilty plea rate and dispositions

The statistics also throw light on the question whether, irrespective of trial capacity, the rate of guilty pleas varies according to the volume of dispositions in the court at any one time. If the caseload hypothesis were correct, we would expect to see the guilty plea rate grow with overall increases in dispositions. In fact, this is not the case. This can be demonstrated by comparing for each year the dispositions per month with the guilty plea rates for each month of that year. On this basis, if the caseload hypothesis were true, we would expect the month with the highest number of dispositions to have the highest rate of disposal by guilty plea and the month with the lowest number of dispositions to have the lowest rate of guilty plea. Table 9.3 accordingly compares the monthly caseload with the guilty plea rate by rank order where '1' equals the highest number of dispositions/guilty plea rate and '12' the lowest.

It emerges from Table 9.3 that the relationship between disposition and guilty plea rate as predicted by the caseload hypothesis is not found. Whilst the highest guilty plea rate is sometimes correlated with the highest monthly dispositions (as in 1840), it also occurs in months where the number of dispositions is the least (1850) or among the least (1845 and 1860) busy. Indeed, if we take the three least busy months we find that the overall guilty plea rate (the combined aggregate of the rank order scores for each of the months) is at least as high as that for the three busiest months in four years out of the six in question (1845, 1855, 1860, 1865).

Trial capacity

The capacity of the court to dispose of cases can also be looked at in terms of its ability to try cases within a given year. Thus, for any year, even if we do not know how many cases the court *could have* tried, we do know that the court should have *at least* the capacity to try in each month the same number of cases that it was able to process by trial in the month with the highest number of trials, assuming the number of trials started and completed per day remained relatively constant as we will show. If, for example, it was able to conduct 50 trials in October, it should have been able to handle in each of the other months at least 50 trials beyond which its capacity to

---

[68] We assume for these purposes that a 'trial' remained more or less the same over the period in question. We return to this point later.

[69] In addition, the court disposed of a further 13 cases by guilty plea in July, 1840.

TABLE 9.3: *General Sessions, Secretary of State Reports, Rank Order of Guilty Plea and Caseload Dispositions on a Monthly Basis, 1840–1865*

Monthly caseload by rank order	Monthly guilty plea rate by rank order					
	1840	1845	1850	1855	1860	1865
1	1	8	1	2	5	8
2	8	10	9	6	6	12
3	2	9	3	4	9	6
4	10	5	4	5	8	5
5	7	2	8	10	4	10
6	4	12	10	11	++2=	1
7	6	3	5	12	++2=	2
8	5	11	7	+7=	12	3
9	3	6	6	+7=	10	11
10	11	4	12	+7=	11	4
11	9	1	2	3	1	9
12	*	7	11	1	7	7

*   No Dispositions are recorded in May 1840.
+   In 1855 the caseload for three months was identical.
++   In 1860 the caseload for two months was identical.

dispose of additional cases by trial might be eroded by increases in caseload thus causing the court to rely on guilty pleas. One way of testing this possibility, is to take the highest number of trials recorded in any month as the court's monthly trial-capacity for that year and calculate what guilty plea rate would have been needed in the other months in order to enable the court to handle the overall caseload demand it actually faced. This is dealt with in Table 9.4 below which shows the actual guilty plea rate for every month in question as compared to the guilty plea rate ('adjusted') that would have been needed to enable to court to dispose of its cases in the month:

It is clear from Table 9.4 that, even if we assume that the month with the highest number of trials in any year represents the court's monthly trial capacity for that year and that no further trials could have been absorbed by the court, the rate of guilty pleas needed to dispose of the residue of cases in many months was not only lower but far lower than the rate of guilty pleas actually entered. Indeed, on many occasions the court's trial capacity would have allowed it to dispose of *all* cases coming into the court in any month. Thus, had the court in 1840 tried in all months cases up to its trial capacity of 63 cases, as it did in July of that year, no reliance on guilty pleas would have been needed to deal with its workload in any other month since the court was not faced with as many as 63 case dispositions (trials and guilty pleas) overall in any month except July. This would also have been true in nine months in 1845, in none of which did the total caseload exceed the number of trials dealt with by the court in January of that year (n=50); in five months in 1850; in six months in 1855; and in two months in 1860. And whilst the trial capacity in 1865 in the busiest trial month of September (n=51) would not have been enough of itself to dispose of the caseload of the court in any given month, it would have *substantially* reduced

TABLE 9.4: *General Sessions, Secretary of State Reports: A Comparison Between the Monthly Actual and 'Adjusted' Guilty Plea Rates, 1840–1865*

Month	1840 Guilty plea rate		1845 Guilty plea rate		1850 Guilty plea rate		1855 Guilty plea rate		1860 Guilty plea rate		1865 Guilty plea rate	
	Actual	Adjusted	Actual	Adjusted	Actual	Adjusted	Actual	Adjusted	Actual	Adjusted	Actual	Adjusted
January	4.2	0.0	12.3	12.3	29.9	29.9	29.4	11.8	39.7	27.0	67.2	12.1
February	8.7	0.0	31.8	0.0	34.7	24.5	37.3	23.7	66.6	47.1	64.8	5.5
March	11.8	0.0	32.4	0.0	43.2	0.0	20.9	0.0	54.0	54.0	52.4	19.0
April	6.6	0.0	10.9	9.1	27.7	21.3	47.7	47.7	50.0	14.8	53.6	9.8
May	–	–	40.9	0.0	60.9	0.0	33.3	0.0	65.2	60.0	66.6	45.2
June	9.4	0.0	12.5	0.0	53.6	33.9	42.6	16.6	56.4	51.0	62.0	60.5
July	17.1	17.1	3.6	0.0	18.2	0.0	47.1	0.0	57.9	0.0	69.0	28.2
August	0.0	0.0	20.8	0.0	23.8	0.0	64.0	0.0	78.3	0.0	80.8	34.6
September	16.4	0.0	22.7	0.0	49.1	32.7	23.1	13.5	62.8	59.3	56.8	56.8
October	5.9	0.0	11.8	2.0	46.2	5.1	33.3	0.0	50.9	19.3	65.5	56.0
November	13.6	0.0	3.1	0.0	40.5	0.0	40.4	13.5	66.3	48.3	51.7	42.7
December	10.7	0.0	32.3	0.0	80.3	47.9	33.3	0.0	66.6	30.3	80.9	42.7

the plea rate needed for clearing the docket in almost every month and virtually eliminated the need for any guilty pleas in two months (February and April).

Courtroom adaptation

Given that there was a general increase in caseload over the period of our research, it was important to examine what structural efforts the court was able to invoke to respond to this increase without the need to change the method of disposition. We found that, from the beginning of the nineteenth century, General Sessions responded to changes in caseload through three principal methods which were unrelated to method of disposition. First, the court expanded the number of sessions per year from six in 1800 to twelve by 1815 such that a session became equivalent to a monthly term of court. Second, the average number of days per session increased from nine in 1800 to 12 by 1850[70] and to between 14 and 17 thereafter. Third, by 1850, the court added additional parts thereby expanding exponentially the number of courtroom actors available to address any increase in caseload. Moreover, throughout this period the hours in the court day remained flexible which enabled the judges to expand the working day dependent upon demand. The increase in court sessions and court days is set out below in Table 9.5:

TABLE 9.5: *General Sessions, Minute Book: The Frequency of Court Sessions and The Number of Non-ceremonial Court Days over the Year, for One Part of Court, 1800–1865*

Year	Number of court sessions	Average number of days per session
1800	6	9.0
1805	7	5.1
1810	7	11.6
1815	12	11.3
1820	12	11.5
1825	12	11.3
1830	12	11.3
1835	12	10.7
1839	12	14.5
1844 (9 months)	9	12.8
1849 (6 months)	6	11.5
1860 (7 months)	7	13.7
1865 (7 months)	7	16.0
1870 (8 months)	8	11.3
1875 (9 months)	9	16.6
1878 (5 months)	5	15.8
1885 (9 months)	9	19.1
1890 (10 months)	10	16.3
1892 (5 months)	5	16.4
1895 (4 months)	4	19.5

Note: From 1844 only the number of months noted in the parentheses could be traced.

[70] Moreover, it was not at all unusual for a court and jury to work into the early hours of the morning in order to complete the cases in progress.

In the period before 1850 General Sessions was perfectly capable of adapting to varying caseload demands through operational changes in court days without abandoning jury trials as the predominant method of case disposition. Prior to the period 1850–1865 when guilty pleas came to predominate, significant increases in caseload were not accompanied by any comparable change in the rate of guilty pleas. For example, the Secretary of State's Reports show that in 1839 there were 18 guilty pleas and 167 trials which meant a guilty plea rate of 9.7 per cent. In the very next year, 1840, although the number of trials and guilty pleas had risen from 185 to 400, the guilty plea rate was effectively unchanged at 10.5 per cent.

Between 1850 and 1865, caseload dispositions (trials and guilty pleas) in General Sessions increased by 132 per cent from n=570 to n=1323. On its face this might tend to support the argument that the guilty plea rate is a function of caseload, since over the same period of time the guilty plea rate increased from 35 per cent to 49 per cent. However, over the same period of time, the capacity of the court to handle cases more than doubled. In addition to increasing the average number of days per court session from 11.5 days in 1849 to 16.0 days by 1865, the court regularly cloned itself into two parts. By 1850, a second full-time judge, the City Judge, convened General Sessions concurrently with the Recorder, thus doubling the number of court parts. In other words, by increasing the number of court parts and thus court days, General Sessions was able to reduce caseload demand per court part at least to pre-1850 levels, when the rate of guilty plea was a much less prominent feature of case dispositions. Thus, for example, in 1844 the Court actually sat for 156 days[71] and disposed of 419 trials and guilty pleas at a rate of 2.7 dispositions per judge day. By contrast, in 1865 the Court, now regularly in at least two concurrent parts, had the capacity to sit for at least 384 days in total[72] to enable it to deal with the 1323 trials and guilty pleas disposed of in that year or a rate of 3.5 dispositions per judge day, less than one case more per day from that of twenty years earlier.

Prosecutorial adaptations

As the number of court days expanded in response to caseload demands so too did the prosecutorial resources which serviced General Sessions. In the first half of the century, the District Attorney was an appointed official who prosecuted cases where the private prosecutor had not retained a private attorney. As the number of publicly-prosecuted cases grew and as the number of court days expanded, so the position of District Attorney came to be one which would

---

[71] This assumes twelve sessions over the year at an average of 12.8 days per session, as depicted in Table 9.5.

[72] Court capacity here has been calculated on the basis of each of the Court Parts sitting for twelve sessions each year on an average of 16 days per session. Actually, our inspection of available Court Minute Books for 1865 showed that, whilst the average number of judge days sat was 16, as depicted in Table 9.5, in at least three sessions one of the two Court Parts actually sat for a period of 20 days per session.

more fully occupy a lawyer's time, unlike the earlier period when public prosecution in General Sessions cases was clearly a part-time activity. Thus, for
example, in 1805, prosecutions in General Sessions occurred during no more
than 36 days of the entire year, whereas by 1839, prosecutions occurred over
174 days.

By 1846 the District Attorney became an elected official with a dedicated
office the resources for which grew steadily as caseload and court days expanded. Thus, the Controller's Reports show that whilst prior to 1847, $3,500 was
allocated annually to the District Attorney, by 1852 that amount had grown to
$8,500. The increase in expenditure occurred through additional salary to the
District Attorney himself, from $3,500 to $5,000, coupled with payment beginning in 1847 to an Assistant District Attorney, initially of $1,000 and by 1852 of
$2,500[73] as seen in Figure 9.8:

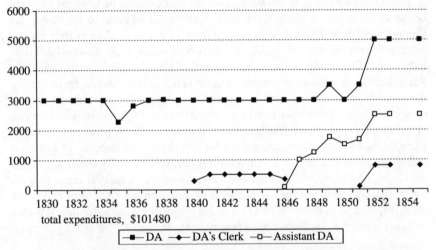

total expenditures, $101480

| ■ DA | ◆ DA's Clerk | □ Assistant DA |

FIGURE 9.8: Controller's Reports—District Attorney Expenditures, 1830–1855

The capacity of the District Attorney's office continued to increase such that by
1865 a third attorney was added to the public prosecutor's staff.[74] In addition,
where necessary to respond to workload demands, the District Attorney may
have hired private counsel to act as Assistant District Attorneys in criminal trials.[75] The growth in resources enabled the Assistant District Attorneys and later
Associate Attorneys to appear and prosecute cases either alone or with the
District Attorney in each of the concurrent court parts.

[73] Support services for the District Attorney's Office also expanded as payment to the DA's clerk
increased from $250 in 1846 to $750 in 1852.

[74] And by 1870, a fourth.

[75] See Carolyn Ramsey (2002) p 1329 who points out that as late as 1896, statutory law em-
powered the District Attorney to hire private counsel as assistants in criminal trials, citing *Revised
Statutes of the State of New York*, Section 204, article 10 (Collin 1896).

However, this increase in capacity of the District Attorney's office might not be conclusive because, as Fisher contends, even as a salaried official the prosecutor might have an incentive to fasten upon a more expeditious method of disposition so as to free up time for an increasingly lucrative civil practice, particularly in the burgeoning area of tort law.[76] Nonetheless, in New York City, this would not seem to have had a direct impact on prosecutors in General Sessions who, through the cloning of court parts and hence the expansion of available court days retained sufficient number of excess days in each court session so as to be able to devote time exclusively to civil practice without impinging on criminal workload should they so choose. Indeed, District Attorney Oakey Hall, as an elected official steeped in Tammany Hall politics, discharged his responsibility in civil law practice by maintaining his name at the head of a law firm as a 'rain maker' whose political connections served to attract clients.[77]

CONCLUSION

After mid century, significant changes in the socio-political character of New York City occurred whereby concurrent with the growth of population came a reorganisation of city government, expanded suffrage and the emergence of professional politicians linked to the Tammany Society which inaugurated an era of 'ward-heeling' and created divisions between elected officials and the mercantile class that otherwise did not exist in the earlier part of the century. Co-ordinate with changes in local government, the figures depicted in this chapter show a sudden and dramatic change in the method of case disposition after mid century-from jury trials to guilty pleas. During this period, when jury verdicts became increasingly dominated by acquittals and convictions to lesser included offences, the overall rate of conviction increased co-ordinate with the dramatic change in the overall method of case disposition through guilty pleas.

Furthermore, it could be argued that the proliferation of non-trial dispositions occurred during a process of professional degradation. The overall result of politicisation appears to have been that the prosecution's case became destabilised, in part, because of the inherent unreliability of a pre-trial process that involved discretionary decision-making, involving Tombs' lawyers and elected Police Justices. As to the latter, some were neither learned in the law nor capable of

---

[76] George Fisher (2000) p 903.

[77] See C Bowen (1869) p 57 where the author indicates that even when District Attorney Oakey Hall became Mayor in 1869 he maintained his law partnership which had value to the other members in and of itself, given his name and connections. Furthermore, there is no evidence that the District Attorney's reliance upon guilty pleas and non-trial dispositions was exercised in order to increase the time and opportunity to devote to private legal practice. As District Attorney, Hall was paid a salary of $4,000 per annum and while he maintained his partnership in his law firm, the latter took up little of his time. This remained the case when he became Mayor in 1869. See Bowen p 57.

organising their office in such a fashion as to reliably provide the District Attorney and Grand Jury with cases that could withstand a challenge in General Sessions. Many cases never reached General Sessions itself and often died a quiet death in the pigeon holes of the Police Court without any further prosecutorial or judicial review.

Moreover, the District Attorney became an operative of Tammany Hall whose constituents were very often those who would be subject to prosecution in General Sessions. This resulted in the District Attorney exercising favour to such a degree that indictments which the Grand Jury returned against Tammany's constituents could be pigeon-holed and never arraigned in General Sessions or prosecuted thereafter. Similarly, in those cases that were prosecuted, General Sessions judges themselves, now nominated and vetted by Tammany loyalists, engaged in criminal misdeeds favouring defendants with political connections.

By contrast, the nature and pattern of offences prosecuted in General Sessions over the period 1850–1865 was similar to that prevailing in the first half of the century when jury trials predominated. While property offences in General Sessions grew proportionately in contrast to crimes against the person (despite the diminution of petit larceny prosecutions), the nature of those property offences tended to be simple opportunistic crimes. Property crimes were commonly committed by servants stealing from their masters, by employees stealing from their employers, by boarders from fellow boarders, by people who slept in the same room as their victims, by prostitutes stealing from their clients, by individuals exploiting their luck where a monied person fell drunk in their presence or a stranger inadvertently dropped a pocketbook or purse. Crimes against the person, now proportionately fewer in number, more often than in the earlier period involved serious crimes of violence within the working class and poorer sections of society. Nonetheless, the vast majority of crime prosecuted in General Sessions was opportunistic rather than planned, simple rather than complex, casual rather than systematic. At the least, most of those caught and thereby featured in our sample of case files were apprehended precisely because they were inexperienced amateurs or habitual but unprofessional criminals.

It is evident from our caseload analysis of General Sessions, that the case pressure hypothesis, which explains the rise in guilty pleas as principally a function of increased volume of cases, cannot be sustained as a direct correlation on either a monthly or yearly basis. During the mid-period of the nineteenth century, the workload, in terms of trials and guilty plea dispositions, varied considerably on a monthly basis and increased gradually over time. Throughout this period, the court was able to respond flexibly to these variable demands without necessitating any dramatic change in the method by which cases were disposed. Indeed, whilst reliance on guilty pleas increased over time, the increase in the rate of guilty pleas between 1840 and 1865 (610 per cent) far outstripped the increase in caseload disposition over the same period (230 per cent). This places into question what appears, to this extent at least, a gratuitous transformation in method of case disposition not born out of necessity related to the demands of increased work load. Indeed, our data demonstrate that there was little relationship between caseload and guilty plea rate predictive of the change in method of case disposition. Whilst overall caseload expanded so did court days and prosecutorial resources such that the expansion in workload did not appear to have overcome the capacity of courtroom actors to continue to dispose of cases through trials.

Of course, one explanation for this transformation may be that the District Attorney was induced into foregoing jury trials because of what he may have perceived as the likelihood of perverse acquittals and unjustified reductions in charges. This, however, is not the principal functionalist explanation advanced for the advent of the guilty plea system. Commentators contend, instead, that enhanced policing led to evidence whose reliability was incontrovertible, thereby inviting an avoidance of trials given the absence of disputable issues whilst the adversarial practices of lawyers so complicated the process as to make trials too cumbersome and time-consuming to be relied upon as a regular method of case disposition.

In the ensuing chapters, we seek to determine the degree to which the transformation in method of case disposition was a function of more reliable and scientific policing and trial complexity. We then consider the nature of litigated processes lawyers employed in cases prosecuted in General Sessions to determine to what extent such practices made trials unworkable in everyday cases. Following this, through an analysis of our case files in which guilty pleas were entered, we consider whether exogenous factors unrelated to the sufficiency of evidence and proof but instead to the wider socio-political economy of the local state have explanatory force.

Chapter 10

Crime Detection and Investigation: 1850–1865

INTRODUCTION

In this chapter we consider whether reorganisation of police in New York City affected the acquisition of evidence and proof in cases prosecuted in General Sessions in light of the argument that after the police became organised into a central force, beginning in New York by 1846, methodological advances in policing improved the quality and reliability of evidence auguring in favour of guilty pleas rather than trials because most prosecutions, in contrast to the earlier period, would now clearly establish the defendant's guilt.[1]

We next consider the effect the mid-century 'judicialisation' of the role of the magistrate had on the evidence-gathering function and on the reliability of the prosecution case. In particular, we address the changing nature of the examination of the accused and the role of the magistrate in the assemblage and co-ordination of the case for the prosecution.

The analysis of our sample of case files therefore seeks to determine, at a macro level, the degree of change in crime detection, apprehension and evidence-acquisition over the period that plea bargaining came to predominate. We analysed our sample according to generic offence type to determine the role of the reorganised police and citizens in the arrest and apprehension of offenders, in contrast to the earlier period. This was followed by an analysis of the role and importance of the Police Justice. We begin, however, with a description of the reorganisation of policing itself derived from the literature and secondary sources.

---

[1] As Vogel has pointed out, this general theory is unpersuasive at a comparative level: 'The ... line of argument, attributing causality [of plea bargaining] to the rise of a professional police force, founders on the fact that the police existed in London prior to their appearance in the United States; thus, if the presence of a professional police force alone were causal, the practice [of plea bargaining] would have arisen first in Britain, which it did not': Vogel (1999) p 167.

REORGANISATION OF POLICE

Between 1840 and 1850 in New York City, efforts were undertaken to reorganise the police and change it into a salaried full-time force that would replace the marshals, constables and watch. These efforts, modelled on the metropolitan police of London, sought by 1845 to create a 'preventive' police by combining day and night patrols into a semi-military force of 800 men with specified qualifications, fixed terms of office, and established pay.[2] At the outset, with the Mayor's approval, each Alderman appointed the police of the ward he represented. The idea was that the investigatory and crime detection work of a regular police force covering the whole of the City would replace that of the various Police Offices under the auspices of Special Justices. This new force was to enhance the visibility of policing since it would be present both in the day and night replacing the more sporadic presence of the night watch.[3]

The reorganisation process was itself highly politicised whereby mayors and governors with different political allegiances contended for control of the police and the population these forces served. Ultimately two forces—the Municipal and Metropolitan Police—vied for control of the policing function with, by 1857, the Metropolitan Police (Governor controlled) replacing the Municipal Police (Mayor and Tammany Hall controlled) as the body that would police the City of New York for the next thirteen years.

This reorganisation had a direct impact both on the identity of those who served as police officers as well as on their competence and capacity.[4] For example, the new appointment process reduced the presence of career officials who as constables had made respectable reputations for themselves as crime fighters in the earlier period.[5] With marked exceptions,[6] some of their successors, at least until 1857, prior to which the police were largely under the direct control of elected Tammany officials, were untrained, had little experience in police work and were responsive primarily to the social concerns of the local ward in which they were situated as articulated by Aldermen and 'ward heelers'.[7]

---

[2] *New York Laws* (1844) Chapter 315.

[3] More detailed accounts of the reform efforts over this period are to be found in: R Fosdick (1920); A Costello (1885); J Richardson (1970); W Miller (1977); G Ketcham (1967).

[4] Wilbur Miller (1973) found that the steady decline in convictions at trial may have been attributed to the jury's views as to the reliability of police evidence: 'In the later sixties the public relations of the Metropolitan Police were at their lowest point since 1857; juries may not have trusted police testimony' (pp 101–02). However, as we will see the greater involvement of the police in the prosecution of indicted cases over the period 1850–1865 was mostly formalistic and there was no measurable increase in the rate at which the police supplied substantive evidence of guilt.

[5] Indeed, following the first efforts at reorganisation, some experienced police officers transformed themselves into private policemen because, for example, they found themselves politically unacceptable to an incumbent administration: see David Johnson (1979) pp 59–60.

[6] George W Walling, for example, was a career officer. Appointed as a patrolman in 1847, he was promoted to superintendent before eventually retiring in 1885: see David Johnson (1979).

[7] See eg, Wilbur R Miller (1977) p 37 describing how detailment for detective work became a means of rewarding political supporters. See also Burrows and Wallace (1999) p 638.

Whilst in one sense policing came under the centralised control of either the Governor or the Mayor, in another, more importantly for the day to day operation of the force, policing became decentralised and autonomous from the Police Justices who, like their English counterparts, now no longer supervised or co-ordinated with law enforcement efforts in acquiring and securing the prosecution's evidence.[8] Thus, the earlier capacity to integrate policing functions through the Police Office now became disassembled with little overall investigative coordination with what now became the Police Court.

Moreover, there is little reported enhancement from the earlier period in methods of detection or in police capacity for increased investigative efficiency.[9] The principal additional instruction received by the new police followed the introduction of drilling, as detailed in the report of the Chief of Police, George Matsell, to the Mayor in 1854:[10]

> Since my last report to your Honor, I have selected a competent policeman to act as drill-sergeant, whose duty it is to take the men appointed by the Commissioners of Police, and instruct them in the military art, and in the rules and regulations adopted for the government of the Police Department. While under instruction they are required to act as a reserve force to attend at fires, etc., and to perform patrol duty in different parts of the city, under the directions of their sergeants; after being thus thoroughly drilled and instructed, they are directed to report themselves to their several captains and are ready to perform any duty he may require of them ...
>
> [T]he policemen in the different districts are now being thoroughly instructed in the military art, and decided improvement is already visible at fires and other places where they are required to act in concert, and in case of riot they will be able to act with increased efficiency and power.

Apart from rudimentary military training throughout the period 1850–1865 the 'new' police had to learn whatever policing skills they acquired on the job. Officers, working alone or in small groups, might pass on knowledge and skills to their comrades but the methods of instruction were haphazard and the skills of a basic character. Thus, William Bell, a New York City patrolman, recorded the following entry in his journal:[11]

> Monday, August 18th, 1851
> On duty. Previous to coming to the office this morning, I went to the station house and signed the book. On my way down I met the notorious *pickpockets* or *knucks* John Baxter, alias Tosh, Jim Bond and a man I suppose Jack

---

[8] See Langbein (2003) p 276.
[9] For a discussion of police detention and interrogation strategies, see Miller (1973) pp 58–62.
[10] Board of Aldermen, Document No 17, February 9, 1854.
[11] S Wilentz (1979).

Roach, in company together going up the 4th Avenue. I put the pipe[12] on them and holded them at the Gothic corner of 32nd Street and 4th Avenue where the cars start from. They took a drink. I went up and spoke to them. They said if I would let them go, they would immediately leave the city. I spotted them to Officer Sutton and several others. They then left and went down 4th Avenue. It was about 9 o'clock when they left.

The 'spotting' of repeat offenders to colleagues,[13] the surveillance of pawn-brokers and junk dealers and the frisking of suspected offenders on the street documented by William Bell were a continuation of policing methodologies whose lineage is directly traceable to the watch and ward system and the office of Special Justice. Indeed, the only 'new' advance was the institutionalising of 'spotting' with the establishment of The Rogues' Portrait Gallery in New York in November, 1857,[14] which generalised and updated a proposal advanced by Special Justice Christian in 1812.[15]

   The assertions of functionalist commentators of increased police professionalisation thus may give credence to a wider and long-discredited myth about the replacement of the 'old' watch and ward with the 'new police'. Contrary to their assertions, the literature suggests that there was no clean break in policing methodologies between the 'old' and the 'new'. In New York, as in London,[16] the new police in their early years were not very efficient or of sufficient numbers,[17] many were inexperienced and some of those skilled in the craft of policing had acquired their experience in the 'old' forces; and problems in appointments based upon patronage, without necessarily regard for fitness for office, graft and corruption were as apparent in the new police as in the old.[18] Tyler Anbinder,[19] for

---

[12] A police expression for 'tailing' or 'watching' or 'tracking' a person.

[13] In a journal entry for Friday, 22 August 1851, William Bell records that Frank Hannock, a local thief, told him that he was leaving for Virginia 'as he could not live respectable here, for the officers were continually spotting him when ever he went to work.' S Wilentz (1979) p 153.

[14] See J Richardson (1970) p 122 who records that by June 1858 the Gallery had some seven hundred photographs of known criminals.

[15] Christian proposed the establishment of 'intelligence offices' for servants under the superintendance of the police, with a register which would contain all the applications of masters and servants within the city and in this way preserve the morals of domestics and 'correct their excesses': Christian (1812, 1970) pp 27–8.

[16] For England, see R Storch (1975, 1976); D Philips (1977); J Styles (1983); P Rawlings (1999). For the USA, see J Richardson (1976); G Ketcham (1976); W Miller (1977); New York, K Spann (1981).

[17] The contemporary commentator, James Gerard, asserted that there was no doubt that amongst the police of New York 'many … do not come up to the proper standard of requirements, either physical, intellectual or moral' and who called for a major expansion in the numbers of police on the force: J W Gerrard (1853) pp 14–15.

[18] After quoting the view of the *New York Times* that an inefficient police force was 'one of the consequences of the rudest health, and the most unbounded prosperity' (*New York Times*, December 9, 1854), Wilbur Miller remarks: 'America's distinctive social and economic mobility made the policeman's career appealing only to those without energy or ability to pursue a more lucrative occupation.' W Miller (1977) p 19.

[19] T Anbinder (2002).

example, found that by mid-century police corruption was a direct corollary of party politics with some officers earning their posts as party loyalists and with others directly bribing local politicians. By 1855, a regular system of police extortion resulted in brothel keepers and owners of disorderly houses complaining of shakedowns to Tammany's Mayor, Fernando Wood.[20]

In March 1857, the legislative Committee on Cities and Villages, referring to the fact that 'grave complaints' had been preferred against the workings of the police in New York and Brooklyn, stated that everyone was agreed that the police system required improvement. The Committee then cited evidence given to it by the District Attorney of New York:[21]

> ... The policemen are not kept on active patrol, but are permitted to lounge and loiter. The day force on duty is excessively unnecessary, and disproportioned to the night watch. The chief of police, from lack of clerkly duty, is compelled nearly all the time to remain at his office. There is really no head of police, but each captain is a head in his own district; and discipline varies, in different wards, according to the captain's attention, or skill and tact. Policemen by constantly acting in a limited sphere, have their haunts! There is an irksome spirit of favouritism ... An enervating system of rewards has been practiced. There is no incentive to promotion, but, on the contrary, captains are taken from the citizens, and placed over lieutenants and sergeants of ten years' experience, depressing the energies of the men. The regulations are mainly dead letter, and are often contemptibly evaded ... There is an irresponsible clashing of interests by the independent police and private watch, often leading to foolish jealousy from the regular police. Excepting *drill*, there is NO SYSTEMATIC INSTRUCTION OF POLICEMEN IN THEIR DUTIES ... (original emphasis)

Nor is there any scarcity in the examples of the continuation of the system of watch although it now appears that watchmen were privately retained as contrasted with most of their predecessors who volunteered from the neighbourhood.[22] Thus, James Gerard commented in 1853 on deficiencies in the policing of New York in these terms:[23]

> We are utterly deficient of a River Police. We have miles of wharves, and millions of property almost entirely unprotected. Our mercantile and business men pay a heavy and private taxation for night watchmen of ships and goods, when they ought to have protection from the public for the tax they

---

[20] T Anbinder (2002) pp 228–29.

[21] *State of New York, Assembly Documents* (1857) No 127, pp 2–3 (original emphasis).

[22] See *Robert Mitchell*, District Attorney's Files, 8 October, 1849 and *Alexander Woolsey and Charles Wilson*, District Attorney's Files, 6 September, 1855.

[23] J W Gerard (1853) p 15. See also *New York Times*, November 23, 1857, giving an account of the William Street murder in which Private Watchman Cohen told the Coroner of his experience as a watchman for six or seven years in the vicinity of Chatham and Frankfurt Streets.

pay for supporting the police. So little confidence have those in the upper part of the city in any benefit from the police in protecting their houses at night from burglars, that a private police or watch is now very generally being established in the region of Union square, Madison square, Gramarcy park, and a large portion of the eighteenth ward, which costs each house six dollars a year, when we pay heavy taxes for that very security.

The available literature on New York City police for 1850–1865 thus strongly supports Harring's characterisation of pre-1880s police departments in the USA:[24]

Paternalistic domination by chiefs, minimal standards for admission and training, poorly defined bureaucratic structure, little specialization among the ranks, weak central structure, and strong precinct structure characterized the pre-1880s departments.

In short, the literature suggests that the transformation from watch and ward to modern policing was a long and complex *process* not an event and was, in any event, at its very early stages during the dramatic shift from jury trial to plea bargaining.

In the rest of this chapter, we analyse the cases in our sample to determine to what extent, following the advent of centralised policing, control of the case for the prosecution became the sole province of the local state after which we consider whether subtle changes in policing methodology occurred in everyday cases which enhanced the construction and reliability of prosecutions in General Sessions.

OWNERSHIP AND CONTROL

We sought to determine to what extent the private prosecutor was the moving force in the first half of the century or whether this changed after 1846 with the reorganisation of policing.[25] As Figure 10.1 shows, however, the private prosecutor or complainant remained the dominant actor in responding to criminal activity subsequent to the movement to centralised policing.

We analysed the responses to criminal activity by the private prosecutor (by mid-century more commonly referred to as the complainant), by civilian bystanders and by law enforcers by considering their involvement in the apprehension of suspects. We distinguished three broad categories of involvement: first, the reaction of a bystander (private person or law enforcement) to a crime in progress by arresting or assisting in the apprehension of the suspected individual; second, the reaction of a private person or law enforcement officer to a request

---

[24] S Harring (1983) p 30.
[25] Reorganisation of policing, proposed in New York by Charles Christian in 1812, became more widespread in the 1830s before an implementation process during the 1850s and 1860s: Johnson (1979) pp 8–11.

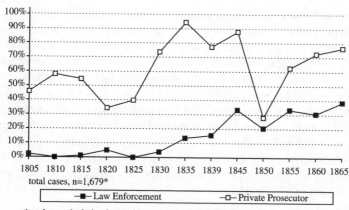

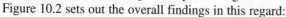

*total cases includes those with no activity and no information.
**includes watchperson, constable, marshall, and police.
***1804 and 1809 included in 1805 and 1810, respectively.

FIGURE 10.1 General Sessions, District Attorney's Files—Percentage of All Cases with
Identifiable Responses to Criminal Activity by Law Enforcement** and Private
Prosecutor Over a Thirty Day Period for One Court Part, 1804–1865***

from a private person for aid in apprehending a suspect who was in flight; and third,
the proactive involvement of private persons or law enforcement in solving criminal activity through the setting of a trap or through surveillance or stop and search.
Figure 10.2 sets out the overall findings in this regard:

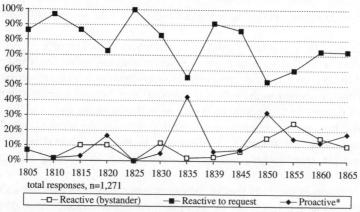

*set trap or set up lookout for person who committed crime in past or considered likely to engage in
criminal activity; stopped and searched based on suspicion.
**includes watchperson, constable, marshall and police.
***1804 and 1809 included in 1805 and 1810, respectively.

FIGURE 10.2 General Sessions, District Attorney's Files—Percentage of Responses to
Criminal Activity by Law Enforcement** and Private Prosecutor Over a Thirty Day
Period for One Court Part, 1804–1865***

Figure 10.2 shows that the dominant response to criminal activity over the entire period 1800–1865 was reactive. As the case files show, this was commonly to a request by a private person who made a 'hue and cry' after having first become a crime victim. Indeed, in so far as there was any proactive engagement with crime this was as or more frequent when constables and marshals undertook this work in collaboration with the Special Justice.

The foregoing is not to suggest that structural changes in the organisation of policing had no effect on capacity of the police to be engaged in the arrest and prosecution of offenders. One effect was expressed in our analysis of the annual reports of the City's chief financial officer, the Controller, between 1830–1858, which clearly showed the growth in rank and file police expenditure over the period, as seen in Figure 10.3:

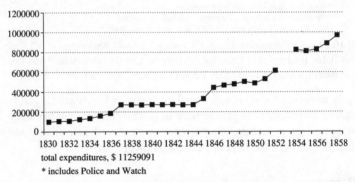

total expenditures, $ 11259091
* includes Police and Watch

FIGURE 10.3 Rank and File Police Expenditures*, Controller's Report, 1830–1858

A second effect was the growth in the numbers of police officers officially associated in the District Attorney's case papers with any given arrest and prosecution. Indeed, ownership or 'property' in individual cases was transferred from the private prosecutor to the police. Complaints now became embossed with the name of the officer assigned to each case as well as with the names of the police officers who were in some way involved in processing the accused, whether as witnesses or as functionaries, as illustrated in the prosecutions of Elizabeth Haviland for grand larceny and of Elizabeth Wilson for keeping a disorderly house.

By contrast, in the early part of the century, our sample of case files showed that neither the indictment nor the complaint contained any indication of police ownership of the case independent of the Special Justice. References to watchmen and constables would occur only in the context of an examination before the Special Justice of the private prosecutor.[26] By 1850, however, the jacket of the complaint indicated that the number of police officers associated with any given

---

[26] Or, exceptionally, of the officers themselves.

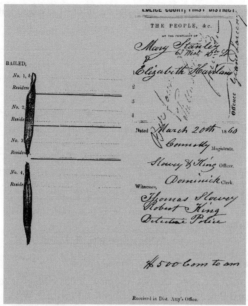

ILLUSTRATION 10.1: Elizabeth Haviland, Complaint Jacket, District Attorney's Files, 10 May, 1860.

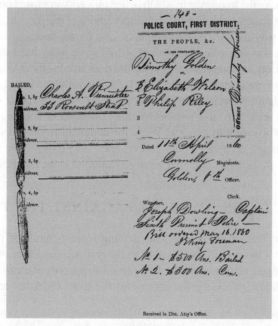

ILLUSTRATION 10.2: Elizabeth Wilson, Complaint Jacket, District Attorney's Files, 18 May, 1860.

case was either equal to or greater than the number of civilian witnesses and complainants, as depicted in Figure 10.4:

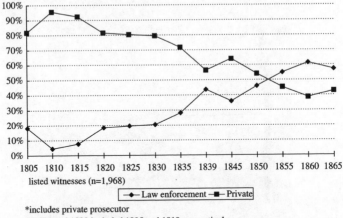

listed witnesses (n=1,968)

[—♦—Law enforcement —■— Private]

*includes private prosecutor
**1804 and 1809 included 1805 and 1810, respectively

FIGURE 10.4 General Sessions, District Attorney's Files—Magistrate's Complaint—
Percentage of Listed Potential Law Enforcement and Private* Witnesses Over a Thirty
Day Period for One Court Part, 1804–1865**

Figure 10.4 tracks the frequency in which police officers were listed on the complaint prepared by the magistrate, upon the initial appearance of the accused. In 1849–50 no specific space was allocated on the complaint form for the designation of a case officer. The result was that whereas the clerk would write in by hand the name of the responsible officer in some cases,[27] in others no responsible officer was designated in the complaint or elsewhere in the file.[28] By 1855, the complaint form had been developed to include a pre-printed 'Officer' section, and from this point onwards cases were routinely designated to a responsible officer whether or not the officer had any substantive involvement in the case. While the complainant remained the predominant witness examined by the Police Justice, after 1845 police came to outstrip private witnesses in the list of potential witnesses attached to the complaint.

PROSECUTIONS OF CRIMES AGAINST THE PERSON

As in the first half of the century, the driving force behind the prosecution of offences against the person continued to be the private prosecutor or complainant. It was the alleged victim who was best placed to identify the offender and provide the evidence necessary for committal for trial. Offences tended to arise

---

[27] See eg, *Ludwig Ginsburg and Carl Gross*, District Attorney's Files, 12 October, 1849 where 'Officer' appears in handwriting on the complaint form; and *John Blaw*, District Attorney's Files, 9 September, 1850 in which 'Officers Willis and Johnson' is endorsed on the complaint.
[28] See eg *Benedict Schmidt*, District Attorney's Files, 10 October, 1849.

between parties known to each other as neighbours, or in the work place[29] or occasionally in a familial setting.[30] In such cases, the complainant provided the principal, and often sole, evidence against the defendant.

By contrast, police officers were rarely involved in any significant way in offences against the person. Indeed, in the period 1850–1865, the police played an active role in providing evidence before the Police Justice in our sample of case files in only 14.0 per cent of these offences, although their role in some instances was clearly subordinate to that of the complainant or other civilian witnesses. The police were central to three prosecutions because, in each instance, the officer alleged that he was the victim of an assault, as illustrated in the prosecution of William Chambert.[31] In that case, Officer Simon Elliott of the Twelfth Ward Police instigated a prosecution against the defendant, a 42 year old German tailor, on the grounds that the defendant had made an attempt 'to take [his] life with a knife—[Elliott] further swears that while attempting to arrest the defendant he cut him on the hand with said knife and also gave him a severe blow on his eye with his fist'.

In three further cases, as illustrated by the prosecution of John Thacker,[32] police officers provided important evidence because they had been witnesses to the incident or because of information discovered on stopping and searching the defendant. In Thacker's case, Officer Henry Whitehead of the 11th Ward Police observed an incident by chance as he was standing opposite a porter house on the corner of 8th Street and Avenue D. According to testimony he gave to the Coroner's Inquisition, Officer Whitehead saw Andrew Ferguson knock John Thacker to the ground in the middle of the street. After arresting Ferguson, however, he learned from Ferguson that Ferguson had been stabbed by the defendant. Two fellow officers at the station house also stated that, when brought to the station, Ferguson stated that Thacker had stabbed him.[33]

As the foregoing examples illustrate, the broad pattern of policing in our sample of offences of personal violence remained unchanged from the earlier period. The moving force behind the arrest and prosecution and the principal provider of

---

[29] See *Richard Clark*, District Attorney's Files, 2 October, 1855 (one neighbour firing his gun out of his window into the house of complainant); *Albert Watson*, District Attorney's Files, 22 May, 1860 (complainant Ellen Smith had tried to restrain the defendant from leaving the house prior to the assault); and *Michael Connolly*, District Attorney's Files, 14 September, 1850 (a fight between men working at the dock).

[30] The recurrent theme in the period 1804–1845 of assault and battery between domestic partners was much less evident in the papers, most probably because they were dealt with in Special Sessions.

[31] District Attorney's Files, 4 September, 1855. See also *Patrick Martin*, District Attorney's Files, 30 May, 1860, in which a police officer accused the defendant of pushing him from a platform breaking both his wrists.

[32] District Attorney's Files, 6 September, 1850.

[33] In other cases involving police evidence, the officer's involvement arose out of a call for assistance by a citizen or out of an administrative performance of arrest. See eg, *Charlotte Morford*, District Attorney's Files, 6 April, 1865 in which the victim claimed to have been cut with a razor by the defendant.

evidence continued to be the private complainant with police involvement limited to assisting the complainant or chancing upon an offence in progress.

PROPERTY PROSECUTIONS

If advances in police science and the production of reliable evidence were not
apparent in the prosecution of crimes against the person, the question arises
whether such advances were more evident in property prosecutions where the
need for detection, tracing of goods and proof of ownership was and is generally
greater. To test this, we analysed our sample of case files to see whether the resolution of the case depended upon civilian evidence or whether the police played
the dominant role.

In only one case, *John McCarty, Richard Garrah and James Sherry*,[34] is there
any indication of the use of technology by the police as an aid in criminal investigation.

> Patrick Gleeson, a driver for James Atkinson, left his coach and horses in
> front of 62 Montgomerie Street when he went to get paid for carrying two
> gentlemen and, on his return 'about five minutes afterwards', discovered the
> coach missing. After a man 'standing on the walk' told him that James
> Sherry had taken the horses for a drive around the block, he waited for some
> 25 minutes but, when Sherry did not return, he tracked the wheels in the
> snow through several streets until he lost sight of them. Gleeson then went
> to the 7th Ward Station House for assistance in tracing the coach. As Gleeson
> stated in his affidavit, after arriving at the Station House he 'telegraphed to
> several station houses, [he] went to the Central Office and telegraphed to the
> station houses on the West Side of the City …' Officer James Parrish of the
> 13th Ward Police stated in his affidavit that the 13th Ward Station house had
> received a telegraph notice at 2.40am, that he had left the station at 3.00am
> together with Officer Senior, and that they found the coach and horses at
> about 3.20am.

While the potential value of the telegraph in co-ordinating police action and in
speeding up police response is clear in the above example, as late as 1865 officers were still summoning each other for assistance by means of an 'alarm rap',
a wooden contraption like a rattle that gave off a rapping noise to which other
officers could respond.[35]

Of course, it might be thought, with the commencement of the reorganisation
of the police in the 1840s in New York, that the police role in the investigation

---

[34] District Attorney's Files, 10 April, 1860.
[35] See eg *Francis West*, District Attorney's Files, 23 March, 1865 in which Officer Martin used the
'alarm rap' after hearing a noise in a store at night, thereby getting the assistance of Officer Carnochan.

and proof of General Sessions' cases might have been enhanced in other ways. To test this, we analysed, as we had done for the first half of the century, our sample of case files to gauge the respective roles of the police and citizens in the resolution of property prosecutions as set out in Table 10.1:

TABLE 10.1: *General Sessions, District Attorney's Files: The Contributions of Citizens and Police to the Investigation of Property Offences Over a Thirty Day Period for One Court Part, 1850–1865*

	1850		1855		1860		1865		Total	
	n	%	n	%	n	%	n	%	n	%
Dominant role played by citizen	26	37.7	29	44.6	33	31.4	50	39.0	138	37.6
Dominant role played by police	13	18.8	20	30.8	16	15.2	28	21.9	77	21.0
Joint citizen-police role	15	21.7	13	20.0	42	40.0	49	38.3	119	32.4
Probable dominance of citizen	5	7.3	2	3.1	9	8.6	0	0.0	16	4.4
Probable dominance of police	10	14.5	1	1.5	5	4.8	1	0.8	17	4.6
Inadequate information	20	–	18	–	34	–	23	–	95	–
Total	89	100.0	83	100.0	139	100.0	151	100.0	462	100.0

The disaggregation of data by year in Table 10.1 demonstrates that there was no significant change in the respective roles of citizens and police in the investigation of property prosecutions prior to or after 1860 by which time the guilty plea had become the dominant method of case disposition. In essence, the production of cases in General Sessions was primarily the responsibility of citizens with the police playing a subordinate, if important, supporting role. This was as true in 1865 when disposition by guilty plea was the prevailing norm as in 1850 when jury trials still predominated. A brief account of some of the broad categories in Table 10.1 will illuminate this.

Dominant role played by citizen

As appears from Table 10.1, in over one-third of property prosecutions for which clear information survives, the principal factor leading to the identification and apprehension of the suspect was the action of a private citizen, usually the complainant. Whilst police officers were involved in all cases in some capacity, the guiding force in these cases was the private citizen.

An analysis of our sample of case files for the period 1850–1865 shows that in no less than 17.0 per cent of all property cases defendants were actually arrested by the complainant or other citizen. Typically, the defendant would be caught in the act, as illustrated in the following cases:

Charles Mullen:[36]
Captain George McGown of the Battery Barracks stated that, on 12 April 1865, while he was standing with his wife in front of Trinity Church watching the funeral ceremonies of Brigadier General Winthrop he felt his watch being removed by the defendant. As a result he seized Mullen who struck McGown in the face and 'endeavoured to get away'.[37]

George Harris and William Wilson:[38]
Stephen Conovan, the agent and controller of the premises at 108 Leonard Street and resident himself at 110 Leonard Street, heard a noise at about 2.00 pm coming from No 108. He went to the door of No 108, unlocked it and found George Harris who 'by great exertions ran away from [his] hold and left a part of his shirt sleeve in [his] hand and ran away'. On searching the premises, Conovan found William Wilson 'secreted in the under cellar ...'[39]

Louis Schmidt:[40]
The defendant entered the store of Gustavus Hessenberg at 119 Broadway at the corner of Cedar Street and picked up three pieces of silk valued at $160.00 each. As Williams Wadsworth, a clerk at the store, arrived at the store from 'up town' he saw Schmidt leaving the store. At this point, Wadsworth made the arrest:

> 'I went after him, over took him, found the silks in his possession & brought him back to the store—I over took him in the same block.'[41]

Indeed, despite the re-organisation of policing, complainant-citizens often had to engage in extensive efforts in response to criminality, as in *Archibald Gilles*:[42]

> At about 7.00 pm on the event of 15 February 1865, James Gault discovered barrels of linseed oil and benzine to the value of $250.00 missing from the sidewalk outside his store at 392 Seventh Avenue. In his evidence at the trial of Gilles, Gault described what happened next:

---

[36] District Attorney's Files, 13 April, 1865.

[37] See also: *Louis Carmozin*, District Attorney's Files, 10 September, 1855; *James Smith*, District Attorney's Files, 18 October, 1855; and *John Rogers*, District Attorney's Files, 22 May, 1860.

[38] District Attorney's Files, 18 October, 1855.

[39] See also: *Charles Henderson*, District Attorney's Files, 10 October, 1849; *Frederick Heisenbuttle*, District Attorney's Files, 3 September, 1850; and *William Fenton*, District Attorney's Files, 11 October, 1850.

[40] District Attorney's Files, 12 October, 1855.

[41] For other examples, see: *Charles Tappen*, District Attorney's Files, 10 October, 1849; *George Harrison*, District Attorney's Files, 7 September, 1855; *Mary Brown*, District Attorney's Files, 5 May, 1865.

[42] District Attorney's Files, 23 March, 1865.

> [I] went round to the station house at 35th street to give notice that I had lost it; they told me that they would send a detective in the morning; I waited till 9 o'clock and the detective did not come. I went round to the paint stores in the neighborhood and warned them against buying anything of the kind in case it was offered them for sale; I went into a place in 26th Street near Ninth Avenue and asked if anything of that kind had been offered for sale; he told me Yes and brought me to the place where it was offered to him for sale—Mr Coyle, 243 Ninth Avenue; I seen the barrels and identified them as mine ...

> On learning of this, James Coyle reported the matter to the beat officer, Officer Fulle, who thereupon arrested Gilles and brought him to the station house, after which James Gault swore out a formal complaint.

Similarly, as in the earlier period, without the complainant's initiative many cases would never have been prosecuted because of the absence of knowledge of the identity of the perpetrator, as illustrated in the prosecution of Eliza Ploss:[43]

> The complainant, Mary Ellen Anthony had her pocketbook taken by the 13-year old defendant after she had dropped it while on the Eight Avenue car. She later learned from the conductor that the girl who had picked up the pocketbook gave her name as Elizabeth Augusta Smith, 524 Tenth Avenue. Mrs Anthony visited this address but found no such person living there. After this, she put an advertisement in the paper, as a result of which she was contacted by Susan Jane Van Tassel who had been in company with the defendant when the pocketbook was taken and she gave the detailed information which led to the arrest and prosecution of Eliza.[44]

Finally, we can note that citizens were crucial to the prosecution where they claimed to have witnessed the crime itself.[45]

Dominant role played by police officers

Although property prosecutions remained private in character and heavily dependent on civilian evidence, the police continued to have a dominant role in

[43] District Attorney's Files, 28 March, 1865.

[44] Eliza left for the country shortly after finding the pocketbook. Once she had been identified, a 'detective policeman' was sent to find her in Nyack, but she was out at Johnstown at the time. The matter was left for 'a week or so' before Mrs Anthony 'had Sergeant Lefferts go down and arrest her ...'. See also *John Tierney*, District Attorney's Files, 8 March, 1865, and *Bernard Brennan*, District Attorney's Files, 8 March, 1865.

[45] See eg, *Elizabeth Coolley and Anne Wilson*, District Attorney's Files, 22 November, 1855. In other cases, officers, though called to give evidence, told the court that they could contribute nothing of value to the evidence, as in: *Mary Ann Bradshaw*, District Attorney's Files, 9 March, 1865, in which Officer James M Tilley told the court 'I know nothing about the case ...'; *William Golden*, District Attorney's Files, 10 May, 1865, in which Officer John McPherson told the trial court, 'I know no more about the affair than that I was called to arrest this prisoner ...'

the identification, apprehension and prosecution of a significant minority of suspects. Their involvement, as in prosecutions in the earlier part of the century, came about primarily through finding the suspects in the act of committing a crime or stopping and searching individuals on the street. The police were aided, as before, by their knowledge of the underworld and by their ability to cultivate informants.

In a variety of different offences prosecuted, the police were the central actors in the case because they had, according to their affidavits, disturbed the defendant in the course of criminal activity. A number of burglary offences were brought to court on the basis of such evidence. Thus, for example, in *Fitch Lockett and Jeremiah Anderson*[46] the defendants were arrested on a charge of burglary of the house of Anthony Bernard by Officer John Brewer of the 18th District Police who stated that he found them in the house which had been 'burglariously broken open'.

Some robberies were also detected by an officer who was alert to suspicious conduct and was able to seize the perpetrator in the act, as in *Henry Williamson and Richard Wilson*:[47]

> The incident began when the defendants 'pretended to be old acquaintances with [the complainant]' and went with him to a vacant lot. After a time there, Wilson put a handkerchief around Esler's neck 'and tried to choke him and as [Esler] firmly believes to rob him'. Officer Farley then arrived and arrested both men. In his affidavit, Officer Farley explained that he had seen the defendants in company with the complainant and his 'suspicions were aroused by their conduct while in the street' and accordingly he followed them arresting them when they attempted to rob Esler.

Similarly, officers also chanced upon or saw in the course of their duties, various crimes of larceny, including stealing from ships while docked at piers,[48] and stealing from the person, as in *Ann Smith and Margaret Spier*,[49] a grand larceny prosecution in which the defendants stole money from John Shannon.[50]

> Shannon, who had recently been discharged from the army, went to Smith's house. Whilst there, he met Margaret Spier and spent the evening drinking before he passed out. The story is taken up by Officer Cornelius Reed of the 27th Precinct Police in his evidence at the defendants' trial:
>
> > '... I saw Shannon on the 23rd of March of this year; I arrested the women. In the morning of the 23 about 5 1/2 o'clock in the morning I

---

[46] District Attorney's Files, 6 September, 1850. See also: *Henry McCarthy*, District Attorney's Files, 12 November, 1850; and *Robert Granger*, District Attorney's Files, 21 November, 1850.

[47] District Attorney's Files, 19 September, 1855.

[48] *James Sheehan and Martin Norton*, District Attorney's Files, 13 March, 1865.

[49] District Attorney's Files, 6 April, 1865.

[50] See also *Thomas Boyle*, District Attorney's Files, 22 March, 1865 in which Officer Lewes Rockwell arrested Boyle after seeing Boyle stealing butter from his employer at the freight depot.

was patrolling my post and saw a light in this woman's basement where these people lived; I walked down very cautiously to the door and looked into a large split and a keyhole; I saw Shannon lying on the floor about twelve feet from where I stood; the woman Smith was bent over him and the woman Spear was by her side holding a candle for her; the woman Smith put her hand in his pocket, drew it up, and put something in the pocket of her dress; the man Shannon moved once or twice and she pulled the hand very cautiously; at another time he made a sudden sort of move; she ordered the woman with a light away; I watched her till she got up; I then halloed to her and told her to open the door; I said if she did not open the door I would break it in; I went in and said to her, what did you do with the money you took from this woman (*sic*); there is no use of your denying it; she hesitated when I said that 'you have better give me that money'; she said she took it for safe keeping.'

The police were sometimes assisted in their investigative or pre-emptive functions by their knowledge of the underworld and by their ability to cultivate informants, a practice which also existed in the first half of the nineteenth century. This practice is illustrated in *William Jones, Peter Butler and Andrew Roberts*:[51]

In the evening of 2nd May and the morning of the 3rd, Officer Lemuel Slater was on patrol when, in his words,

'... he saw William Jones alias 'Little Candy', Peter Butler alias 'Ikey' and Andrew Roberts alias 'Big Candy' ... talking together—[he] well knowing their bad character suspected some thing wrong and watched their movements and followed them and saw them in the morning of the 3rd day of May 1860 enter the house of Mary McHugh who ... washed for them ...'

Officer Slater went for assistance and on his return searched McHugh's room with Officer Barry and found a bundle of property stolen from a jewellry store that same night which, according to Mary McHugh, the defendants had brought with them and asked her to leave the bundle there until they came back for it.[52]

The police also benefited from information provided by informants, as illustrated in the application for an arrest warrant in the case of *Otis Foster*:[53]

[51] District Attorney's Files, 18 May, 1860.
[52] In a few other cases police suspicion was based upon knowledge of the defendant's character, as, eg, in *Robert Mitchell*, District Attorney's Files, 8 October, 1849 in which Judge Osborn and Constable McCleester arrested the defendant, 'a thief', on suspicion of burglary; and *George Hoyt*, District Attorney's Files, 16 September, 1850 in which several men were acting suspiciously, one of whom, when Captain James Leonard was informed, he 'immediately identified as an old thief named George Hoyt' and directed his arrest.
[53] District Attorney's Files, 22 May, 1860.

The case arose some time after a burglary on February 8, 1860 at Ann Henry's house at 854 Broadway, a crime for which Malvina Francis and Isadora Smith were convicted in March 1860. Following the conviction, Officer John Bennet swore an affidavit on 26 March 1860 against Otis Foster who, he alleged, was involved in that burglary. Officer Bennet's affidavit spelled out the basis of his suspicion:

> '... Upon information received by [him] and which [he] verily believes to be true [he] has reason to believe that John Otis Foster—now here— was a participant in the commission of the said felony—and that a portion of the said property so taken and stolen ... has been seen in the possession of ... Foster—whereupon [he] prays that said Foster may be held and detained for a reasonable time to enable [him] to produce such witnesses as [he] verily believes may be obtained to testify against the said Foster ...'

After Police Justice Connolly acceded to this application, an affidavit was sworn by Elizabeth Havelow, then detained in the City Prison, in which she implicated Foster in the crime.[54]

Joint citizen-police role

Overall, in almost one-third of all property prosecutions in our sample of case files over the period 1850–1865, the responsibility for identifying the suspect and bringing him or her before the magistrate was the joint responsibility of citizens and police. In almost all of these cases, as in the earlier period, the matter was initiated by a citizen (usually complainant), and it was the citizen who usually played the key role in giving evidence at trial. Nonetheless, the part played by the police was also significant and the case would never have got to trial without such official action. The most common example of joint citizen-police involvement occurred where the police actually executed the arrest following a hue and cry initiated by a citizen or where a citizen called on the police to arrest someone, as illustrated in the prosecution of Mary Beehman:[55]

> Coats, vests, cups, spoons and other items went missing from the house of Jennie Burdett in her absence in Brooklyn. On her return Jennie found the things gone and, suspecting the defendant, she 'got an officer and had [Mary Beehman] arrested'. She then went with Officer McGloin in search of the property and 'found part of it in Second Street'; Jennie telling the court: 'I found a breast pin on a girl down in the Bowery in a lager beer saloon; that girl admitted to me in the presence of others that [Mary Beehman] gave it to her'.[56]

---

[54] The file records do not indicate that Havelow was held as a witness.

[55] District Attorney's Files, 27 March, 1865.

[56] For other similar cases, see: *Elizabeth Hamilton*, District Attorney's Files, 18 October, 1855; *Peter Lewis*, District Attorney's Files, April 27, 1860; *Luman Hawes*, District Attorney's Files, 9 May, 1860.

Similarly, as in the earlier period, there were occasions in which citizens collaborated with the police prior to the commission of the crime with a view to catching the culprit red-handed, as in the prosecution of Alfred Tarte:[57]

> The complainant William J Brown said that, at various times since 1 December 1859 different items of 'merchandize' had been stolen by Tarte and others.[58] Brown's accusation was based on the fact that Tarte, a porter in his employ, had 'keys to the store and access to the store day or night' and that, over a period property was stolen. According to Brown's affidavit, as a result of this
>
> > '... he caused watch and surveillance to be kept upon [his] store—; and that upon the night of the first day of March instant the said Alfred Tarte was caught and detected in the act of taking and stealing from [his] premises—two cheeses—the property of [Brown]; and that ... Tarte was arrested by policeman Joseph W Cornell—now here—in the act of leaving said store—and that ... Tarte had then and there in his possession— ... two cheeses ...'
>
> James Cornell of the 24th Precinct (Harbor) Police confirmed this account stating that he caught Alfred Tarte in the act of leaving the store.

THE JUDICIALISATION OF THE MAGISTRATE

By 1850, significant changes had occurred in the formal role of the magistrate in the investigation of criminal activity prosecuted in General Sessions and in the interaction with the accused. Whereas, in the earlier period, Special Justices combined both policing and judicial functions in the investigation and prosecution of indicted offences, by mid-century, with the advent of the Police Justice, magistrates, as in England,[59] were divested of their investigative responsibilities and were instead confined, in indicted cases, to conducting committal proceedings. With the reorganisation of the police and the virtual elimination of the system of watch, constables and marshals, the locus of the criminal investigation became the police precinct (under the control of the Police Captain) rather than the Police Court (under the control of the magistrate). Police Justices became isolated from everyday policing activities and could no longer demand that officers be detailed to the Police Court. Nor were the wider problems associated with

---

[57] District Attorney's Files, 8 May, 1860.

[58] The cases against four other defendants were dismissed at the magistrates' court because of insufficient evidence. See also *William Shanks*, District Attorney's Files, 16 May, 1860.

[59] See Henry Smith (1997). Whilst English magistrates such as Henry and John Fielding had previously undertaken investigative functions, a reform movement, culminating in the Jervis Acts during the 1840s, led to their judicialisation. See: D Freestone and J Richardson (1980); Bruce Smith (1996) pp 441–54.

criminal activity designated and addressed from a policy perspective by the
Police Justice or his Clerk based upon their experience in examining witnesses,
accused persons and informants and interfacing with officers on the beat. This
change mirrored the limitations on magistrates imposed by the Jervis Acts in
England in the late 1840s, whereby the role of the magistrate was sought to be
constrained to the courtroom rather than to be conjoined in the policing function.

As the separation of the judicial and policing functions evolved, moreover, attitudes began to change regarding the propriety of the continued role of the Police
Justice in the examination of the accused.[60] By 1850, reformers contended that
there should be a clear division between the investigatory function of the police
and the judicial function of the magistrate in the examination of the accused. In
New York, Commissioners, like David Graham and David Dudley Field, who
were assembled to rationalise existing criminal procedure discovered, in the
examination of the accused, 'principles which they [deemed] at war with the
rights of the accused'.[61] They stated:

> The very term 'examination', which is used in the statute, and the proceed-
> ings pointed out as the mode in taking it, all seem to be a departure from the
> spirit of the constitutional declaration, which provides that 'no person shall
> be compelled, in any criminal case, to be a witness against himself.'[62]

The Commissioners believed that the object of the magistrate's examination of
the accused had become perverted from its original purpose. They argued that the
purpose of such an examination was 'not to place the defendant in the hands of a
cross-examining magistrate, who might, according to the principles of the French
Practice, by the exercise of ingenuity, extract from him evidence of his guilt ...'[63]
Instead, they contended that the examination was designed 'in the humane and
benign spirit of the common law, to give the defendant an opportunity, by a voluntary explanation, to exculpate himself from the charge.'[64] Whilst the concern
of the Commissioners was with the magistrate's interrogation practices, our
sample of case files shows, in fact, that the examination of the accused became
by mid-century mostly a 'pro-forma' bureaucratic inquiry, as detailed below and
in Illustration 10.3:

> '... being duly examined before the undersigned, according to law, on the
> annexed charge; and being informed that he was at liberty to answer, or not,
> all or any questions put to him states as follows, viz:';

---

[60] And, as we have seen, in the process by which Police Justices were selected.
[61] Committee on Criminal Code, 1855, p 99. See further, C Cook (1981); H Field (1898).
[62] *Ibid.*
[63] *Ibid.*
[64] *Ibid*, pp 99–100.

'What is your name?' 'How old are you?'; 'Where were you born?'; 'Where do you live?'; 'What is your occupation?'; and

'Have you anything to say, and if so, what—relative to the charge you preferred against you?'[65]

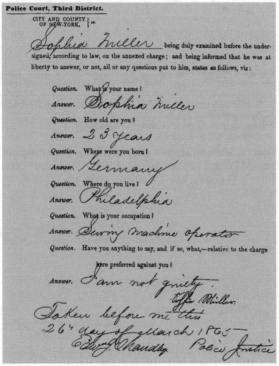

ILLUSTRATION 10.3: Sophie Miller, District Attorney's Files, 28 April, 1865.

Throughout the period, whilst the defendant was 'examined' in the vast majority of cases, by 1850, this simply meant that the Police Justice asked the defendant, as in Illustration 10.3, whether he or she desired to make a statement after which the accused either responded briefly without detail or declined. As the Illustration also shows, pro-forma inquiry most likely to obtain substantive responses related to the defendant's origins and occupation. Our analysis of the nature of the examination of the accused by police magistrate over the entire period of the research appears in Figures 10.5–10.7.

Figure 10.5 shows that from 1835 onwards, following the mandate of the 1829 Statute, our sample of case files record in virtually every case the advice of rights contrasted with the earlier decades when the advice of rights was not recorded with any frequency. As the frequency of admissions declined significantly from 35 per

[65] *Ibid*, p 98.

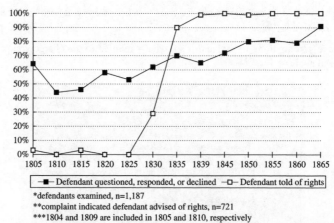

*defendants examined, n=1,187
**complaint indicated defendant advised of rights, n=721
***1804 and 1809 are included in 1805 and 1810, respectively

FIGURE 10.5 General Sessions, District Attorney's Files—Percentage of Cases where
Magistrate Examined Defendant* and Advice of Rights Recorded** Over a Thirty Day
Period for One Court Part, 1804–1865***

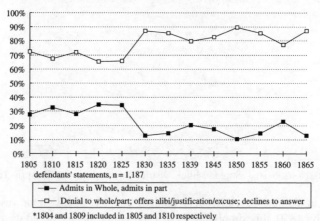

*1804 and 1809 included in 1805 and 1810 respectively

FIGURE 10.6 General Sessions, District Attorney's Files—Percentage Type of Statements
Defendants Made to Magistrate Over a Thirty Day Period for One Court Part,
1804–1865*

cent in 1825 to between 10 and 20 per cent thereafter, the defendant's response
more often became either self-serving or exculpatory. Indeed, should the accused
respond with a proffer of facts relevant to innocence, as is evident in the data dis-
played in Figure 10.6, the Police Justice no longer questioned the authenticity of the
account. Instead, as Figure 10.7 shows, the focus of the Police Justice's concern
was obtaining responses to inquiries related solely to the defendant's community
roots which, between 1850 and 1865, occurred in virtually all cases in contrast to
the period prior thereto where it occurred in between 40 and 70 per cent of cases.

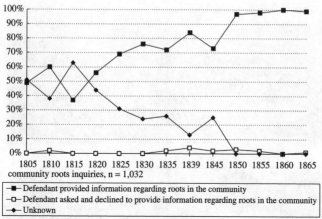

community roots inquiries, n = 1,032

- ■— Defendant provided information regarding roots in the community
- □— Defendant asked and declined to provide information regarding roots in the community
- ◆— Unknown

*1804 and 1809 included in 1805 and 1810, respectively

FIGURE 10.7 General Sessions, District Attorney's Files—Percentage Responses to Magistrate's Inquiries Regarding Community Roots for One Court Part, 1804–1865*

Whilst the relevance and admissibility of confessions remained, the responsibility for obtaining these now passed to the police. Indeed, the belief existed, as expressed by the Commissioners, that the 'law [had] been too tender in this respect' in guarding against involuntary admissions. They contended that whilst police interrogations should not be 'made under the influence of fear produced by threats,' the policy of the law should tend toward greater admissibility of confessions 'to let in all the light possible, trusting to the discretion of juries to distinguish between the false and the true.'[66]

By 1860, examinations came to be depicted as 'hearings' with the following pro-forma recitation preceding the recorded statements of witnesses at the committal proceedings: 'At a hearing held on —day of — 18—, before Justice—,' thus further disassociating the work of the Police Court from that of the Police Justice. The Police Justice, however, continued as in the earlier period to examine the prosecution's witnesses to determine whether the evidence gathered by the police was sufficient to bind over the defendant for the action of the Grand Jury and to reduce into writing the statements of the witnesses and preserve any tangible evidence, as in Illustration 10.4 of counterfeit notes introduced at the committal proceedings.

Presence of counsel

On occasions, at the committal or preliminary hearing before the Police Justice, the testimony of the witnesses came to be in response to a direct, cross and re-direct examination by lawyers, replacing what had previously been a witness's

---

[66] *Ibid,* p 225.

ILLUSTRATION 10.4: George Myers, District Attorney's Files, 3 October, 1855.

statement, supplemented by the magistrate's inquiries. While in the earlier part of the century the Special Justice might take it upon himself to produce additional witnesses where the defendant either refuted the allegations or provided an alibi or other innocent explanation, the case files after 1850 reveal that defence counsel might take on this task and produce and call witnesses himself. Although this occurred in only a few cases in our sample, when coupled with the absence of such activity by the Police Justice, it also suggests the relative inertness of the magistrate at this stage of the process. Table 10.2 depicts the occasional presence of counsel in some participatory manner at Police Court hearings.

Whilst Table 10.2 cannot measure counsel's participatory presence with exactness, it appears that if counsel was present in cases other than those listed, counsel was inactive or, at most, outside the presence of the magistrate advising the

TABLE 10.2: *General Sessions, District Attorney's Files: Cases in which there is Evidence of the Presence of Defence Counsel at the Police Court Hearing Over a Thirty Day Period for One Court Part, 1850–1865*

Year	Number of cases[1]	Police court hearings counsel present	
	n	n	%
1850	90	11	12.2
1855	83	4	4.8
1860	140	8	5.7
1865	139	18	12.9

[1] Table 10.2 records the presence of counsel by case rather than by defendant because, in joint prosecutions, it was not clear whether counsel was acting for more than one of the defendants. However, the frequency of appearance barely changes if it is assumed that counsel, if present, acted for all defendants, the proportions being 12.0 per cent for 1850; 4.7 per cent, 1855; 5.1 per cent, 1860; and 16.9 per cent for 1865.

defendant only as to how to respond to the accusation, mostly by asserting the right to silence.[67]

CONCLUSION

Reorganisation of the police did not mean the presence of any significant methodological advances which so improved the quality and reliability of the prosecution's evidence as to make trials redundant. Indeed, politics intervened with a dispute over who should control the police many of whom, under Tammany Hall's control, lacked the competence of their predecessors and were unco-ordinated as they had been, by the Police Office and Special Justice. Patronage abounded and the key to appointment was not a test of competence but rather, up to 1853, the approval of the alderman who, as ward heeler, served to ensure that the police were indistinguishable from the local population;[68] and afterwards, approval of

[67] Between 1850 and 1865, however, in a few other cases questioning of the complainant or witnesses is recorded as having been undertaken where it is clear that the accused was the questioner, as in *John Blaw*, District Attorney's Files, 9 September, 1850. On a charge of incest on the complaint of the defendant's daughter Margaret Jane Blaw, after swearing her original affidavit of complaint on July 1, 1850, Margaret was 'sworn & cross examined' on July 3 and stated 'that John Blaw now present, is the person referred to in the foregoing affidavit and the statements in said affidavit made are true. By Defendant X You used me very well at first but afterwards ill-treated me as I have stated ...'

[68] The reorganisation and further politicisation of the police did, however, affect significantly the nature of cases in misdemeanour court, the Court of Special Sessions, where no public prosecutor and no jury was present. Whilst prior to 1855 these cases were similar in type to those processed in General Sessions in that crimes against property (petit larceny) were 70 per cent or more with the residue comprising minor assault and battery, by 1860 these offences were overwhelmed by an explosion in the prosecution of morals offences, principally prostitution, bawdy house and liquor law violations. The increase in case load from n=5,000 between 1839 and 1850 to n=36,200 between 1855 and 1865 was accommodated through an expansion of Special Sessions courts whereby magistrates or police justices came to preside, with the Recorder and City Judge presiding only in General Sessions. The Recorder along with aldermen had previously presided in Special Sessions.

members of the Board of Police Commissions (Mayor, City Recorder, and City Judge). As Luc Sante comments, the 'only major difference this made was to determine who would get the graft'.[69]

Our case file analysis showed that the degree of engagement of the new police in investigation and prosecution of criminal activity in cases in General Sessions was not significantly different from that of their predecessors. The greatest number of prosecutions with police involvement resulted from requests for assistance made by the private prosecutor or complainant. Sometimes the police worked together with private citizens in an effort to solve a crime and apprehend the accused. In other instances, as in the past, the investigation was initially undertaken by the private citizen before handing it over to the police for prosecution. There were examples of pro-active policing, yet none of this was different, either qualitatively or quantitatively, from the either period.

Our data demonstrate that the evidential basis of prosecutions in General Sessions, derived as it was from crime detection and investigation, was essentially unchanged over the period of system transformation from jury trials to plea bargaining. As in the first half of the century, the principal prosecution evidence consisted of the oral testimony of citizens who claimed to have caught the defendant in the act, witnessed the crime in progress, or discovered stolen, forged or otherwise illegal goods in the defendant's possession. In short, prosecutions stood or fell on the persuasiveness of ordinary witness evidence.

The transformation that did take place occurred in relation to the management and 'ownership' of the prosecution's case. After 1850, responsibility for the management of prosecutions in the court decisively shifted away from the private citizen to state actors. As police administration became more bureaucratised so the police became identified with the prosecution and responsible for marshalling the witnesses and overseeing the case as it progressed through court. This transformation was most apparent in the official file documentation which was increasingly embossed with the names of police officers, irrespective of the testimonial contribution they were able to make. However, none of this resulted in the production of tighter or more reliable cases for the prosecution. Forensic science, in so far as it was employed, had not advanced beyond the earlier period.

In addition, the structural constraints imposed by the judicialisation of the magistrate and the separating of policing functions reduced the capacity of the Police Justice to acquire and memorialise relevant evidence of guilt. Not only did the frequency of admissions decline as the recording of rights increased following the adoption of the 1829 Statute, so did the earlier practice of the magistrate's questioning of whatever statement the defendant made relative to the charge. Since the overwhelming majority of defendants, when accorded the opportunity to speak, simply declined or proclaimed their innocence in conclusory terms, the defendant's voice was in real terms silenced. The magistrate

[69] L Sante (1991) p 238.

and/or his clerk thus ceased to be principal witnesses in General Sessions regarding the statements and behaviour of the defendant. What remained of the examination of the accused were skeletal responses to truncated questions related to the individual's roots in the community. Thus, Police Court became solely the locus of a preliminary hearing proceeding, and thus an intermediate formalistic link between the actors at either end of the process who would henceforth control the case for the prosecution.

Chapter 11

Litigation Practice in General Sessions: 1850–1865

INTRODUCTION

In this chapter, we explore the nature of litigation practice in cases prosecuted in General Sessions after mid-century as contrasted with the earlier period to determine whether the practice of lawyers enhanced the complexity of the proceedings and thus had a significant effect both on the conduct of trials and on the method of case disposition. In particular, we consider whether any structural changes within the lawyered event could support the contention that trials suddenly became so unworkable as to compel their replacement by plea bargaining or other form of non-trial disposition.

We first utilise quantitative measures to consider such issues as to what extent there were significant changes from the earlier period in the frequency of legal representation, motion practice and the time consumed from initial appearance to final disposition. We also test whether there were changes in the structure of the indictment, the frequency of trial witnesses and the length of the trial. Thereafter, we use separate quantitative and qualitative measures to analyse to what extent there were any significant changes, after 1850, in the pattern, style, focus and effectiveness of cross-examination such that heightened adversariness could render litigated proceedings cumbersome and serve to reduce the rate of conviction and thereby render the trial more problematic in everyday cases.

We focus on cross-examination because it tends to demonstrate whether competing theories were propounded other than overall pleas to lenity and mercy and concern for simple reasonable doubt, arising out of the sufficiency and persuasiveness of the prosecution's evidence. This issue is addressed by Millender who contrasts trials of the earlier period with those of mid-century and concludes that lawyers began to spin alternative theories through cross-examination and, in particular, reliance on leading questions that emphasised the circumstantial nature of the prosecution's case and suggested the possibility of alternative scenarios of innocence for the jury's consideration.[1]

[1] Michael Millender (1996) p 19.

PRESENCE OF LAWYERS

We begin with an analysis of the presence of lawyers in General Sessions in both the earlier and later period, to determine whether an increase in their presence occurred which could have complicated cases because of the greater frequency of litigated issues. Thus, we analysed our sample of Minute Book entries to determine the frequency in which General Sessions' clerks recorded the presence of defence lawyers at trial to see to what extent the frequency of lawyers may have had an impact upon the overall rate of guilty pleas.[2] We controlled for defence lawyers because at the outset of the century either the District Attorney or private lawyer represented the prosecution in every case at General Sessions. The results are set out in Figure 11.1:

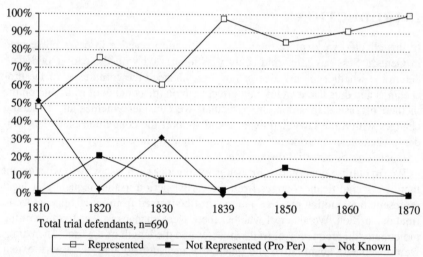

Total trial defendants, n=690

| ─□─ Represented | ─■─ Not Represented (Pro Per) | ─◆─ Not Known |

FIGURE 11.1 General Sessions Minute Book—Percentage of Trial Representation Over a Thirty Day Period for One Court Part, 1810–1870

Figure 11.1 shows that Minute Book entries recorded defendants as represented by lawyers in a predominant proportion of trials in the earlier period prior to the rise of guilty pleas with little change thereafter particularly after mid century when the guilty plea system emerged as the principal method of case disposition. Thus, by 1820 lawyers were recorded as representing defendants at trial in over 70 per cent of cases and beginning in 1839 and continuing thereafter in almost 100 per cent of all cases in General Sessions.

---

[2] Clerks often did not make Minute Book entries regarding the presence of lawyers in 1804 or 1815 and in most guilty pleas over the period 1800–1850. We know, however, from both the case files and the nominative reports that lawyers were regularly present in court from 1810 on behalf of both prosecution and defence.

However, after 1850 private lawyers no longer represented the interests of the private prosecutor. Whilst the District Attorney may have hired private lawyers to act as Assistant District Attorneys when necessary, for the most part private lawyers became identified with defence work and therefore reliant upon what funds they could receive from the accused or his family. Whilst prominent defence lawyers continued to be present at trial in General Sessions after mid century, the practices of other lawyers in the criminal process came to attract considerable criticism by reformers. Indeed, the 'shyster' approbrium was attached to some defence lawyers by the Prison Association in its 1859 report, which described the effect that such lawyers had not only on the representation of defendants but on the justice system as a whole:[3]

> It will be readily conceded that *some* are improperly charged; that *some*, while innocent, are in danger of being condemned by false or vindictive witnesses, through inadvertance, or for want of the aid of honest lawyers; that *some* are stripped of all they possess by 'shysters', without receiving any beneficial services in return; and that *some* by reason of circumstances difficult to be explained at the time of conviction, are made to suffer punishments which might be properly mitigated, if the matters in extenuation were reliably brought to the notice of the court, but which, owing to the fears, confusion or friendless situation of the accused, cannot be furnished without timely aid, volunteered on the spot...

> It is indeed to be deplored that there are creatures who engage to defend men on their trial, who extort from them every dollar which they or their families can collect or scrape together, and then abandon them to their fate. Such characters ought *themselves* to be sent to prison, and kept at hard labour, instead of those who are so frequently the dupes and sufferers by their evil practices, and who would in many cases be acquitted were it not for the bad advice of these unscrupulous leeches. (original emphasis)[4]

Furthermore, fee-paying practices which had evolved in the earlier period and had secured the presence of reputable lawyers in General Sessions were now being exploited, at least in Police Court, to the detriment of the prosecution's evidence as well as the autonomy of the accused.[5] 'Skinning' practices and 'Tombs lawyers' were a constant source of degradation under which lawyers would be connected to the accused through police officers, gaol-keepers and the Police

---

[3] Prison Association Report (1859) pp 10, 19. George W Pearcey, a magistrate, told the 1855 hearings that it was difficult to distinguish between lawyers and that 'clan of men who hover about the Tombs' (pp 12–13).

[4] Report of the Prison Association, 1859, p 19.

[5] During the 1840s, the reduced state of at least sections of the Bar was commented upon by grand juries, committees of the Common Council and reports of aldermen. See eg, Board of Aldermen, *Report on the Reorganisation of the Police Department* (1844) p 800; Grand Jury Presentment (1842) p 972.

Justice's clerk. In return, these lawyers would 'kick back' to those involved in the reference of the case from whatever monies were received through a process widely known as 'percentage' or 'division'.[6]

Not only did 'skinning' of the defendant result in a two-tier system of justice, whereby intervention by lawyers before magistrates occurred only in those cases where the accused or his family could raise the lawyer's fee, but the inter-relationship of the lawyer, police, gaol-keeper and clerk meant that only certain individuals who represented themselves as counsel would appear on behalf of the accused before the Police Justice. This favoured group could also benefit by way of a tailoring or structuring of the police evidence to minimise the accused's involvement and maximise the opportunity for discharge by the magistrate or a dismissal or acquittal of all charges in General Sessions.[7]

Motion practice

Of course, defence lawyers may over time have become more litigious raising a greater number of issues of law and fact requiring a response by the prosecution or judge. One way of measuring increased lawyering activity leading to increased complexity would be an increase in the number of motions put by lawyers to the courts. A plethora of legal motions (claims requiring judicial intervention) could create a disincentive for reliance on legal formalism and an incentive to avoid litigation altogether and/or negotiate a deal.

An analysis of our sample of the Court Minute Book of the frequency of recorded motion practice in all defence lawyer cases showed that for the entire period, 1810–1865, in more than 80 per cent of cases, no filed motion had been recorded by the court clerks. Where motions were recorded, variations in their frequency did not correspond to the increase in dispositions through guilty pleas over the critical period 1850–1865. Indeed, there was a greater percentage of cases in which motions were recorded in 1835 and 1839 than in 1856, 1862 or 1865 when guilty pleas came to predominate, as depicted in Table 11.1.

No clear pattern is evident from these statistics because recorded motion practice was as frequent if not more so in the earlier period. Nor does the picture get any clearer once the nature of the motion, where this is known, is taken into account, even though there is evidence here of a shift in emphasis (and perhaps in adversariness) over the years.

Recorded motion practice in the period 1810–1835, as depicted in Figures 11.2–4, was heavily dominated by motions relating to delay, constituting between 59.0 per cent (1835) and 87.0 per cent (1821) of all known motions. Thereafter, the proportion of recorded motions concerned with delay fell away steeply, constituting only one-third of all known motions in 1839, 4.6 per cent 1862, and 2.8

---

[6] See eg, testimony of Abraham Beale, Prison Agent, James Welch Police Justice and George Walling, Police Captain of 18th Ward, Assembly Documents 1855 pp 55–6.

[7] *Ibid.* see testimony of Napoleon Montfort, a former Police Justice.

TABLE 11.1: *General Sessions, Court Minute Book: Number of Recorded Motions Over the Year in All-Lawyer Cases in One Court Part, 1810–1865*

	Known lawyer cases n	Recorded motions n	% of cases in which motions made n
1810	380	24	6.3
1821	968	53	5.5
1825	549	21	3.8
1830	438	50	11.4
1835	375	71	18.9
1839	408	60	14.7
1846	611	67	11.0
1850	462	101	21.9
1856	235	33	14.0
1860	532	65	12.2
1865	506	72	14.2

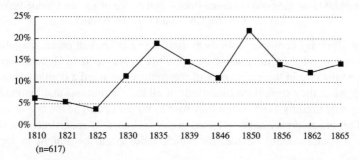

FIGURE 11.2 General Sessions Minute Book—Percentage of All Defence Lawyer Cases with Recorded Motion Practice Over the Year for One Court Part, 1810–1865

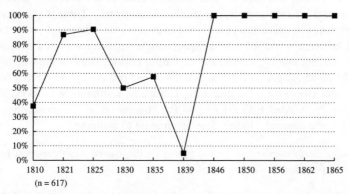

FIGURE 11.3 General Sessions Minute Book—Percentage of Known Motions to Recorded Motions Over the Year, All Defence Lawyer Cases, for One Court Part, 1810–1865

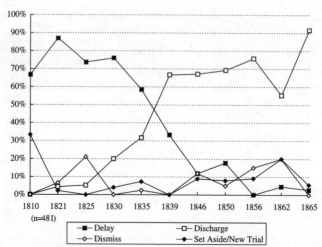

FIGURE 11.4 General Sessions Minute Book—Percentage of Known Motion Practice Over the Year, for One Court Part, 1810–1865

per cent 1865. By contrast, motions to discharge a defendant on an allegation of wrongful committal by the magistrate or failure to prosecute in General Sessions which, whilst rare in the early years of the century, assumed a dominant position by 1839 when they comprised two-thirds of all known motions and maintained a majority role until by 1865, when they rose to 90 per cent. The change in record-ed motion practice may have reflected greater reliance by magistrates on deten-tion as a social control device, for which relief could be sought in General Sessions.

Moreover, our sample of case files containing trial transcripts for 1865 (only those ending in conviction) revealed that references to non-recorded motions tended to be brief and give no convincing picture of the extent to which these applications were spontaneous, prepared or documented.[8] There is some evidence of oral motions in which lawyers moved to dismiss the indictment on the grounds of legal sufficiency and we would expect similar application at trial to those con-tained in the nominative reports for the earlier period. Thus, in the trial of Harry Howard,[9] on an allegation that the defendant had received goods stolen from the Lawson and Goodnow Manufacturing Company, testimony was received from the complainant, Abel F Goodnow. At the conclusion of the prosecution's evi-dence, defence counsel, 'Judge' Stewart, moved to dismiss:

> Judge Stuart objected to the indictment on the ground that there must be some proof that it was a corporation.

---

[8] There were, of course, objections made to evidence which appeared occasionally in the trial tran-scripts, as in the prosecution of *John Wyman and Lizzie Beriden*, District Attorney's Files, 13 April, 1865 where, after objection, a special policemen did not testify for the prosecution.

[9] District Attorney's Files, 8 March, 1865.

The judge sustained the indictment and gave the counsel the benefit of the exception.

Time-lapse in prosecution

Another measure of case complexity is the time that elapses between initial court appearance before the examining magistrate and final disposition in General Sessions. First, there is the time consumed once the Police Justice reviews the evidence and binds over the defendant to the Grand Jury. The time consumed involves the transfer of papers and Grand Jury presentation the latter of which throughout the entire period 1805–1865 occurred on the day the indictment was filed or within a day prior thereto. As Figure 11.5 shows, the predominant period of time consumed to indictment was one week but less than four weeks and this would vary dependent upon the availability of a Grand Jury to review the evidence.

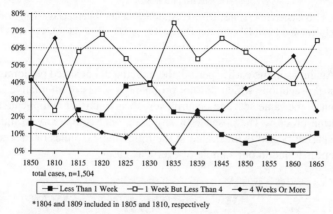

total cases, n=1,504

Less Than 1 Week   1 Week But Less Than 4   4 Weeks Or More

*1804 and 1809 included in 1805 and 1810, respectively

FIGURE 11.5 General Sessions, District Attorney's Files—Percentage Time Between First Court Appearance and Indictment Over a Thirty Day Period for One Court Part, 1804–1865*

A second time-lapse measure is the time between indictment and final disposition since this is the period during which pre-trial motions would be made and evidence assembled for trial purposes. As Figure 11.6 shows, the predominant time to disposition over the period 1805–1865 was less than one week.

Indeed, the greatest delay in time to disposition (four weeks or more) pre-dates the dramatic rise of guilty pleas and is evidence that, in so far as this is a measure of case complexity, there was no greater complexity in the period 1850–1865 than in any of the years predating the rise of the guilty plea.

Form of the indictment

As in the earlier period, indictments continued to employ tried and trusted forms requiring the District Attorney only to insert basic information such as names, dates, locations and description of property stolen or identity of the victim of the

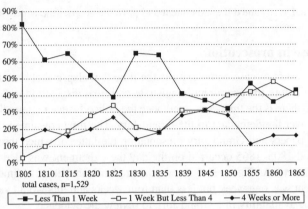

FIGURE 11.6 General Sessions, District Attorney's Files—Percentage Time Between
Indictment and Final Disposition Over a Thirty Day Period for One Court Part,
1804–1865*

assault. Again, as in the earlier period, the indictment consisted predominantly of
top count prosecutions which did not propound a series of alternative scenarios
arising out of the same acts and occurrences, so as to further complicate the decision-making process. The absence of any additional complexity in indictments
from the earlier period is illustrated in the following examples of the most common offences found in our sample of everyday cases:

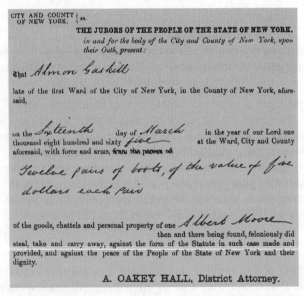

ILLUSTRATION 11.1: Almon Gaskill, District Attorney's Files, 5 April, 1865.

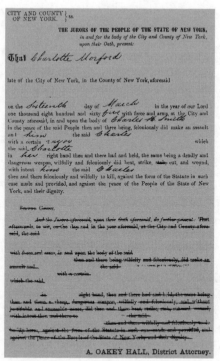

ILLUSTRATION 11.2: Charlotte Morford, District Attorney's Files, 6 April, 1865.

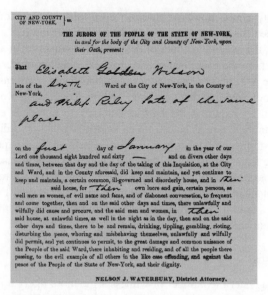

ILLUSTRATION 11.3: Elisabeth Wilson, District Attorney's Files, 5 June, 1860.

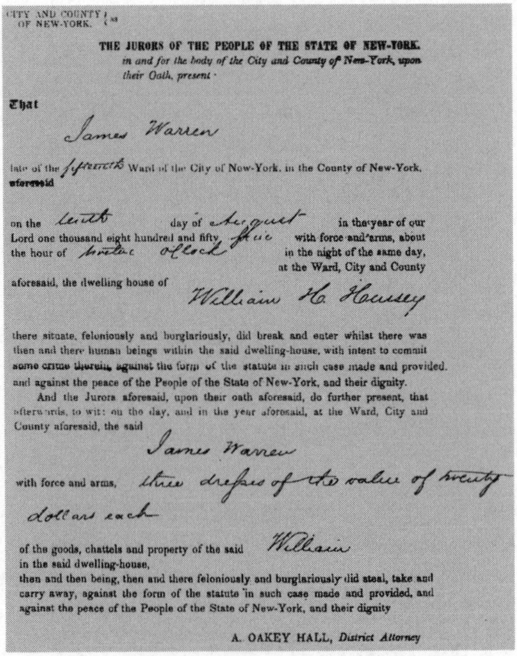
CITY AND COUNTY OF NEW-YORK, ss

THE JURORS OF THE PEOPLE OF THE STATE OF NEW-YORK.
in and for the body of the City and County of New-York, upon their Oath, present

That

James Warren

late of the fifteenth Ward of the City of New-York, in the County of New-York, aforesaid

on the tenth day of August in the year of our Lord one thousand eight hundred and fifty five with force and arms, about the hour of twelve o'clock in the night of the same day, at the Ward, City and County aforesaid, the dwelling house of William H. Hussey

there situate, feloniously and burglariously, did break and enter whilst there was then and there human beings within the said dwelling-house, with intent to commit some crime therein, against the form of the statute in such case made and provided, and against the peace of the People of the State of New-York, and their dignity.

And the Jurors aforesaid, upon their oath aforesaid, do further present, that afterwards, to wit: on the day, and in the year aforesaid, at the Ward, City and County aforesaid, the said

James Warren

with force and arms, three dresses of the value of twenty dollars each

of the goods, chattels and property of the said William in the said dwelling-house, then and then being, then and there feloniously and burglariously did steal, take and carry away, against the form of the statute in such case made and provided, and against the peace of the People of the State of New-York, and their dignity

A. OAKEY HALL, *District Attorney*

ILLUSTRATION 11.4: James Warren, District Attorney's Files, 20 September, 1855.

Multiple defendants and multiple counts

Case complexity could, however, increase even when the predominant offence charged remained constant and even when the practices of lawyers were unchanged if, for example, the average number of defendants or witnesses in a trial increased thereby lengthening the examination and cross-examination process. Accordingly, we analysed the percentage of single-defendant and single-count cases on the basis that an increase in multiple-defendant and multiple-count cases would complicate any prosecution by requiring the District Attorney to introduce evidence which would satisfy multiple targets both from an evidentiary and procedural standpoint, to say nothing of the compounding of lawyering tasks and assignments. As Figure 11.7 shows, the recording of single-defendant and single-count cases amounted to more than 90 per cent of all prosecutions over the entire period from 1810–1870, with, in particular, no change in this distribution of cases between 1850 and 1870.

On this basis, after mid-century, cases were no more complex than those at the outset of the century.

Trial witnesses

Of course, the greater the number of witnesses the more likely it is that conflicts would emerge in the evidence which might in turn be the focus of increased

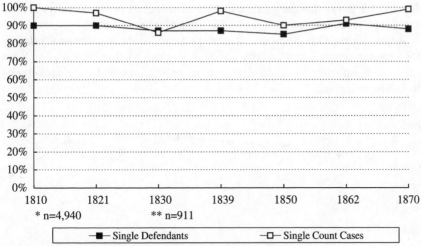

*as a percentage of all defence lawyer cases over the year.
**as a percentage of total trials and guilty pleas over a 30 day period.

FIGURE 11.7 General Sessions Minute Book—Percentage of Single Defendants* and
Single Count Cases**, for One Court Part, 1810–1870

lawyering activity at trial and deliberation time by the jury. To test whether this
had occurred, we analysed the Court Minute Book for the number of witnesses
called to testify over a 30-day period from 1800 to 1870 at ten-year intervals. Our
findings on this are set out in Figure 11.8:

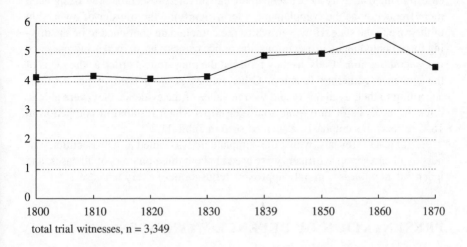

total trial witnesses, n = 3,349

FIGURE 11.8 General Sessions Minute Book—Average Number of Trial Witnesses Over
a Thirty Day Period for One Court Part, 1800–1870

Figure 11.8 shows that the average number of witnesses per trial barely changed from 1800 when it stood at 4.00 to 1870 when it stood at 4.50.

And as Figure 11.9 shows, the percentage of recorded trial witnesses called by the prosecution remained broadly constant over the whole research period and only fell significantly once the defendant in 1869 was provided the opportunity to testify under oath.

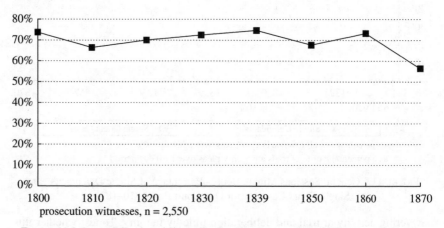

prosecution witnesses, n = 2,550

FIGURE 11.9 General Sessions Minute Book—Percentage of Trial Witnesses Called by the Prosecution Over a Thirty Day Period, for One Court Part, 1800–1870

As we have seen, over the period 1850–1865, the initiation of the prosecution case remained heavily dependent upon the private prosecutor now designated more frequently as the complainant, a term signifying the transfer of ownership of the case to the state. However, whilst the complainant continued to be the driving force behind many prosecutions, the police came to be an increasing presence in General Sessions' trials, as they replaced the magistrate's office as the locus of the evidence gathering function. Other witnesses were used in prosecutions according to their availability and the relevance of the evidence they were able to offer. An analysis of thirty-one trial transcripts which resulted in conviction in 1865 reflects this emphasis, as can be seen in Table 11.2.

As Table 11.2 reveals, whilst the complainant was called as a prosecution witness in all cases, police officers were used in about three-quarters of all cases, and independent witnesses in only approximately six out of every ten cases.

PRESENTATION OF DEFENCE WITNESSES

Complexity is measured not only by the number and frequency of witnesses for the prosecution but also by the frequency in production of witnesses for the

TABLE 11.2: *General Sessions, District Attorney's Files: Status of Witnesses Called by the Prosecution in 1865 Lawyered Trials by Case Over a Thirty Day Period for One Court Part*

Status of witness	n	%
Complainant	31	100.0
Police officer	23	74.2
Independent witness[1]	19	61.3

[1] 'Independent witnesses' for present purposes includes one case in which the witnesses, other than the compainant and police, were co-operating witnesses giving state's evidence.

defence. Thus, we measured the production of defence witnesses in our sample for the whole of the period 1804–1865. Our findings on this are set out in Table 11.3:

TABLE 11.3: *General Sessions, District Attorney's Files: The Production of Defence Witnesses at Trials Over a Thirty Day Period for One Court Part, 1804–1865*

Year n	Total trials n	Cases ending in conviction n	Trials where defence witnesses n	%	Cases ending in acquittal n	Trials where defence witnesses n	%
1804	93	67	19	28.4	26	19	73.1
1810	76	47	22	46.8	29	13	44.8
1815	160	108	35	32.4	52	23	44.2
1820	92	54	13	24.1	38	15	39.5
1825	72	52	12	23.1	20	8	40.0
1830	83	61	7	11.5	22	11	50.0
1835	103	71	17	23.9	32	12	37.5
1839	113	77	24	31.2	36	14	38.9
1845	92	51	12	23.5	41	17	41.5
1850	49	24	11	45.8	25	10	40.0
1855	61	40	11	27.5	21	3	14.3
1860	63	30	14	46.7	33	17	51.5
1865	58	34	10	29.4	24	11	45.8

[1] The Table includes only trials in which all defendants were convicted or all acquitted. The figures are based upon trials whether the defendant was represented or acted *pro se*.

As Table 11.3 shows, no consistent pattern emerges in the production of defence witnesses which clearly distinguishes the period after mid-century period from the earlier decades. Whilst, in conviction cases, defence witnesses were produced at a higher ratio over the period 1850–1865 (36.0 per cent) than over the earlier period 1804–1845 (27.0 per cent), the reverse was true in the case of acquittals where the equivalent figures for 1850–1865 were 40.0 per cent contrasted with the earlier period, 45.0 per cent. Indeed, if the trial figures are aggregated without reference to outcome, there was a greater incidence in the production of defence witnesses at trial in 1804 (41.0 per cent) as against that in 1865 (36.0 per cent). Table 11.3 also makes clear that there is no consistent correlation between the production of defence witnesses and outcome. Whilst in most years there was a tendency for the defence to produce its own witnesses more frequently in cases that resulted in an acquittal, the opposite was true for 1810, 1850 and 1855. In so far as these are measures of contested and hence more complex trials, the figures lend no support for the view that complexity increased coordinate with the transformation to plea bargaining.

Overall, perhaps the most striking feature of Table 11.3 is the failure of the defence to produce witnesses of any kind in a majority of all cases. Indeed, in our entire sample of case files over the period 1800–1865, no defence witnesses were produced in 66.0 per cent of cases. Given that no defence witnesses were offered in trials for the period 1850–1865 in 62.0 per cent of cases, as against 67.0 per cent of cases for the period 1804–1845, it is hard to see how this measure would support any serious claim that complexity based upon the frequency of defence witnesses increased in any significant way after 1850.

What these figures cannot tell us is the kind of witnesses relied upon by the defence. Such information is available only for 1865 and then only in respect of conviction cases where the trial transcript has been preserved. Analysis of these transcripts, however, confirms the picture which emerges in the nominative reporters' accounts of the earlier period: there was a heavy reliance (in 1865, it was 50.0 per cent) on witnesses attesting to the good character of the defendant but who otherwise had no substantive knowledge of the incident in question.[10]

Length of trial

Increase in length of trial would, of course, be a factor in complicating case disposition, because it would reduce the capacity of a court to adjudicate by trial in any given day. Indeed, should argument and witness examination, procedural and evidentiary objections expand and become more time consuming this would naturally cause a back log in cases awaiting disposition and, in a cost-efficient environment, could certainly influence a decision to find an alternative to jury trial. Accordingly, we analysed the total number of started and completed jury trials to determine whether this issue had any application to our data set. Our analysis is depicted in Figure 11.10.

As Figure 11.10 shows, there was a significant change in the number of trials started and completed. However, this occurred twenty years prior to the advent of the guilty plea system over which time it remained broadly constant. It is only with this understanding that one can begin to approach a raw count of jury trials

---

[10] A striking example of this in reported appeal cases occurs in *Moses Lowenburg v The People* (1863). On a trial for murder, the defence produced eleven witnesses, all of whom sought to establish the good character of the defendant. The emphasis on good character contrasted with hypothetical theories of innocence which Millender and others contend marked the jury trial by mid-century is further evidence of the straightforward nature of these proceedings and their lack of complexity: see Millender (1996) pp 4–6.

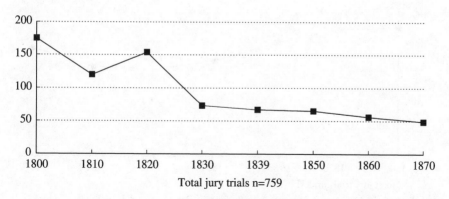

FIGURE 11.10 General Sessions Minute Book—Total Number of Started and Completed Jury Trials Over a Thirty Day Period for One Court Part, 1800–1870

started and completed over a 30 day period, as indicative of changes in workload resulting from increases in the length of trials. Whilst the raw count, as depicted in Figure 11.10, would seem to imply that trials succumbed to workload concerns, a closer examination, which we undertook in chapter 9, demonstrates that when compared with the patterns of case disposition there is no correlation between jury trials started and completed and the rate of guilty pleas. In particular, in the earlier period when trials were the principal method of case disposition, there was considerable variance in the number of jury trials over a thirty-day period without any significant change in the residual number of guilty pleas. By contrast, after 1850 when there was a sea-change in method of disposition and guilty pleas largely replaced jury trials, there was by comparison very little by way of change in total number of jury trials over the same period of time.

Deliberation time

Deliberation time may be a measure of increased case complexity because it would be expected that the more complex the case the greater the likelihood that the jury would retire and deliberate. However, our analysis of verdicts returned with or without retirement of the jury shows that while in 1800 in 90 per cent of all cases juries returned verdicts without retiring, between 1839–1860 the proportion remained at about 60 per cent, while in 1870 almost 80 per cent of all jury verdicts were also returned without retirement.

What is of special note in Figure 11.11 is that in the period 1850–1870 when guilty pleas came to predominate, the rate of verdicts returned without retirement actually increased in those trials that remained. These data would appear of themselves to contradict the notion that guilty pleas winnowed out straightforward 'dead-bang' cases leaving only those problematic cases with triable disputes for jury deliberation.

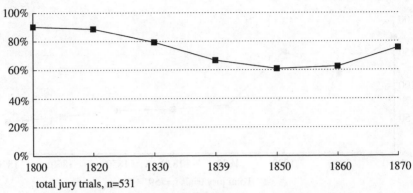

total jury trials, n=531

FIGURE 11.11 General Sessions Minute Book—Percentage of Jury Trials in which Verdicts Were Returned without Retiring Over a Thirty Day Period for One Court Part, 1800–1870

Jury trial days

Further evidence that case complexity did not overcome the courtroom actors appears upon analysis of the pattern of trial days in which a single jury dealt with one or more cases. The greater the number of cases a single jury could try in a given day the more likely that the cases lacked complexity. Our analysis of the Court Minute Book showed that over the critical period 1850–1870, when the court was starting and completing approximately two trials per day, the percentage of trial days with a single jury deliberating over all cases increased from 40 per cent to 65 per cent as shown in Figure 11.12:

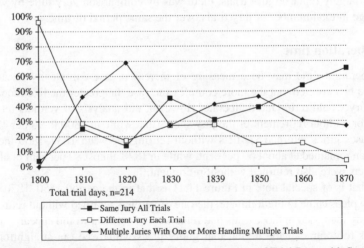

Total trial days, n=214

—■— Same Jury All Trials
—□— Different Jury Each Trial
—◆— Multiple Juries With One or More Handling Multiple Trials

FIGURE 11.12 General Sessions Minute Book—Percentage of Trial Days with Same or Different Juries Over a Thirty Day Period for One Court Part, 1800–1870

Court work days

Moreover, our data suggest instead that trials were relatively straightforward events allowing any individual court part to process several trials and pleas in any given day, even after the guilty plea system was entrenched. Thus, for example, in 1860 when some 60 per cent of cases were disposed of by guilty plea, the court was commonly able to process in a single day several trials, involving significant numbers of witnesses. This is shown in Table 11.4 which documents the daily business in one court part for all the cases falling within our sample in the month of May, 1860:

TABLE 11.4: *General Sessions, Court Minute Book: Daily Court Business for May 1860 in One Court Part*

Date	Number of trials n	Witness called prosecution n	defence n	Guilty pleas n	Defendants n
May 7, 1860	0	0	0	1	1
May 8, 1860	2	5	5	3	5
May 9, 1860	1	1	0	1	3
May 10, 1860	0	0	0	7	8
May 11, 1860	2	11	5	5	7
May 14, 1860	2	8	8	5	8
May 15, 1860	1	7	2	5	6
May 16, 1860	1	2	1	3	4
May 17, 1860	3	11	4	4	8
May 18, 1860	3	11	0	5	10
May 21, 1860	3	8	8	3	9
May 22, 1860	8	26	5	6	14
May 23, 1860	3	10	10	5	9
May 24, 1860	3	14	10	3	6
May 25, 1860	1	3	0	2	4
May 29, 1860	3	8	2	1	4
May 30, 1860	3	8	8	2	6

These data, which are broadly representative of case disposition patterns for 1860, show that a single court part was able to handle a considerable volume of work, disposing of 2.3 trials, 3.6 pleas, 6.6 defendants and hearing 11.8 witnesses on an average day.[11] The fact that one court part was able on average each day to undertake, on its eight busiest days in May 1860, three or more trials, involving 17.9 witnesses, as well as 3.6 guilty pleas shows convincingly that, for the most part, trials tended to be uncomplicated and uninvolved rather than elaborate, complex and drawn out.

Transcribing cross-examination

There are considerable difficulties in trying to discover how lawyers actually performed at trial over the period 1850–1865, when the separation between plea and trial

[11] Our analysis of the General Sessions Court Minute Book at ten-year intervals produced broadly similar results with, for example, one court part handling in 1850 an average of 2.2 trials per day and receiving the testimony of 10.7 witnesses; the equivalent figures for 1860 being 1.9 trials per day and 10.4 witnesses.

cases began to be laid down in a systemic and widespread manner. The richest source
is cross-examination and it occured in our sample of 1865 case files which contain
trial transcripts of the testimony of witnesses, and includes records of the course
of questioning (examination and cross-examination) to which the witness was subject, as exemplified in the trial of William Thompson described in Illustration 11.5:

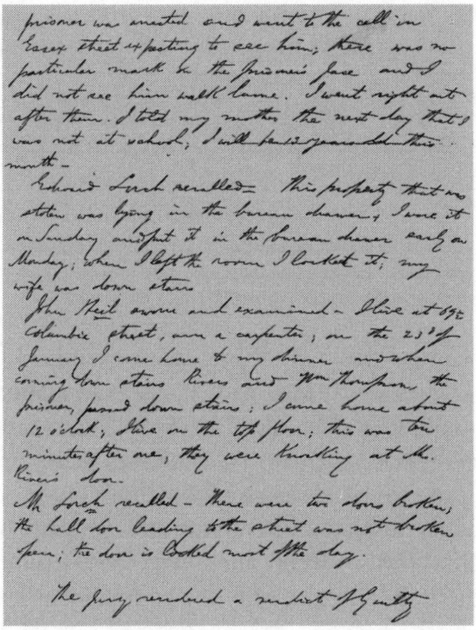
prisoner was arrested and went to the cell in
Essex street expecting to see him; there was no
particular mark on the prisoner's face and I
did not see him walk home. I went right out
after them. I told my mother the next day that I
was not at school; I will [illegible] this
month –
Edward Loesch recalled – This property that was
stolen was lying in the bureau drawer; I saw it
on Sunday and put it in the bureau drawer early on
Monday; when I left the room I locked it; my
wife was down stairs
John Theil sworn and examined – I live at 69½
Columbia street, am a carpenter; on the 23d of
January I came home to my dinner and when
coming down stairs Rivers and Wm Thompson, the
prisoner, passed down stairs; I came home about
12 o'clock; I live on the top floor; this was two
minutes after one, they were knocking at Mr.
Rivers' door.
Mr Loesch recalled – There were two doors broken;
the hall door leading to the street was not broken
open; the door is locked most of the day.

The jury rendered a verdict of guilty

ILLUSTRATION 11.5: William Thompson, District Attorney's Files, 10 March, 1865.

Whilst the transcripts are a rich data source, they were preserved in the District Attorney's files only in cases of conviction, presumably to provide a record for any appeal. This means, however, that with few exceptions[12] we have no data on the performance of lawyers on cross-examination at trials in which the defence case prevailed.[13] To balance the sample, therefore, we examined those instances of cross-examination at the preliminary hearing before the Police Justice that were embedded in the committal proceedings in Police Court. Although the frequency of lawyer participation at the preliminary hearing stage was limited, deficient as they may be, the combined records enable us to gain insights into the quality of cross-examination including the manner in which lawyers framed their questions and directed their challenges.

The frequency of cross-examination

The extent to which the defence responded to the prosecution case through cross-examination was heavily influenced by the status of the witness. As a general rule, cross-examination was focused on the testimony of the complainant, with little questioning of other witnesses evident in the papers. This is illustrated in our analysis of the trial transcripts for 1865, as set out in Table 11.5.

[12] The exceptions are confined to multiple-defendant trials in which one or more of the defendants obtained an acquittal or discharge, while others were convicted.

[13] Additionally, while the trial transcripts refer to defence motion practice, the reasoning behind the motions is not set out routinely and there is no reference to any legal authority that might have been cited.

TABLE 11.5: *General Sessions, District Attorney's Files: Cross-examination of Prosecution Witnesses in Trial-Convictions, 1865 by Witness Over a Thirty Day Period for One Court Part*

Status of witness	Testifying n	Cross-examined n	%
Complainant	31	25	80.6
Police	31	4	12.9
Independent witness[1]	29	5	17.2

[1] 'Independent witnesses' for present purposes includes one case in which the witnesses other than the complainant and police, were co-operating witnesses giving state's evidence.

The proportion of prosecution witnesses cross examined in General Sessions revealed by Table 11.5 is consistent with cross-examination before the Police Justice in our entire sample of case files for 1865. Thus, in relation to guilty plea cases for thirty days of that year (n=91), witnesses were cross-examined at the Police Court hearing in five cases, three of which involved cross-examination of the complainant[14] with the residue involving independent witnesses.[15] In trials resulting in an acquittal (n=26) where there was cross-examination of witnesses in one case before the Police Justice only the complainant was questioned.[16]

The necessity of cross-examination

Before any conclusions about the use of cross-examination by defence lawyers can be safely drawn, it is important to go beyond the frequency of cross-examination to consider the context in which cross-examination may be effectively conducted. Cross-examination is not only a difficult task to perform well, it is an adversarial skill to be used when necessary and not reflexively.[17] Cross-examination at a preliminary hearing before a magistrate may be directed to discovery of the prosecution's evidence including committing the witness's testimony in enough detail so that if their recollection changes at trial they may be impeached. It may also be an opportunity to directly impeach or discredit the prosecution's case. By contrast, the decision to cross-examine at trial is based on the foreknowledge of the preliminary examination and, in turn, the general thrust of the prosecution case. Whether at hearing or trial, however, criminal defence work has to be reactive in response to the capacity of the prosecution witnesses to either satisfy the burden of proof at that stage or be able and willing to provide evidence accrediting and supporting an alternative scenario of innocence. Indeed, at whatever stage, cross-examination may be unnecessary for a whole variety of reasons:

[14] *William McDermott et al*, District Attorney's Files, April 5, 1865; *Thomas Burke*, District Attorney's Files, May 9, 1865; *Mary Walker*, District Attorney's Files, May 10, 1865.

[15] *James Cleary et al*, District Attorney's Files May 3, 1865 (involving a co-operating witness); and *Patrick Quinn and James McCormick*, District Attorney's Files, May 15, 1865 (where three independent witnesses were cross-examined before the Police Justice).

[16] *John Williams and Davis Casey*, District Attorney's Files, 8 March, 1865 in which the complainant was held as a witness in the House of Detention.

[17] The values and dangers of cross-examination are discussed in D Napley (1975).

the witness may have said nothing which harms the defence case; the witness may have made an unconvincing impression, through demeanour or otherwise; or the testimony given by the witness may be accepted in its entirety if it is capable of bearing an interpretation favourable to the defence.

Our sample of 1865 trial transcripts strongly suggests that it would not have been necessary or wise to have cross-examined prosecution witnesses in a number of instances because their testimony caused no harm to the theory of defence. This was particularly true in respect of police evidence because whilst officers over time became increasingly involved in the prosecution their presence in court, as we have seen, was often of limited value because their own role was mostly administrative, such as identifying property taken from the accused. Similarly, in some cases, complainants and independent witnesses were called to give evidence for limited purposes, such as identifying ownership of property allegedly stolen, without the witnesses having any other evidence connecting the defendant to the offence. The following trials involving police evidence are examples where the nature of the police testimony was such that it obviated the need for cross-examination by defence counsel:

Mary Ann Bradshaw[18]
The defendant was alleged to have picked the pocket of the complainant in the Washington Market where the principal prosecution witness, who arrested the defendant, kept a butter and cheese stall. When Officer James M Tilley of the Third District police was called by the prosecution, he made clear his inability to contribute anything of real evidential value to the case:

> 'I dont know anything about the case; I was in the station house when the pocket book was handed to me; the complainant said there was twenty shillings in the pocket book—I found one dollar and 50 cent currency stamp in it.'

William Golden[19]
The defendant was apprehended by the complainant's husband after he had allegedly tried to steal her watch. At trial, Officer John McPherson described his role in the case in these terms:

> 'I am an officer; I know no more about the affair than that I was called to arrest the prisoner; when I got up there this lady's husband and another man was holding him; the watch was still in her pocket:-
>
> Q You identify this as the man that they had hold of?
> A Yes sir.'

On the basis of our evaluation of witness testimony in our sample of trial transcripts, we concluded that it was not necessary for the defence to cross-examine a large group of police officers acting in an administrative capacity (45.0 per cent

---

[18] District Attorney's Files, 9 March, 1865.
[19] District Attorney's Files, 10 May, 1865.

of officers called at trial), a smaller number of independent witnesses whose evidence did not directly incriminate the defendant (11.0 per cent of independent witnesses called), and a few complainants who could give no direct evidence connecting the defendant to the crime but merely reported what others had told them (6.5 per cent of complainants). If these witnesses are left out of account, however, the remaining witnesses were all ones whose evidence tended to directly connect the defendant to the offence charged and, in respect of whom, a failure to cross-examine would seem to suggest an absence of adversariness characteristic of a more protracted and contested proceeding. Table 11.6 sets out the proportion of cross-examination practices when only the latter cases have been taken into account:

TABLE 11.6: *General Sessions, District Attorney's Files: Cross-examination of Prosecution Witnesses where the Witness Incriminates the Defendant, Over a Thirty Day Period for One Court Part, 1865*

Status of witness	Witnesses directly incriminating defendant n	Cross-examined n	%
Complainant	29	25	86.2
Police	17	4	23.5
Independent	27	5	18.5

As Table 11.6 shows, there was a substantial absence of cross-examination of police and independent witnesses directly incriminating the defendant as might have been anticipated in trials with heightened adversariness. We set out below some examples from our trial transcripts in which evidence of a witness directly implicating the defendant went untested:

John Gallagher[20]
The complainant, Susan Le Roy, stated that Gallagher and another person unknown came to her house on the pretext of inspecting it for the purposes of renting the property and, whilst there, had stolen various items. Gallagher was arrested over four weeks after the alleged larceny. In addition to Le Roy, two individuals who had been her servants at the time of the incident gave evidence directly identifying Gallagher. Although Le Roy was cross-examined, in neither case were the servants cross-examined regarding the reliability of the identification including the time lapse between the incident itself and the apprehension of the accused who, after all, was a stranger to the witnesses or as to the effects of what may have been a 'confrontation' at the precinct:

> 'Margaret Barrett sworn. On the 21st of January I lived with Mrs Leroy; I let two persons in—one of them was the prisoner whom I recognise by his general appearance; I left him in the parlor; he gave his name as

[20] District Attorney's Files, 3 May, 1865.

> Dodd Dart; I saw him three times, and when I went to the station house Mrs LeRoy was not their (*sic*) the first time I went down. I identified the prisoner before anybody pointed him out to me. I told Mrs LeRoy the name they had given at the station house.

> Mary Veitch sworn and examined—In January last I lived with Mr Leroys' in Twenty Third Street as a domestic; I was there on the 21st of January between the hours of 3 and 4 in the afternoon. I was going into Mrs Le Roy's room and I saw two gentlemen there; the prisoner looked very earnestly at me; he was standing looking at me from the dressing room in the hall which adjoins the bed room; there was no doubt in my mind that the prisoner is the man when I saw him; I was down at the station house and at the Police Court the day before Mrs Le Roy went down; I said nothing until one of the gentlemen told us to pick out if we thought there was any man there that we saw up at our house; this and another man stood at the furthest part of the room: I recognised the prisoner at once and I had not seen the other. The man I saw in the room had no whiskers but black hair and was dressed in dark clothes; he did not say anything to me; I was only a short distance from him.'

In the absence of cross-examination of the servants, defence counsel relied upon the testimony of Jeremiah Simonson, a machinist and engineer on the ship *Daniel Webster* who stated that Gallagher was at sea at the time of the crime, and Charles Andre, a well-known thief under conviction, who stated that 'he knew that Gallagher was not a party to the larceny at Mrs Leroy's.' Two days after Gallagher's trial, Austin Baldwin drew up a memorandum on behalf of several of the jurors and forwarded it to Judge Russell expressing their concern over the conviction. In the course of this memorandum, the jurors stated that a 'reasonable doubt' had arisen in their minds

> in regard to the identity of the Prisoner with the party who committed the act in conjunction with Andre, and that his conviction arose not only from the very positive evidence on the part of the prosecution but the very lame defence of the prisoner and the absence of all but the very questionable testimony in his behalf, his counsel appears to have relied too much on his own assertion of the prisoner's innocence, and very little upon the nature and character of the evidence brought forward by him.[21]

Police evidence which went unchallenged included stating that officers had found incriminating articles on searching the defendant,[22] heard the defendant make a

---

[21] The author of the note, Austin Baldwin, explained to the judge in a separate note that he had drawn up the note 'in accordance with the wishes of several of the jury but too late to submit to them until Monday'. It is not clear whether the lawyer, Stuart, was at fault or whether, if he was at fault, this was an exceptional case. If he did fail in his duties it would be worrying since he represented the defence in 15 separate trials in the 1865 sample of cases.

[22] *James Foster*, District Attorney's Files, 24 March, 1865.

damaging admission;[23] or that they had seen the crime committed[24] as illustrated in the following case:

James Best[25]

Following a burglary committed on February 28, 1865, during which paper currency and silver and copper coins were stolen, Officer Richard Field was called for the prosecution and told the court that he had arrested Best on 1st March, seized coins and currency in Best's possession and obtained an admission from Best. The latter was a critical piece of evidence linking the accused to the crime, the reliability of which might have been challenged. Yet, there was a total absence of cross-examination of the officer who testified as follows:

'I took hold of him and told him to come along; I was informed that the prisoner had silver around him showing it. I told him to come to the station house, I searched him there and found three half dollars in silver and one American quarter; I asked him who was with him when he entered the store that was robbed; he told me 'Desperate Mike' was with him; his name was Micheal Williams; he said he was on the corner of West Broadway and Worth Street on the 28th of Feb. Desperate Mike came up West Broadway and said, 'Jim, dont you want to make a raise? He said he had no objections; then they went together. Mike went into the alley while he (the prisoner) stood in front of the store; after the robbery they went to different places and had coffee and cakes.'

In other trials, a similar absence of cross-examination occurred of independent witnesses who gave evidence that the defendant was in possession of stolen goods and that the defendant had offered to supply the thief with a special jacket to conceal the goods[26] and that stolen goods had been found in the area to which only the defendant had access.[27]

The style and focus of cross-examination

The style of witness examination at both the preliminary hearing stage and at trial was, for the most part, indistinguishable. Questions were directed to the subject matter of direct examination in a measured, non-repetitive and non-aggressive manner. The emphasis was to elicit a full account from the witness either because the lawyer was searching for information or checking the reliability of the testimony itself. Witnesses were treated with respect, even deference, and given licence to tell their stories or elaborate on them, although, as in the earlier

---

[23] *Eliza Ploss*, District Attorney's Files, 28 March, 1865.
[24] *Ann Smith and Margaret Spier*, District Attorney's Files, 6 April, 1865.
[25] District Attorney's Files, 15 March, 1865.
[26] *Harry Howard*, District Attorney's Files, 8 March, 1865.
[27] *John McMahon*, District Attorney's Files, 10 May, 1865.

period, closed questions and more infrequently leading questions were employed to pin down the witness and develop the theory of defence.

Table 11.7 and Table 11.8 set out the overall findings regarding the general focus of the questioning of prosecution witnesses at the preliminary hearing in Police Court[28] and at trial in General Sessions:

TABLE 11.7: *General Sessions, District Attorney's Files: The Focus of Preliminary Hearing Cross-examination at Police Court Over a Thirty Day Period for One Court Part, 1850–1865*

Principal focus of cross-examination	Witness examined	
	n	%
Information-seeking	22	46.8
Checking testimonial reliability	17	36.1
Accrediting defence account	6	12.8
Discrediting witness character	2	4.3
Total	47	100.0

TABLE 11.8: *General Sessions, District Attorney's Files: The Focus of Cross-examination in Trials Over a Thirty Day Period for One Court Part, 1865*

Principal focus of cross-examination	Witnesses cross-examined	
	n	%
Information-seeking	11	31.4
Checking testimonial reliability	17	48.6
Accrediting defence account	4	11.4
Discrediting witness character	3	8.6
Total	35	100.0

At the preliminary examination stage and at trial, counsel asked questions to determine the details of what witnesses had observed and whether there was any ambiguity or mistake in what they were saying. In addition, counsel asked questions regarding the reliability of the witness himself either because of a lack of competence or inebriation. Whilst the latter focus of questioning was more frequent at trial, the style of questioning was the same at both proceedings, as illustrated by the responses to cross-examination at the preliminary hearing of Margaret Crane and Mary O'Donnell:[29]

> The defendants were charged with larceny of money from William Douglas, a sailor from Mystic Connecticut, who had come to the city on the Sloop 'Active'. Douglas went out on the town on Saturday night after being paid by the Captain of the Sloop. Upon examination by the magistrate, Douglas stated that the two accused were the only persons in the room with him when

---

[28] For this purpose, we have categorised cases in terms of the dominant thrust of the questions. Whilst in a few cases counsel may have had several objectives in mind, the general focus of the examination is clear from the questions or answers.

[29] District Attorney's Files, 21 September, 1865.

he fell asleep and when he awoke they were gone. He was told that the accused gave the houseowner money to keep which he believed was his. Douglas was questioned as to capacity to reliably state that he had lost $54.00 in bills to which he made the following responses:

> After I received the money on Saturday night I was cruising about the city. The first place I went to was in Water Street. Nobody was with me —I drank several times. I believe I treated somebody once or twice—I had one bill changed in a store that was about 9 o'clock. I drank after that. The bill that I changed I took out of my pocket book. I did not have all my money together—it was in different parcels in my pocket book —it was in three parcels ... As near as I can calculate I had from $75 to $80 when I started out.

He was then questioned to establish that he had gone into a house of ill repute and that he was much the worse for drink, to which he responded:

> As far as I can tell it was 10 or 11 o'clock when I first saw the defendants—I saw them both at once—it was in a house in Water Street—up 4 flights of stairs. I was enticed to go up by another girl whom I saw at the door. I stood and talked with her probably 5 minutes and we went right up stairs—she took me into a room where there was a man and his wife—I sat down and she wanted me to give her some money to get some liquor and I gave her a $5 bill, when she went out and I never saw her again ... I did not count my money when I took out that last $5 bill —I was a little the worse for liquor. I put my pocket book in either my pantonloons or coat pocket after I took out the $5 bill—I did not feel drowsy while in that room—We were all sitting still while I was in the room ... I found the girl was not coming back and went out and met these defendants on the stairs or landing and they took me into another room ... I sat down on a chair. We talked about different things. My pocket-book was in my pocket at this time. Margaret was to sleep with me she said ... I then laid down upon the bed after taking my clothes off and laying them on a chair at the foot of the bed. I went into the bedroom to pull off my clothes and the girls remained in the room where they were. I then dropped asleep. When I awoke there were no girls there ... When I awoke I got up and dressed myself and found the girls gone and my pocket book and money also ...

Whilst it was exceptional for any attempt to be made to discredit the general character of a witness at a preliminary hearing, cross-examination of another witness in this case sought to attack his character by suggesting that he was a pimp who managed various prostitutes in a house of ill-repute:

> Andrew O'Brien, who lived in the same house as the defendants, stated before the Police Justice that the defendants came to his room a little after midnight, and gave him $54.00 to keep for them. He said that he later learned that the money had been stolen, refused to return it when requested,

and afterwards told the police about it. The following responses to cross-examination are indicative of the focus of the questioning:

> I had not got to sleep when the girls came to my door—I had a girl with me—it was not my wife—I did not reside at the house—it is a bed house—it was next to the corner of Cherry & James next door to the Clothing store—I have been acquainted with Margaret about two years & seven years with Mary. During my acquaintance with Margaret I have received money from her at different times to keep for her. I am in the habit of receiving money from three or four girls for safe keeping ...

The reliability of witnesses also might be called into question on the basis of bias and interest. Thus, for example, where the police sought to rely upon the evidence of accomplices in a crime, cross-examination before the magistrate might seek to establish whether the evidence of the witness was or might be contaminated by an offer or inducement from the police, as in *James Cleary et al*:[30]

> Several witnesses for the prosecution had, on their own admission, been a party to stealing from the factory of the complainant. Each of these was asked about promises of leniency in exchange for co-operation. Thus, after James Lucky told how he had confessed to the police his role in the thefts, he was asked whether any promises had been made to him in return for his evidence to which he made the following responses:
>
> > Did not tell me that it would be better for me to tell the whole truth. I knew that I would get put up on the Island and thought I might as well tell the truth and I wanted to have company with me. The Captain said nothing to me when I got to the Station House except to ask my name. I do not expect to get clear by being State's evidence ...
>
> His fellow approver, Andrew Villig, responded to cross-examination to the same effect:
>
> > I had no promise of favour made to me upon consideration of my turning States Evidence ... They made no promises but simply said it would be better for me but did not say I would or could get clear and I do not know whether I shall get clear or not by becoming States Evidence ...

In another group of cases, counsel sought to accredit the accused's version of events learned in advance of the magistrate's proceedings, by asking questions of the witness which would tend to support that version, as in *Francis R Crussell*.[31] In that case, an alternative account was advanced, in part, directly through a series of questions to the witness which sought both to accredit the accused's version of

---

[30] District Attorney's Files, 3 May, 1865.
[31] District Attorney's Files, 16 May, 1860.

events and to call into question the reliability of the complainant's assertion that the accused did not act in self-defence. Here, cross-examination by counsel for the defendant provoked a re-direct by counsel for the complainant[32] regarding the answers elicited on cross and this was followed by a *re-cross-examination* by defence counsel:

> Crussell was employed to take timber from the carpenter's yard of Hennessey and Walsh and, on the day in question, was being assisted by Hennessey in loading the timber onto his cart. According to John Hennessey, the defendant 'appeared to get wrathy' about the help Hennessey was giving, that words passed between them and that shortly afterwards, Crussell threatened Hennessey with a cart rung. Hennessey said that he took hold of the cart rung with his left hand and Crussell with his right before being separated by Walsh. Afterwards, according to Hennessey, Crussell 'passed towards me a distance of seven or eight yards and struck me down as I was standing near the curb-stone'. He said that he was badly cut and 'bled a pail-full', was taken to the station house before having three stitches put in the wound. He was adamant that he was not the aggressor: 'I did not strike Crussell at any time. I did not shake him or use any other violence than to take hold of him and the cart rung—to protect myself'. The circumstances leading to the altercation were challenged under cross-examination by Mr S Davison, Esq., 'of counsel for the defence,' the initial response to which appear below:
>
> > Crussell did not ask me to assist him in loading his cart. I can not say that he told me several times to go away and leave it alone—I can not say that he did not tell me so. I do not recollect having refused to do so—and calling him a son of a bitch, I might have used the words.
> >
> > Q Did you not pursue him around his cart—several times—making the circuit several times—threatening him with personal violence and making use of opprobrious language, before he took out the cart-rung from his cart to strike you?
> >
> > A I do not recollect having done so. I will answer positively that I did not. I saw him take the rung but once out of his cart—that is all I know—that was not at the time he struck me, it was at the time I approached him in self-defence—and before we were separated—it was after Walsh separated us that he struck me. I did not chase him up after we were separated—I was retiring away at the time ... I do not recollect that Mr Walsh said I ought to be ashamed of myself ... I do not believe I was under the influence of liquor at the time—I can not tell at what time of day it was: it was in the afternoon somewhere between twelve and three o'clock—I might have drank half a dozen times in the

---

[32] Although it is clear that in *Crussell's Case* the District Attorney, Nelson J Waterbury, prosecuted the case in General Sessions, a review of the case papers does not reveal the identity of the lawyer for the prosecutor/complainant who conducted the direct and re-direct examination before Police Justice Connolly.

course of the day—I drank cold whisky: I do say positively that I was not intoxicated at the time: I say positively that I do not recollect any words that were spoken between him and me during the affray—

Re-direct

I can not swear positively to any words that passed between the defendant and me—I think my memory must be impaired to the extent that I can not remember any thing in the shape of words—My partner, Mr Walsh, was present during the entire occurrence—and other parties besides—who I presume heard all that was said and saw all that was done—

Re-cross-examination

I am now a partner of Mr Walsh—and was then. I can not tell how many persons were present and witnessed this affray: there were others present besides Mr Walsh. I can not account why I remember some things that were done, and not others—I distinctly remember his drawing the cart rung—but what else was said and done I have no recollection of, excepting as I have already stated

> Q Have you offered—or authorized any person—to settle this matter for money?
>
> A I authorized my partner to settle it, as it would appear to him the best

Re-direct Examination

> Q What caused you to authorize your partner to do any thing in the matter?
>
> A The defendants brother waited upon me—and represented to me that his (defendants) friends were poor and were anxious to settle it with me by paying the expenses of my confinement—the doctor's bills—I told him I would let it rest with my partner and whatever he would say I would agree to—I did not name any sum of money—I did not authorize my partner to name any sum of money—I left it to his discretion to settle—

The foregoing is typical of the non-aggressive style employed by lawyers as in the earlier period, with little effort made to control the witness so as to preclude a fulsome response beyond that required to answer the question put to the witness. In the following examples of cross-examination at trial, similar to those at preliminary hearings, the focus of the questioning was directed to the witness's capacity to observe and recount the events in question and, hence, to the reliability of the testimony. For example, in *Julius Weinhold*,[33] one of the issues raised on cross-examination of the complainant was the witness's ability to identify, as his goods, leather which was allegedly stolen and found in the defendant's house.

---

[33] District Attorney's Files, 16 May, 1865.

The nature of the questioning throughout can be gauged from looking at defence counsel's interrogations in respect of the first issue:

> Q Where did you get this leather?
> A Well, I suppose some of it came from Philadelphia: I know it was Philadelphia and New York leather; there was also sheepskin and carpeting.
> Q Did you purchase it yourself in Philadelphia?
> A Yes sir
> Q Did you see it when it was brought to your store?
> A I did not see it all; you cannot classify leather; I know it is my leather, tanned for me and got up for me. It is pretty hard to tell what particular pieces I had on the 4th January when a man has three or four hundred sizes of leather in his store.
> Q There was no particular marks?
> A We can tell by the curer's marks
> Q You dont know when the leather was taken?
> A No sir. I know when it was found though.
> Q You do not know in what quantities it was taken?
> A No sir.
> Q When did you miss it?—at any particular time.
> A At no particular time; it is very hard to miss it in a quantity of leather in a building like mine.
> Q You stated before the police magistrate that you identified what was found from general appearance and nothing else?
> A Yes sir, marks on the leather.

Here the issue of ownership and recognition of the leather was explored through non-argumentative open and closed questions, including occasional leading questions, which were succinct and limited in scope.

In *Fanny Wells*[34] the intention of counsel at trial appears, at least in part, to have been to impeach the character of the complainant, Ida Slate, and to cast doubt upon her assertion that the alleged larceny of a silk dress took place on 24 February 1865. 'Ann' or 'Fanny' was arrested on the complaint of Ida who stated that she had handed the officer a pawn ticket that enabled the police to recover the property. We begin with direct examination of Ida followed by cross-examination:

> Ida Slight (*sic*) *sworn and examined* testified as follows:-
> Q Where do you live?
> A I did live in 8 Pell Street, but I live at 7 Duane Street now.
> Q Where did you reside on the 24th of Feb. last
> A 8 Cherry Street

---

[34] District Attorney's Files, 22 March, 1865.

Q Did you have any property in that house on that day?

A Yes sir

Q What was that property?

A A plaid silk dress

Q What was the value of that plaid silk dress.

A Eighty one dollars.

Q To whom did the plaid silk dress belong.

A To me.

Q Was it stolen on the 24th day of February.

A Yes sir.

Q Have you since discovered where the frock is.

A Yes sir. I went with another to the pawn brokers and identified my dress, it was handed over to the property clerk the Judge said. I went to the pawn brokers with officer Woolwich and seen the dress.

Q What day of the month was that—the larceny was on the 24th?

A It was on the Sunday evening before that, I do not know what day of the month it was.

Q How many days after the larceny was committed did you find the pawn ticket on her?

A On the third day.

Cross Examined

Q Did this girl live in the same room with you.

A Yes sir, she boarded with me.

Q Where did you say you lived?

A 8 Pell Street.

Q How many persons lived in that house?

A I do not know how many persons live in that house. I had my own room.

Q What do you do for a living?

A I work.

Q Where do you work?

A I have been working in a saloon.

Q What saloon?

A On Broadway

Q How long have you been working there

A I worked there nine months.

Q Were you working there at the time of the occurrence?

A No sir.

Q How long had you been working there?

A I do not know

Q Had you been working there a year before this occurrence?

A No sir.

Q Two years before this occurrence?

A No sir; two years before this occurrence I was home

Q Where?

A Philadelphia.

Q Who were you living with there?

A   With my husband.
Q   Is your husband in New York now?
A   No sir. I was never in New York before this time and I have been here
      since. I have been here some fifteen months. I have been working at a
      concert saloon since I have been here to New York. I have been working
      here inside of fifteen months.
Q   Was it a year before you lost your dress
A   No sir, it was not a year.

It is important to note that while limited, the foregoing is the entirety of the
witness examination of the complainant at trial, on both direct and cross-examination. It demonstrates, as in the earlier period, the fact that the length of examinations themselves did not change and it enabled the court and jury to try
multiple cases in any given day. Whatever the precise objective of counsel on
cross-examination above—to discredit the general character of the complainant by
implying that she was a prostitute in a saloon, separated from and unsupported by
her husband; to question her reliability as a witness in respect of when the incident
occurred; or to show that others had an opportunity to take the dress—the style of
cross-examination remained non-aggressive and not dissimilar from the earlier
period and from that which may have occurred at a preliminary hearing.

The occasional attempts to impeach the witness, again, as in the earlier period,
occurred where it appeared that the witness may have had a criminal background
or was a person of low moral worth. In *Harry Howard*[35] for example, James
Conway, a boy who had originally been joined in the complaint with Howard,
was cross-examined on the basis of his general character, as can be gathered from
his answers to unrecorded questions: '… I have never been convicted of stealing
before; am 16 years old, my parents are not living, have not been at the House of
Refuge …' Similarly, when Mary Beehan[36] was charged with grand larceny on
the complaint of Jennie Burdett, the clear implication of the questioning was that
the complainant was lacking in credibility because she lived in or ran a house
(Sinclair House) of ill-repute:

> … my husband is at the war; he went about the 1st of January; my husband
> has supported me ever since I have been married to him; I make no money
> myself by any other means; I have two rooms at the Sinclair House, and
> nobody resides there beside myself … I dont know anything about the char-
> acter of the Sinclair House.

In four instances in our sample of trial transcripts, the focus of questioning was
directed towards supporting or accrediting the defence theory of how the incident
occurred. This, too, was not dissimilar from the earlier period or from that which

---

[35]   District Attorney's Files, 8 March, 1865.
[36]   District Attorney's Files, 27 March, 1865.

occurred, as we have seen, at the preliminary hearing. A good example is the trial of Michael Cannaven,[37] on a charge of rape against Mary McBride. It was undisputed that Cannaven and McBride, both of whom worked at the Fifth Avenue Hotel, went out together on Sunday afternoon on 15 March, 1865, visited Mary's brother's house and stayed there until after 10.00 pm. According to McBride, Cannaven then induced her to go to a house in Greene Street on the pretext of having to see a man and, once inside the house, raped her. The course of the cross-examination was directed to establish a different version consistent with innocence: that the parties knew each other well and had contemplated marriage; that she went to the house knowing that it was used for the purposes of illicit sex; and that intercourse had taken place with her consent. The following extracts from the responses to counsel's inquiries show how counsel sought to accredit the theory of the defence that what occurred was consensual:

> The defendant and myself were quite friendly together; have not thought of marrying him and have not spoken to others about marrying him; I often sent messages to him down stairs; we have been to the theatre before and kept up a correspondence; my brother's house is in Sixth Street between First Avenue and Avenue A; we had something to drink there; I know the way to the hotel, but he would not let me go; the number of the house was 153 Greene Street; I did not see anybody when I went into the house; there was light burning in the room and in the entry. I did not see him give any woman three dollars; I did not holla till he misused me; I told him I wished to go and he said I had to stay with him; he had two small pitchers of oysters handed into him through the door; I told him I did not relish anything where I was ...

> I made the complaint on the 30th; he has not married me, I do not care any more for him than to have my own and family name redeemed; I am 27 years old and was never married; I was not intoxicated that Sunday night.

Advancing triable issues

In addition to the foregoing, our sample of trial transcripts for 1865 offers a basis on which to evaluate the extent to which cross-examination at trials was founded in a genuine concern over reliability and contested issues of fact, which was the practice in the earlier period, or whether, in contrast to the ethics of advocacy of the earlier period, in the absence of any actual defence, counsel was simply thrown back on attacking the complainant. It is difficult to tell whether cross-examination based, for example, on misidentification, was expressing a real concern, albeit with limited skills, or was merely verifying that the elements of the offence were satisfied, or was the futile effort by a lawyer who was grasping at straws. This is not, however, a significant limitation since our evaluation is principally concerned with the performance of lawyers on cross-examination and

---

[37] District Attorney's Files, 11 April, 1865.

their ability to raise or advance triable issues. On this basis, we were able to determine whether the lawyer's cross-examination raised triable issues or whether the cases were 'dead bang'. Our overall findings on this are set out in Table 11.9:

TABLE 11.9: *General Sessions, District Attorney's Files: Lawyered Trials in which Cross-examination Raised or Failed to Raise Triable Issues Over a Thirty Day Period for One Court Part*

Whether triable issues raised	n	%
No triable issue raised: case is dead bang	21	60.0
Triable issues were raised	9	25.7
Triable issues raised in respect of some defendants	5	14.3
Total	35	100.0

We classified a case as 'dead bang' where no substantial issue existed as to proof of the elements of the offence including the identity and culpability of the defendant, where only inconsequential evidential or procedural points were raised on cross-examination, or where no attempt was made to challenge the prosecution evidence. An illustration from our 1865 sample of trial transcripts shows our reasons for classifying cases in this manner:

James Foster[38]
The defendant was charged with burglary and grand larceny from John Owen, having been arrested at 4.00 am on the morning of the burglary in possession of the stolen property by Officer Benjamin Bates. This evidence went entirely unchallenged. Indeed, the only intervention by defence counsel came in respect of the complainant's evidence. John Owen testified as to the loss of his property from his house telling the court he had last seen it at dinner on the night of the burglary and had discovered the window broken the next morning. The response to defence counsel's cross-examination, which is reproduced below in full, raised what appeared to be the only available but futile question as to the culpability of the defendant, given the proximity in time to the finding of evidence of the burglary and the defendant's recent possession of the stolen property:

'Cross-examined—I saw the window broken open and found the pieces on the floor; the ordinary fastening of the sash was broken in two pieces and laid on the floor; I saw this myself about 61/2 or 7; I do not know when the window was broken open or who did it.'

CONCLUSION

Our data show that the nature of litigation practice remained essentially unchanged from that prevailing in the first half of the century, except that lawyers now

---

[38] District Attorney's Files, 24 March, 1865.

participated, albeit infrequently, in the conduct of the preliminary examination of witnesses. Overall, however, the frequency of lawyers at trials remained constant with the earlier period. The cases prosecuted, as in the earlier period, remained predominantly property offences involving few witnesses, a single-count and a single-defendant indictment. Throughout the entire period 1800–1865, delay was not a factor and cases moved expeditiously, taking little more than a month from initial appearance before the magistrate to final disposition, with cases usually being tried within a week of indictment. There was little recorded pre-trial practice with those motions being confined to requests for delay (in the earlier period) or the discharge of the accused (during the later). Further, there was no significant increase in the overall number of witnesses or the percentage and/or type of witnesses called by the prosecution. The private prosecutor or complainant remained the dominant witness relative to conduct of the defendant which established the elements of the offence. However, by mid century, police officers came to replace the Special Justice and clerk as the principal witnesses to tangible evidence seized upon search and arrest and to those incriminating statements the defendant made at the time of arrest and at the precinct (albeit infrequently in our sample). In addition the number and proportion of defence witnesses was not significantly different from the earlier period with continued heavy reliance on character witnesses. Indictments themselves, as in the earlier period, were for the most part for a single top count against a single defendant and continued to rely upon the identical form of words utilised in pre-printed documents.

When looked at from the perspective of the degree of adversariness, evidenced by the cross-examination, we found that defence counsel did not engage in cross-examination at trial with any greater frequency or purpose than in the earlier period so as to raise or advance triable issues. Indeed, the style and focus of cross-examination did not make the trial any more problematic. Cross-examination provided the complainant an opportunity to clarify and complete the narrative. For the most part, defence counsel tended to avoid outright attacks on prosecution witnesses, was parsimonious in the questions put, and omitted to challenge much of the evidence of the police or independent witnesses. Whilst the advent of lawyers for the accused participating in the preliminary hearing at Police Court may have presaged the introduction of a more adversarial pre-trial process, the infrequency in which this occurred is a limiting factor in any understanding of the dramatic transformation from jury trials to guilty pleas during this period of time.

Chapter 12
Structure of Guilty Pleas:
1850–1865

INTRODUCTION

In this chapter, we examine the structure of the guilty pleas that came to replace jury trials and to predominate after mid century. We first consider the extent to which guilty pleas were to uncharged lesser included offences and attempts. We then ask whether the evidence in guilty plea cases sufficiently distinguished those cases from the remaining cases so as to serve as a meaningful basis for sorting both the 'dead bang' from the triable in a lawyers' negotiation, concerned as it might be with the sufficiency and persuasiveness of the prosecution's proof. Further, we consider to what extent mitigating factors or explicit intervention by the District Attorney or judge may have induced the plea. Thereafter we consider the degree to which pleas to lesser included offences and attempts may have been without any explanatory force related to the facts and circumstances of the prosecution itself.

LESSER PLEAS

It is generally accepted by researchers that a principal indicator of plea bargaining is a proliferation of guilty pleas to uncharged lesser-included offences or attempts. As Friedman states:

> Can we be sure we know plea bargaining when we see it? The answer, for the most part, is yes. Some cases have unambiguous signs—most notably a change in plea from *innocent* to *guilty of a lesser charge* (emphasis in original).[1]

However, in General Sessions in New York, already by 1829 a clear mechanism—indeed a recipe formula—existed to dispose of cases through pleas to

---

[1] (1979) p 249.

lesser-included offences and attempts when the legislature divided all principal offence types into degrees of seriousness. Yet, when we considered the reliance on lesser offences and attempts as a percentage of all guilty pleas, our data show that this became a dominant practice only after the middle of the century, almost thirty years after the adoption of the Code and fifty years after defence lawyers were recorded as regularly present in criminal cases:

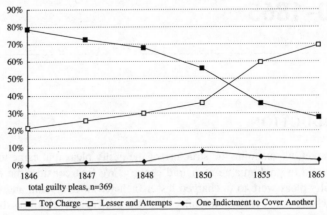

FIGURE 12.1: General Sessions, District Attorney's Files—Lesser Degree, Attempt and Covered Convictions as a Percentage of All Guilty Pleas Over 6 Months (1846–1848) or Thirty Day (1850, 55, 65) Period for One Court Part

As Figure 12.1 shows, even by 1846, lesser pleas and attempts were only approximately twenty per cent of all guilty pleas. The dramatic increase in reliance on lesser pleas and attempts occurred between 1850 and 1855 when the percentage grew to some sixty per cent and by 1865 to seventy per cent of all guilty pleas.

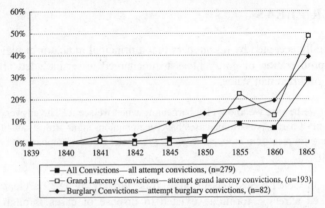

FIGURE 12.2: General Sessions, Secretary of State Reports—Percentage of Attempt Convictions Over the Year, 1839–1865

Perhaps the greatest increase in reliance on lesser offences as a method of case disposition can be seen in the increase in reliance on attempt convictions as depicted in Figure 12.2.

As Figure 12.2 shows, by 1865 attempts became approximately 30 per cent of all convictions with particular dominance evidenced in grand larceny and burglary cases.

The rationale for lesser pleas

In looking at guilty pleas over the period 1850–1865, we sought to determine whether these cases were structurally distinguishable from trial cases in General Sessions on the basis of our appraisal of evidence and proof as documented in our sample of case files. We analysed all case papers for that period including some or all of the following material: the complaint sworn by or on behalf of the complainant; the record of the examination of the complainant and witnesses; the transcript of the proceedings at any hearing convened to examine or further perpetuate the testimony of prosecution witnesses; any notes or briefs by the District Attorney regarding the availability, relevance and persuasiveness of the prosecution's evidence; the record of the defendant's examination; the record of any letters written by or on behalf of the defendant to the prosecuting authorities; the record of any motion or stipulation filed by counsel for the defendant; together with the indictment and the record of the final plea entered by the defendant as recorded on the file jacket and in the Court Minute Book.

Despite the richness of the available data, the reasoning of the prosecuting authorities and of the defence is rarely disclosed. Additionally, we are confined to material disclosed in the documentary evidence which frequently excludes factors that might have played a part in the decision-making of the actors, such as the District Attorney's assessment of the credibility of witnesses. Nor do the case papers systematically account for the presence of defence lawyers whose involvement might be reported only by chance, as in Illustration 12.1, the prosecution of Mary Taylor[2] where the lawyers' card was included in the District Attorney's files.

Having said this, the files routinely record testimony introduced at Police Court examinations and this information appears to have formed the basis for the prosecution case and, for the most part, that of the defence. Based upon our analysis for the period 1850–1865 we concluded that whilst a proportion of lesser pleas might be explicable in terms of the available evidence and proof, in the vast majority of cases a plea to a lesser offence did not appear to be consistent with the nature, strength and sufficiency of the evidence available.

Table 12.1 sets out our overall findings on this:

[2] Mary Taylor, alias Jane Philips, having been charged with grand larceny from the person and alleged by the police to have had a large inside pocket 'generally carried by female thieves (known as "shop lifters") upon their person' eventually pleaded guilty to attempted grand larceny.

ILLUSTRATION 12.1: Mary Taylor, District Attorney's Files, 10 May, 1865.

TABLE 12.1: *General Sessions, District Attorney's Files: The Reasons for Lesser Pleas 1850–1865 Over a Thirty Day Period for One Court Part*

	Nature of offences					
	Property		**Person**		**All offences**	
Reason for lesser plea	**n**	**%**	**n**	**%**	**n**	**%**
Equivocal facts	22	16.9	4	21.0	26	17.4
Mitigating factors	11	8.5	6	31.6	17	11.4
Explicit official intervention	2	1.5	3	15.8	5	3.4
No evident reason	95	73.1	6	31.6	101	67.8
Inadequate information	22	–	1	–	23	–
Total	152	100.0	20	100.0	172	100.0

We detail below the kinds of cases that constitute the categories in Table 12.1

Equivocal facts

We begin with cases in which there might be a plausible reason for the acceptance of a guilty plea. In about one in every six such cases, information in the file suggests a degree of uncertainty about the sufficiency of the available evidence and proof that might have persuaded the District Attorney to offer a lesser plea. Whilst few required such a reduction, the facts alleged can be read in such a way as to be consistent with the lesser plea in most cases. The cases give rise to two different kinds of uncertainty: whether the defendant did the basic acts constituting the original charge; and whether the value of the property taken supported conviction for the top count (as charged) or a lesser-included offence (as pleaded).

In the vast majority of cases falling within this equivocal fact category (85.0 per cent), the uncertainty concerns whether the defendant's conduct fulfilled the requirements of the completed offence. Typically, the question posed by the allegation was whether, when a defendant was discovered in possession of stolen goods, there was sufficient evidence to prove that the defendant was the burglar or was simply a thief or receiver; or whether a defendant had done enough to warrant conviction for the full crime or whether he or she had only reached the stage of an attempt. Thus, in the absence of direct evidence that the defendant had been in the house of the complainant, successful prosecution for burglary might be difficult if based solely upon possession of goods stolen from the house thus suggesting to the District Attorney that a guilty plea to a lesser offence was appropriate. An illustration of this is the prosecution of Robert Adams[3] who was indicted with burglary in the first degree (punishable by not less than ten years in state prison) and pleaded guilty to grand larceny (punishable by not more than five years in state prison):

> The case arose out of a complaint by Hetty Coursen of 282 Fourth Street who claimed that her house had been burglariously entered 'by means of violently forcing open a rear door opening upon the yard with an augur and chisel on the night of the 20th day of August, 1850 or thereabouts ...' and spoons, clothes and other items of property stolen. The defendant, together with Robert Davis, was arrested by William H Martin of the 5th Patrol on the 21st of August, 1850 with the property described in Hetty Coursen's complaint in their possession.

Whilst possession of recently stolen goods no doubt raised an inference of knowledge that the property was stolen, Adams' guilty plea to grand larceny may have represented the best outcome in the absence of direct evidence that he had broken into Coursen's house,[4] although in the earlier period cases with identical facts were disposed through trial of the top count.

Other examples were cases reduced to an attempt in relation to burglary prosecutions where the defendants were caught inside the premises before the asportation of property occurred. An example is *John Scully and James McCann*,[5] where the top count of the indictment was for burglary in the third degree and the defendants pleaded guilty to an attempt (punishable by one half, 2.5 years, of the maximum sentence available for the top count):

> Officer Patrick Smith of the 11th Precinct Police discovered at between 3.30am and 4.00am the basement door of 128 Avenue C standing open. Together with Officer Prout he went into the basement and found 'four pairs of boots piled up in the middle of the floor, and on searching further found in the back basement, hidden away in a coal bin, John Scully and James McCann ...' The defendants, both youths, who had effected entry by forcing the front door, openly admitted the offence, Scully stating at his examination: 'I can't say anything more than that we did it' and McCann saying:
>
> > 'There were two big boys who took me along with them and put me into it. John Scully was one of them'.

---

[3] District Attorney's Files, 8 October, 1850.

[4] As a matter of interest, Davis went to trial on the original charges of burglary and grand larceny and was acquitted of both: District Attorney's Files, 8 October, 1865.

[5] District Attorney's Files, 15 May, 1865.

The guilty plea to attempted burglary may be explained by the fact that the only property which appeared to be the object of the burglary were the four pairs of boots, and these had not been removed from the basement,[6] although in similar circumstances, other defendants were convicted after trial of or pleaded guilty to the completed offence of burglary.[7]

A similar evidential problem may have been behind a plea to a lesser offence in certain cases of theft from the person where, although the defendant was caught in the act, there may have been a question as to whether he had done sufficient acts to prove the completed offence or whether there was only proof of a lesser included offence or attempt, as illustrated in the prosecution of James McLaughlin.[8]

> The defendant was indicted for robbery in the first degree (punishable by not less than ten years in state prison). According to the complainant, Michael Shaw of Greenwich Avenue, he was approached by two persons, one of whom he believed to be the defendant, whilst walking along Eighth Avenue at 6 o'clock on the morning of 7 April, 1860. In his examination before the magistrate, Shaw stated that the two individuals:
>
> > feloniously assaulted him—and snatched the watch from his vest pocket or attempted to and in the act broke the chain of said watch of the value of ten dollars leaving the hook fast to his vest and the chain broken ...

It appears from this statement of Shaw that his watch may not in fact have been taken, confirmation of which is provided by the deposition of Stephen Mitchell a bystander who witnessed the incident and, on asking Shaw if his watch was gone, was told 'that his chain was stolen or attempted to be stolen ...' Given this evidence, McLaughlin's plea of guilty to the lesser offence of assault with intent to commit robbery (punishable by not more than five years in state prison or not more than one year in county gaol) may have been viewed by the actors as more consistent with the available evidence.

A similar set of issues arose in the prosecution for grand larceny (punishable by not more than five years in state prison) of Thomas Burke,[9] who pleaded guilty to an attempt:

> The defendant was arrested on the complaint of Thomas Knudson arising out of an incident that took place in the City Hall Park on Monday, 24 April

---

[6] See also *Andrew Fitzgerald and James Tigue*, District Attorney's Files, 16 May, 1865.

[7] See eg, *Abram Hecht*, District Attorney's Files, 22 March, 1865 a fourteen year old 'segar maker' who pleaded guilty to burglary even though he did not take any goods off the premises, the complainant householder catching him in the act. Moreover, in this case, the complaint accurately stated that Hecht had 'attempted' to take the goods.

[8] District Attorney's Files, 22 May, 1860.

[9] District Attorney's Files, 9 May, 1865.

1865 when crowds were gathered on the occasion of the reception of the remains of the late President Abraham Lincoln. It is clear that, from the very outset, the nature of the allegation was consistent with attempted larceny. The complaint itself, sworn to by Knudson before magistrate Mansfield, alleged that a book containing bills in the value of $35.00 'was feloniously taken and attempted to be carried away' by Thomas Burke. According to Knudson, when examined before the magistrate, feeling someone's hand in his pocket he 'seized hold of the hand while it was actually in his ... pocket and found that his Pocket Book had been nearly pulled out from his pantaloons pocket by ... Burke whom he held on to until the arrival of officer Edward Powers of the 7 precinct to whom he delivered him over ...' Knudson added that he was able to identify Burke as the person who 'attempted to pick his ... pocket ...'

It seems clear that Mr Osborn, counsel for the defence,[10] felt it necessary to ensure that the attempt and not the completed offence had been committed.[11] Accordingly, in what appears to be a continuation of the examination before the Police Justice, Knudson was re-sworn and cross-examined two days later.[12] Knudson repeated his earlier charge telling the court that 'he did not actually lose anything' having caught hold of Burke's hand 'before he had or could get his hand out of my pocket ...' All of this was corroborated by Officer Edward Powers who described how the struggle had taken place in front of him with Knudson charging Burke with 'having attempted to pick his pocket ...'

Whilst these cases can be explained on the basis of an incomplete crime, other defendants, in identical circumstances, were convicted after trial or on a plea of guilty to the full offence.[13]

In another group of cases, the equivocal facts relate to uncertainties as to the value of the property taken and, thereby, as to the appropriate level of the offence committed, whether, for example, petit larceny (value of item $25 or less and punishable by not more than six months in county gaol) or grand larceny (punishable by not more than five years in state prison). An illustration is the

---

[10] B W Osborn of 68 Essex Street is listed on the indictment jacket in the place where defence counsel is usually annotated.

[11] Whilst Thomas Burke said 'I am not guilty' when asked by the Police Justice if he had anything to say to the charge of attempted larceny from the person, a letter he wrote to the Judge from the Tombs prison on 9 May 1865, the day of his plea, shows that he did not dispute guilt. In that letter he expressed sorrow 'for that rash act when it is too late', telling the judge that he had 'not always been a dishonest man' and asking if 'your honor would only be a little merciful towards me for the sake of my poor wife and sisters which are living in Boston.'

[12] The questions put to Knudson are not disclosed.

[13] See eg, *John Ravel*, District Attorney's Files, 5 May, 1865 who was also arrested on Broadway by the complainant, William Redfield, who stated that he 'caught him in the act of taking [his] watch & chain from his person while he was looking at the procession near 14th Street on Broadway'. Despite the apparently inchoate nature of the offence, Ravel was convicted on his plea of the full offence charged of grand larceny and sentenced to state prison for 3 years and 4 months.

prosecution of Amanda Chambers,[14] who was indicted for grand larceny of various items to the value of $82.50 the property of Mary Smith and pleaded guilty to petit larceny:

> In her original complaint, Smith alleged that Chambers had stolen items to the value of $52.00. Although the value of the property in the complaint alone would have supported a charge of grand larceny, it seems likely that the prosecution might have had difficulty in proving that Amanda had taken all the items alleged given the testimony which was offered before the magistrate. Chambers had been apprehended by Officer Joseph Webster eleven days after the original theft 'with part of the property named in the affidavit of Smith in her possession'. The impression that the complaint might have been inflated[15] is given further credence by Chamber's response when asked if she had anything to say to the charge preferred against her: 'I have nothing to say only I am charged with more than I took'.[16]

Equivocal facts were also present in offences against the person where uncertainty arose as to whether a greater or lesser offence was supported by the evidence, as illustrated by the prosecution of Patrick Quinn and James McCormick,[17] where the defendants pleaded guilty in General Sessions to simple assault and battery (punishable by not more than one year in county gaol) on a charge of assault with intent to kill (punishable by not more than ten years in state prison) on the complaint of James Ryan. The latter said that, on 5 December, 1864 in Mr Tietjen's store, the defendants and five others struck him several blows with their fists and kicked him with their feet and that Quinn 'drew an open knife' and inflicted serious bodily injury on him:

> At a hearing held on 9 January, 1865 before the magistrate, defence counsel sought to establish that there was no evidence of any knife being used in the fight. Thus, when cross-examined, one witness, Patrick Delaney, stated: 'I did not see Mr Quinn have a knife in Mr Tietjin's store', and John Tietjen himself stated under cross-examination that: 'I did not see any body have any knife there—I think I would have seen it unless it was a very small knife—so that he covered it all with his hand.' In the absence,

---

[14] District Attorney's Files, 4 October, 1855.

[15] Occasionally, a defendant might be charged with having stolen all of the items of property in a room in which he or she had been discovered, even though none of the items had been physically removed. See eg *John Hessian*, 21 September, 1855 in which the indictment documents all items in the room totalling over $300.00 in value though none had actually been removed.

[16] See also *Abraham Riap*, District Attorney's Files, 13 September, 1850 in which Riap admitted taking various goods which had been entrusted to him to take to the steamboat landing but stated, contrary to the claim of the loser John Elton, that the pocket book had no money in it. The presence or absence of money was probably crucial to the appropriate level of charge, Riap's plea of guilty to petit larceny being accepted on an indictment charging him with grand larceny.

[17] District Attorney's Files, 15 May, 1865.

therefore, of any corroborative evidence independent of the assertion of James Ryan and, given the evidence to the contrary, proof of an intention to kill would have been difficult at trial and a plea of guilty to the misdemeanour of simple assault and battery appeared more consistent with the available evidence.

Mitigating factors

In another group of cases, involving about one in every nine lesser pleas (n=17), the reason for the reduced plea may plausibly be located in the presence of some factor which mitigated the seriousness of the offence or promoted a sense of leniency towards the defendant. Most of the cases in this category involved a claim as to the defendant's state of mind at the time of the incident or a claim of remorse.

The most frequently occurring mitigating factor was a claim by the defendant to have been drunk at the time of the incident, as in the prosecution of Thomas Boyle[18] in which the defendant was indicted on a charge of grand larceny of a firkin of butter valued at $60.00 the property of Willet G Vandemark.

> The evidence presented before the magistrate showed that Boyle, who was employed by Vandemark at the freight depot of the Hudson River Rail-road company, hired a cartman, Collins, to come to the depot and cart the butter away. At his examination before the magistrate, Boyle set out the mitigating circumstances as follows:
>
> > 'I have nothing to say. I was under the influence of liquor and had no intention of stealing the butter. I am perfectly friendless and have no one to intercede for me.'

Boyle reinforced his plea for lenient treatment in two letters he later wrote from the Tombs where he was incarcerated whilst waiting for his trial. In a letter to Judge Hoffman dated 10 February 1865 Boyle repeated his claim to have been 'in liquor at the time [of the offence],' stating that he 'was unconscious of what [he] was doing' and swearing that he would 'never taste it again as it is the forerunner of all misfortune and trouble.'[19] His second letter of 19 February 1865, addressed to the 'District Attorney Presiding', repeated his earlier claims and directly raised the question of a reduced plea: 'I will offer a plea of Petit Larceny in my case if you will please to accept it.' Whilst Boyle's direct offer of a plea to petit larceny was not accepted, it is possible that his various entreaties induced

---

[18] District Attorney's Files, 22 March, 1865.

[19] In his claim for merciful treatment, Boyle also said that it was his first offence, that his 60 year old mother needed his support and that, if the Judge did not pass a sentence of imprisonment, he would willingly join the army or navy.

sympathetic feelings which led to acceptance of his plea of guilty to attempted grand larceny.[20]

Nonetheless, a claim of drunkenness or disturbed mental state did not invariably secure a reduction in the charge, as illustrated in the prosecution of Henry Bellamy,[21] in which the defendant ultimately pleaded guilty to the full offence of grand larceny even though there was clear independent evidence that he was heavily intoxicated at the time and made such a claim at his examination before the magistrate.[22] Moreover, Bellamy wrote from the City Prison to General Sessions' Judge Russell seeking his mercy for the 'unpardonable act' which, he said, would never have occurred had he 'not been so much intoxicated as scarcely to know what [I] was doing.' Bellamy also enclosed a testimonial from Mr Richardson, an accountant of Russell Street, London in which he recommended Bellamy on the basis of his trustworthiness.

In some cases, the reduction in plea may have been attributable to evidence that the defendant was truly remorseful or had made some efforts towards reparation, as illustrated by the prosecution of Andrew Larssen,[23] who pleaded guilty to petit larceny having been charged with grand larceny of various items of clothes from Louis Henry Buggely.

> Buggely asserted that Larssen 'acknowledges that he committed the offence
> … charged and has caused a large portion of the property to be returned to
> [Buggeley's] possession.' The evidence of remorse appears in Larssen's
> examination before the magistrate, during which he stated:
>
> > I acknowledge commission of the offence. The only evidence of my
> > guilt was furnished by myself at the solicition (*sic*) of the complainant
> > who assured me as a consideration that I would not be prosecuted. After
> > I caused the property to be delivered up, he preferred this complaint.

Larsen's reduced plea to a misdemeanour was presumably based on the fact that the crime was self-reported and that the defendant voluntarily surrendered the residue of the property taken, as well as, perhaps, the fact that the loser had or might have broken a promise not to prosecute at all.

In other cases, the only evidence of repentance is the fact that the defendant gave up the residue of the property once he or she had been discovered, as in the

---

[20] For other examples, see: *Cornelius Dodge*, District Attorney's Files, 20 September, 1850 in which the defendant's guilty plea to petit larceny was accepted to a charge of grand larceny where the evidence showed he had stolen a watch and sold it to a third party after Dodge told the magistrate: 'I was intoxicated at the time I took the watch & did not know what I was doing'; and *Henry Fulton*, District Attorney's Files, 11 October, 1850 in which a plea of guilty to petit larceny on a charge of Burglary in the Third Degree and Petit Larceny was accepted after the defendant stated at his examination: 'I done it, but I was intoxicated at the time.'

[21] District Attorney's Files, 8 May, 1865.

[22] The goods stolen had, in fact, been given by Bellamy to the Hotel clerk for safe keeping at the request of the clerk who had seen Bellamy's drunken actions.

[23] District Attorney's Files, 14 November, 1850.

grand larceny prosecution of John Casey,[24] where the defendant pleaded guilty to petit larceny.

> The defendant stole a watch worth $50.00 from John Masterson when Masterson was asleep in an oyster saloon and pawned it. Casey, a waiter in the saloon, stated at his examination that he 'gave up the pawn ticket for the watch and all the money [he] received for it except twenty five cents.'

Whilst, as we have seen, repentance did not invariably lead to lesser pleas and the surrender of undisposed property is itself equivocal, such factors are the only evidence in the files to explain the reduction in plea in this and similar cases.[25]

Explicit official intervention

In a small group of cases (n=5), there is explicit reference to the District Attorney's or trial judge's involvement in some way in the plea argreement. Whilst this evidence is of itself too patchy to suggest systematic involvement in plea settlements by judges or prosecutors, it does show that, at least occasionally, there was some space outside conventional courtroom procedures for involvement of courtroom actors in the settlement of guilty pleas.

A case illustrative of the existence of prosecutorial discretion over charge and plea and of the rationale of the District Attorney in settling cases without going to trial, even where there were triable issues, is the prosecution of William Smith.[26] There, following a charge of murder in the first degree (punishable by death), the defendant's plea of guilty to manslaughter in the fourth degree (punishable by not more than two years in state prison or one year in county gaol) was accepted:

> In the course of an inquisition before the coroner, Edward Collin, and jurors, Emma Weilds gave a graphic account of the day in question in which she, Smith and the deceased, Daniel Lawrence had visited various saloons on Saturday, 25 February 1865. Lawrence was very keen on Wields and jealous of her relationship with Smith. At about 1.30am, just before they left for home, Lawrence said to Wields: 'some of you will cry to night' and when asked if he meant Wields, replied: 'No, Emma, I would not hurt you, but one very close to you' which Wields took to mean Smith. As they walked home, Lawrence fell behind and on arriving home, Wields and Smith locked the doors, Wields telling Smith not to let anyone in because she was afraid for her life after the threat issued by Lawrence earlier in the evening.

---

[24] District Attorney's Files, 30 May, 1860.
[25] See also: *Felix Kennedy*, District Attorney's Files, 21 September, 1855 where the defendant admitted that he was given $35.00, part of the proceeds of a burglary, adding that he 'gave the Officer Arnoux Twenty Five Dollars back.'
[26] District Attorney's Files, 10 April, 1865.

Lawrence eventually arrived there and on failing to gain entry, uttered various threats including 'you son of a bitch, if you dont open the door, I'll murder you.' They kept the door locked and the lights out but eventually
'Lawrence came through the hall bedroom window and fell onto the bed.' A
scuffle developed and Wields went next door to Mrs Barry, thereby escaping
the attentions of Lawrence who tried to catch her after coming out of her
room. Mrs Barry gave an account which corroborated Wields' description of
Lawrence's behaviour stating that he knocked 'awful hard' to gain entry to
the room and 'swore all sorts of vengeance if he did not get in.' As a result
of this evidence the District Attorney, A Oakey Hall, appended the following
note to the file:

> Upon the testimony of Emma, and Barry, and the reticence of Prisoner,
> this case looks exceedingly like self defence, a plea of manslaughter
> 4th degree is tendered & I receive it.[27]

The prosecution of George Sloan[28] is an example of a guilty plea case in which
explicit judicial intervention (after a conversation with the arresting officer) is
documented. In Sloan, the defendant was charged with assault and battery with
intent to kill Officer Ralph Barker of the 15th Precinct Police but pleaded guilty
to simple assault and battery:

> The incident began after Barker arrested Sloan on a complaint that he
> had stolen a gold watch and chain from a liquor store on Sixth Avenue.
> According to Barker, Sloan persuaded Barker to take him home so that
> Sloan could inform his wife of his arrest. Barker alleged in his examination
> before the magistrate that, when at the defendant's home, 'Sloan opened a
> bureau drawer and took therefrom a pistol with which he threatened to shoot
> [me]—said Sloan at the time made the following remark to [me] 'You son
> of a bitch leave my house or I'll blow your brains out'.

> Barker said that he thereupon took Sloan into custody. For his part, Sloan, a
> 35-year old Scottish sailor, denied the substance of Barker's allegation, stat-
> ing at his examination before the magistrate:

>> I made no assault on the officer and am innocent of the charge. I had no
>> weapon of any description in my hand.

> There is no record of any weapon being produced in support of Officer
> Barker's allegation. The matter was resolved with the acceptance of the
> reduced plea a week later, General Sessions' Recorder John Hoffman then
> writing the following note to the Clerk to the Court of General Sessions:

---

[27] In this case, for example, medical evidence from Dr Woolsey Johnson of the New York Hospital
revealed that Daniel Lawrence had suffered twenty stab wounds varying from $/$ " to 1" in depth; and
Emma's credibility was perhaps reduced by the fact that she was the girlfriend of the defendant who,
on her own evidence, intended to marry her. The wording of the District Attorney's note might indicate that the initiative for the reduced plea came from the defence.

[28] District Attorney's Files, 28 April, 1865.

> After conversing with Officer Barker in relation to the complaint against
> George Sloane I have concluded to suspend sentence. Let it be so entered.

The outcome in this case suggests that there may have been no real prospect of
proving the officer's original allegations against Sloan in full.

NO EVIDENT REASON

Crimes against property—lesser pleas

Commonly in property prosecutions, a plea of guilty to petit larceny was accepted
where the value of goods stolen supported a charge of grand larceny, a plea of guilty
to larceny where there was clear evidence of burglary, or a plea of guilty to grand
larceny or simple assault where the evidence showed that the victim had been the
subject of a robbery. This is illustrated in the prosecution of William McDermott
et al, [29] in which four defendants pleaded guilty to the misdemeanour of assault and
battery having been indicted for robbery in the first degree of Newman Cowen.

> In his examination before the Magistrate, on the same day as the alleged
> offence, Cowen said that the four defendants 'took forcible hold of [him],
> knocked him down & while he was down the money was taken from him ...'
> The money allegedly taken consisted of $100.00 which had been in his
> pocket book. When cross-examined the next day, Cowen maintained his
> story that he was assaulted and importantly that his money was taken:
>
> > The whole four struck me ... I couldn't call for assistance. I was sur-
> > prised. I did not strike back or call out as I was unable. They all struck
> > me & kicked me at one time. I was coming to my store from the house.
> > After I got up my money was gone & they all ran away into a cut in
> > Mulberry Street. I did not see my pocket book taken, it was taken when
> > I was on the ground ...
>
> It is clear from this that Cowen maintained that the money was taken in the
> course of the assault, a point that was reiterated during his re-direct exami-
> nation:
>
> > I had my money when I was struck in my outer coat pocket & while
> > down I felt them at my pocket.
>
> Despite this, a plea to the misdemeanour was accepted.

A further illustration occurred in the prosecution of James McAnany,[30] where
the defendant pleaded guilty to petit larceny after having been indicted for grand

---

[29] District Attorney's Files, 5 April, 1865.
[30] District Attorney's Files, 15 November, 1855.

larceny of six hundred pounds of iron to the value of $120.00,[31] the property of
Daniel L Pettee. Here, a guilty plea to a lesser included offence was entered, as
frequently occurred in our sample, where the magistrate's examination showed sufficient evidence to convict of the top count, but the defendant denied any involvement. Such a denial, if believed by the District Attorney in the earlier period, would
have resulted in a *nolle prosequi* or, if disbelieved, in a trial. In *McAnany*:

> The complainant Pettee stated in his examination before the magistrate that
> he was informed by Thomas Lane that the latter had bought the pig iron from
> McAnany, sold it on in turn to Patrick McBride and that he, Pettee, 'this day
> found said iron in the yard of said McBride'. Thomas Lane, in his examina-
> tion, corroborated Pettee's account telling the court 'that he bought the iron
> claimed by Daniel L Pettee from James McAnany and sold the same to
> Patrick McBride'. When examined, James McAnany denied involvement,
> stating: 'I am not guilty of the charge preferred against him (*sic*)'.

In the absence of evidence that only a part of the property was stolen or that
the property taken was of much less value than that claimed, there would appear
to be no justification for the acceptance of the defendant's plea of guilty to petit
larceny.

Kate Dickson[32] is another case in which the evidence against the defendant for
the principal offence seemed clear, although the defendant denied any involvement before the Police Justice. There, the defendant, a prostitute, pleaded guilty
to petit larceny having been indicted for grand larceny of a pocketbook and
money to the value of $32.00 from Smith Clark.

> After Clark met Dickson on Sixth Avenue, they went into a saloon on the
> corner of 28th Street and 6th Avenue in company with another girl and took
> a private box. Ten minutes later Dickson left the box after which Clark
> 'found that he had been robbed of [the] pocketbook containing [his]
> money…'. According to Clark he then procured the assistance of Officer
> Gilpin of the 29th precinct and 'had said Kate arrested and conveyed to the
> … station House and then searched and while in the act of searching said
> Kate the aforesaid Pocketbook dropped upon the floor, that [he] identifies
> said pocketbook as belonging to and which have been stolen from his pos-
> session as aforesaid …'
>
> Dickson when questioned before the magistrate stated: 'I do not know any-
> thing about his money'.

---

[31] The original complaint did not specify the exact quantity of iron stolen, stating only that 'a large
quantity of pig iron of the value of sixty dollars' had been stolen. Even if the amount of property taken
was that described in the original complaint this more than satisfied the requirements for a charge of
grand larceny: see eg *Matthias Dodd*, District Attorney's Files, 14 November, 1855 who was tried for
grand larceny where the property stolen was valued at $30.00.
[32] District Attorney's Files, 4 May, 1865.

Guilty pleas also became disassociated from the sufficiency of evidence and proof in some more serious prosecutions where the defendant entered a denial before the magistrate despite strong evidence of guilt. This is illustrated by the prosecution of Thomas Stack alias Lloyd,[33] who pleaded guilty to grand larceny having been indicted for robbery in the first degree despite evidence provided by the victim George H Grenville that force had been used. Grenville set out his complaint in the following terms:

> ... at about 3 oclock in the morning of the 17th April 1860 when returning from a Ball in company with his wife and while passing along Canal St in the vicinity of Lawrence St he was feloniously assaulted by Thomas Stack alias Lloyd now present and two other persons who struck [him] in the breast and at the time took stole and carried away from his possession and from his person a Gold Watch of the value of Fifty Dollars.
>
> [He] further says that at the time officer Mount of the 8th Ward came to his assistance. He saw ... Stack alias Lloyd throw away the said Watch which he picked up, when the other two persons fled and ran away ...

Officer William H Mount gave an account which corroborated Grenville's story. Mount said that, while on duty in Canal Street at about 3 o'clock in the morning:

> he heard the cry of Watch and on running towards the place met Thomas Stack alias Lloyd ... running towards him and arrested him and took him back to the place on the corner of Lawrence St where Mr Grenville and his wife were standing and when there ... Stack dropped the watch on the side walk which Mr Grenville picked up and identified as his property ...

For his part, Stack told the magistrate: 'I am not guilty'.

Similarly, on an indictment for burglary in the first degree in the prosecution of Daniel Doolan,[34] the defendant pleaded guilty to the misdemeanour petit larceny despite available evidence sufficient to establish the felonious breaking and entering.

> In this case, the complainant, Jeremiah Curtin, alleged that his house at 234 Greenwich Street had been burglariously entered by means of a false key and a silver cup valued at $5.00 stolen. Jeremiah stated that this offence had been committed by Daniel Doolan and another man who had escaped as his son Michael Curtin had found Doolan inside the house. This account was supported by Michael Curtin who said that, on discovering them in the house, both men ran away and he pursued them, with Doolan being arrested by Officer Sullivan. Doolan, told the magistrate: 'I am innocent of the charge'.

[33] District Attorney's Files, 14 May, 1860.
[34] District Attorney's Files, 23 May, 1860.

In the grand larceny indictment of Michael Crowley, however, the defendant admitted culpability of the offence before the magistrate[35] and the independent evidence seemed sufficient to convict. In General Sessions, nonetheless, the defendant pleaded guilty to petit larceny. The charge arose on the complaint of Andrew Brown of 188 Cherry Street who alleged that gold coins and bank bills to the value of $50.00 were stolen from his possession by Michael Crowley. The basis of Brown's complaint was that Crowley:

> '... now acknowledges that he saw [Brown] drop said money out of [his] pocket and picked it up—he also acknowledges that the twenty five 10/100 Dollars now here is a portion of said money and that he spent the remainder for himself and another boy also for the chain now produced.'

At his examination before the magistrate Crowley effectively conceded his guilt, stating:

> 'I only knew it was his by seeing him drop it.'

Crimes against property—attempts

In another group of cases (n=39) a plea of guilty to attempt was accepted on evidence which suggested that the completed crime had been committed and which, in the earlier period, resulted in conviction for the full offence. This was common in indictments for grand larceny.

In *Catharine Carroll*,[36] for example, the defendant was charged with grand larceny from Charles G Cornell of 68 Third Street. Carroll admitted to Cornell that she had stolen his gold coins to the value of about $100.00 'and had bought a lot of articles with a part of the money and had thrown the Ballance in the sink'. At her examination before the magistrate, Carroll admitted that she had taken the money telling the court: 'I have nothing to say. I gave all I had back again'.

Similarly in *Caroline Engleman*,[37] the complaint drawn by Sarah Ward of 402 Fourth Avenue, alleged that Engleman had stolen a black silk dress, cashmere shawl and muslin skirt totalling in value $47.00 in the following manner:

> [Sarah] discovered the said Caroline in [the] premises coming from the apartment in which the said property was contained and that [Sarah] questioned her as to what she was doing there, that the said Caroline stated that she was looking for a dress maker and that if [Sarah] thought that she ... had stolen any thing [Sarah] might search her basket which she was carrying with her. [Sarah] then went to the front room and discovered the door leading to [her] apartment .... was open and that [she] discovered that the ... silk dress had been carried off—[Sarah] then went in search of ... Caroline and

---

[35] District Attorney's Files, 16 May, 1860.
[36] District Attorney's Files, 22 November, 1855.
[37] District Attorney's Files, 22 March, 1865.

found her in 29th Street near the corner of 4th Avenue. [Sarah] requested her to go to the police station house when she … then acknowledged to [Sarah] that she had the said dress in her basket and that if [Sarah] would let her go she would give anything that [Sarah] might ask of her. That in the 29th police station house Officer Henry Roberts searched the basket belonging to … Caroline & in the same found the said silk dress & the said shawl & skirt which [Sarah] identified as the property of her & her husband …

Officer Henry Roberts swore a deposition in which he corroborated Sarah's account of the search of Caroline's basket. When questioned, Engleman told the magistrate that she was guilty of the crime of grand larceny, stating: 'I did steal the property'.

Other examples of pleas to attempted grand larceny occurred where there was sufficient evidence of the completed act but, as in uncharged lesser pleas, the defendant denied any involvement. An illustration is provided by the case of *William Blunt*,[38] which arose out of the theft of a gold watch and ebony wood chain from William Harris while on board the steamer *Electri* as it travelled from Providence to New York City. In his complaint before the magistrate, William Harris described what happened on board the steamer:

… he placed the … property in his vest pocket and when he retired to bed placed the vest … at the head of the bed in which [he] slept in, that … Blunt was employed on board of the same Steamer and occupied the same apartment in which [Harris] slept in—that [Harris] on awaking discovered that the said property had been abstracted from his … vest—that on the 16th day of February 1865 [Harris] was informed by Joseph Tines of No 51 East Houston Street that he … purchased the said watch & chain of the said Blunt. [Harris] has seen the said watch & chain so purchased by said Tines and identifies the same as his property … [T]hat [he] caused the said Blunt to be arrested by Officer James Curley of the 8th precinct police on the 19th day of February 1865 and the said Blunt admitted to [Harris] that he sold the said property to [Joseph Tines] …

Blunt stated in answer to the charge: 'I found the watch and sold it to Joseph Tines. I did not steal it'.

Crimes against property: aggravating factors

It might be expected that aggravating factors would militate against a reduction in charge severity and instead stimulate the District Attorney to seek conviction for the top count. However, in a small number of cases the entry of lesser pleas occurred where there were no evidential justifications for reducing the crime and where there were factors which aggravated it, as in theft offences involving

---

[38] District Attorney's Files, 28 March, 1865.

breach of trust by employees, as illustrated by the prosecution of John Standring,[39] who pleaded guilty to petit larceny having been indicted for grand larceny.

> The complaint was based upon a pattern of thefts over a long period of time by Standring a clerk in the store of the complainant, Thomas Douglass. The indictment for grand larceny charged Standring with theft of nails, files, tools and nippers of value in excess of $2,500.00. The evidence suggested that Standring had systematically stolen goods from his employer, selling them on to hardware dealers, some of whom appeared as prosecution witnesses. Further, Standring had employed Edward Phillips to travel about the City to sell different kinds of hardware, falsely representing to Phillips that he, Standring, had an interest in the firm of Thomas Douglass. According to Phillips, he paid over to Standring the proceeds of the sales every evening which, he said, totalled between $15-25 each day from 26 May 1855 to 7 August 1855.

A different kind of aggravating feature was present in the prosecution of John Jones,[40] who pleaded guilty to attempted grand larceny after having attempted to bribe the arresting officer. The grand larceny indictment arose on the complaint of John K Martin, a driver for Kinsley's Express, who had left his Express Wagon in front of 447 Broome Street when John Jones was seen by independent witnesses to take a bundle of goods from the wagon. Jones was later arrested by Officer John Andre in Broadway as he made off with the goods. According to Officer Andre:

> … Jones admitted having stolen [the] property, and offered [me] five dollars to let him go, which [I] refused …

Crimes against the person

The practice of accepting lesser pleas for reasons unrelated to evidence and proof was also prevalent in crimes of violence directed against individuals. Our sample of case files in which defendants were indicted for crimes of felonious assault and battery *with intent* illustrates the practice. One example is the prosecution of Heinrich Böhme alias Henry Dutcher,[41] who was indicted for assault with intent to kill with a deadly and dangerous weapon, and the defendant pleaded guilty to the misdemeanour of assault and battery. Dutcher was arrested on the complaint of Alexander Shepherd of the same address. Shepherd said that he had been assaulted by Dutcher

---

[39] District Attorney's Files, 21 September, 1855.
[40] District Attorney's Files, 19 April, 1860.
[41] District Attorney's Files, 11 May, 1860.

'…who pursued [Shepherd] for a distance of about twenty feet with the knife here shown—in the hand of him, the said Dutcher: that said Dutcher overtook [Shepherd] and, with the said knife, then and there struck at [Shepherd]—and inflicted upon [his] hand a wound: that said wound was received by [Shepherd] while in the act of warding off the said blow, so struck by said Dutcher, as aforesaid—'

When examined before the magistrate, Dutcher denied responsibility, stating: 'I am not guilty of the charge'.

If Shepherd's testimony were to be believed, then a top count conviction would seem to have been justified given his evidence that Dutcher used a knife in striking at him.

Overall data analysis

In spite of the fact that a minority of guilty pleas to uncharged lesser included offences and attempts might be explained because of equivocal facts, mitigating circumstances or the direct involvement of the District Attorney and trial judge, in the vast majority of cases in our sample, we could identify no factors which might explain the reduction in offence. On the contrary, in these cases the facts alleged in the indictment and supported by the testimony of prosecution witnesses given before the Police Justice would, if accepted, have supported a conviction of the offence charged. Nonetheless, the frequency of these cases suggests that it had by now become a common feature of the system of prosecutorial discretion that cases which a few decades earlier would have gone to full trial for the full or completed offence were now regularly disposed of by guilty pleas to lesser offences or attempts. As in the earlier period, single count indictments were returned charging a defendant with either the most serious offence prosecutable or a lesser offence itself, given the available evidence and proof. The difference occurred in the seemingly routinised practice over the period 1850–1865 of accepting guilty pleas to uncharged lesser included offences for no evident reason, whereas guilty pleas in the earlier period were almost invariably to the top count which was the offence originally returned by the grand jury.

The cases in which guilty pleas became separated from the available evidence and proof occurred in two principal ways: where a plea of guilty to a lesser included offence was accepted on facts which suggested quite clearly that the greater offence had been committed; and where a guilty plea to an attempt was accepted despite evidence also clearly showing that the full crime had been completed.[42] In the larger group of cases (n=59), the prosecution was disposed of on the basis of the defendant's plea of guilty to a lesser-included offence.

---

[42] In a few cases (n=3), the defendant pleaded guilty to a lesser degree of crime than that originally charged.

The practice of accepting pleas to uncharged lesser included offences was not limited to crimes against property. Indeed, no fewer than twenty of the twenty one felonious assault cases in our sample were settled by the entry of a guilty plea to a lesser offence mostly without any evident reason related to the facts and circumstances of the case itself. Moreover, in most assault with intent prosecutions, the lesser plea was to simple assault and battery, a misdemeanour. Taken on their own, these figures suggest a routine willingness to accept lesser pleas, often misdemeanours, in indictments for serious violent felony offences.

CONCLUSION

The new plea bargaining regime based upon offers of lesser offences and attempts with statutory caps replaced the earlier regime in which convictions whether by plea or trial were generally to the top count of the indictment and where the judge, after hearing the witnesses and reflecting upon the culpability of the accused, including any prior criminal activity, would impose a sentence within a maximum statutory range. Our analysis of the District Attorney's case files supports the conclusion that, for the most part, after mid-century, as in the earlier period, the indictment reflected the seriousness of the allegations made by witnesses or the admissions made by the defendant. In some instances there was counter evidence either through a claim by the defendant denying the offence or offering mitigating circumstances or through the testimony of witnesses that the activity the subject of the indictment was of lesser seriousness. Nevertheless, had this been the period 1800–1845, the presence of counter evidence would have suggested that the case was suitable for trial on the original charge and would not have justified acceptance of a guilty plea to a lesser charge.

What developed after mid-century was a separation between the facts established in support of the allegations and those implicit in the lesser plea. In contrast to the earlier period, where the synchronisation between the facts alleged and the plea entered demonstrated the personal character of criminal justice, the lack of a firm factual foundation for the lesser plea over the period 1856–1865 is evidence of the transformation towards a system of aggregate justice.

Thus, we examined our sample of case files to determine to what extent lesser pleas, as Friedman and Percival contend, were 'almost unmistakeably the sign of a bargain'.[43] Of course, one would expect that such an outcome, to provide a meaningful inducement to the actors in relation to the facts and circumstances of the case, would be based upon some rational assessment of the sufficiency and persuasiveness of the evidence and proof and character of the defendant. As our data have shown, however, for the vast majority of guilty plea cases in this transformative period, this explanation is unavailing. Of greater explanatory force is

---

[43] Friedman and Percival (1981) p 176.

the politics of ward-heeling which impacted upon the role of the District Attorney resulting in the diversion of indictments and so-called plea bargaining. Such practices assured the continued election of the District Attorney who, as Tammany Hall's candidate, depended upon an underclass of constituents many of whom themselves were engaged in ongoing activity in violation of the criminal law.

New York City's justice system, controlled as it was by the Tammany machine, thus came to symbolise the emergent politics of discretion. As Wilbur Miller has stated;[44]

> Whether the district attorney was lenient on political supporters or bargained for briefer sentences than an offender deserved, legal standards of argument and evidence were replaced by personal discretion. The district attorney's honesty or dishonesty was more important than the rule of law.

Such discretionary practices as the offering of uncharged lesser pleas and attempts or the reliance on *nolles prosequi* and pigeon holing to eliminate entire indictments assured that clientelism and discretion often separated from the sufficiency of evidence and proof in any individual case would become the principal characteristic of prosecutions in General Sessions.

[44] Wilbur Miller (1973) p 80.

Chapter 13

Aggregate Justice and Social Control

INTRODUCTION

In this chapter, we situate the transformation to a plea bargaining system in the prevailing political economy of criminal justice after mid-century. Once the ethnicity of defendants had changed, and the foreign-born and poor came to be viewed by reformers concerned with the underlying causes of crime as criminogenic, there evolved a collective interest in crime control and with it a concern for aggregate justice. Ironically, from the perspective of reformers, the emergent positivist criminology also reinforced reliance on uncharged lesser pleas and attempts since it enabled the District Attorney to contend that he had achieved a high overall rate of conviction in the face of public criticism that plea bargaining was a causative factor of crime itself.

Thus, we first consider the dichotomy between the District Attorney as political operative and the criticisms the reform movement made of the guilty plea system itself. We then consider the link between the new positivist criminology and the need to achieve aggregate justice defined, as it was, by the prosecution of dangerous classes where ethnicity and country of origin were of greater importance than a formal trial and separate sentencing proceeding. Thereafter, we consider the efforts by charitable organisations, such as the Prison Association, to ameliorate the harsh edges of aggregate justice by focusing upon individual cases worthy of special concern based upon the background and character of the accused.

LEGITIMATION AND CRITICISM

Despite the obvious departure from the public airing of evidence and proof, which was the hallmark of the earlier period, to a closed guilty plea system, where the rationale for case disposition was no longer transparent, the District

Attorney was capable of legitimating his actions politically by pointing to the high rate of conviction that plea bargaining secured. To accomplish this, the District Attorney utilising his ward-heeler's capacity, arranged pleas to uncharged lesser offences and attempts rather than prosecuting the top charge of the indictment. Of course, conviction of the top count at trial had substantially lessened, as we have seen, given the frequency in which juries exercised their power to return compromise verdicts. This, in turn, may have related to the composition and attitudes of the jury as well as an increasingly flawed process of evidence acquisition. Furthermore, the assurance that a trial judge, as in the earlier period, would direct a verdict of guilty appropriately justified by the evidence was less certain after the election of judges. Under these circumstances, the guilty plea not only reduced the harshness of the criminal sanction, a concern of the underclass that were Tammany's constituents, but it created, as well, a certainty in outcome for the District Attorney, as Raymond Moley was later to note:[1]

> Equally important is the advantage which a plea of guilty gives to the prosecuting attorney. He is not compelled to carry through an onerous and protracted trial. He does not run the risk of losing his case in the trial court. He runs no risk of having to oppose an appeal to a higher court in case he wins the trial … What is much more important to the prosecutor is the fact that in such records as most prosecutors make of the work which they have performed, a plea of guilty of any sort is counted as a conviction, and when he goes before the voters for re-election he can talk in large terms about securing convictions when, in reality, these 'convictions' include all sorts of compromises. The district attorney's 'record', as he usually interprets it to the public, rests upon the ratio of convictions to acquittals and means as much to him as a batting average means to a baseball player.

The District Attorney now determined whether indictments were worthy of further prosecution, and, if so, at what level, a decision which came to be exercised with political considerations in mind. Regardless of the available proof, guilty pleas to lesser included offences enabled the District Attorney to assert to the middling classes that he had provided society with a temporary respite from fears of criminality without the risk of non-conviction, by expeditiously placing defendants out of sight and out of mind.

In this context, District Attorney Oakey Hall spoke out about the effectiveness of policing, expressed enlightened views on the penal system and was prepared to call the attention of General Sessions' judges to deficiencies in the system, particularly when private complainants were concerned, as appears in Illustration 13.1:

---

[1] Raymond Moley (1928) p 103.

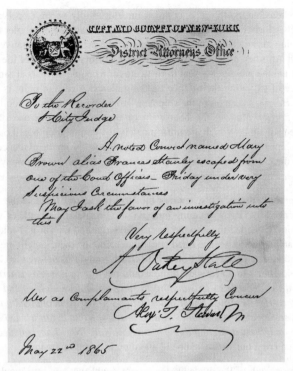

ILLUSTRATION 13.1: Mary Brown, District Attorney's Files, 5 May, 1865.

Moreover, Hall presented himself as someone learned and knowledgeable in criminological matters, and through lectures and speeches to lawyers and civic groups he became officially identified with what later reformers termed 'the certainty and celerity' of the criminal sanction[2] (as social meaning came to be attributed to rates of conviction and acquittal), for example, by calling for a reduction in the 'excessive' number of peremptory challenges available to the defence and vilifying 'perverse acquittals, and ignoble juries'.[3]

Nevertheless, plea bargaining practices of the District Attorney became a matter of adverse public comment among those who opposed what they believed to be unbalanced, corrupt and unprofessional exercise of discretion by Tammany's office holders. In 1866, for example, the reformist *New York Times* used the murder prosecution of James Harris in Oyer and Terminer, as a basis for a wider denunciation of the lesser plea practices of Tammany's District Attorney:[4]

[2] F H Norcross (1911) p 600.
[3] R M Ireland (1962) p 57.
[4] *New York Times*, December 9, 1866.

A reprehensible indifference, to put the matter mildly, seems to pervade the District-Attorney's office. Instead of bringing a clear case of murder to trial, and doing all he can to convict the culprit, the acting representative of the District-Attorney is content to receive a plea of manslaughter of the lowest grade, and the murderer is sent to rusticate for a couple of years at Sing Sing in place of expiating the offence on the gallows. A case in point is that of *James Harris*, a seaman of the ship *New World*, who in July last foully murdered *Patrick Mullan*, the boatswain of the vessel, during one of those drunken squabbles which are unfortunately too common on board our merchant ships on the eve of their departure from port. From the evidence taken before the Coroner, a few days after the murder, we cull the testimony of one witness, which is corroborated by others, setting forth the facts.

Jos Marshall, one of the seamen of the *New World*, testified that the trouble commenced by Harris' blaming him (witness) for taking a bottle of whisky from him; he called me into the forecastle and asked me for it; I told him I had drank no whisky since I had been in hospital; he then, caught me by the hair and kicked me several times; the officer brought us before the Captain, who told Harris to go forward or he would put him in irons; *as Harris went forward the deceased was standing looking up aloft, with his hand on the sail, when Harris turned round suddenly, drew a knife and plunged it into his breast, saying at the same time, 'You—! It was you that did it.' He twisted the knife round, drew it out and threw it away, saying, 'Now I am satisfied'*. The deceased cried out, 'I am stabbed,' and died in twenty minutes.

On the strength of the evidence we do not doubt that any jury would have convicted Harris of homicide of the degree of wilful murder. But for some reason a jury has not been allowed to pass upon the facts. Assistant District-Attorney Hutchings, representing the people in the Court of Oyer and Terminer, on Friday accepted a plea of manslaughter in the fourth degree from the accused, and the presiding Justice necessarily imposed the light sentence of two years in the State Prison. This case of Harris, is a marked instance of many that are brought to our notice, where sheer indifference or criminal indolence on the part of the prosecuting attorneys results in criminals escaping the law's penalty for their offences. It is precisely such a course as that pursued by Mr Hutchings, in the case of Harris, which tends to cheapen human life in the estimation of ruffians, and holds out a premium to murderers.

Lesser pleas were not the only method of non-trial dispositions employed by the District Attorney which attracted public criticism. With the apparent consent of General Sessions' judges as required by statute,[5] the public prosecutor utilised the *nolle* power to abruptly terminate the prosecution of entire indictments. Such dispositions could and did occur because of the public prosecutor's capacity to

---

[5] 1829 *Revised Statutes of the State of New York*, Part IV, Chapter II, Title IV, Section 54, p 726.

create 'loopholes' in the indictment which could easily be spotted by defence counsel or which could result directly from the actions of a District Attorney who might demand a trial on a day he knew that witnesses would be out of town,[6] as documented by the reformist Prison Association Report on Common Jails in 1866:[7]

> Under the existing laws the district attorney, and no one else, is charged with the duty of putting the machinery of the law in operation. It is on his power to wink at offences, and notwithstanding the indictments of grand juries, the complaints of sufferers, and the urgencies of communities, if he so desires to shield an offender, he can do so with impunity, and no one else can tell how it was effected. The most acute lawyers with the most upright intentions often make such errors in drawing indictments, that they are quashed on demurrer; if the district attorney *voluntarily* makes such an error, who can tell whether it was intentional or not? Who can successfully fasten the charge of corrupt intent upon him? How easy it is for him to leave some latent point unproved, which, when detected by the lynx-eyed counsel for the defendant, is fatal to conviction! He can state that in his opinion the evidence in a given case is insufficient to procure conviction; there is no one to call the statement in question, and the court will, without hesitation, direct a *nolle prosequi* to be entered in the case ...
>
> The district attorney is also generally a politician. He has been indebted for his election to the exertions of many individuals who are not enrolled among the saints. He, in most cases, looks forward to future political preferment, and hence he naturally desires to remain on good terms with his old friends, which frame of mind is not altogether propitious to the stern and impartial administration of justice.
>
> We have often heard it asserted by men of veracity that candidates for this office have pledged themselves, in advance, to deal lightly with certain classes of offences, especially those against the excise laws; and their conduct after election has been exactly what it would have been, if the charge were true. We have also been assured that active politicians have usually been dealt with far more leniently than those who were friendless and without influence ...

The District Attorney also 'pigeon holed' indictments returned by the Grand Jury which, in consequence, were never calendared in General Sessions. Whilst in his fourteen years as District Attorney, Oakey Hall had prosecuted 12,000 indictments in General Sessions, by the end of his term, one of his chief critics, Superintendent Kennedy of the 'upstate' controlled anti-Tammany Metropolitan

[6] W Miller (1973) p 80.
[7] J S Gould *et al, Twenty-First Annual Report of the Prison Association of New York* (1866), reprinted in New York Assembly Doc No 50, *Report on Common Jails*, pp 149–50 (emphasis in original).

Police, contended that Hall had also pigeon-holed ten thousand indictments. Hall acknowledged that he was not disposed to prosecute liquor law violators, and hence tavern-owners, an important group of Tammany constituents, were secure under his administration with the knowledge that licensing violations, whether or not they resulted in an indictment, would not be prosecuted.[8] In addition, prosecutions for keeping disorderly houses, owners and patrons of which were also among Tammany's constituents, were undertaken at little more than a token level in General Sessions.[9]

Critics argued, as we have seen, that the District Attorney's pigeon-holing practices went far beyond licensing violations and houses of ill-repute. Some contended, for example, that the District Attorney's practices encouraged any criminal who wished to carry arms to do so, in the almost certain knowledge that if they were apprehended they would go scot-free. The *New York Times*, for example, attacked the pigeon-holing of indictments and the utilisation of what Fisher has described as 'on-file' bargaining[10] whereby convictions were obtained but the District Attorney deferred or suspended sentence indefinitely by not prosecuting the case further:[11]

> It is calculated by competent observers that there is now in the pigeon holes of the District-Attorney's office *ten thousand* untried indictments or indictments on which convictions have been obtained and sentence suspended. Up to the point of obtaining the indictment indeed nothing can exceed the ardor with which our indomitable legal functionaries push prosecutions; but the bill once found and the criminal arraigned, a kind of langour steals over the proceedings; the case is never ready for trial; witnesses are not forthcoming, or something happens which causes it to disappear from view and the culprit resumes his usual avocations. In nine charges out of ten in this City, it happens somehow that the accused is a politician; in fact the close connection between politics and shooting, stabbing and drinking, is very remarkable, and we are satisfied, although we believe no statistics are obtainable on the subject, that there are very few active ward politicians whom it would not be in the power of our District Attorney to arraign on some old offence and send to Sing Sing any day he pleased. The District Attorney, however, hoping they will reform, refrains from bringing them and waits year after year for the benign improvement of our Christian civilisation to soften their hearts. They naturally feel grateful for this forbearance, and depraved though they be, appreciating the purity of his motives, testify their gratitude by working for him at elections …

---

[8] C Bowen (1956) p 51.

[9] See T Gilfoyle (1992) pp 125ff. Gilfoyle points out that, during the 1850s, only seven establishments were charged with any type of disorderly conduct even though there were 143 different addresses advertised in the city's leading guidebooks: p 125.

[10] Fisher (2000), pp 936–57.

[11] *New York Times*, Sunday, December 12, 1869.

Aggregate positivist criminology

By mid-century, a growing concern had emerged about the rise of what later became denominated as 'dangerous classes,' whereby reformers sought to impose social control on segments of society believed to have a propensity for crime based on race, class and ethnicity. The official reconstruction of offenders, utilising taxonomies of dangerousness in which the poor were classified and categorised, became the basis for a new criminology in which centralised statistics and social surveys attributed social ills to the underclass in society.

This criminology augered in favour of a new method of case disposition informed by stereotypical views as to the type of individual likely to commit the offence charged in the indictment. Case disposition statistics themselves gave legitimacy not only to a concern over crime as a society-wide problem[12] but more importantly to an emergent state ideology of crime control that came to focus on the poor and foreign born. In this way, poverty became equated with crime and justified social intervention in the lives of the poor and uniform treatment of them.[13]

New York City's mercantile and propertied elite had always been acutely aware of the problems of urban life and, as they perceived it, those who were responsible for crime: the poor, the idle, vagrants, immigrants and, generally, those who dwelt in the most destitute areas such as Five Points, Hell's Kitchen and Corlear's Hook. After all, the propertied classes inhabited a City in which their lives dramatically contrasted with those of the poor and this was evident to them on a daily basis.[14] Yet, with the explosion of immigration at the end of the 1840s and the ending of apprenticeships as artisan craftshops collapsed, the poor became more visible on the streets and the underclass came to be viewed by the middling and upper classes as an endemic source of social problems. This perspective was untempered by the empathetic appreciation of the predicament of the poor which personal involvement in charitable work had aroused in the earlier mercantile and propertied class governing the city. Thus, the victims of social dislocation and poverty became its architects and a new response emerged which synthesised the scientism of positivist criminology with an enduring concern for moralistic reform.

At the forefront of this new ideology were the Chief of Police, George Matsell and evangelical reformers such as Charles Loring Brace, John Griscom and

---

[12] The very production of criminal statistics created a picture of society under threat. As Martin Weiner observes, commenting on the same phenomenon in England, crime now became a central metaphor of disorder and loss of control in all spheres of life: Weiner (1990) p 11.

[13] For an overview of the development of criminological science and state interest, see Garland (1985), especially pp 77ff.

[14] Stansell (1987). See Philip Hone, *The Diary of Philip Hone*, 1825–1851 (ed A Nevins) (1927).

Robert Hartley.[15] As Christine Stansell indicates:[16]

> The common enemy of the tenement classes brought these men together. A precursor to the 'dangerous classes' ... the tenement classes were conceived as a source of both moral and physical contagion—agents, not victims, of social distress, active allies of 'sickness and pauperism' ... With the invention of the tenement classes, however, the distinctions between people and their surroundings began to blur, and humanitarian sentiment faded away. The tenement classes and the tenements themselves appeared equally loathsome.

By 1856 official concerns were given expression in the report of the Secretary of State that commented on the groups of individuals believed to be responsible for crime:[17]

> A large proportion of these are shipped as criminals. Foreign monarchies and despotisms find it cheaper to pay the passage of criminals to this country, than to support and guard them at home, and so empty their jails and prison houses upon our coasts, to swell the records of crime, and shock the public sentiment with deeds of violence. These men enter at once upon a life of crime, and by their course demoralize the crowded communities in which they dwell, oppress our courts with criminal cases, and levy an enormous tax on the industrious and virtuous classes of the State for their support. Out of 6,744 convicted criminals, all but 1,648, or more than three fourths, are foreigners.
>
> The character of the class of human beings we are yearly compelled to absorb in our midst, is clearly shown from this statement. Out of a little more than a million and a half of foreigners in the State, 5,076 *are criminals*. If the same ratio held good with the native born, there would have been this year nearly 14,000 convicted criminals in the State. (original emphasis)

The shift in emphasis toward groups of individuals identifiable by class, race and ethnicity represented a watershed in social thinking about the relationship of the state to those prosecuted for criminal activity. After the middle of the century, the emphasis was with expeditiously confining the dangerous classes, who were identified as outsiders and immigrants, in order to provide a measure of security to the wider society.[18] The emergent centralised state's interest

---

[15] Matsell's alarmist views on the rootless classes was set out in his report of 1849: 'Semi-Annual Report of the Chief of Police', *Documents of the Board of Aldermen* (1850) 17(4): 58. For social reformers see Isaac S Hartley (ed) (1882); Clifford S Griffin (1957, 1960); T Smith (1957); M J Heale (1976).
[16] Stansell (1987) p 200.
[17] *Report of the Secretary of State of New York* (1856) p 5.
[18] D Rothman (1971) p 254.

fuelled and was part of an ideology that altered perceptions of the poor and their relationship to the ills of the City. As Marie-Christine Leps summarised the change:[19]

> First, statistical studies of various kinds, originating from penal and government institutions as well as from private societies, afforded a broad view of criminality as a social phenomenon, correlated to such factors as climate, race, sex, and education. Second, empirical studies undertaken by journalists who ventured into the infamous rookeries to then sell their stories to an interested middle-class audience provided knowledge about criminality as the manifestation of degeneration and disease in regions excluded from the purifying influences of civilisation. Similar narratives were also produced by those employed by the criminal justice system, either as police officers or as ex-criminals turned informants. Finally, medical studies focused on the bodies of those manifesting the symptoms of criminality, and searched for the physical determinants of their condition. These various analytical grids (from general statistics to first-hand exchanges to the examination of skull formation) eventually delineated the discursive space from which a science of 'criminal man' would emerge.

The underpinnings of positivist criminology were first manifested by disposition statistics collected by the New York Secretary of State in 1838 and published annually, beginning in 1839.[20] The impetus for gathering these statistics, already a feature of government concerns in England,[21] underpinned by the very idea of 'crime prevention',[22] was the project of reformers who sought to quantify criminal cases in terms of outcome and to classify convicted criminal defendants in terms of demographic characteristics and offence type. In this way these 'moral statistics' comparing crime data in all jurisdictions within New York state with other countries (principally England and Wales, and France) would serve the interests of the 'science of government and the cause of philanthropy' alike in

---

[19] M-C Leps (1992) p 24.

[20] Whilst it is right to recognise that it was not until the last part of the nineteenth century that modern criminology as an identifiable independent discipline emerged with the writings of Lombroso and Ferri (see David Garland, 1994) it is also true that the emergent state interest in understanding and controlling criminality was already evident in the Secretary of State's Reports. These reports adopted the views of Adolf Quetelet, one of the most important social scientists in Europe and certainly its leading statistician: M J Cullen (1975) pp 78–9. It also reflected the views of A M Guerry, *Essay Sur La Statistique Moral de la France* (1833).

[21] Official statistics on crime, albeit of a limited character, appeared fitfully over the first three decades of the nineteenth century: see, Radzinowicz and Hood (1986) pp 92–112. This had been preceded by the writings of the English stipendiary magistrate, Patrick Colquhoun (1795 and 1800) who sought to provide a quantitative account of criminality and the loss of property thereby caused.

[22] As David Johnson put it: 'Prevention implied prior decisions as to whom society regarded as prone to crime.' Johnson (1979) p 13.

identifying and removing 'the impediments which are in the way of [countries']
social improvement'.[23]

General Sessions, like other courts of record, after 1839, was required to record
and report to the Secretary of State two principal types of aggregate data: one,
whether the prosecutions were successful (measured by the rate of conviction);
and, second, the categories of persons convicted of these offences by gender,
race, ethnicity, educational background, history of inebriation, and country of origin. These data not only became a measure of the success of the District
Attorney's efforts in any locale, but also a basis for wider state law enforcement
strategies.

The first significant building block of an emergent state ideology of dangerousness and crime control appeared in the Secretary of State's Report of 1839.[24] These
data ultimately came to legitimate the District Attorney's adoption of a guilty
plea system which assured a high rate of conviction as well as what state-wide
public officials came to decry as the emergence and identification of a
'dangerous class',[25] based, as it was, on aggregate justice. The essential message of
the report, like that of its predecessor, was optimistic: the increase in population
had outrun the increase in crime, and there was the hope that the constantly increasing temptations to crime presented by a state in the process of rapid internal transition would be counterbalanced by forces which would 'confine the current of
disorderly passions within its accustomed bounds'.[26] Of more enduring significance, however, was the Report's adoption of the observation of Adolphe Quetelet,
one of the most important social scientists in Europe and at that time certainly its
leading statistician,[27] that 'the race or origin of the convicted person is deemed an
essential ingredient in the statistics of crime.' Successive Annual Reports prepared

---

[23] *Report of the Secretary of State of New York* (1839) pp 4–5. The term 'moral statistics' was first
coined by the French lawyer and statistician, A M Guerry in 1833, *Essai sur la statistique morale de
la France*. See also H Westergaard (1932) esp pp 164 ff, P Beirne (1986); P Beirne (1993); P Beirne
(ed) (1994).

[24] The Report drew attention to the alleged deficiencies of the state's statistics in these terms:
It deserves to be considered, that of the four cases of murder committed in this State in the year
1838, two were by negroes, and one by a Canadian, who had been but a short period in the State.
In the able work of Mr Quetelet, on man, referred to in last year's report, the race or origin of
the convicted person is deemed an essential ingredient in the statistics of crime. In a state like
this, having a mixed population, and attracting from its commercial importance large numbers of
persons from other countries, it is of great consequence that our tables should show to what
extent crimes are committed by those who have recently become inhabitants of the State, or who
are temporarily sojurning in it. As was stated in last year's report, our tables are exceedingly
defective in other respects also. They do not show the ages of the convicted persons, their habits,
or the degree of instruction that they have received (p 9).

[25] See Monkonen (1975). As Wilbur Miller (1973) observes: 'Like their London counterparts,
respectable New Yorkers knew who the 'dangerous classes' were. They were foreign-born, largely
Irish, unskilled workers who possessed ominous political influence because of universal male suffrage' (p 142).

[26] *Report of the Secretary of State of New York* (1839) p 12.

[27] M Cullen (1975) pp 78–9.

by the Secretary of State distinguished between those born in the United States and the 'foreign born' as well as those convicted who were 'coloured'

Thus, in 1840 the Secretary of State's Report for New York published the number of cases falling within each type of offence prosecuted to conviction in General Sessions, in the City and County of New York, as follows:[28]

CITY AND COUNTY OF NEW-YORK.

	Murder.	Arson.	Perjury.	Forg'ry & burg.	Manslaughter.	Assault,&c. with int. com. rape.	Bigamy.	Petit larceny, 2d offence.	Forgery.	Burglary.	Grand larceny.	Petit larceny.	Attempt to commit burglary.	Receiving stolen property.	Assault,&c. with intent to kill.	Assault and battery.	Publicly exposing nak. person.	Total.
Number reported,	1	1	2	1	2	1	2	1	4	11	39	29	2	2	2	5	1	106
Males,	1	1	2	1	2	1	2	1	4	11	33	25	2	2	2	5	1	96
Females,											6	4						10
14 years of age,												2						2
15 do											1							1
16 do											1							1
17 do											2		1					3
18 do								1		2	1							4
19 do										1	2	4						7
20 do							1			2	4	1						8
21 do										1	2					1		4
22 do											4					1		5
23 do										3		3				1		7
24 do											3	1						4
25 do											3	2		1				6
26 do									1		3		1	1				6
27 do									1		1							2
28 do									1		3	1				1		6
29 do									1		2	2				1		6
32 do				1							1	2						4
33 do		1										2						3
34 do					1							1						2
35 do											1	2					1	4
36 do			1															1
38 do			1		1						1	1						4
39 do												2						2
40 do						1												1
43 do											1							1
45 do										1	1	1						3
48 do										1								1
49 do															1			1
50 do															1			1
51 do	1																	1
58 do											1							1
Unknown,							1				1	1						3
Married,	1		2		1	1		1	3	3	16	13	1	2		2		48
Single,		1		1	1			1	1	8	21	15	1		2	3	1	56
Unknown,						1					2	1						4
Had children,	1			1	1	1			2	1	11	10		1		2		31
Had no children,		1							1	1	5	3	1	1				13
Unknown,			1							1								2
United States,	1		2	1		1	1	1	2	10	25	17	2	2		2	1	68
England,				2						1	1	2						6
Ireland,									1		9	8				3		21
Scotland,											2							2
France,															1			1
Germany,		1							1									2

[28] A similar classification was given for all other counties in the State.

NEW-YORK.—CONTINUED.

	Murder.	Arson.	Perjury.	Forgery&burgly.	Manslaughter.	Assault,&c. with int. to com. rape.	Bigamy.	Petit larceny, 2d offence.	Forgery.	Burglary.	Grand larceny.	Petit larceny.	Attempt to commit burglary.	Receiving stolen property.	Assault,&c. with intent to kill.	Assault and battery.	Publicly exposing nak. person.	Total.
Sweden,											1		—		1	—		1
Canada,											1							1
Unknown,							1				1	2						4
Can read and write,		1	1	1	1	1			1	3	18	9		1	2	1	1	41
Cannot read or write,			1							4	7	10	1			3		26
Can read but not write,	1									4	6	5	1	1				18
Tolerably good education,							1	1	2		7	3				1		15
Well educated,					1				1		1							3
Unknown,							1				1	1						3
Had religious instruction,	1	1	1		1		1	1	4	8	28	19		2	1	4	1	73
Had no religious instruction,				1		1				2	10	8	2		1	1		26
Unknown,			1		1		1			1	1	2						7
Lost both parents,	1	1		1	1				2	4	15	8		2	1			36
Father and mother living,										3	12	8	1			2		26
Father only living,		1		1		1				1	2	1						7
Mother only living,		1			1			1	1	3	9	8	1			3		28
Unknown,							1		1		1	4			1		1	9
Never before imprisoned,		1	2	1	2	1	1		4	8	31	15	2	2	1	3	1	75
Imp. before in city or co. pris. or fin'd										2	4	11				2		19
Imprisoned before in State prison,	1					1			1	3	1				1			8
Unknown,							1				1	2						4
Occasionally intemperate,									4	4	6				2	1		17
Habitually do	1									2	5							8
Temperate,				1					2	5	4							12
Not intemperate,		1	2	1	1	1	1	1	4	5	26	13	2	2	2	2		64
Unknown,							1				2	1				1		5
Coloured,			1						7	10	4	2	1		2			27
Crime committed when intoxicated,					1						1							2

ILLUSTRATION 13.2: The Secretary of State's Report for New York, 1840.

Our analysis of country of origin data in the Secretary of State's reports shows that in 1855 General Sessions' clerks reported that the foreign-born represented 65 per cent of convicted defendants with the greatest percentage of Irish descent in that year even outstripping those convicted who were born in the United States. This is depicted in Figures 13.1–13.3.

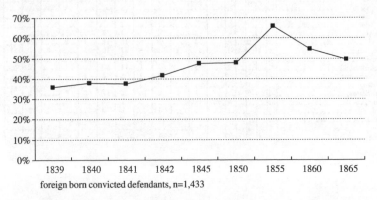

FIGURE 13.1 General Sessions, Secretary of State Reports—Percentage of Convicted Defendants who are Foreign Born, Over the Year, 1839–1865

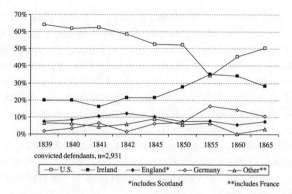

FIGURE 13.2 General Sessions, Secretary of State Reports—Percentage of Convicted Defendants According to Country of Origin Over the Year, 1839–1865

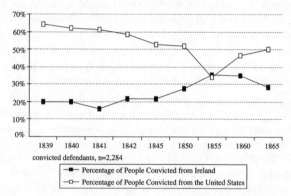

FIGURE 13.3 General Sessions, Secretary of State Reports—Percentage of Convicted Defendants from Ireland and the United States Over the Year, 1839–1865

The very reporting of these data by the clerk of General Sessions and their publication by the Secretary of State is itself indicative of an evolving criminal justice system specifically concerned with classes of individuals and offence types that were considered detrimental to the overall quality of life of the wider society.

Individual amelioration

The sharper edges of the emergent state concern with aggregate justice and the infusion of politics into the court and the office of the District Attorney, were themselves the subject of concern of reformist bodies, principal among which was the Prison Association. Beginning in 1845, the agents of the Prison Association, sought to identify those individuals prosecuted in General Sessions who because of their antecedents—prior good character and personal circumstances—were viewed as more than a statistic and were deemed to be deserving of individual justice either through a lesser plea, special sentence reduction or discharge from any further penalty.[29] In some instances, the background facts themselves identified by the Prison Association agents persuaded the District Attorney to reduce the charge and judges to recommend leniency and mercy in sentencing. For example, a person's antecedents and motivation, upon recommendation of the Prison Association, might serve to reduce a charge of grand larceny to petit larceny or forgery in the second degree to forgery in the fourth degree, in return for the entry of a guilty plea. Thus, in the case of a German woman indicted for grand larceny, the Prison Association agent intervened in an effort to place the commission of the criminal offence in the context of the personal plight of the individual, as detailed in the Association's Annual Report of 1857 and 1858:[30]

> No 1 A German woman was indicted for grand larceny, for stealing a bank book, valued by complainant at $40. When brought into court, the association, by its agent, informed the judge that he had made diligent enquiries of her past history and antecedents. These are the facts:
>
> > About seven months since, she arrived in New York, from Hamburg, having $600 in her possession; she expected to find a portion of her family here, but they had gone west, she know not where.
> >
> > At the boarding house where she stayed, a young man also lived, who formerly resided in a neighboring town, in Germany, near to that she had so recently left. An intimacy grew up between them, and they married; he proposed they should start west, find their friends, and then with her $600, and the money he expected to receive from his parents, they should buy a farm, live happy, and become rich. To this she heartily assented, handing him over all her money. Within a few hours, this unprincipled scoundrel disappeared, and left for parts unknown. She was left with her few clothes only, without the means to pay even one day's board. A situation was suggested by the woman with whom she had stayed since her arrival; she accepted it, but found it to be a house of bad repute. She determined instantly to leave, and return to her fatherland. She saw this bank book, and was tempted to take it, concluding could she draw out the $40, it would defray her expenses home. The theft was discovered, and the plans she had laid were frustrated, and she expressed great contrition. On recommendation of the agent, a plea of petit larceny was accepted by the district attorney, when the judgment was suspended, and she was discharged. A situation was subsequently obtained for her.

[29] In some respects, the agents of the Association followed closely the tradition of the prison inspectors of New York's Auburn penitentiary in their search for and reporting on the root causes of deviant behaviour. For an account of the methodologies of these prison inspectors, see D Rothman (1971) pp 64ff. It is here that Garland's (1994) statements relevant to antecedents became substantiated some fifty years prior to his estimation of the time of its inception, ie the start of the twentieth century.

[30] Annual Report 1857–1858 p 21.

In another case, as detailed in the 1857–1858 Annual Report, the agent secured a reduction in charge from forgery to forgery in the fourth degree due to the failing health of the defendant, the destitution of his family and the sympathy of the complainant.[31]

> No 25 Indicted for forgery; that he had obtained the sum of $17.50 by feloniously personating a shipmate to whom that sum was due as prize money.
>
> This unfortunate creature had been in prison nearly four months, suffering sadly from chronic rheumatism, whilst his wife and two infant children were literally starving. The complainant felt more anxious to alleviate their distress than to have him punished saying, 'He did not do it; Rum did it.'
>
> The District Attorney humanely accepted a plea of forgery in the fourth degree, and then asked the court to suspend the judgment.
>
> They called at our office the day following his discharge, expressing their unfeigned thanks for the interest the Association had shown in their behalf. They both signed a pledge to abandon the use of strong drinks.

Similarly, where a child committed theft on the advice of an adult and had restored the property to the complainant, the Prison Association agent moved the Recorder to suggest that the District Attorney accept a plea to attempted grand larceny on the basis of the extenuating circumstances.[32]

> No 26 A young girl, aged 16, was indicted for grand larceny. She had, under bad advice, committed this crime; the wife or mistress of the complainant being more in fault than this child. The money was all restored.
>
> The agent ascertained that this juvenile offender had lived at home with her parents, except for the last few weeks. Her departure from home had well nigh broken her mother's heart. Her parents are poor, but of sober, industrious, thrifty habits. The father refuses to see his child, she having brought disgrace upon his name and family.
>
> When brought into court to plead, we submitted all the facts to his honor the Recorder. With his characteristic discrimination, he suggested that a plea of an attempt at grand larceny be accepted. The mother then begged that her daughter be now restored to her. We succeeded in convincing her that to obtain her discharge would probably complete her ruin. We urged her to seek for her daughter, and to persuade her child to seek admission to the Magdalen asylum for one year; in which case we would solicit the Recorder to show her mercy. They both thankfully consented to this proposition. We then waited on the court, representing that, for the interest of this young

---

[31] Annual Report, 1857–1858 p 27.
[32] Annual Report of the Prison Association, 1863 p 128.

creature, she should be placed under wholesome restraint, kind treatment, and regular family discipline in one of our benevolent reformatories. At our suggestion, his honor sent her to the Magdalen.

Ironically, this process of individual amelioration reinforced the ideology of discretion which the courtroom actors heretofore relied upon to justify treating cases typically for policy reasons separated from the circumstances which gave rise to the prosecution in the first place. In reinforcing discretion, which itself was the basis of policies of typicality, the disposition of criminal disputes in which the Prison Association intervened became related to worthiness and blame measured not on standards of legal culpability—a principal measure of legal formalism—but instead upon the politics of subjectivity which itself was a function of the values and interests of the various actors. Thus, 'mercy' and 'lenity' could be extended to individuals identified as 'inexperienced in prison life', and 'penitent', and those who manifested a desire to make restitution, as well as for those attracting the sympathy of the complainant[33] and those first offenders and youths where there was no aggravation and where there were 'circumstances of extenuation'.[34] Those, by contrast, who did not possess characteristics which commended themselves to the actors would not be assisted.[35] As the Prison Association Annual Report for 1859 stated:[36]

> And in no solitary case have we lent ourselves directly or indirectly to assist an old offender or professional thief, that he might escape the punishment due to his transgressions. On the contrary, we have invariably contributed our aid in securing to them their deserts. With all such we have no complicity whatever.

CONCLUSION

The confluence of the District Attorney's concern for a high rate of conviction, while addressing the needs of Tammany's constituents, and the focus of positivist

[33] From time to time, the Prison Association Reports make explicit reference to the view of the complainant. Thus, for example, the Annual Report for 1861 describes a plea of guilty to attempt being entered to a charge of grand larceny where the 'complainant felt a strong sympathy for [the defendant]' (Report, p 36) and a plea of attempt to a charge of burglary in the third degree was entered '[w]ith the consent of the complainant ...' (p 37). See also Annual Report 1857–1858 at p 32.

[34] Prison Association Report 1859, p 19.

[35] The Annual Report of 1855 for example described one of its cases in the following terms:

No 36 Was committed to the city prison on charge of stealing a $5 bill from an unfortunate girl living at No—West Broadway; He solemnly protested his innocence and begged the [Prison Association] agent to see the girl at this brothel, to this application a decided negative was given. If men will frequent such places, they must pay the penalty. We would not interfere; he deserved more than he suffered. (Report, p 35)

[36] *Ibid.*

criminology on the so-called dangerous classes, enabled social interests to take precedence over legal interests and inaugurated a system of aggregate justice which replaced legal formalism as the context in which lesser plea convictions came to dominate. The politics of ward-heeling resulted in plea bargaining and the diversion of thousands of indictments without any adjudicatory process whatsoever, as well as the failure to prosecute guilty plea convictions to sentence by keeping these cases on file. Nonetheless, clientilism and legitimation were incorporated within the larger framework of societal concerns over the foreign born as a suspect population which served to underpin a new criminology and the emergent state system of crime control. Concurrently, the values of self-rectitude, industriousness, familial ties, and penitence became important ameliorative measures for reformers who sought to petition the justice system to divert from the aggregate method of normative processing and to exercise lenity and mercy.

Chapter 14
Understanding System Transformation

INTRODUCTION

Our research was conducted against the backdrop of the thesis of leading American commentators, namely that the guilty plea system emerged to displace jury trials when professionals, police and lawyers, entered the fray and set the system right, ie with due regard to notions of cost efficiency and justice. Such a theory that explains change purely in functionalist terms within the courtroom ultimately reduces systemic transformation, as Drew Humphries and David Greenberg observe, to a 'spontaneous and unwitting convulsion', so that it appears disconnected from the 'meanings and goals of the members of … society'.[1] Changes in the political economy of society, thus, would have little or no bearing on the operation of the justice system, the social, economic and political neutrality of which is assumed.

The development of plea bargaining interfaces with contentions of other commentators that the application of law serves as a means of maintaining the social, political and economic status quo at a time when large parts of the population were expected to be governed by 'representatives' in whose election they played no part. We thus analysed the persuasiveness of contentions regarding episodic leniency by a privileged class who sought to secure their own position in society by extracting obedience and deference to authority from an underclass. After all, criminal law practice in the Northeastern part of the United States in the early part of the nineteenth century was essentially adopted from the English common law, sparsely codified with a system of harsh penalties including at the outset a liberal availability of the death penalty and public executions, all of which these commentators point to as reasons for the exercise of episodic leniency by a ruling elite. On its face, therefore, key attributes of the English system between the

---

[1] D Humphries and D Greenberg (1981) p 210.

seventeenth and eighteenth centuries, were present such that one could expect a similar relationship between law, authority and obedience.

In this final chapter, therefore, we reflect upon the general theoretical explanations posited for the emergence of plea bargaining compared with our data findings over the period 1800–1865. We then turn to a consideration of the historical methodology that must serve for any generalisable theory of dramatic system transformation. Thereafter, we propose an alternative theoretical explanation for the displacement of the jury with the abrupt rise of plea bargaining locating it within the prevailing political economy.

FUNCTIONALIST CRITIQUE

The localised system of community justice which resulted in prosecution of indicted offences in New York City in the first half of the nineteenth century was individually-based and responsive to private prosecutors. Despite the fact that the earlier system was not driven by a state ideology of crime (except for the obvious point that it sought to protect people and property), it was in every sense a professional system based on rational legal considerations and in no way resembled a 'rag-tag' amateur-hour which functionalist commentators ascribe to an era in which reliance on jury trials was the dominant method of case disposition in everyday cases. Procedures and practices controlled by lawyers protected indicted defendants against over-reaching. In this way in the first half of the nineteenth century, law was reified, raised above the political economy in an effort to guarantee, through its form and practice, a measure of equality and protection against arbitrary and capricious judgment.

In reflecting on the abrupt transformation after 1850 from jury trials to guilty pleas, we sought to determine whether, as applied to these circumstances, the professionalisation hypothesis would be that lawyers suddenly emerged and came to represent the parties in indicted criminal cases thus causing the system to turn on its head. We sought to test whether lawyers could have suddenly acquired the skills of evidence assessment or to have become organised enough to rapidly gain monopoly of a process from which they were said to have been previously excluded. Of course, given the transformation, there would have to have been time for a massive education process to produce the lawyers simultaneously to staff and complicate criminal disputes. Yet the sudden emergence of professional dominance itself appears to contradict the literature on professional classes.[2] The latter suggests that lawyers' transcendance occurred over time in response to market forces which fostered the notion that an organised body of lawyers was needed to complete the rationalisation of the evidence-gathering process.

---

[2] Feeley (1982) p 350 where he cites Magali Larson (1977). See also A Abbott (1987).

Our data show that lawyers were regularly present from the outset of the century in General Sessions as judges, prosecutors and defence lawyers. Certainly, the lawyers servicing General Sessions in the early decades of the nineteenth century functioned in sociological terms as a professional formation, whatever theory of the professions is applied. Considered from the viewpoint of the 'trait theory',[3] these lawyers possessed core characteristics which evidence professionalism: formal educational, training and entrance requirements; a monopoly over technical expert knowledge and trade skills; relative autonomy over the terms and conditions of practice; a commitment to a service ideal; and a *de facto* professional association.[4] Similarly, if a profession is understood not as an occupation with inherent defining properties but instead as group which has successfully claimed the right to organise and control work, there can be no doubt that the lawyers then operating in General Sessions constituted a profession.[5] Whilst, therefore, the self-legitimating encrustations of 'bar associations' and their 'Canons of Ethics' and large corporate law firms were more than fifty years away, an identifiable professional group of lawyers with a commitment to a service ideal, ethics of practice and the rule of law held sway in the legal marketplace of the court.

Furthermore, litigation practice and the jury process itself were narrowly constrained and rule-bound, limiting the discretion that any of the actors could employ. The lawyers discharged their responsibilities in conformity with the basic adversarial principles of the common law whilst the presiding judges, the mayor and recorder, espousing the traditional values of independence and impartiality,[6] brought learning, authority and dignity to court proceedings and thereby set a standard that the attorneys appearing before them sought to emulate.

Rules of formalism whilst a regular feature of the conduct of everyday trials were animated by notions of justice to assure against miscarriages and to protect society against acquittals secured only on the basis of disembodied technicalities. Ethics of advocacy constrained the prosecution and defence in the conduct of the proceedings. As our data show, lawyers would not continue where to do so would either be futile or undermining of what they saw as a fair and just outcome. This distinguished the lawyers in the first half of the nineteenth century from what some reformers later contended became hyper-adversarial sporting events by the start of the twentieth century.

---

[3] See especially A Carr-Saunders and P Wilson (1933); W Goode (1957); C Greenwood (1957); W Goode (1969); A Abbott (1983); M Waters (1989).

[4] Whilst social theorists of this tradition are not in agreement over the essential or core traits of a profession, those enumerated in the text conform to the common acceptation of professional identity in the literature.

[5] For this approach to professionalisation, see T Johnson (1972); M Larson (1977); R Abel and P Lewis (eds) (1988); K Macdonald (1995).

[6] The judge would recuse himself in cases of personal interest as in *Amos Broad* (1818) Rogers, vol 3, p 7.

While commentators have noticed that the guilty plea system replaced jury trials approximate to the Civil War,[7] trial complexity which allegedly rendered the jury system unworkable, is expressed by the same commentators as evolving over a period stretching from the eighteenth to the twentieth century.[8] Thus, the rapid mid-nineteenth century transformation to guilty pleas, as shown by our data analysis, contradicts the evolution of any process of professionalisation emerging from the role of lawyers in the creation of case complexity. Whilst the case complexity contention might appear compelling if one were to compare nineteenth century with twentieth/twenty-first century racketeering, narcotics and white-collar conspiracy cases, there is no basis for such a comparison over the period in which the transformation to guilty pleas actually occurred during which the frequency of jury trials per day remained relatively constant and the majority of jury verdicts were entered without retiring. Indeed, whilst those litigation practices after mid century continued to involve questions of fact and law, the participants were no longer mostly members of a barrister class whose politics augered in favour of trial proceedings that would be decided in conformity with accepted norms derived from the application of legal formalism. Nor did increases in adversariness substantially reduce the organisational capacity of the court to try everyday cases with the same frequency as it had in the earlier period.

Our data analysis also shows a lack of correlation between growth in caseload and method of case disposition. The Court was able to increase the number of court work days as well as the number of courtroom actors to adapt to the caseload demands while maintaining its trial capacity, and we found no direct correlation between the monthly and annual workload and the day to day reliance on guilty pleas. Thus, workload, case complexity, and professionalism can serve superficially as broad brush stroke claims for the rise of the guilty plea system that are arguable only through reliance on end-point data without any temporal reference for the period in which the transformation occurred and that supplant and are unanchored in any continuous dataset. Under such an approach, end-point data are necessarily relied upon to impute reasons for change to a past that has no time-frame.

Indeed, the guilty plea system extant after mid-century represented a substantial reduction of professional tasks by creating a structural disincentive to engage in formal adversarial advocacy and the use of conventional legal skills. In a culture in which lesser pleas became the currency, litigation of an indictment became an increasingly perilous task, itself reducing the options available to lawyers and auguring for a narrower range of lawyering skills. Indeed, by 1860, lawyers possessing litigation skills could exercise them at trial only by placing their clients at

---

[7] See sources cited in Chapter 1 above.
[8] Feeley and Lester (1994). See also Langbein (1992) p 123.

risk of greatly enhanced sentences or, in the case of the District Attorney, acquittals or convictions of lesser offences by juries which so diverted from the top count as to create a hue and cry in the press and among reformers against the elected office holder. Furthermore, with the transformation from trials to plea bargaining the voice of the accused was effectively silenced. The plea allocutus lacked transparency and detail whilst the pro-forma examination of the accused by the police magistrate became little more than an exercise in the right to remain silent, without being replaced by regular statements being made in response to police interrogation. Thus, in and of itself, plea bargaining created a substantial incentive to utilise the justice system as a wider avenue of social control given the new found facility for aggregate disposition.

CONTEXTUALIST CRITIQUE

Whilst a mercantile class and classically educated barristers comprised the principal actors of the Court of General Sessions in the earlier period, our data show that these actors did not exploit class differences through manipulation of the method of case disposition or sentencing practices. Private prosecutors were given considerable deference as the initiating party and these individuals, as a group, came from every walk of life and circumstance oftentimes bereft of any property themselves or none of substance. What these prosecutors sought to achieve in the criminal dispute which was the subject of indictment, and what the court sought to further, was the personal security and capacity of ordinary people to engage in everyday affairs.

Furthermore, our analysis of the court proceedings, when trials predominated, shows that trial outcomes, when empirically tested, were explicable in terms of evidence and proof as well as settled rules of law rather than ideological presuppositions of guilt dependent upon notions of class, race or ethnicity. Though, in structure, the system was in some ways dominated by a type of elite (given the education, background and character of the judicial and legal actors), given the diverse socio-economic background of the lawyers, prosecutors, judges and jurors, it was not simply responsive to the concerns of a propertied class. Fidelity to the constraints of formalism contrasted with the naked assertion of deference to propertied interests provides a more fulsome and reliable account of the quality of justice and its purposive content in the earlier period. Whilst class differences, as between master and servant, superficially might account for the method of prosecution in cases involving crimes of property, our data show that access to prosecution was not limited to those with substantial means or status; rather the disputes and their judicial treatment showed that the principal purpose of the prosecution was to assure fidelity to legal sufficiency and procedural form. This meant that in the earlier period directed verdicts of acquittal could and did occur regularly and not episodically despite the disparate background of the parties and what might be viewed by some as essential class interest.

Historical method

The foregoing has shown the importance of historical method and the care that needs to be taken before arriving at a theoretical explanation for the dramatic social transformation in criminal justice. We contend that theory should not precede but be dependent upon and arise out of an empirical method of data collection which can be defended not by pointing to disparate end points but because it sheds light on the reasons for continuity and change at all times proximate to the system transformation itself.

A theory of system change that is empirically based is the method by which notions of romanticism and ideology are avoided. Such arguments, as advanced by Roscoe Pound and others, that the 'formative era' of American law[9] occurred in the nineteenth century and replaced a practice extant in the colonial era which was little more than one of 'frontier justice,'[10] are but tenets of a wider ideological view of American legal history uninformed by any systematic empirical analysis and founded in romanticism. The problem with reliance on ideology contrasted with an empirically-based analysis was forcefully asserted by Julius Goebel and Raymond Naughton in their criticism of the frontier justice hypothesis.[11] The data they carefully reviewed demonstrated that law enforcement in New York in the early eighteenth century was:[12]

> not in the hands of ignoramuses but of people who...[were] using English law for the good government of the Province. If one must speak solemnly of a formative era it begins in 1684 [with the advent of the Dongan Charter] when English indictments, English process and English forms of recordation moved in to stay. There were few who at that moment knew the import of these devices or how they were to be used, but on all sides, the magistrates and attorneys set about to cut a substantive law to fit what they had to use as due process.

Hendrik Hartog, in reviewing the frontier justice contentions correctly observes that Goebel and Naughton left the 'theory of a rude, crude indigenous administration of criminal justice in colonial America ... in ruins.'[13] Similarly, it is wrong to assert without a systematic review of the available data, that the first half of the nineteenth century represented either a 'golden age' of jury trials or a feckless

---

[9] See R Pound (1938).
[10] See R Pound (1912); (1930, republished 1972).
[11] Julius Goebel Jnr and T Raymond Naughton (1944; reprint 1970) p xx.
[12] Goebel and Naughton (1944) p xxiv.
[13] Hartog (1981).

'amateur' hour. Certainly neither characterisation can square with our data in everyday cases in which a culture of real people—lawyers, judges and jurors—struggled to ensure integrity in a process that always had wider overtones.

We also emphasise the importance of contextualising research on law practice with the then existing political economy of the local state to avoid drawing generalisable conclusions based upon a micro-analysis of the variables of practice alone. The latter, such as the presence and availability of lawyers, the complexity of cases, and growth in overall workload might not cause any significant alteration to the overall administration of criminal justice and, in particular, to the method of case disposition without a concomitant change in the local socio-political culture. Thus, events occurring in other venues, even those remote from the Northeast such as Alameda County, California and Leon County, Florida, would be best understood with reference to the composition, nature and structure of the jurisdiction in which they were situated rather than confining analysis to courtroom docket entries alone. Such a method of analysis would help explain whether events inside these courtrooms are likely to be generalisable to courtrooms in venues such as New York City, Philadelphia and Boston and vice versa.

Moreover, to consider law courts as hermetically sealed from the wider society and outside of the history and politics of the local state ignores the relationship between law and society. Such a decontextualised legal theory can be defended only through generalities which seek to demonstrate, as Feeley contends, that 'disposition by means of guilty pleas are (sic) phenomena of the late nineteenth and twentieth centuries'[14] coincident with the emergence of organised bar associations or, as Langbein[15] maintains, although 'the potential was ever present to deal with caseload pressure by encouraging guilty pleas, so long as the jury trial remained rapid and lawyer free there was usually no disposition to do it.'

Rethinking system transformation

Our study has certainly shown that, whether one concludes that law and its practice are subordinate to politics or vice versa, the structure of society, including government, and its relationship to law courts must be significant in any searching inquiry.[16] However, there is no reason to conclude that one form of governance is more capable of responding to the needs of the population than another simply because of the passage of time or the growth in population. The culture of local government, the principles upon which it operated and the way it manifests relations between people would seem to be critical variables which one must

---

[14] Feeley (1982) p 343.
[15] Langbein (2003) pp 19–20.
[16] The link between law and politics has been underscored by a number of writers. See eg: J Brewer and J Styles (1980); and E P Thompson (1975).

consider before characterising the demise of trials and the abrupt dominance of guilty pleas, and attempting to derive some contextual understanding of the reasons for its occurrence. The capacity of the courts to respond to increases in workload and the absence of significant changes in offences and offending in indicted cases, the competence of the police and courtroom actors, or indeed the class relations between the private prosecutor or complainant and the defendant, in light of the changing roles of courtroom actors over the critical period 1800–1865, therefore, necessitates a rethinking of explanations which have heretofore been advanced for the transformation from jury trials to plea bargaining.

As this study demonstrates, law and its institutions are not autonomous. While it is generally accepted that law is an important element in creating or sustaining an ideology of consent, thus securing the legitimacy of the state, our data show that over the entire period of our study the form of legitimacy attributed to law practice changed as did the structure and nature of the local state. Machine politics and the emergent state's concern for aggregate justice conjoined to transform the courtroom, catapulting the office of the District Attorney over all other actors, by shifting control over case disposition from private prosecutors to elected state agents, thus giving rise to an institutionalised system of guilty pleas described by some as 'plea bargaining,' but ultimately one manifestation of the triumph of the politicisation of crime and crime control.

In the first half of the nineteenth century, New York City society was based upon principles of mercantilism that shaped both individual interaction and the system of local governance. In formal terms, the post-colonialist state continued to be viewed in terms of its potential to encroach upon the rights of its citizens, thereby justifying a set of protections for the individual embodied in the judicial process. In the context of prosecutions in General Sessions, procedures and practices were adopted which sought to secure the sanctity of the individual against the coercive potential of the state. Courtroom actors ensured that these practices had meaning for the individual: private prosecutors and defendants both were represented by lawyers irrespective of their standing in society or their ability to pay; judges ensured that disputes were resolved with due regard to principles of legality; and juries, while broadly representative of the diverse mercantile class, were screened to remove case-related bias. At trial, collective interests were concerned not only with the protection of property and the person but also with issues of quality of life and other issues that needed to be resolved in order to ensure certainty in commerce.

After mid century, a new political process headlined by Tammany Hall's ward heelers provides explanatory force for the dominance of plea bargaining and the degradation of legal formalism. This inversion of the political landscape gave rise to a new ideology of criminal justice. Law became instrumentalised to secure against crises of social order, while providing aggregate justice to the newly-formed electorate for whom the 'excesses of law' could prove to be the undoing of the elected class of officials and judicial actors. In this new social context, machine politics not imbued by the ideology of the mercantile era, exalted discretion which, in General Sessions, fostered reliance on lesser pleas in everyday cases. Thus, plea bargaining characterised the role of the District Attorney whose unfettered discretion and relationship with a new social order undermined the hierarchical relationship of that office which pre-existed machine politics and which were characteristic of the mercantile era. Law therefore became a resource by which local politics sought to reconcile contradictory notions of social control and clientelism through both the certainty and celerity of the criminal sanction—the rate of conviction—and the reduction in charges, concomitant (in a ward heeler's mentality) with the foregoing of formal prosecution.

By the 1860s, therefore, criminal justice came to be marked by lines of authority organised along different socio-political interests. This underscores the importance of structural factors which might explain events within the courtroom in terms of wider forces in society. In this new environment, prosecutorial policies often became subordinate to the electoral politics of the local state. Process began to be valued primarily in so far as it could guarantee the emergent state's interest in outcome measured in terms of throughput and the rate of conviction. While the mercantile era trial procedures and the concern for individual decision-making remained on the books, the role of the courtroom actors in General Sessions diverted to a form of aggregate justice through plea bargaining.

Discretion in this context came to be based upon ascribed characteristics and general notions of worthiness and blame. Such practice, however, left little room for consideration of the individual circumstances that ordinarily would comprise the proof adduced in the course of a formal trial and at a separate sentencing proceeding. In so categorising disputes and individuals based upon factors unrelated to the actual circumstances themselves, an understanding of outcome in terms of sentence became the capstone of thought in ascertaining the appropriate case disposition. Thus, pleas to lesser offences and attempts (with limited sentence exposure) could come to replace trials despite the fact that reliance on evidence and proof could either sustain a conviction of the top count or result in an acquittal. Nor was the ascendant plea bargaining informed necessarily by a rational legal system which winnowed out dead bang cases because individual issues of legal sufficiency, persuasiveness of evidence and, indeed, culpability were no longer dispositive.

Our data show that episodic leniency, if that term may be properly applied to plea bargaining, occurred after the middle of the century with the emergence of reformist organisations imbued with the desire to ameliorate the harsh edges of the guilty plea system. This occurred against the backdrop of positivist criminology when a new ruling class came into being whose legitimacy was derived from the ballot box rather than the paternalism and political sensibility of a class based elite.

The movement to a guilty plea system is thus indicative of significant structural changes in the attitude and approach towards and method of defining crime and attributing culpability. The system of social control that plea bargaining came to replace was, at its creation, a bottom-up system dependent upon the initiating acts and capacity of the private prosecutor who sought to persuade the judicial process to engage in formal prosecution. Contingencies were largely limited to persuasiveness of the facts offered as proof and their admissibility given formal evidentiary and procedural challenges. Should the evidence and proof be sufficient, convictions of the offence would follow after which a punishment regime would be set in train. In this system, therefore, facts relevant to the ambit of sentencing—the degree of punishment—would become more expansive from the initiating facts which triggered the prosecution. Thus, the presence or absence of antecedents—previous convictions, a person's upbringing and background (separate from character evidence at trial)—as well as mitigating and aggravating circumstances of the offence, could all be brought to bear on the sentencing decision. It was at this stage, therefore, that issues of worthiness and blame and the generalised concern for the seriousness of the offence and levels of dangerousness to society would be factored into the equation.

The effect of replacing a system of individualised justice with one of aggregate justice based upon plea bargaining was to reduce reliance on the rule of law and concomitant legal rationality based on evidence and proof. The new system sought certainty in outcome by substituting the presumption of guilt for any factual or legal dispute and discriminated among cases for policy reasons unrelated to legal sufficiency, while legitimacy was accorded the state through reporting the rates of conviction and detailing of personal characteristics of convicted defendants, along socio-demographic lines. This, in turn, gave prominence to a criminology that tended to define dangerousness through class, race and ethnicity and other characteristics unrelated to the facts and circumstances which gave rise to the culpability of any individual offender.

Underpinning the local state's increased involvement in criminal justice was a set of ideologies and interests separate from those which in the earlier period had sought to improve the quality of life of individuals and to ensure a stable environment in which commerce could thrive. With the advent of the Secretary of State's reports in 1838, official depictions of segments of the defendant population occurred often focusing on the conduct and behaviour of the 'foreign-born'. In this way, a new state ideology emerged which, in turn, came to legitimate the politicised role of courtroom actors. Thus, whilst lesser pleas came to predominate in a culture of compromise, the ideological objects of societal vilification were 'perverse' acquittals, compromise verdicts, 'ignoble' juries, and the 'foreign born'. Indeed, the continued reliance on formalism itself was viewed as both inefficient and ultimately anti-democratic. In this context, plea bargaining is but one example, albeit the most widely discussed, of a statist movement towards aggregate justice legitimated as it is by rates of conviction, cost-effectiveness and stereotypical thinking about crime and offending.

CONCLUSION

A clear understanding of the origins of the guilty plea system must occur before anyone can look critically at the modern practices of plea bargaining and decide whether such practices are worth further refinement and adoption in venues which have not as yet accepted the guilty plea system as a standard method of case disposition. Such an approach would also permit more objective considera-tion of the trial process which preceded reliance on guilty pleas in venues such as New York City and which may indeed have greater application in everyday cases in many venues—from the perspective of legal and organisational rationality—than the system that came to replace it. It is one thing to refine and improve upon plea bargaining when its origins are based upon rational legal thought and day to day operational pressures; it is another matter entirely to attempt to redefine in rational legal terms this method of disposition when its origins are obfuscated and its methods gratuitous and dubious in nature.

Our analysis of the transformation in the method of case disposition in General Sessions thus views courtroom actors as relational entities whose ideological pur-pose changed over time and shows why explanations for systemic transformation must be located in structural changes within the wider political economy of the state. In retrospect, systemic reliance on guilty pleas in the second half of the cen-tury appears purposive, having occurred contemporaneously with the judicialisa-tion of magistrates, the reorganisation of police, the politicisation of courtroom actors and the marginalisation of juries. Thus, the 'vanishing jury' and the rise of plea bargaining, together with a new construction of the nature of crime and offending, are better understood in terms of an emerging state interest, with the ability to rationalise and achieve its own social and political agenda through new legal forms and practices and to establish legitimacy through the discourse of positivist criminology.

Bibliography

Abbott, A 'Professional ethics', *American Journal of Sociology* 88 (1983) 855.

—— *The System of Professions: an essay on the division of expert labor.* (Chicago, University of Chicago Press, 1988).

Abel, R *American Lawyers.* (New York, Oxford University Press, 1989).

—— and Lewis, P (eds.) *Lawyers in Society.* (3 vols) (Berkeley, University of California Press, 1988).

Abramson, J *We the Jury: The Jury System and the Ideal of Democracy* (New York, Basic Books, 1994).

Albion, R G *The Rise of New York Port (1815–1860).* (New York, Scribner, 1939).

Alschuler, A 'Plea Bargaining and its History.' *Law & Society Review* 13 (1979) 211.

—— 'The Defense Attorney's Role in Plea Bargaining.' *Yale Law Journal* 84 (1975) 1179.

—— 'The Prosecutor's Role in Plea Bargaining.' *University of Chicago Law Review* 36 (1968) 50.

—— 'The Trial Judge's Role in Plea Bargaining.' *Colorado Law Review* 76 (1976) 1059.

Anbinder, T *Five Points: The 19th Century New York Neighborhood that Invented Tap Dance, Stole Elections and Became the World's Most Notorious Slum,* (New York, Free Press, 2002).

Asbury, H *The Gangs of New York: An Informal History of the Underworld* (New York, Knopf, 1928).

Ascoli, D *The Queen's Peace: The Origins and development of the Metropolitan Police 1829–1979* (London, H Hamilton, 1979).

Auerbach, J *Unequal Justice* (New York, Oxford University Press, 1976).

Bacon, D *The New York Judicial Repository* (New York, Gould and Banks, 1818–1819).

Barak, G *In Defense of Whom?* (Berkeley, Anderson, 1980).

Barbour, O *A Treatise on Criminal Law of the State of New York* (New York, Gould, Banks, 1852).

Barnes, H 'The Origins of Prison Reform in New York State'. *Quarterly Journal of the New York State Historical Association* 2 (1921) 89.

—— *The Repression of Crime: studies in historical penology* (New York, G H Doran, 1926).

Barnes, Thurlow W *Memoir of Thurlow Weed* (Boston, Houghton Mifflin and company, 1884).

Battestin, M C *Henry Fielding: A Life* (London, Routledge, 1989).

Beaney, W *The Right to Counsel in American Courts* (Ann Arbor, University of Michigan Press, 1955).

Beattie, J M 'Crime and Courts in Surrey, 1736–1753' in J S Cockburn (ed.) *Crime in England, 1550–1800* (London, Methuen, 1977).

—— *Crime and Courts in England, 1660–1800* (Oxford, Clarendon Press, 1986).

—— *Policing and Punishment in London, 1660–1750* (Oxford, Oxford University Press, 2001).

Beirne, P *Inventing Criminology: Essays on the rise of 'Homo criminalis'* (Albany, State University of New York Press, 1993).

—— 'A note on Quetelet and the Development of Criminological statistics', *Journal of Criminal Justice* 14 (1986) 459.

—— (ed) *The Origins and Growth of Criminology: Essay on Intellectual History, 1760–1945* (England, Dartmouth, 1994).

Bentham, J 'Theorie des Peines et des Recompense', 43 *Edinburgh Review*.

Bloomfield, M *American Lawyers in a Changing Society, 1776–1876* (Cambridge, Mass, Harvard University Press, 1976).

Blumberg, A *Criminal Justice* (Chicago, Quadrangle Books, 1967).

Bodenhamer, David J *Fair Trial: The Rights of the Accused in American History* (New York, Oxford University Press, 1992).

Bowen, C *The Elegant Oakey* (New York, Oxford University Press, 1956).

Brewer, J and J Sykes (1980) *An Ungovernable People: The English and Their Law in the Seventeenth and Eighteenth Centuries* (New Brunswick, NJ, Rutgers University Press).

Bridges, A *A City in the Republic—Antebellum New York and the Origins of Machine Politics* (Cambridge, Cambridge Press, 1984).

Brooks, J W *History of the Court of Common Pleas of the City and County of New York with Full Reports of All Proceedings* (New York, Subscription, 1896).

Brown, R M (Ed.) *American Violence* (Englewood Cliffs, Hemel Hempstead, Prentice-Hall, 1970).

Buntline, N *The Mystery and Myseries of New York* (New York, W F Burgess, 1848).

Callahan, Raymond E *Education and the Cult of Efficiency: A Study of the Social Forces that Have Shaped the Administration of the Public Schools* (Chicago, University of Chicago Press, 1962).

Callow, A B (1966) *The Tweed Ring* (New York, Oxford University Press).

Carr-Saunders, A and Wilson, P *The Professions* (Oxford, Clarendon Press, 1933).

Casper, J *American Criminal Justice: The Defendant's Perspective* (Englewood Cliffs, Prentice-Hall, 1972).

Chadwick, Kathryn and Scraton, Phil 'The theoretical and Political Priorities of Critical Criminology' in (eds) K Stenson and D Cowell, *The Politics of Crime Control* (London, Sage Publications, 1991).

Chester, A *Legal and Judicial History of New York* (New York, National American Society, 1911).

—— *Courts and Lawyers of New York, A History, 1609–1925* (New York, Historical Society, 1925).

Christian, C *A Brief Treatise on the Police of the City of New York* (New York, Southwick & Pelsue, 1812).

Colby, John H *A Practical Treatise Upon the Criminal Law and Practice* (Albany, W C Little, 1868).

Cole, George F 'The Decision to Prosecute.' *Law & Society Review* 4 (1970) 331.

Cole, S A *Suspect Identities: A History of Fingerprinting and Criminal Identification* (Cambridge, Mass, Harvard University Press, 2001).

Cook, C *The American Codification Movement: A Study of Antebellum Legal Reform* (Westport, Conn, Greenwood Press, 1981).

Cooley R (1958) 'Predecessors of the Federal Attorney General: The Attorney General in England and the American Colonies' *American Journal of Legal History* 2 (1958) 304.

Colquhoun, P *A Treatise on the Police of the Metropolis* (London, 1795).

—— *A Treatise on the Commerce and Police of the River Thames* (London, 1800).

Conley Carolyn, A *The Unwritten Law: Criminal Justice in Victorian Kent* (New York, Oxford University Press, 1991).

Costello, A *Our Police Protectors: History of the New York Police from the Earliest Period to the Present Time* (New York, Chas F Roper & Co, 1885).

Crapsey, E *The Netherside of New York* (Montclair, 1872, Reprint 1969).

Cray, R *Paupers and Poor Relief in New York City and its Rural Environs, 1700–1830* (Philadelphia, Temple University Press, 1988).

Critchley, T A *A History of Police in England and Wales* (London, Constable, 1978).

Cullen, M J *The Statistical Movement in Early Victorian Britain: The Foundations of Empirical Social Research* (Hassocks, Harvester Press, 1975).

Curtis C P 'The Legal Aid Society, New York City—A Review' *The Record* 9 (1924) 224.

Curry L P *The Corporate City: The American City as a Political Entity, 1800–1850* (Westport, Conn, Greenwood Press, 1997).

Daly C P *Historical Sketch of the Judicial Tribunals of New York, From 1623 to 1846* (New York, J W Amerman, 1855).

Donnan, George R *Annotated Code of Criminal Procedure and Penal Law of the State of New York* (Albany, H B Parsons, 1887).

Downie, L *Justice Denied* (New York, Praeger, 1971).

Dunn, Thomas L *Democracy and Punishment: Disciplinary Origins of the United States* (Madison, University of Wisconsin Press, 1987).

Durey, M 'Thomas Paine's Apostles: Radical Emigres and the Triumph of Jeffersonian Republicanism' *William and Mary Quarterly* 44 (1987).

Eisenstein, J and Jacob, H *Felony Justice*, (Boston, Little, Brown, 1977).

Ekirch, A E Jr 'Thomas Eddy and the Beginnings of Prison Reform in New York' *New York History* 24 (1943) 376.

Emsley, C *The English Police: A Political and Social History* (London, Pearson) (1991).

Ernst, R *Immigrant Life in New York City: 1825–1863* (New York, Octagon Books, 1949).

Faulds, H 'On the Skin Furrows of the Hand' *Nature* 22 (1880) 605.

Feeley, M 'Legal Complexity and the Transformation of the Criminal Process: The Origins of Plea Bargaining', *Israeli Law Review* 31(1–3) (1997) 183.

—— 'Plea Bargaining and The Structure of The Criminal Process.' *Journal of Justice Systems* 73 (1982) 338.

—— 'The Concept of Laws In Social Science: A Critique and Notes On An Expanded View', *Law and Society Review* 10(4) (1976) 497.

—— *The Process Is The Punishment: handling cases in a lower criminal court* (New York, Russell Sage Foundation, 1979).

—— 'Two Models of the Criminal Justice System: An Organizational Perspective.' *Law and Society Review* 7 (1973) 407.

Feeley, M and Lester, C 'Legal Complexity and the Transformation of the Criminal Process' *Subjektivierung des Justiziellen Beweisverfahrens* 334. (André Gouron *et al*, eds,) (Frankfurt, Vittorio Klostermann, 1994).

Feldberg, M *The Turbulent Era: Riot and Disorder in Jacksonian America* (New York, Oxford University Press, 1980).

Ferdinand, T *Boston's Lower Criminal Courts 1814–1850* (Newark, University of Delaware Press; London, Cranbury, NJ, Associated University Presses, 1992).

Field, H *The Life of David Dudley Field* (New York, Charles Scribner's Sons, 1898).

Fisher, G 'Plea Bargaining's Triumph', *Yale Law Journal* 109 (2000) 857.

—— *Plea Bargaining's Triumph: A History of Plea Bargaining in America* (Stanford, Stanford University Press, 2003).

Fishman, E *New York City's Criminal Justice System 1895–1932* (Ann Arbor, University Microfilm, 1980).

Fogelson, R *Big City Police* (Cambridge, Mass, Harvard University Press, 1977).

Foltz, C 'Public Defenders' *American Law Review* 31 (1897) 393.

Fosdick, R *American Police Systems* (New York, The Century Co. 1920).

Freestone, D and Richardson J (1980) 'The Making of English Criminal Law: Sir John Jervis and his Acts' [1980] *Criminal Law Review* 5.

Friedman, L and Percival R, *The Roots of Justice: Crime and Punishment in Alameda County, California, 1870–1910* (Chapel Hill, University of North Carolina Press, 1981).

Friedman, L *A History of American Law* (New York, Simon and Schuster, 1973).

—— 'Plea Bargaining in Historical Perspective', *Law & Society Review* 13 (1979) 247.

—— 'Courts Over Time: A Survey of Theories and Research' in (eds. K O Boyum and L Mather) *Empirical Theories About Courts* 38 (1983).

—— *Crime and Punishment in American History* (New York, Basic Books, 1993).

Garland, D 'The development of British Criminology' in (eds) M Maguire, R Morgan and R Reiner *The Oxford Handbook of Criminology*, (Oxford, Clarendon Press; New York, Oxford University Press, 1994).

—— *Punishment and Welfare: A History of Penal Strategies* (Aldershot, Gower, 1985).

Gatrell, V *The Hanging Tree* (Oxford, New York, Oxford University Press, 1994).

Gawalt, G W (ed) *The New High Priests: Lawyers in Post-Civil War America* (Westport, Conn, Greenwood Press Westport, 1984).

Gerrard, J W *London and New York, Their Crime and Police*, (New York, W C Bryant, 1853).

Gilfoyle, T *City of Eros, New York City, Prostitution and the Commercialization of Sex, 1790–1920* (New York, W W Norton, 1992).

Gilje, Paul A *The Road to Mobocracy: Popular Disorder in New York City 1763–1834* (Chapel Hill, NC, University of North Carolina Press, 1987a).

Gilje, P *Mobocracy: Popular Disturbances in Post-Revolutionary New York, 1783–1829* (Chapel Hill, London, University of North Carolina Press, 1987b).

Goebel, J and Naughton, R *Law Enforcement in Colonial New York* (New York, Commonwealth Fund, 1944, reprinted, Patterson Smith, 1972).

Goode, W 'Community Within a Community: The Professions', *American Sociological Review* 20 (1957) 194.

—— 'The Theoretical Limits of Professionalization', in A Etzioni (ed) *The Semi-Professions and their Organization: Teachers, Nurses, Social Workers* (New York, Free Press, 1969).

Gould, J S *et al*, *Report on Common Jails and the Administration of Criminal Justice* (1866) reprinted in N Y Assembly Doc No 50.

Graham, H and Gurr, T *The History of Violence in America* (New York, F A Praeger, 1969).

Greenberg, D *Crime and Law Enforcement in the Colony of New York, 1691–1776* (Ithaca, London, Cornell University Press, 1976).

Greenwood, C 'Attributes of a profession', *Social Work* 2 (1957) 45.

Griffin, C 'Religious Benevolence as Social Control, 1815–1860' *The Mississippi Valley Historical Review*, 44(3) (1957).

—— *Their Brothers' Keepers: Moral Stewardship in the United States, 1800–1865* (New Brunswick, New Jersey, Rutgers University Press, 1960).

Griffith, Ernest S *A History of American City Government: The Conspicuous Failure, 1870–1900* (New York, Praeger, 1974).

Guerry, A M *Essay Sur la Statistique Moral de la France* (Paris, Didot, 1833).

Haller, Mark H 'Plea Bargaining: The Nineteenth Century Context.' *Law & Society Review* 13 (1979) 273.

Handlin, O *Race and Nationality in American Life* (1941) [Race and nationality in American life. [1st ed.], Publisher, Boston, Little, Brown, 1957 / Race and nationality in American life / by Oscar Handlin, Publisher Garden City, New York, Doubleday, 1957].

Harring, Sidney L *Policing a Class Society: The Experience of American Cities 1865–1915* (New Brunswick, New Jersey, Rutgers University Press, 1983).

Hartley, Issac S (ed) *Memorial of Robert Milham Hartley* (New York, Utica, 1882).

Hartog, H *Public Property and Private Power: The Corporation of the City of New York in American Law, 1730–1870* (Chapel Hill, University of North Carolina Press, 1983).

Harts, L *Economic Policy and Democratic Thought in Philadelphia, 1776–1860* (Cambridge, Mass, Harvard University Press, 1948).

Hay, D 'Property, Authority, and the Criminal Law', in D Hay, *et al Albion's Fatal Tree: Crime and Society in Eighteenth-Century England* (New York, Pantheon Books, 1975).

Headley, J *The Great Riots of New York, 1712–1873* (New York, E B Treat 1873).

Heale, M 'From City Fathers to Social Critics: Humanitarianism and Government in New York, 1790–1860', *The Journal of American History*, 63(1) (1976) 21.

—— 'Humanitarianism in the Early Republic: The Moral Reformers of New York, 1776–1825', *Journal of American Studies*, 2 (October) (1968)161.

Heumann, M *Plea Bargaining: The Experience of Prosecutors, Judges and Defense Attorneys* (Chicago, University of Chicago Press, 1978).

—— 'A note on plea bargaining and case pressure' 9 *Law and Society Review* 515.

Hill, M W *Their Sisters' Keepers: Prostitution in New York City, 1830–1870*, (Berkeley, University of California Press, 1993).

Hindus, M S *Prison and Plantation: Crime, Justice, and Authority in Massachusetts and South Carolina, 1767–1878* (Chapel Hill, University of North Carolina Press, 1980).

—— 'Crime and History': Book Review of The Root of Justice, 34 *Stanford Law Review* (1982) 923.

Hirsch, L H 'The Negro and New York', *Journal of Negro History* 16 (1931) 382.

Homberger, E *Scenes From the Life of a City: Corruption and Conscience in Old New York* (New Haven, London, Yale University Press, 1994).

Humphries, D and Greenberg, D F 'The Dialectics of Crime Control' in *Crime and Capitalism* (1981).

Hunt, C H *Life of Edward Livingston* (New York, D Appleton & Co 1870).

Ireland, R M 'The Nineteenth Century Criminal Jury: Kentucky in the Context of the American Experience', *Kentucky Review* 4 (1962) 55.

—— 'Privately Funded Prosecution of Crime in the Nineteenth-Century United States', *American Journal of Legal History* 39 (1995) 43.

—— 'Publically Funded Prosecution of Crime in the Nineteenth-Century United States', *American Journal of Legal History* 39 (1995) 43.

Jackson, F *The United States 1830–1850* (New York, Henry Holt & Co, 1935).

Jacoby, Joan E *The American Prosecutor: A Search for Identity* (Lexington, Mass, Lexington Books, 1980).

Johnson, David R *Policing the Urban Underworld, The Impact of Crime on the Development of the American Police, 1800–1887* (Philadelphia, Temple University Press, 1979).

Johnstone, T *Professions and Power* (London, Macmillan, 1972).

Jones, M A *American Immigration* (Chicago and London, University of Chicago Press, 1960).

Katz, J *Poor People's Lawyers In Transition* (New Brunswick, Rutgers University Press, 1982).

Kaye, B *Science and the Detective* (Weinheim, VCH, 1995).

Ketcham, G *Municipal Police Reform: A Comparative Study of Law Enforcement in Cincinnati, Chicago, New Orleans, New York and St. Louis 1844–1877* (Ms. PhD Dissertation, 1967).

King, P 'Decision Makers and Decision Making in English Criminal Law', *Historical Journal* 27 (1984) 25.

—— 'Prosecution associations and their impact in eighteenth-century Essex' in D Hay and F Snyder (eds) *Policing and Prosecution in Britain, 1750–1850.* (Oxford, Clarendon, 1989).

—— *Crime, Justice, and Discretion in England, 1740–1820* (Oxford, New York, Oxford University Press, 2000).

Knapp, S L *The Life of Thomas Eddy* (New York, Conner & Cooke, 1834).

Knight, B 'Murder in the Laboratory', *New Scientist 23 December 1986.*

Kress, J M 'Progress and Prosecution', *The Annals of the American Academy of Political and Social Sciences* 423 (1976) 100–116.

Kross, M and Grossman, M, 'Magistrates' Courts of the City of New York: History and Organization', *7 Brooklyn Law Review 133 (1937).*

Kuntz, W F *Criminal Sentencing in Three Nineteenth Century Cities: Social History of Punishment in New York, Boston, and Philadelphia 1830–1880.* (New York, Garland Publishing, 1988).

Lamb, M *History of the City of New York,* 3 vols (New York, A S Barnes and company, 1877–1896).

Landsman, S (1990) 'The rise of the contentious spirit. Adversary procedure in eighteenth century England' *Cornell Law Review* 75:497.

Lane, R *Policing the City: Boston 1822–1855.* (Cambridge, MA, Harvard University Press, 1967).

—— 'Crime and Criminal Statistics in Nineteenth Century Massachusetts', *Journal of Social History* 2 (1968) 156–63.

—— 'Crime and Industrial Revolution: British and American Views', *Journal of Social History* 7 (1974) 287–303.

Langbein, J H (1973) 'The Origins of Public Prosecution and Common Law', *American Journal of Legal History* 17: 313.

—— (1978) 'The Criminal Trial Before Lawyers', *The University of Chicago Law Review.* 45: 263.

—— (1978) 'Torture and Plea Bargaining', *The University of Chicago Law Review.* 46:3.

—— (1979) 'Understanding The Short History of Plea Bargaining', *Law & Society Review* 13: 261.

—— (1983) 'Albion's Fatal Flaws', *Past and Present*, 98: 96.

—— (1992) 'On the Myth of Written Constitutions: The Disappearance of the Criminal Jury Trial', *Harvard Journal of Public Law and Policy* 15: 119.

—— (1994) 'The historical origins of the privilege against self incrimination at common law' *Michigan Law Review* 92: 1047.

—— *The Origins of Adversary Criminal Trial* (Oxford, Oxford University Press, 2003).

Larson, M *The Rise of Professionalism: A Sociological Analysis* (Berkeley, University of California Press, 1977).

Lempert, R 'More Tales of Two Courts: Exploring Changes in the 'Dispute Settlement' Function of Trial Courts' 13 *Law and Society Review* 91 (1978).

—— 'Docket Data and Local Knowledge: Studying the Court and Society Link Over Time' (1990) 24 *Law and Society Review* 321–32.

Leps, M-C *Apprehending the Criminal: The Production of Deviance in Nineteenth Century Discourse* (Durhman, Duke University Press, 1992).

Levett, A *Centralization of City Police in the Nineteenth Century* (Ann Arbor, Mich, University Microfilms International, 1975).

Lewis, O F *The Development of American Prisons and Prison Customs, 1776–1845* (New York, Prison Association of New York, 1922).

Lewis, W David, *From Newgate to Dannemora: The Rise of Penitentiary in New York, 1796–1848* (Ithaca, Cornell University Press, 1965).

Linebaugh, P *The London Hanged: Crime and Civil Society in the Eighteenth Century* (Harmondsworth, Penguin, 1991).

Little, Craig B 'The Criminal Courts in 'Young America': Bucks County, Pennsylvania, 1820–1860' with some comparisons to Massachusetts and South Carolina' (1991) *Social Science History* 15(4):457–78.

Lincoln, C *The Constitutional History of New York* (5 vols) (Rochester, Lawyers' Cooperative Publishing Co 1906).

Livingston, E 'Introductory Report to the Code of Criminal Procedure' in *The Complete Works of Edward Livingston on Criminal Jurisprudence* (New York, National prison association of the United States of America 1873).

Macdonald, K *The Sociology of the Professions* (London, Sage Publications, 1995).

Martin, E *The Secrets of the Great City: A Work Descriptive of the Virtues and Vices, the Mysteries, Miseries and Crimes of New York City*, (Philadelphia, Chicago, Jones brothers & Co, 1868).

Martin, G *Causes and Conflict: The Centennial History of the Association of the Bar of the City of New York, 1870–1970* (Boston, Houghton, Mifflin Co 1970).

Masur, L (1987) 'The Revision of the Criminal Law in Post-Revolutionary America' *Criminal Justice History* 8:21.

Mather, L 'Comments on the History of Plea Bargaining', *Law & Society Review* 13 (1979) 282.

Mather, L *Plea Bargaining or Trial* (Lexington, MA, Lexington, 1979).

Matsell, G W *Vocabulum; or the Rogue's Lexicon* (New York, G W Matsell & Co, 1859).

McAdam, D Bischoff, H *et al* (eds) *History of the Bench and Bar of the City of New York* (2 vols) (New York, New York History Company, 1897–99).

McConville, M and Mirsky, C L 'Criminal Defense of The Poor In New York City', *New York University Review of Law & Social Change*, 15 (1986–1987) 582.

—— 'Criminal Defense of the Poor in New York City', *Occasional Papers from The Center for Research in Crime and Justice*, New York University School of Law (Ed, G Hughes) (1988).

—— 'Guilty Plea Courts: A Social Disciplinary Model of Criminal Justice', *Social Problems* 42 (1995) 216.

—— 'The Rise of Guilty Pleas', *Journal of Law and Society* 22(4) (1995) 443.

—— 'Understanding Defense of the Poor in State Courts: The Sociolegal Context of Non-Adversarial Advocacy', A Sarat and S Silby (eds) *Studies in Law, Politics and Society* 10 (1990).

—— 'The State, the Legal Profession, and the Defence of the Poor', *Journal of Law and Society* 15 (1988).

McDonald, W F 'The Prosecutor's Domain' pp 15–51 in *The Prosecutor* (ed) W F McDonald (Beverly Hills, Sage, 1979).

—— 'In Defense of Inequality: The Legal Profession and Criminal Defense.' pp 13–38 in *The Defense Counsel*, (ed) W F McDonald (Beverly Hills, Sage, 1983).

—— 'Towards A BiCentennial Revolution in Criminal Justice: The Return of the Victim', *American Criminal Law Review* 13 (1976) 649.

McGowen, R 'The body and punishment in Eighteenth Century England', *Journal of Modern History* 59 (1987) 651.

Millender, M *The Transformation of the American Criminal Trial, 1790–1875* (1996) UMI Dissertation Services.

Miller, W R *Cops and Bobbies: Police Authority in New York and London 1830–1870* (1973) (Chicago, University of Chicago Press, 1977).

Moglen, E (1994) 'Taking the Fifth: Reconsidering the origins of the privilege against self incrimination' *Michigan Law Review* 92: 1086.

—— (1997) 'The privilege in British North America: The Colonial Period to the Fifth Amendment' pp 109–144 in R H Helmholz *et al* (eds) *The Privilege Against Self Incrimination* (Chicago, University of Chicago Press, 1997).

Mohl, R *Poverty in New York 1783–1825* (New York, Oxford University Press, 1971).

Moley, R 'The Vanishing Jury', *Southern California Law Review* 2 (1928) 97.

Monkkonnen, E H *The Dangerous Class: Crime and Poverty in Columbus, Ohio 1860–1885* (Cambridge, Harvard University Press, 1975).

—— *Police in Urban America, 1860–1920* (New York, Cambridge University Press, 1981).

—— 'The Organized Response to Crime in Nineteenth and Twentieth Century America', *Journal of Interdisciplinary History* 14 (1983) 113.

Munger, F 'Trial Courts and Social Change: The Evolution of a Field of Study', *Law and Society Review* 24 (1990) 17.

Mushkat, J *Tammany, The Evolution of a Political Machine, 1789–1865* (Syracuse, Syracuse University Press, 1971).

Napley, D *The Technique of Persuasion* (London, Sweet and Maxwell, 1975).

Nelson, W E *Americanization of the Common Law: The Impact of Legal change on Massachusetts Society, 1760–1830* (Cambridge, MA, Harvard University Press, 1975).

New York City, *Documents of the Board of Aldermen* 8 (1842) 57 (New York, Bryant & Boggs).

New York Law Institute, *Catalogue of the Books in the Library* (New York, Martin's steam printing house, 1874).

New York State, *Annual Reports of the Secretary of State on Statistics of Crime 1836–1819* (Albany).

—— *Revised Statutes 1829–1865*.

Nivens, A *The Diary of Philip Hone 1821–1851* (New York, Dodd, Mead & Company, 1927).

Norcross, F 'The Crime Problem' *Yale Law Journal* 20 (1911) 599.

North American Review, 'The Judiciary of New York City' *North American Review* vol.ccxvi (1867, July) 148–176.

Oaks, D and Lehman, W 1968. *A Criminal Justice System and The Indigent* (Chicago, University of Chicago Press, 1968).

Ottley, R and Weatherby, W J *The Negro in New York* (New York, Oceana Publications, Inc, 1967).

Packer, H *The Limits of the Criminal Sanction* (Stanford, Stanford University Press, 1968).

Padgett, J F 'The Emergent Organization of Plea Bargaining', *American Journal of Sociology* 90 (1985) 753–799.

—— 'Plea Bargaining and Prohibition in the Federal Courts: 1908–1934.' *Law & Society Review* 24 (1990) 413.

Paley, R 'An imperfect and wretched system? Policing London before Peel' *Criminal Justice History* 10:102.

Parker, A J (1855–1877) *Reports of Decisions in Criminal Cases*, (vols 1–6) (Albany, William Gould and Son, 1860–1868).

Parmalee, M 'A New System of Criminal Procedure', *Journal of Criminal Law & Criminology* 4 (1913–1914) 359.

Patterson, E *Catalogue of the Books in the Library of the New York Law Institute* (New York, Martin's Steam Printing House, 1874).

Pessen, E *Riches, Class, and Power Before the Civil War* (Lexington, Mass, D C Heath, 1973).

Phelps, I N *Iconograph of Manhattan Island, 1498–1909*, vol V (New York, Arno Press, 1967).

Phillips, D 'Good men to associate and bad men to conspire: associations for the prosecution of felons in England' pp 113–70 in D Hay and F Snyder (eds) *Policing and Prosecution in Britain, 1750–1850* (Oxford, England, Clarendon Press, New York, Oxford University Press, 1989).

—— *Crime and Authority in Victorian England: The Black Country 1835–60* (London, Croom Helm, Totowa, N J, Rowman and Littlefield, 1977).

Pomerantz, S *New York: An American City, 1783–1803* (New York, Columbia University Press, 1938).

Porter, R *English Society in the 18th Century* (Halmondsworth, Penguin, 1912).

Pound, R. 'The Causes of Popular Dissatisfaction with the Administration of Justice', *American Bar Association Reports* 29 (1906).

—— *The Formative Era in American Law* (Boston, Little Brown and Co 1912).

—— *Criminal Justice in America* (New York, Brown University Press, 1930, republished by Da Cappo Press, 1972).

—— *Organization of Courts* (Boston, Little Brown and Co 1940).

—— *The Lawyer from Antiquity to Modern Times* (Minnesota, West Publishing Co, 1953).

Pound, R and Frankfurter, F *Criminal Justice in Cleveland: A Report of the Cleveland Foundation's Survey of the Administration of Criminal Justice in Cleveland Ohio* (Cleveland, Ohio, The Cleveland Foundation, 1922).

Pred, A 'Manufacturing in the Mercantile City', *Annals of the Society of American Geographics* 56 (1966) 307–25.

Proctor, L B (1870), *The Bench and Bar of New York* (New York, Diossy & Co).

Radzinowicz, L and Hood, R A *History of English Criminal Law and Its Administration since 1750*, vol 5 (London: Stevens, 1986).

Ramsey, C (2002) 'The Discretionary Power of "Public" Prosecutors in Historical Perspective' *American Criminal Law Review* 1309.

Rawlings, P J 'The Idea of Policing: a History, *Policing and Society* 5 (1995) 129–149.

—— *Crime and Power: A History of Criminal Justice 1688–1998* (London, New York, Longman, 1999).

Reed, A *Training for the Public Profession of the Law* (Bull No 15 New York Carnegie Foundation, 1921).

Reith, C *The Blind Eye of History* (London: Faber and Faber, 1952).

Report of the Trial of Henry Bedlow for Committing a Rape on Lanah Sawyer, New York, 1793.

Reynolds, E A (2002) 'Sir John Fielding, Sir Charles Whitworth, and the Westminster Night Watch Act, 1770–1775' pp 1–19 in Louis A Knafla (ed), *Policing and War in Europe* (Westport, CT, Greenwood Press).

Richardson, J F *The New York Police* (New York, Oxford University Press, 1970).

Robertson, B and Vignaux, G *Interpreting Evidence* (Chichester, John Wiley, 1995).

Rock, H 'A delicate balance: The mechanics and the city in the age of Jefferson', *New York Historical Society Quarterly* 63 (1979) 93.

Rogers, D *The New York City Recorder*, (vols 1–6) (New York, C N Baldwin, 1817–1822).

Rosenburg, C *Religion and the Rise of the American City: The New York City Mission Movement,* 1812–1870 (Ithaca, London, Cornell University Press, 1971).

Rosenwaike, I *Population History of New York City* (Syracuse, NY, Syracuse University Press, 1972).

Rothman, D *The Discovery of the Asylum: Social Order and Disorder in the New Republic* (Boston, Little Brown, 1971).

Salvelsberg, J J 'Law that Does Not Fit Society: Sentencing Guidelines as a Neoclassical Reaction to the Dilemmas of Substantive Law' *The American Journal of Sociology* 1346 (1992).

Sampson, W *Trial of Robert Goodwin* (New York, John Low, 1820).

Sanger, W W *The History of Prostitution* (New York, Arno Press, 1859).

Schneider, John C *Detroit and the Problem of Order, 1830–1880* (Lincoln, University of Nebraska Press, 1980).

Scott, H W *The Courts of the State of New York* (New York, Wilson publishing Co, 1909).

Shapiro, B J *Beyond Resonable Doubt and Probable Cause* (Berkeley, University of California Press, 1991).

Sidman, A 'The Outmoded Concept of Private Prosecution' *American University Law Review* 25 (1976) 754.

Skillman, J *New York Police Reports* (New York, Ludwig & Tolefree, 1830).

Sklansky, D (1999) 'The Private Police', *UCLA Law Review* 46: 1165.

Smith, B *Circumventing the Jury: Petty Crime and Summary Jurisdiction in London and New York City, 1790–1855*. Unpublished PhD Dissertation; UMI: 9714304 (1996).

Smith, Henry E 'The modern privilege: Its nineteenth-century origins' pp 145–80 in R H Helmholz *et al* (eds) *The Privilege Against Self Incrimination* (Chicago, University of Chicago Press, 1997.

Smith, T *Revivalism and Social Reform in Mid-Nineteenth Century America* (New York, Abingdon Press, 1957).

Spann, E *The New Metropolis: New York City 1840–1857* (New York, Columbia University Press, 1981).

Spitzer, S and Scull, A 'Privatization and Capitalist Development: The Case of the Private Police', *Social Problems* 25(1) (1977) 18.

Stansell, C *City of Women: Sex and Class in New York, 1789–1860* (Urbana, University of Illinois Press, 1987).

Steinberg, A *The Criminal Courts and the Transformation of Criminal Justice in Philadelphia 1815–1874*. (Ann Arbor, University Microfilm, 1983).

—— *The Transformation of Criminal Justice, Philadelphia, 1800–1880* (Chapel Hill, University of North Carolina Press, 1989).

—— 'From Private Prosecution to Plea Bargaining: Criminal Prosecution, The District Attorney and American Legal History', *Crime & Delinquency* 30 (1984) 568.

—— 'The Spirit of Litigation: Private Prosecution and Criminal Justice in Nineteenth Century Philadelphia', *Journal of Social History* 20 (1985) 231.

Stevens, R *Law School: Legal Education in America from the 1850s to the 1980s*. (Chapel Hill, University of North Carolina Press, 1983).

Storch, R 'The Plague of Blue Locusts: Police Reform and Popular Resistance in Northern England 1840–57', *International Review of Social History* 20 (1975) 61.

—— 'The Policeman as Domestic Missionary: Urban Discipline and Popular Culture in Northern England, 1850–1880', *Journal of Social History* 9(4) (1976) 481.

Styles, J 'Sir John Fielding and the Problem of Crime Investigation in Eighteenth-Century England', *Transactions of the Royal Historical Society* (5th Series) 33 (1983) 127.

—— Brewer, J *An Ungovernable people: The English and Their Law in the Seventeenth and Eighteenth Centuries* (New Brunswick, NJ, Rutgers University Press, 1880).

Swaine, R T *The Cravath Firm: 1819–1947* (3 vols) (New York, Priv. print. At Ad Press, 1946–48).

Taft, H *Century and A Half at the New York Bar* (New York, Priv. print, 1938).

Thayer, J V *A Preliminary Treatise on Evidence at the Common Law* (London, Sweet & Maxwell, 1898).

Thompson, E P *Whigs and Hunters: The Origins of the Black Act* (New York, Pantheon Books, 1975).

Train, A *Courts and Criminals*, (New York, Scribner's, 1925).

Twomey, R *Jacobins and Jeffersonians* (London, New York, Garland Publication, 1989).

Untermeyer, S 'Evils and Remedies in the Administration of the Criminal Law', *The Record*, 36 (1910) 145.

Utz, Pamela *Settling The Facts*, (Lexington, Mass, Lexington Books, 1978).

Van Alstyne, W F 'The District Attorney—A Historical Puzzle', *Wisconsin Law Review,* (1952) 125–138.

Vogel, M *Courts of Trade: Social Conflict and the Emergence of Plea Bargaining in Boston, Massachusetts, 1830–1890.* (Unpublished PhD Dissertation, Harvard University, 1988).

Vogel, M 'The Social Origins of Plea Bargaining: Conflict and the Law in the Process of State Formation, 1830–1860', *Law and Society Review* 33(1) (1999) 161.

Warren, C *A History of the American Bar* (Boston, Little, Brown, 1911).

Waters, M 'Collegiality, Bureaucratization and Professionalization: A Weberian Analysis', *American Journal of Sociology* 94 (1989) 945.

Weinbaum, P *Mobs and Demagogues* (Ann Arbor, UMI Research Press, 1979).

Weiner, M *Reconstructing the Criminal: Culture, Law and Policy in England, 1830–1914* (Cambridge, Cambridge University Press, 1990).

Westergaard, H *Contributions to the History of Statistics* (London, P S King, 1932).

Wheeler, Jacob D *Reports of Criminal Law Cases* (New York, Banks and Brothers, 1851–1860).

White, S 'A Question of Style: Blacks in and around New York City in the late Eighteenth Century', *Journal of American Folklore* 102 (1989) 24.

White, S *Somewhat More Independent: The End of Slavery in New York City, 1770–1810.* (Athens, GA, 1991).

Wilentz, Sean 'Crime, Poverty and the Streets of New York City. The Diary of William H Bell 1850–1851', *History Workshop Journal* 7 (1979) 126.

—— *Chants Democratic: New York City and the Rise of the American Working Class 1788–1850* (New York, OUP, 1984).

Williamson, C *American Suffrage from Property to Democracy 1760–1860* (Princeton, Princeton University Press, 1960).

Wilson, J G *Memorial History of the City of New York*, (4 vols) (New York, New Yok History Co 1893).

Wines, E C *Transactions of the National Congress on Penitentiary and Reformatory Discipline* (Albany, Weed, Parsons, 1871).

Wunder, John *Inferior Courts, Superior Justice: A History of Justices of the Peace on the Northwest Frontier 1853–1899.* (Westport, Greenwood Press, 1917).

Younger, R D *The People's Panel: The Grand Jury in the United States*, 1634–1941 (Providence Rhode Is. Brown University Press, 1963).

Index